Complex AI Dynamics and Interactions in Management

Paula Cristina Nunes Figueiredo
Universidade Lusófona, Portugal

A volume in the Advances in Logistics, Operations, and Management Science (ALOMS) Book Series

IGI Global
PUBLISHER of TIMELY KNOWLEDGE

Published in the United States of America by
IGI Global
Business Science Reference (an imprint of IGI Global)
701 E. Chocolate Avenue
Hershey PA, USA 17033
Tel: 717-533-8845
Fax: 717-533-8661
E-mail: cust@igi-global.com
Web site: http://www.igi-global.com

Library of Congress Cataloging-in-Publication Data

Names: Figueiredo, Paula Cristina Nunes, 1978- editor.
Title: Complex AI dynamics and interactions in management / edited by Paula Figueiredo.
Description: Hershey, PA : Business Science Reference, [2024] | Includes bibliographical references and index. | Summary: "It is a very important scientific topic in today's world, namely the challenges and implications for organizations. It is not believed that robots or Artificial Intelligence and digitization will diminish the need for Humans in organizations; quite the contrary, it is believed that the so-called 5.0 revolution will only increase the need for a more developed human potential"-- Provided by publisher.
Identifiers: LCCN 2023049129 (print) | LCCN 2023049130 (ebook) | ISBN 9798369307120 (hardcover) | ISBN 9798369307137 (ebook)
Subjects: LCSH: Management. | Artificial intelligence. | Technological innovations--Management.
Classification: LCC HD30.2 .C6389 2024 (print) | LCC HD30.2 (ebook) | DDC 658--dc23/eng/20231102
LC record available at https://lccn.loc.gov/2023049129
LC ebook record available at https://lccn.loc.gov/2023049130

This book is published in the IGI Global book series Advances in Logistics, Operations, and Management Science (ALOMS) (ISSN: 2327-350X; eISSN: 2327-3518)

British Cataloguing in Publication Data
A Cataloguing in Publication record for this book is available from the British Library.

All work contributed to this book is new, previously-unpublished material.
The views expressed in this book are those of the authors, but not necessarily of the publisher.

For electronic access to this publication, please contact: eresources@igi-global.com.

Advances in Logistics, Operations, and Management Science (ALOMS) Book Series

John Wang
Montclair State University, USA

ISSN:2327-350X
EISSN:2327-3518

MISSION

Operations research and management science continue to influence business processes, administration, and management information systems, particularly in covering the application methods for decision-making processes. New case studies and applications on management science, operations management, social sciences, and other behavioral sciences have been incorporated into business and organizations real-world objectives.

The **Advances in Logistics, Operations, and Management Science** (ALOMS) Book Series provides a collection of reference publications on the current trends, applications, theories, and practices in the management science field. Providing relevant and current research, this series and its individual publications would be useful for academics, researchers, scholars, and practitioners interested in improving decision making models and business functions.

COVERAGE

- Decision analysis and decision support
- Marketing engineering
- Information Management
- Political Science
- Computing and information technologies
- Networks
- Services management
- Organizational Behavior
- Finance
- Risk Management

IGI Global is currently accepting manuscripts for publication within this series. To submit a proposal for a volume in this series, please contact our Acquisition Editors at Acquisitions@igi-global.com or visit: http://www.igi-global.com/publish/.

The Advances in Logistics, Operations, and Management Science (ALOMS) Book Series (ISSN 2327-350X) is published by IGI Global, 701 E. Chocolate Avenue, Hershey, PA 17033-1240, USA, www.igi-global.com. This series is composed of titles available for purchase individually; each title is edited to be contextually exclusive from any other title within the series. For pricing and ordering information please visit http://www.igi-global.com/book-series/advances-logistics-operations-management-science/37170. Postmaster: Send all address changes to above address.

Titles in this Series

For a list of additional titles in this series, please visit:
http://www.igi-global.com/book-series/advances-logistics-operations-management-science/37170

Critical Examination of the Recent Evolution of B2B Sales
Joel G. Cohn (Everglades University, Boca Raton, USA)
Business Science Reference • © 2024 • 300pp • H/C (ISBN: 9798369303481) • US $255.00

Perspectives on Innovation and Technology Transfer in Managing Public Organizations
Luan Carlos Santos Silva (Federal University of Grande Dourados)
Business Science Reference • © 2024 • 371pp • H/C (ISBN: 9781668498330) • US $275.00

AI and Machine Learning Impacts in Intelligent Supply Chain
Binay Kumar Pandey (Department of Information Technology, College of Technology, Govind Ballabh Pant University of Agriculture and Technology, India) Uday Kumar Kanike (Independent Researcher, USA) A. Shaji George (Crown University International, Saudi Arabia & Chartered International Da Vinci University, Nigeria) and Digvijay Pandey (Department of Technical Education, U. P., India)
Business Science Reference • © 2024 • 314pp • H/C (ISBN: 9798369313473) • US $275.00

Convergence of Industry 4.0 and Supply Chain Sustainability
Muhammad Rahies Khan (Bahria University Karachi, Pakistan) Naveed R. Khan (UCSI University, Malaysia) and Noor Zaman Jhanjhi (Taylor's University, Malaysia)
Business Science Reference • © 2024 • 320pp • H/C (ISBN: 9798369313633) • US $275.00

Achieving Secure and Transparent Supply Chains With Blockchain Technology
Mustafa Rehman Khan (UCSI University, Malaysia) Naveed Rehman Khan (UCSI University, Malaysia) and Arsalan Mujahid Ghouri (London South Bank University, UK)
Business Science Reference • © 2024 • 345pp • H/C (ISBN: 9798369304822) • US $275.00

Strategies and Approaches of Corporate Social Responsibility Toward Multinational Enterprises
Erum Shaikh (Shaheed Benazir Bhutto University, Sanghar Campus, Pakistan)
Business Science Reference • © 2024 • 400pp • H/C (ISBN: 9798369303634) • US $275.00

IGI Global
PUBLISHER of TIMELY KNOWLEDGE

701 East Chocolate Avenue, Hershey, PA 17033, USA
Tel: 717-533-8845 x100 • Fax: 717-533-8661
E-Mail: cust@igi-global.com • www.igi-global.com

Table of Contents

Detailed Table of Contents

Decision-making is a high-risk process for businesses' life cycle worldwide. Wrong decisions by business leaders may lead to business closure in critical situations for all firms, including small and medium-sized enterprises. Leaders invest in artificial intelligence to improve their decision-making capabilities and contribute to their businesses' sustainability. Grounded in Herbert Simon's decision-making theory, the purpose of this chapter's multiple case study was to explore why artificial intelligence may enhance business leaders' decision-making. Three business leaders from different organizations in the United States and UAE's real estate properties industry participated in this research. Data were collected through semi-structured interviews and from a review of previous literature. A key recommendation for firms is to invest in artificial intelligence. Artificial intelligence may allow business leaders to improve decision-making, reduce the potential risk of closure, extend business opportunities, and positively contribute to communities' stability and growth.

In the information age, organizations are more powerful as they have more information. However, having information is not enough. It needs to be compiled and organized so that it can be used. This compiled information can be used in many areas of an organization, including the recruitment of new employees. Organizations are always looking for ways to improve productivity and profitability. The COVID-19 pandemic has made this even more important. To do this, they need employees with the right skills for the job. This is where data science comes in. Data science is the field of study that analyses and processes data so that it can be used to make and create informed decisions. This study aims to investigate how data science can be used to help organizations hire new employees. The project will explore how data science can be used to identify the skills and qualifications that are most important for a particular role, screen candidates more effectively, and make better hiring decisions.

Uncertainty, innovation, competitive advantage, globalization, and digitalization are some of the changes that have forced managers to rethink the way they manage their

enabling the customers to access financial products and lending even in remote areas of the country.

The chapter embarked on a comprehensive exploration of robotic process automation (RPA) and its merge with building information modeling (BIM) in revolutionizing the construction industry. By investigating the applications, benefits, challenges, and opportunities associated with RPA and its integration with BIM, this research has shed light on the immense potential for transforming productivity, efficiency, safety, decision-making, and sustainability in construction processes. Moreover, the merge of RPA with BIM represents a paradigm shift in collaboration, data management, and decision-making within the construction industry. By combining the strengths of these two transformative technologies, stakeholders can achieve unprecedented levels of coordination, efficiency, and accuracy throughout the project lifecycle. RPA, when integrated with BIM, empowers real-time monitoring, safety analysis, clash detection, risk assessment, and advanced simulations, allowing for proactive identification and resolution of issues.

Foreword

Although a mature scientific field, with discussions and events for more than sixty years, artificial intelligence became a daily topic only in the last three years, with the emergence of large language models environments and the immense offer of data analytics and knowledge production tools. The usage of "chatbots", for instance, is now a routine for any bank customer, healthcare patient, student, traveler or, simply speaking, citizen. Communication about one of our simple transactions with public or private service, as one good purchase, document retrieval, requirement for an administrative intervention or even an emergency such as a hospital demand is frequently resulted of "artificial intelligence" action or process.

Several organizations, from the smaller commerce, shops, liberal autonomous providers reaching to big companies, as airlines, banks, and media, not excluding many others, are implementing solutions based on AI to improve their knowledge about their markets, about customers and citizens profiles and their preferences and to better understand market developments. In general, these implementations present a business risk if they were not a result of a plan or a project. Unfortunately, as markets are always pressured, businesses managers must answer and react to these critical movements with unplanned fashion, resulting in partial or even inefficient AI positioning.

In this scenario, the book *Complex AI Dynamics and Interactions in Management*, proposed and led by editor Paula Cristina Nunes Figueiredo, brings a significant help to the readers. As it was edited by an experienced professional, this book project gathered different experiences, cases and background around real events approaching AI, both from the planning and usage side, composing an accessible panorama with useful results for the reader, allowing he or she as to completely absorb experiences, fundamentals, elements and intended results of AI projects.

From the perspective of an editorial balance, *Complex AI Dynamics and Interactions in Management* presents an opportune approach, which address technological basics and demands, along with its results, not restricted to usually narrowed tech discussion, widening the view of AI projects requirements and goals. Topics such as skills development to use, deal and lead AI plans, organizational and professional leadership, recruitment processes and decision-making are presented along with technological points of view and associated management, composing a rich, deep and diverse contribution to improve the understanding of AI projects and its outcomes for any type of organization, both public and private.

The challenge on bringing a comprehensive view of disruptive AI project was faced by editor Paula Figueiredo, as the book coverage range from topics such as organizational environment to tangible application, such as robotization of construction sites in a quite balanced way. This open view, needed nowadays to discuss AI in the needed detailed way, results in a useful, inspirational experience for the reader, as he or she will receive solid knowledge about the demands, intentions, interests for specific applications, along with results from projects and decisions which really performed in these real scenarios.

This way, *Complex AI Dynamics and Interactions in Management* is a title which must deserve reader´s special attention as it definitely contributes to help managers and decision-makers to efficiently and precisely apply AI for solutions, with scientific, experienced and market oriented base.

George Leal Jamil
FUMEC University, Brazil

Preface

Welcome to *Complex AI Dynamics and Interactions in Management*, an edited reference book that delves into the profound challenges and implications of Artificial Intelligence (AI) on contemporary business management. In an era where AI is seamlessly integrated into our daily lives, it becomes imperative for leaders and organizations to comprehend the intricacies of AI dynamics and strategically navigate this transformative landscape.

As the Editor of this compilation, Paula Figueiredo, hailing from Universidade Lusófona, Portugal, I am thrilled to present a volume dedicated to unraveling the multifaceted aspects of AI in management. The objective is not merely to address the future of work or the potential takeover of jobs by robots but to foster a comprehensive understanding of how AI can be harnessed for the benefit of humanity. It is crucial that societies at all levels are adequately prepared for this technological revolution.

Leaders play a pivotal role in steering organizations through this transformative journey. Their commitment and strategic preparation are essential for leveraging AI to enhance productivity and improve the quality of life for communities. In "Complex AI Dynamics and Interactions in Management," we aim to assist leaders and organizations in this transition by providing insights into successful AI initiatives. This involves prioritizing opportunities, building diverse teams of experts, conducting strategic experiments, and designing solutions that have a positive impact on both organizations and society.

In the contemporary context, making concrete business decisions involves the application of AI and machine learning to maintain competitiveness and sustainability. This book addresses the pressing need for leaders and organizations to make informed decisions in the dynamic landscape of AI and technology.

The main objectives of this book are outlined as follows:

- Analyze the state of the art of AI applied to Business Management.
- Investigate the factors promoting AI development dynamics in organizational contexts.
- Examine organizational AI development systems, processes, and practices.

- Evaluate the impact of AI on the lives of individuals, organizations, and societies.
- Suggest systems, processes, and organizational practices for finding solutions through AI applications.
- Explore changing management approaches influenced by AI and technology.

Complex AI Dynamics and Interactions in Management is a significant scientific contribution to the challenges and implications faced by organizations in the contemporary world. We firmly believe that AI and digitization will not diminish the need for humans but rather increase the demand for a more developed human potential during the so-called 5.0 revolution.

This book serves as a valuable resource for managers and decision-makers, offering insights on strategically preparing organizations and sustainably developing talent in the AI era. Researchers from diverse disciplines, spanning business, social and human sciences, computer, and data sciences, are invited to engage in the study of complex AI dynamics and interactions. This project provides a platform for pushing the boundaries of respective disciplines and fostering collaboration among professionals, academics, and researchers from various countries.

I extend my gratitude to the contributors who have enriched this volume with their expertise, making *Complex AI Dynamics and Interactions in Management* a cornerstone for understanding the evolving role of AI in organizational contexts.

Chapter 1: The Use of Digital and Disruptive Technologies in the Artificial Intelligence Era – A Critical Analysis

Authored by José G. Vargas-Hernandez, Selene Castañeda-Burciaga, Omar Alejandro Guirette-Barbosa, and Omar C. Vargas-Gonzàlez, this chapter critically examines emergent and disruptive digital technologies in the AI era. It emphasizes the opportunities and challenges these technologies pose to individuals, organizations, institutions, and society. The study advocates for ethical control and leadership to guide the ethical disruption of digital technologies, recognizing that the ongoing digital transformation requires continuous human guidance.

Chapter 2: The Integration of Artificial Intelligence in Developing Human Resources

Written by Tarinni Kakar, Verley V.J Lanns-Isaac, and Cindy L. Crowder, this chapter explores the transformative potential of AI applications in Human Resource Development. Focusing on fostering a supportive organizational culture, data-driven decision-making, employee growth, and open communication, the authors showcase how AI can enhance routine cycles, making HR functions more efficient, objective, and thorough. The chapter offers insights into leveraging AI to adapt to changing environments and technological advancements for sustained organizational stability and renewal.

Chapter 3: Reskilling in the Artificial Intelligence Era

Authored by Paula Cristina Nunes Figueiredo, Maria João Justino Alves, and José Carlos Rouco, this chapter delves into the profound impact of AI on the workforce. It emphasizes the need for reskilling and upskilling to stay relevant and competitive in an era of increasing automation. The essay focuses on the technological impact of AI on skills management, learning, and development, offering a glimpse into the changing landscape of education and skills acquisition in the age of AI.

Chapter 4: Art of Leading in the AI Age – Portrait of a Leader

In this chapter, Alamelu R analyzes the strategic transformation of leadership in the AI age. With the rise of cyber-physical systems and connected IT systems, the volume of available data has increased significantly. The chapter explores distinct leadership needs and challenges posed by the widespread adoption of AI, emphasizing the importance of effective leadership for successful AI deployment. It provides practical instructions and ideas for creating a better AI culture by improving skills and competencies required in the AI arena.

Chapter 5: Investing in Artificial Intelligence (AI) for Business Leaders to Enhance Decision-Making

Authored by Ahmed Sedky, this chapter explores the impact of AI on business leaders' decision-making capabilities. Grounded in Herbert Simon's decision-making theory, the chapter presents a multiple case study examining why AI may enhance decision-making for business leaders. The research, based on interviews and literature review, reveals the benefits of AI investment in improving decision-making, reducing risks, extending business opportunities, and contributing to community stability and growth.

Chapter 6: Data Science in the Employee Recruitment Process

João Farinha and Maria Fatima Pina discuss the application of Data Science in the recruitment process in this chapter. Focused on how Data Science can help organizations hire new employees more effectively, the study explores the use of data analysis to identify crucial skills, screen candidates, and make informed hiring decisions. The project investigates the role of Data Science in improving productivity and profitability, especially in the context of the challenges posed by the COVID-19 pandemic.

Chapter 7: Happiness Management – How Artificial Intelligence Can Help Managers

Natália Costa and Marisol Guadalupe Moreira Costa delve into the evolving field of Happiness Management in organizations. The chapter explores how AI, with its learning capabilities, is contributing to organizational culture by promoting positive experiences and emotions in the workplace. Despite opinions on its effects, the chapter highlights the increasing innovation in using AI to enhance employee well-being and happiness within organizational contexts.

Chapter 8: Organizational Psychology and the Impact of Artificial Intelligence on Psychosocial Risks and Technostress Levels

Authored by José Baptista, this chapter addresses psychosocial risks in the workplace, a critical challenge for organizations in the AI era. As technological advances, including increased usage of AI, bring transformations to workplaces, the chapter focuses on understanding psychosocial risks and their consequences for individual well-being and organizational productivity. Recognizing the broader impact on society, the chapter emphasizes the need for organizations to address these risks proactively.

Chapter 9: Transformative Power of Artificial Intelligence in Decision-Making, Automation, and Customer Engagement

Nalini R explores the transformative power of AI in decision-making, automation, and customer engagement. Focused on the integration of data, technology, design, and people to foster innovation, the chapter highlights AI's efficiency in processing vast datasets objectively. It emphasizes the role of AI in enhancing decision accuracy, aligning strategies with market trends, and driving transformative growth in organizations.

Chapter 10: The Effects of Artificial Intelligence (AI) on Marketing

Ana Filipa Vieira Lopes Joaquim investigates the profound effects of AI on marketing strategies, customer segmentation, personalized advertising, and customer relationship management. With AI promising to disrupt customer experience, the chapter explores the transformation brought about by generative AI in reshaping the marketing landscape. Ethical considerations and challenges associated with AI implementation in marketing are also examined.

Chapter 11: AI Powered Supply Chains Towards Greater Efficiency

Shobhana N explores the integration of AI technologies, including Big Data, Machine learning, Cloud computing, Block chain, Chatbots, and Chat GPT, in supply chain management. Emphasizing the potential contributions of AI to the global economy, the chapter discusses the wide-ranging applications of AI-powered supply chains across various sectors. It explores the benefits and limitations of these technologies in enhancing efficiency and customer satisfaction within supply chain processes.

Chapter 12: An Upshot of Artificial Intelligence on Customer Engagement in Banking

Amudha R discusses the significant impact of AI on customer engagement in the banking sector. Recognizing AI as a foundation for stimulating human intelligence, the chapter explores how machine learning models contribute to managing daily banking operations. It anticipates continued innovation and partnerships between financial institutions and AI specialists, enabling improved services, increased efficiency, and competitiveness in the evolving digital landscape.

Chapter 13: Adopting Robotic Process Automation (RPA) in the Construction Industry

Fuad Abutaha and Ceren Dinler explore the integration of Robotic Process Automation (RPA) with Building Information Modeling (BIM) in the construction industry. The chapter comprehensively examines the applications, benefits, challenges, and opportunities associated with RPA and its merge with BIM. It sheds light on the transformative potential of RPA-BIM integration in enhancing productivity, efficiency, safety, decision-making, and sustainability within construction processes.

Complex AI Dynamics and Interactions in Management serves as a comprehensive exploration of the intricate challenges and implications brought about by Artificial Intelligence (AI) in the realm of contemporary business management. This book is not just about thinking about the future of work or talking about how robots might eventually replace humans in the workforce. Rather, our goal is to present a comprehensive knowledge of how AI might be deliberately used to advance humankind. In a time when artificial intelligence is pervasively incorporated into our daily lives, it is critical for leaders and companies to understand the nuances of AI dynamics and successfully navigate this dynamically shifting terrain with strategic acumen and foresight.

Leadership in this transformative journey plays a pivotal role, requiring commitment and strategic preparation to leverage AI for enhancing productivity and improving the quality of life for communities. *Complex AI Dynamics and Interactions in Management* aims to assist leaders and organizations in this transition by offering insights into successful AI initiatives. This involves prioritizing opportunities, building diverse teams of experts, conducting strategic experiments, and designing solutions that positively impact both organizations and society.

In the contemporary context, making concrete business decisions necessitates the application of AI and machine learning to maintain competitiveness and sustainability. This book addresses the pressing need for leaders and organizations to make informed decisions in the dynamic landscape of AI and technology.

The outlined objectives of this book encompass analyzing the state of the art of AI applied to Business Management, investigating factors promoting AI development dynamics, examining organizational AI development systems, evaluating the impact of AI on various aspects of life, suggesting systems and practices for finding solutions through AI applications, and exploring changing management approaches influenced by AI and technology.

Complex AI Dynamics and Interactions in Management stands as a significant scientific contribution to the challenges and implications faced by organizations in the contemporary world. We firmly believe that AI and digitization will not diminish the need for humans but rather increase the demand for a more developed human potential during the so-called 5.0 revolution.

This book serves as a valuable resource for managers and decision-makers, offering insights on strategically preparing organizations and sustainably developing talent in the AI era. We extend our heartfelt gratitude to the contributors who have enriched this volume with their expertise, making it a cornerstone for understanding the evolving role of AI in organizational contexts.

To researchers from diverse disciplines, spanning business, social and human sciences, computer, and data sciences, we extend an invitation to engage in the study of complex AI dynamics and interactions. This project provides a platform for pushing the boundaries of respective disciplines and fostering collaboration among professionals, academics, and researchers from various countries.

"Complex AI Dynamics and Interactions in Management" is more than a compilation of chapters; it is a testament to the collective effort of experts contributing to our understanding of the profound implications of AI on the future of management. May this book serve as a catalyst for further exploration, discussion, and innovation in the dynamic intersection of AI and business management.

Paula Cristina Nunes Figueiredo
Universidade Lusófona, Portugal

Acknowledgment

The Editor would like to acknowledge each reviewer and author for their contribution and committed interaction, which resulted in this book. I also thank all IGI Global professionals involved in the opportunity to publish this book.

Chapter 1
The Use of Digital and Disruptive Technologies in the Artificial Intelligence Era:
A Critical Analysis

José G. Vargas-Hernandez
Tecnológico Nacional de México, Mexico & Budapest Centre for Long-Term Sustainability, Hungary

Selene Castañeda-Burciaga
https://orcid.org/0000-0002-2436-308X
Universidad Politécnica de Zacatecas, Mexico

Omar Alejandro Guirette-Barbosa
https://orcid.org/0000-0003-1336-9475
Universidad Politécnica de Zacatecas, Mexico

Omar C. Vargas-Gonzàlez
https://orcid.org/0000-0002-6089-956X
Tecnològico Nacional de Mèxico, Ciudad Guzmàn, Mexico

ABSTRACT

This study aims to analyze the emergent and disruptive digital technologies in an era of artificial intelligence (IA). It departs from the assumption that the emerging technologies create both opportunities and challenges with an impact on individuals, organizations, institutions, and society at large in terms of bias, surveillance, hacking, etc. The method employed is the critical analysis based on the recent developments reported in scientific literature. It is concluded that control over the ethical disruption of digital technologies and more specifically artificial strategy must require a digital conversation and leadership about acceptable ethical behaviors under the assumption that digital transformation cannot be interrupted and must be guided by humans.
DOI: 10.4018/979-8-3693-0712-0.ch001

INTRODUCTION

Human development in recent decades has been accompanied by emergent and rapid disruptive technological changes leading to a growing proliferation of digitized devices and services. Emergent and disruptive digital technologies have become intrinsic to our current way for life and will be part of our future lifestyle, from mundane routines and activities to improvement of productive, contributing to manage the requirements of an economic growth in a more competitive and dynamic environment, and evaluating the balance of power for a more collective security.

Artificial intelligence (IA) has a significant impact on individuals, organizations, and societies by offering systematic capabilities of learning and reasoning based on inputs and the differences with the expected outputs, predicting and adapting to changes in the socio- ecosystems from its received external environment stimulus. Artificial intelligence is a digital transformation led by emerging technologies that have burst into all fields and sectors worldwide leading to benefits in terms of agility, efficiency, transparency, and social welfare, so it can be said that emerging and disruptive digital technologies play a leading role in our environment and can do everything for us!

Artificial intelligence (IA), internet of things (IoT), blockchain and Chat GPT, among others, are emergent and disruptive digital technologies that aid human beings and societies in quick and efficient way to increase economic productivity, support the social wellbeing by providing a more educated, productive and healthier lifestyle of individuals, anticipate and prevent responses to crisis and disasters, absorbing shocks, etc. (Sharifi et al., 2021). An increased level of research in chatbots designed to respond to queries of the user by mapping the best possible response in real time feedback, are based on adopted language models and deep learning to address natural language processes (NLP) (Lokman & Ameedeen, 2018; Kushwaha & Kar, 2021).

This paper provides an insight into the development and incorporation of emerging and disruptive digital technologies and how they have impacted the everyday world to provide an easier life, thus enabling the transformation of the technological socio-ecosystem. Furthermore, it is possible to envision technological innovation as a support to routine work activities, not only as direct competition with human beings, since dealing with the other is still preferable; therefore, it is required that man and machine work in a complementary way to optimize value creation, as long as there is an ethical regulation governing such interaction.

THE EVOLUTION OF EMERGING AND FRONTIER TECHNOLOGIES

The pace of change is likely to accelerate because of the "frontier technologies" that are redefining our world, taking advantage of digitization and connectivity, include artificial intelligence (IA), big data, blockchain, the Internet of Things (IoT), 3D printing, robotics, drones, biotechnology, and nanotechnology. Frontier technologies are those that take advantage of digitization and connectivity (UNCTAD, 2021). Emerging and disruptive technologies evolution has become the buzzword of the current economic and productivity growth, geopolitical landscape, and security architecture, to build resilience leading to conclude that there is a strong link between them. The design of future digital technologies is bound to change the technological socio-ecosystem and the society at large.

Organizations and states remain the major actors in technological innovation designing and implementing policies, strategies, tactics, and instruments, although the leading technological edge is currently and will be lead in the future by private firms, university research centers and academia while extending the possibility to involve the whole of society approach in operations. The emerging technologies create both opportunities and challenges with an impact on individuals, organizations, institutions, and society at large in terms of bias, surveillance, hacking, etc. Digital technologies enhance economic, societal, and socio-ecological resilience in terms of health, education, connectivity, communication, etc. Emerging technologies are a highly innovative tool that seeks to become integrated as a dominant competence (Castro, 2021).

Innovation and competition are the drivers of an emerging and disruptive digital technologies raising challenges and threats based on dynamic and organic processes that require creative destruction of established technologies and industries that takes considerable time in revealing its true features and ultimate effects (Schumpeter, 1949, 1994). Thus, the organic process of creative destruction applies to a new cycle of emerging and disrupting digital technologies that will win the competition leading to the entire transformation of the technological socio-ecosystem. A positive impact of these technologies is the promotion of resilience with the identification of maintenance needs by inspecting critical infrastructure leading to respond to the emergencies with assistance of recovery efforts in crises and disasters, for example.

WHY IS THE DIGITAL ERA GOING WRONG? WHO CONTROLS THE FUTURE?

Any emergent technological outcome is a neutral tool before receiving connotations depending on how is being used. However, in this era of emerging and disruptive digital technologies we are witnessing heated debates on legal frameworks, standards, recommendations, methods, practices, problems, etc., marked by lack of agreement among the main actors due to divergent interests for control without a clear how to provide solutions. According to Castro (2021), emerging digital technologies emerge as tools are required to provide a solution to a given problem.

Emerging, and disruptive digital technologies such as big data, biotechnologies, quantum, autonomous systems require separate international standardization principles of responsible use, which may require various regulatory levels in the space domains. However, the debate on whether ChatGPT's use must be restricted, legislated, and regulated is split. Technological innovation must be stalled by global standards to ensure performance and interoperability between the different emerging technological socio-ecosystems. In the elaboration of this standards must be driven by global governance mechanisms with the participation of other sectors such as private sector and academia. Obviously, it is difficult to know how far human evil can go, incapacity and stupidity. Suffice it to remember that the largest sources of profit are related to death: war and drugs. Thus, the human being does not seem very trustworthy, as stated by Marín (2023).

What Is the Focus of Artificial Intelligence?

The focus of emerging and disruptive digital technologies has been on automation and not in creating jobs must be amended. Artificial intelligence has been focused on automation and this focus should be changed to the net increase of jobs and job creation. The focus of long-term artificial intelligence directions must have an impact on the greatest value of implementation by augmenting people in the jobs, enrichment of jobs and tasks, reimagine and redefine old tasks to create new job activities and transform culture to adapt artificial intelligence threats into new opportunities. According to Corvalán (2019), as long as the workforce is sufficiently prepared with the necessary skills for the changing work environment, there should be no fear of replacement.

Warnings of job losses confuse artificial intelligence with automation overshadowing the augmentation benefit of a combination and complementation of human and artificial intelligence, where both combine and complement each other. As Corvalán (2019) points out, despite the emerging technologies brought about by the Fourth Industrial Revolution, statistics on increased robotization do not have an impact on unemployment rates globally. Artificial intelligence has already a negative impact on the workplace by applying to highly repeatable routine tasks requiring copious quantities of data observations and decisions to be analyzed searching for patterns.

Applying artificial intelligence to less-routine with low repeatability and more varied tasks is yielding higher benefits in job creation and greater value. Using auto-generative artificial intelligence have different impacts depending on the industry sector such as to select data or curing diseases. The retailing industry sector is already expanding digital technology, artificial intelligence and human operation activities aimed to improve productivity the in- store check-out process while creating greater value. Applying artificial intelligence to nonroutine tasks tends to combine and complement humans and machines each other to perform more efficiently than either human experts or AI-driven devices and machines working alone. Artificial intelligence augments the workforce by complementing human capabilities as it provides new tools to enhance their artificial intelligence (Ovanessoff & Plastino, 2018).

Investments in artificial intelligence-enable technologies must evaluate the jobs lost, job creation and transformation of co-working collaboration and decision-making processes between workers and digital technologies. As Del Pozo and Fernández-Sastre (2021) point out, the introduction of new technologies positively influences employment growth; however, investment in innovation activities without the introduction of new technologies does not affect employment growth in companies. Technological innovations are associated with a transition period of job loss followed by a recovery. Affected jobs by artificial intelligence varies according to the industry sector with manufacturing and services such as education and healthcare hit the hardest by eliminating middle- and low-level positions, but also creating more new positions of highly skilled, management, the entry-level and low-skilled variety.

Research suggests consumers still prefer the interaction with a knowledgeable human salesperson than using artificial intelligence in more specialized areas who make a significant impact on customer satisfaction. These efforts of applying artificial intelligence and robotics in retailing to replace human tasks prove not be successful to eliminate this job at all despite that operational activities are disrupted, reducing labor, making labor savings, and prompting to reinvest on training to enhance customer experience and satisfaction, creating higher value.

The impact of artificial intelligence and digital technologies in outsourcing are pressured to fundamental changes aimed to reinvent and invest on business models with the symbiosis of human activities instead of only automating practices to create new business opportunities. Improvement of nonroutine work by applying artificial intelligence and robotics must concentrate on leveraging knowledge of digital technologies about general purpose tools to be incorporated into work processes leading to develop a competitive relationship of intelligent employee-robot automation processes to identify and optimize labor-intensive and repetitive activities currently performed by humans. The potential of artificial intelligence must be harnessed, but accompanying and alphabetizing the worker so that he or she can acquire new skills and build fertile ecosystems so that people are not left behind (Corvalán, 2019).

This improvement resulting from expanding digital technologies, applying artificial intelligence and robotics combined and complemented with humans increment elevated levels of productivity, reducing labor costs and the most important, crate higher levels of value with the creation of new jobs. The entire decision process based on the interaction between human and machines driven by artificial intelligence and other digital technologies must be redesigned to have the advantage of combining and complementing strengths each other to increase agility and optimize the value creation. According to Ovanessoff and Plastino (2018), artificial intelligence offers a range of possibilities for economies to address their productivity deficit and improve their dynamism on a more sustainable basis.

Automation, robotics, artificial intelligence, and other digital technologies have a multiplier effect which requires to redefine and create more jobs to create higher value than displacing and killing them, to the extent that should augment the workforce, increasing the productivity and quality of their work, freeing up time to be employed on more strategic priorities. Artificial intelligence, robotics and other digital technologies improves the productivity of many jobs that already has become a positive motivator. Artificial intelligence, robotics, and automation in manufacturing as in any other sectors rather than removing humans from task processes, contribute to augment customer experiences of workers leading to improve productivity by reducing costs, reducing frictions in value chains, optimizing supply chains, and creating higher value opportunities.

ChatGPT Could Make These Jobs Obsolete: 'The Wolf Is at the Door'

The subtitle of this section is taken from Mitchell (2023) on a recent article of analysis, which I borrowed because it is very illustrative of the situation. Concerned with the emergence of a disruptive tool ChatGPT capabilities, surprising intelligent chat bot upended from and based on artificial intelligence, which since its release on the 30th of November 2022, proving to be a tool with capabilities to perform complex tasks and simplify them (Sagarikabiswas, 2023). Higher education, finance and banking, hospitality and tourism, and information technology industries are sectors in which artificial intelligence and its most recent tool ChatGPT are enhancing business management and marketing activities, among others (Yogesh, et al. (2023).

A competing battle is taking place between artificial intelligence chatbots already released such as ChatGPT, BARD powered by Google, Microsoft-powered Bing, ChatSonic and Ernie powered by China's Baidu App, which are leading to employees and workers to dreadful feelings of losing or getting replaced on their jobs. OpenAI-powered ChatGPT and released GPT-4 fueling fear among the informational technology due to the replacement of programmers and other informational technology professionals by current ongoing massive layoffs (Sagarikabiswas, 2023).

OpenAI's ChatGPT extends the capabilities through the integration of natural language models and deep learning based on a Generative Pre-training Transformer (GPT) architecture (Radford et al., 2018) of neural networks aimed to predict the sequence of words in human interactions through generative and discriminative algorithms (Vaswani et al., 2017) used to generate responses to queries that resembles a human expert. The ChatGPT system is designed on a huge data set and continually improves itself using a simple text prompt to generate the ability to work through any problem and answer to any question with certain varying accuracy depending on its task Experts and analysts are warning that the improvement of these and other capabilities of the ChatGPT tool could spell doom for numerous job fields in industry.

According to the analysis of Sagarikabiswas, (2023) by April of 2023, 503 technological companies worldwide have laid off 139,165 employees in 2023, in part due to the release of the artificial intelligence chatbot. However, other analysts such as Goldman Sachs, are more pessimistic concluding that at least three hundred million jobs are getting obsolete and replaced. Technology engineering and software design has undergone massive staff layoffs at the Silicon Valley (figure 1). Large firms like Microsoft have announced a large investment in the revolutionary technology of artificial intelligence replacing a substantial portion of its global well-paid white-collar workforce while leaving many employees and industries currently vulnerable, from the financial, health care and publishing sectors. Microsoft has already laid off thousands of workers (Mitchell, 2023).

Large firms, such as Microsoft left out of work ten thousand employees while at the same time investing on partnership with OpenAI to accelerate artificial intelligence breakthroughs in abroad set of products aimed to drive growth (Potter, 2023). Other technological firms going through the layoff of white-collar employees to achieve cost-cutting measures, includes Amazon, Facebook, Apple, and Meta (Figure 1).

Technology analysts and experts are warning that the artificial intelligence tool ChatGPT are making white collar jobs obsolete and putting millions of people out of work (Potter, 2023). Humans must learn how to harness ChatGPT as a mind-blowing tool of the artificial intelligence technology which is rocking practices on the academia and social media, and leading to the risk that jobs in certain sectors can be supplemented and even replaced such as high education, financial services, journalism, software design engineering and graphics, etc., just to mention some of the affected sectors.

Figure 1. The job losses across the Silicon Valley

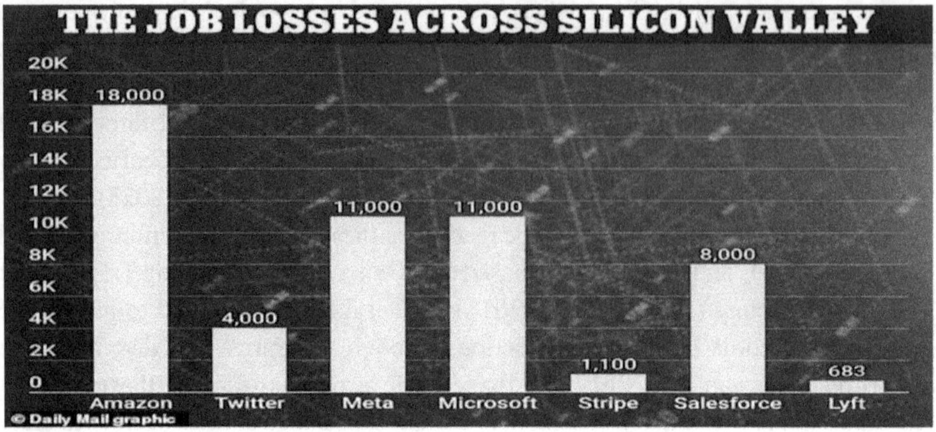

However, the efficient performance of ChatGPT in finding answers to complex questions and solutions to difficult problems in many working tasks and diverse roles of professional fields, there are some tasks and jobs requiring human interaction and empathy, critical thinking, and creativity that artificial intelligence cannot replace. Artificial intelligence cannot replace humans before it has consciousness, autonomy, the ability to act with intent, creativity. There are some job roles that artificial intelligence is not able to replace in the current and future scenarios. Some of these jobs analyzed by Sagarikabiswas (2023) are programming, hardware technology, network engineering, cyber security analysis, risk analysis, project management and information technology training, among others.

Using ChatGPT is transforming the nature of work, in terms of knowledge, capabilities, competencies and roles of employees. Due to the disruptions already created ChatGPT as it stands today has been already banned or blocked the access in some schools concerned over cheating actions.

CONSEQUENCES OF AUTOMATION FOR JOBS, WAGES, AND INEQUALITY

Automation reduces human intervention in job performance by creating machines capable of replacing human attributes in the execution of more complex and repetitive operations with more certainty and security to work more efficiently by reproducing human tasks and leading to fully substitute workers in some cases. Regarding research on the effects of automation, many studies forecast that in the following next years there will be a huge job destruction, reduction of wages and thus an increasing level of inequality (See figure 2).

Figure 2. Existing jobs at potential risk of automation

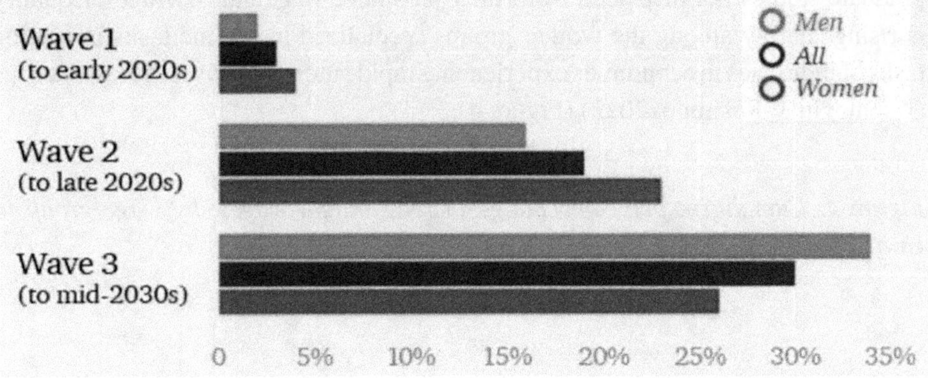

Automation is often associated with job destruction. Automation of tasks will change with advances in artificial intelligence (Acemoglu et al., 2022). Following automation is a decline in routine jobs (Acemoglu et al., 2020; Humlum, 2020). Research on automation documents that is easier to implement it in routine tasks (Levy & Murnane, 2003) (Figure 3).

Figure 3. Existing jobs at potential risk of automation

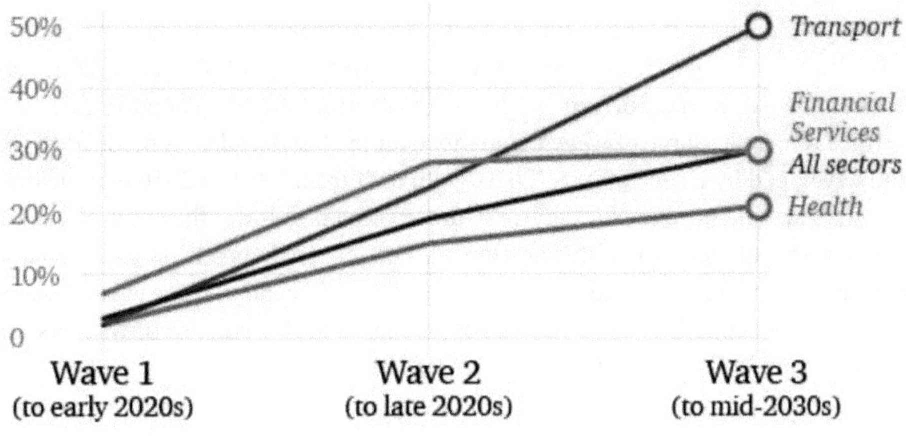

Digital automation technologies tend to expand the tasks performed by the efficient capital, while displacing jobs of certain worker groups for which they have comparative advantage or by reducing the relative and real, wages of workers specialized in routine tasks in manufacturing industries undergoing digital automation, such as the blue-collar jobs and clerical workers. In contrast, workers with post-graduate studies not displaced from their jobs have wage gains. Wage inequality is rising sharply among the worker groups specialized in routine tasks in routine tasks of industries in economies experiencing rapid automation over the last decades (Acemoglu & Restrepo, 2022) (Figure 4).

Figure 4. Cumulative per cent change in real annual wages, by wage group in United States

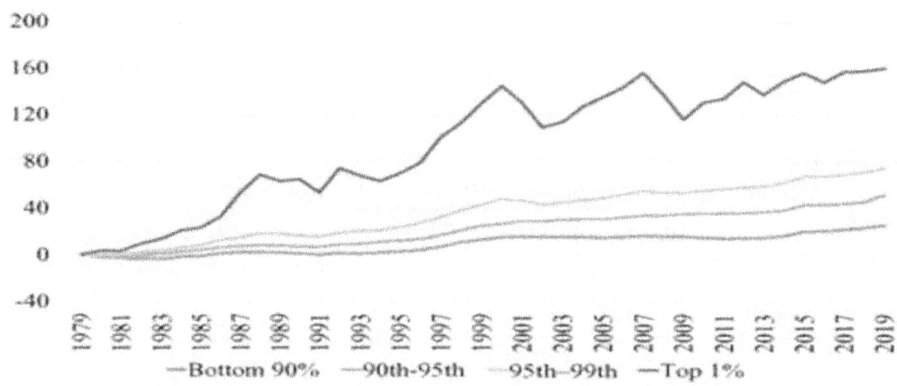

Wage inequality is the result of task displacement, rather than productivity growth and overall capital intensity. According to Acemoglu & Restrepo (2022) task displacement of workers driven by automation from employment opportunities has a defined role in the surge of wage inequality over the last decades. A model designed and developed by Brito & Curl, (2020) with data from 1984 to 2016 demonstrates that the most important consequence of automation is to lower the share of workers in real wages of medium-skilled and low-skilled jobs in domestic production which has steadily declined. Task allocation to diverse types of capital, labor and automation technologies expands tasks performance of capital at the expense of workers. Tax displacement leads to increase in wage inequality.

THE POTENTIAL OF GENERATIVE ARTIFICIAL INTELLIGENCE

Artificial intelligence may reverse the trends of slowing global productivity, increasing the gap of inequality, and diminishing the worker power, undermining advancement of living standards. The living standards of people determines the wealth of nations which can be raised by lifting productivity, as the amount of output produced per worker.

Productivity is barely growing and will continue for some years due to economic and geopolitical uncertainty and the rising capital costs leading to holdback increases in economic growth and wages while widening the gap of inequality. Workplace shifts due to pandemic and investments into generative artificial intelligence eventually will produce compelling results unleashing an era of productivity growth despite that will take more than a decade to reap the benefits. There is an optimism on the use of digital technologies for the creation and development of new business models and workers switching tasks and jobs to yield better results in increasing productivity, augmenting wages, and reducing the inequality wage gap. The implementation of the diverse tools of artificial intelligence in the productivity revolution will take a long-term period to pay off (Strauss, 2023).

Artificial intelligence tools like ChatGPT are easy to adopt ensuring integration with other everyday use apps, which can amplify inequality of resource access leading to asymmetric use and marginalizing groups that will not have represented data (Chen & Wellman, 2004; Weissglass, 2022).

Gopinath (2023) from the International Monetary Fund foresees a boost of economic growth and benefits workers raising productivity by automating cognitive tasks and giving rise to new higher-productivity tasks to perform with machines taking care of routine and repetitive tasks. Humans could spend more time on being creative innovators and analytical people. Artificial Intelligence can spread the knowledge of experienced and productive workers (Figure 5).

Figure 5. The trend of productivity growth has been lower since fiscal crisis.

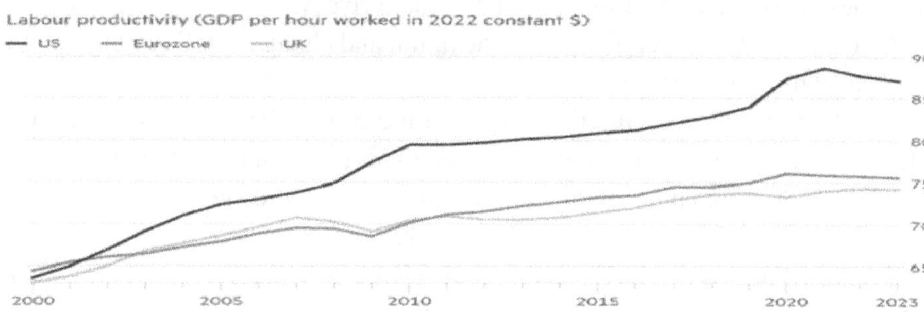

The potential of generative artificial intelligence as more tools are developed, brings about sweeping changes to the global economy, driving about 7%, or almost $7 trillion increase in global GDP lifting productivity growth by about 1.5 percentage points over a 10-year period. Generative IA tools could enhance productivity at office, sales, design building, manufacturing parts, improving healthcare in patient diagnosis, cyber fraud detection, etc. benefiting the global economy. Figure 6 shows the impact of IA on labor productivity, which depends on its capacity and the adoption period. This figure also shows the effect of IA adoption on the annual growth of labor productivity, considering a 10-year adoption period (Sacks (2023)

Figure 6. IA´s impact on labor productivity

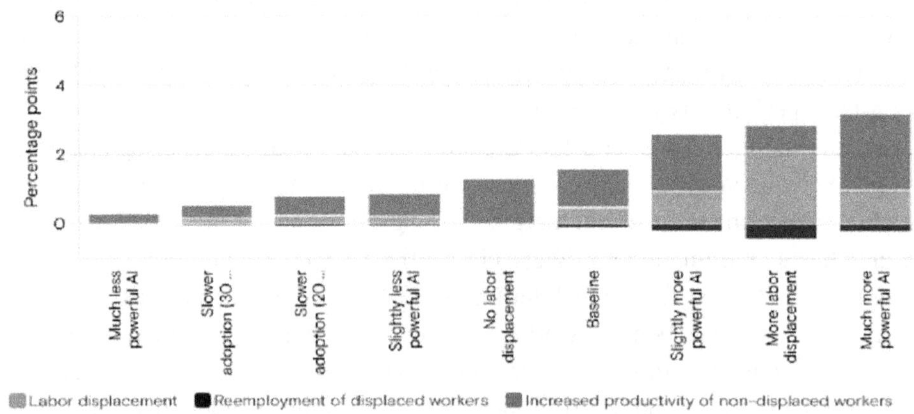

Surveillance Intensifies

A negative impact of the emerging technologies may be the empowerment of malicious actions and the erosion of individual privacy.

Actions to redirect technological innovation and change.

Change the narrative.

At international level, the discussion on the standardization in the present of future digital technologies exists between communities considering that the measures must be evolutive and most of the times the narratives collide leaving space to black swan scenarios and uncertainties lurking back.

Some of the issues that should be considered in changing the narratives are the optimism instead of realism on strategies for technological supremacy among nations, governance, regulations, and standards, competing and cooperation values, congruent coordination of planning, patterns of interactions between governments, technological firms, start-ups, academic and scientific researchers, global market demand, inadequate protocols, revenues, etc., to address operational needs, solve challenges, create benefits for the actors involved and significant impact for the society at large.

Focus on machine learning and intelligence instead than on machine usefulness!

Artificial intelligence systems are characterized as machine-based systems with certain varying levels of autonomy which give support to humans in their objectives and tasks, making predictions, recommendations, decisions, etc., using data analytics also referred as big data based on a massive amount of alternative data sources. Artificial intelligence and machine learning in several industries build applications to take advantage of connections between artificial intelligence and machine learning, helping the companies to transform them processes and products. Machine learning models are techniques of artificial intelligence increasingly deployed in the use experience in big data automatically to learn and improve predictability in performance without being programmed by humans (OECD, 2021). Artificial intelligence and machine learning today are being used in a wide range of applications.

Artificial intelligence and machine learning are used to optimize inventories of retailers, in health organizations in image processing for improved cancer detection; in banking and finance are used for detecting fraud, predicting risk, and proactive financial advice; in sales and marketing for sales forecasting, campaign optimization, sentiment analysis, etc.; in cyber security protect organizations and their clients by detecting anomalies; in customer services, the use of chatbots and cognitive search to gauge customer intent, virtual assistance and answer questions; in transportation improve the efficiency of routs, predictive analysis, traffic forecasting, etc.; in manufacturing, artificial intelligence are used for predictive maintenance and efficiency of operations, etc.

Behind the scenes, the engine of machine learning attempts to reinforce known patterns in the member's behavior and adjusting accordingly when the member change patterns (Burns, 2023). The "Chat Generative Pre-Trained Transformer" (ChatGPT) is a tool of artificial intelligence, with usefulness as machine to overcome resistance to change resulting from the implementation process of digital innovations. As with most tools of artificial intelligence, ChatGPT sometimes works great and simply fine becoming an especially useful learning machine to provide support to human tasks.

An artificial intelligence chatbot performs some cognitive functions, like analysis and interpretation, better than human brains, with more efficiency, effectiveness, and quality, discerning some patterns that elude the human mind to become more useful in contributions to knowledge. Is in this sense, that from a more cheerful outlook, it is required to move from machine learning to machine usefulness.

Enhance Human Capabilities

The relationship between humans and the artificial intelligence ecosystem is one of enhancement of human capabilities and not replacement. Artificial intelligence can be leveraged to enhance cognitive functions and human behavior in the analysis, interpretation, and decision-making. However, the digital traces of artificial intelligence require a knowing subject to interpret, analyze, and validate the outcomes.

Humans are uniquely adapted to constantly create becoming good at it, but when it comes to analyzing, interpreting, and understanding data, the larger the data set becomes, the worse humans perform (Williams, 2023). Humans visualizing data miss the smaller trends that have been averaged out besides that are innately biased through past experiences and preexisting assumptions such as spotting correlations to assume causations. While artificial intelligence takes care of the details data analysis and interpretation, humans can concentrate on creating what he-she does best, making best decisions and empowering to implement them, driving behavior change, improving the abilities to inspire, create habits and true accountability. It is difficult to hold accountability in artificial intelligence systems for any errors and problems with generated content because they lack awareness and consciousness as humans have.

Humans have a limited ability to scale only focusing on one item at a time while in comparison, artificial intelligence does not have limitations regarding scalability processing thousands of tasks in a fraction of a second. Thus, humans can have on artificial intelligence scalability as a trait.

Create Countervailing Powers

The future of edge digital technologies from artificial intelligence to quantum information science have not clear definition which complicates the standardization and regulation because the global competition of major players to gain the largest global market share (Neaher, et al. 2021).

The new standards and regulations for the emerging and disruptive digital technologies must rise from a creative destruction of outdated advances leading to an overall scientific revolution to fully occur to instate no longer emergent the emerging technologies. This argument is supported by Kuhn (1962: 11) who stated that men whose research is based on shared paradigms are committed to the same rules and standards for scientific practice. That commitment and the apparent consensus it creates are prerequisites for normal science.

A new model of cooperation in partnerships between governments and firms sharing both risks and responsibilities, will enable to deliver more value in the digital technologies field by creating more benefits for the involved partners by ensuring proper alignment of interest involving the society at large. Private public partnership cooperation becomes the new structure and a tool for creating economic growth, social development, and socio-ecological resilience, while providing opportunities to balance the advantages for all the involved actors and the society at large.

Convergence of stakeholders in emerging and disruptive digital technology brings new conceptualizations and types of instrumentation of end products and services that will enable major changes in productivity and lifestyles for the wellbeing of the whole society.

Alignment Ethics

It is difficult to imagine how far the evil and stupidity of the human being can go. The rise of ChatGPT and their effects on individuals and society is an opportunity to discuss ethical issues when using these and other similar tools. In the field of artificial intelligence (IA) alignment ethics aims to steer artificial intelligence systems towards ethical principles based on humans' intended goals and preferences. An artificial intelligence system is considered ethically aligned if it advances the intended objectives of human development. Preceded debates are conducted with moral and ethical considerations on specific technologies, as for example, the Ethics of Artificial Intelligence Recommendation of UNESCO.

Artificial intelligence is a digital technology different from all previous technologies including neural networks, dep learning through algorithms and automatic learning, which have presented new and different risks and ethical concerns (Blackman, 2020) considering that humans have control over the machines, turning on and turning off. Humans need to make decisions on what is an acceptable behavior in the use of digital technologies and more precisely on the tools of artificial intelligence, to design, enact and enforce policies.

Avoiding biases on data and models of IA. Artificial intelligence is already here to stay forever and from ethical alignment to be used responsible which requires the commitment to act and behave ethically at every turn. The increasing use of artificial intelligence is risen significant ethical alignment concerns sparking debates regarding issues from human data privacy to the use of algorithms in chat bots and chatGPT that not only perpetuates but tend to emphasize religious, ethnic, racial, gender and other bias. The ethics of responsible artificial intelligence has an orientation from utilitarianism to justify some threats posed by tools such as the ChatGPT, and similar chat bots that include black- box algorithms to validate copyright, infringement discrimination and biases, vulgarity, plagiarism, fake media, fabricated unauthentic textual content, among others.

These ethical issues are being already reported by academics, organizations, and institutions worried with these developments and some measures are being proposed to deal with them. Among other measures to put into place and enforce to mitigate the negative effects, are the claims of disclosing data collected and transparency of what is done with that data, to establish committees dedicated to overseeing the use of artificial intelligence, to identify intelligent agents and chatbots as non-human entities, etc. (Carufel, 2019).

Ways to conduct additional training. Academic, institutional, and organizational leaders are worried and concerned about the effect of artificial intelligence replacing the workforce and the ways to conduct additional training to employees that are rightly worried about being displaced from their jobs. Organizations adopting artificial intelligence must understand, analyze, manage, assess, and mitigate risks, monitor, and evaluate ethical reviews and bias screening considering the evolution of algorithms in nature which require training on the heterogeneous algorithm models that possess high velocity and variability. The diverse ways to conduct additional training is an issue that raises ethical concerns.

Permission to use millions of words and material on artificial intelligence training. Reputation and legal risks of artificial intelligence using copyrighted or offensive content, loss of privacy, spreading false information, fraudulent transactions, lack of transparence, misuse, bias, etc. Regarding the integrity issues, to identify the actual scriptwriter by comparing the text created by ChatGPT is still elusive now. There many legal concerns and issues around copyright and ownership of content generated by artificial intelligence.

Laws and regulations are concerned with these ethical issues dealing with the content created by learning machines which create legal disputes over the ownership of rights to use and profit from the generated content. However, generative artificial intelligence content poses an elevated risk for intellectual property rights and copyright protection, which has serious implications for research to avoid potential infringement caused by the use. OpenAI has already declared that it does not take any responsibility for any infringement that may occur.

Long term implications of artificial intelligence are not clear. Artificial intelligence risk management frameworks must consolidate in the long-term the ethical theory to integrate socially responsible judgments leading to ensure reasoned, purposeful, cautious, and ethical leverage alignment to generative artificial intelligence models. Identification of artificial intelligence and management risks lead to design and implement ethical models to be used long-term to determine a path (Ashok et al., 2022). Utilitarism is an ethical approach used to decision making based on the positive and negative impact of actions that does best good and least harm to individuals, organizations, environment (B ohm et al., 2022).

Control over the ethical disruption of digital technologies and more specifically artificial strategy must require a digital conversation and leadership about acceptable ethical behaviors, under the assumption that digital transformation cannot be interrupted and must be guided by humans in in following years of the near future.

CONCLUSION

Machine learning in artificial intelligence tools, such as the chat GPT can offer prompt responses with an unforeseen combination of innovative and valuable texts produced from digital traces, with the likelihood of an exceptionally low selection subject to quality of data sources and training. These traces require a knowing subject to interpret, analyze, and validate the outcomes. As a stochastic and algorithm parrot, most of the tools of artificial intelligence are unconscious and not be able to produce self-knowledge, which by themselves do not constitute meaningful, valid, and legitimated scientific knowledge.

The development of ethical codes, law, and regulations for the governance of generative artificial intelligence systems is required aimed to minimize ethical concerns such as discrimination, false data and information, plagiarism, copyright infringement, etc. Further, questions regarding the copyright ownership, intellectual property rights, regulations for acceptable use norms, etc., are issues that must be raised, discussed, analyzed, and addressed.

Research and practice must be extended to explore innovative approaches for using artificial intelligence tools and other digital disruptive and breakthrough technologies for finding solution to all ills leading to potential enhancement of human development, creating social and environmental benefits, increasing productivity. These opportunities to conduct future research calls for more transdisciplinary approaches with implications in educational programs that must be challenged using an ethical perspective of digital technologies and artificial intelligence tools aimed to benefit humanity.

REFERENCES

Acemoglu, D., Hazell, J., & Restrepo, P. (2022). Artificial Intelligence and Jobs: Evidence from Online Vacancies. *Journal of Labor Economics*, *40*(S1), S293–S340. doi:10.1086/718327

Acemoglu, D., Lelarge, C., & Restrepo, P. (2020). Competing With Robots: Firm Level Evidence from France. *AEA Papers and Proceedings. American Economic Association*, *110*, 383–388. doi:10.1257/pandp.20201003

Acemoglu, D., & Restrepo, P. (2022). Tasks, automation, and the rise in U.S. wage inequality. *Econometrica*, *90*(5), 1973–2016. doi:10.3982/ECTA19815

Ashok, M., Madan, R., Joha, A., & Sivarajah, U. (2022). Ethical framework for Artificial Intelligence and Digital technologies. *International Journal of Information Management*, *62*, 102433. doi:10.1016/j.ijinfomgt.2021.102433

Blackman, R. (2020), *A Practical Guide to Building Ethical IA*. Retrieved from https://hbr.org/2020/10/a-practical-guide-to-building-ethical-ai

Bohm, S., Carrington, M., Cornelius, N., de Bruin, B., Greenwood, M., Hassan, L., & Shaw, D. (2022). Ethics at the centre of global and local challenges: Thoughts on the future of business ethics. *Journal of Business Ethics*, *180*(3), 835–861. doi:10.1007/s10551-022-05239-2 PMID:36212626

Brito, D., & Curl, R. F. (2020). *Automation Does Not Kill Jobs. It Increases Inequality*. Baker Institute Report no. 11.06.20. Rice University's Baker Institute for Public Policy.

Burns, E. (2023). Machine Learning. *TechTarget network*. https://www.techtarget.com/searchenterpriseai/definition/machine-learning-ML

Carufel, R. (2019). *Companies embrace AI, but execs cite challenges on alignment, ethics*. Agility, PR Solutions. https://www.agilitypr.com/pr-news/public-relations/companies-embrace-ai-but-execs

Castro, A. (2021). Tecnologías emergentes. Uso y aplicación en instituciones públicas de Colombia: Sistematización de Experiencias. *International Education Technologies Review*, *8*(2), 127–139. doi:10.37467/gkarevedutech.v8.3024

Chen, W., & Wellman, B. (2004). The global digital divide within and between countries. *ITandSociety*, *1*(7), 39–45.

Corvalán, J. (2019). The impact of Artificial Intelligence on employment. *Direito Econômico e Socioambiental*, *10*, 35–51. doi:10.7213/rev.dir.econ.soc.v10i1.25870

Del Pozo, D., & Fernández-Sastre, J. (2021). Empleo e inversión en actividades de innovación sin introducción de nuevas tecnologías: Un estudio sobre Ecuador. *Estudios de Economía (Santiago)*, *48*(2), 219–248. doi:10.4067/S0718-52862021000200219

Gopinath, G. (2023). *The Power and Perils of the "Artificial Hand": Considering IA Through the Ideas of Adam Smith Speech to commemorate 300th anniversary of Adam Smith's birth University of Glasgow*. International Monetary Fund. https://www.imf.org/en/News/Articles/2023/06/05/sp060523-fdmd-aiadamsmith?cid=em-COM-123-46688

Humlum, A. (2020). *Robot Adoption and Labor Market Dynamics*. Working paper, University of Chicago.

Kuhn, T. (1962). *The structure of scientific revolutions*. University of Chicago Press.

Kushwaha, A. K., & Kar, A. K. (2021). MarkBot A Language Model Driven Chatbot for Interactive Marketing in Post-Modern World. *Information Systems Frontiers*. Advance online publication. doi:10.1007/s10796-021-10184-y

Levy, D. H. F., & Murnane, R. J. (2003). The Skill Content of Recent Technological Change: An Empirical Exploration. *The Quarterly Journal of Economics*, *118*(4), 1279–1333. doi:10.1162/003355303322552801

Lokman, A. S., & Ameedeen, M. A. (2018). Modern chatbot systems: A technical review. In *Proceedings of the Future Technologies Conference* (pp. 1012–1023). Cham: Springer, 10.1007/978-3-030-02683-7_75

Marín, F. M. (2023). *De las humanidades digitales a la Inteligencia Artificial General*. University of Texas.

Mishel, L., & Bivens, J. (2021). The Productivity-Median Compensation Gap in the United States: The Contribution of Increased Wage Inequality and the Role of Policy Choices. *International Productivity Monitor*, (41). https://link.gale.com/apps/doc/A689169156/AONE?u=anon~10ba8f08&sid=googleScholar&xid=5119dfa8.

Mitchell, A. (2023). ChatGPT could make these jobs obsolete: 'The wolf is at the door.' *New York Post*. https://nypost.com/2023/01/25/chat-gpt- could-make-these-jobs-obsolete/

Neaher, G., Bray, D., Mueller-Kaler, J. & Schatz, B. (2021). *Standardizing the future: How can the United States navigate the geopolitics of international technology standards?* Atlantic Council Report.

OECD. (2021). *Artificial Intelligence, Machine Learning and Big Data in Finance: Opportunities, Challenges, and Implications for Policy Makers,* https://www.oecd.org/finance/artificial-intelligence-machine-learning-big-data-in-finance.html

Ovanessoff, A., & Plastino, E. (2018). Una explosión de productividad. *Integración & comercio, 44*, 28-48. https://dialnet.unirioja.es/servlet/articulo?codigo=6551930

Potter, W. (2023) 'This is not crying wolf... the wolf is at the door': Fears AI could make white collar jobs obsolete as Microsoft pumps multibillion-dollar investment into ChatGPT after laying off 10,000 workers. *Dailymail.com*. https://www.dailymail.co.uk/news/article-11683901/ChatGPT-make-white-collar-jobs-obsolete-Microsoft-pumps-billions-AI.html

Radford, A., Narasimhan, K., Salimans, T. and Sutskever, I. (2018) *Improving Language Understanding with Unsupervised Learning*. Technical Report, OpenAI.

Sacks, G. (2023). *Generative IA could raise global GDP by 7% Artificial Intelligence.* https://www.goldmansachs.com/intelligence/pages/generative-ai-could-raise-global-gdp-by-7-percent.html

Sagarikabiswas. (2023). *ChatGPT: 7 IT Jobs That IA Can't Replace.* https://www.geeksforgeeks.org/chatgpt-7-it-jobs-that-ai-cant-replace/

Schumpeter, J. (1994). *Capitalism, Socialism and democracy.* Routledge.

Schumpeter, J. (1994). *The Theory of Economic Development, An Inquiry into Profits, Capital, Credit, Interest and the Business Cycle.* Harvard University Press.

Sharifi, A., Khavarian-Garmsir, A. R., & Kummitha, R. K. R. (2021). Contributions of smart city solutions and technologies to resilience against the COVID-19 pandemic: A literature review. *Sustainability (Basel), 13*(14), 1–28. doi:10.3390/su13148018

Strauss, D. (2023). *Generative AI's 'productivity revolution' will take time to pay off.* Financial Times. https://www.ft.com/content/21384711-3506-4901-830c-7ecc3ae6b32a

UNCTAD. (2021). *Algunos países en desarrollo bien situados en tecnologías de frontera, pero la mayoría se queda atrás.* Conferencia de las Naciones Unidas sobre Comercio y Desarrollo. https://unctad.org/es/news/algunos-paises-en-desarrollo-bien-situados-en-tecnologias-de-frontera-pero-la-mayoria-se-queda

Vaswani, A., Shazeer, N., Parmar, N., Uszkoreit, J., Jones, L., Gomez, A. N., & Polosukhin, I. (2017). *Attention is all you need. Advances in neural information processing systems.* 31st Conference on Neural Information Processing Systems, Long Beach, CA. https://proceedings.neurips.cc/paper/2017/file/3f5ee243547dee91fbd053c1c4a845aa-Paper.pdf

Weissglass, D. E. (2022). Contextual bias, the democratization of healthcare, and medical artificial intelligence in low and middle income countries. *Bioethics, 36*(2), 201–209. doi:10.1111/bioe.12927 PMID:34460977

Williams, J. (2023). How AI Will Enhance Human Capabilities. *Forbes.* https://www.forbes.com/sites/forbescommunicationscouncil/2018/03/19/how-ai- will-enhance-human-capabilities/?sh=1d37cd1e366f

Yogesh, K. (2023). "So, what if ChatGPT wrote it?" Multidisciplinary perspectives on opportunities, challenges, and implications of generative conversational AI for research, practice, and policy. *International Journal of Information Management, 71*, 102642. doi:10.1016/j.ijinfomgt.2023.102642

Chapter 2
The Integration of Artificial Intelligence in Developing Human Resources

Tarinni Kakar
Indiana State University, USA

Verley V. J. Lanns-Isaac
Indiana State University, USA

Cindy L. Crowder
Indiana State University, USA

ABSTRACT

Even an organization that has reached its limit of growth needs to adapt to the changing environment and technological advancements. Artificial intelligence applications can help transform routine cycles into ones that are more competent, objective, and thorough and will increase its capabilities for stability and renewal. This chapter will explore the beneficial work of AI-based insight on human resource development functions by promoting a supportive organizational culture, encouraging data-driven decision making, fostering employee growth and development, and encouraging openness and communication.

There seems to currently be a lot of excitement surrounding artificial intelligence (AI). For some, it may be a welcome part of modern life in that it opens the way to infinite possibilities and wonders. To others, it is met with trepidation and much pushback. Still others could not care less about AI. Regardless of which side of the AI spectrum of interest one stands, it is evident that AI-based technology is being integrated into

DOI: 10.4018/979-8-3693-0712-0.ch002

our personal and professional lives. What exactly is this AI that is generating such interest suddenly? According to Ketter (2017), artificial intelligence is the theory and development of computer systems that are geared towards the performance of tasks that require the intelligence of humans under normal circumstances.

Martinez (2019) recognized AI as encompassing a system, program, software, or algorithm that can exercise self-governance to the extent that it can think rationally, behave independently, think humanely, act rationally in a beneficent manner, and arrive at decisions, or provide output. Larkin et al. (2022) defined AI as "An advanced computer system that uses algorithms and statistical models to rapidly analyze large amounts of data in order to perform perceptual, cognitive, or conversational functions that are akin to speech or visual recognition, reasoning, and problem solving exhibited by humans" (p. 407). Clearly, while there is no one definition of AI, a commonality that can be deduced from the given definitions is that AI is a branch of computer science that attempts to mimic human intelligence, and it entails a variety of facets in its application.

Types of AI

Under the broad umbrella of AI there are two main types: narrow artificial intelligence and general artificial intelligence. The former, as its name depicts, is narrow in its scope in that it is created to solve one given problem, or one task at a time – it performs only one task at a time in a single domain such as conducting internet searches. In that regard it is constrained to that one task it is programmed to perform. Hence, it is not an independent thinker, and it can only simulate human behavior based on given rules, parameters, and contexts, thus making it 'weak' (Hole & Ahmad, 2021). However, this is not to say that narrow AI is limited in its scope of usefulness, for according to Thomas and Busenhart (2021), "Narrow artificial intelligence is an increasingly integral part of utility, emergency, industrial, transportation, communication, entertainment, financial, medical, and governmental infrastructure systems" (p. 16-17). Carson and Hruska (2023) declared that the majority of current AI experiences stem from narrow intelligence, and businesses use it to transition from standardized to adaptable processes for the purpose of increasing efficiency and automation of routine tasks. With AI being so vastly applied, it is easy to understand why Larkin et al. (2022) considered AI as being poised to be in the category of the most transformative technology in the history of mankind. Indeed, AI has penetrated a wide array of businesses and global markets, and it is thus influencing the lives of humans on a grand scale. This seems to be by design, as Rajakishore and Vineet (2020) stated, the primary aim of AI is to develop advanced programs targeted at finding solutions to the problems of man, and to reproduce mental qualities in machines.

General AI systems, on the other hand, are endowed with commonsense knowledge which equip them to make application of knowledge and skills in numerous contexts. Therefore, general AI is more flexible, and better able to adapt to new situations in less time. Additionally, general AI systems can comprehend abstract concepts, and achieve goals through their ability to manipulate the environment. Since general AI has all these abilities, and can solve any problem that requires AI, it is considered as 'strong' AI (Hole & Ahmad, 2021).

Applications of AI

Amongst some of the applications of AI are in robotics, automation, natural language processing (NLP), machine translation, computer vision and image recognition, data inputting, analysis and predictive modeling, and virtual assistants. It is very likely that any product consumers order online arrives at the doorstep having been in contact with a robot. Warehouses and logistics centers are increasingly dependent on advanced automation technology such as robots, machines vision systems, and AI-based software to automate processes (Kinney, 2023). With use of AI-based technology, companies can function efficiently while they maximize their personnel even during e-commerce surge and labor shortage problems. This was evident during the COVID-19 pandemic (Kinney, 2023).

The use of robotic arms provides a more appealing process of recycling for humans because the robots do the dirty work of sifting through piles of garbage (EverestLabs, 2023). Another application of AI is in the use of ensuring the safety of workers who work in automated factories. Through the employment of tiny-object detection algorithms, YOLOv4, abruptly stops (about 50ms) a robotic arm workstation when a person is within dangerous range. Such quick response to detection of a human's presence can significantly improve the safety in automated workspaces (Lee, Jheng, et al., 2023).

Application of AI is seen in use of autonomous vehicles. Technological advancement is at a level where people who do not delight in driving, but still want to be transported safely from point 'A' to 'B' without maneuvering a vehicle can do so. According to Banks and Liu (2023), there are vehicles today that can operate at highly autonomous levels, allowing the driver to input a destination and relax. In fact, the driver can even go to sleep. The only provision is that the vehicle must remain on traditional roads. For example, Tesla AV vehicles have features built-in that allow them to correspond to stop signs, lane markings, and other vehicles, making hands-free driving possible (Banks & Liu, 2023). Further development of these types of vehicles can significantly benefit humans in that children can be dropped off to school by means of a ride-hailing system – by an AV. These vehicles would therefore free up time for people to read, sleep or engage in other activities (Banks & Liu, 2023). Through AI-powered parking navigation systems, seaports can use "Parknav" to ensure parking solutions. The use of Parknav makes forecasting parking demands possible as well as identifying free spaces and guiding vehicles to these available spaces. With the use of seaports being so crucial to successful international trade, they can help to ensure safe and steady transportation of products across borders to sustain global economies (Lee, Chatterjee, et al., 2023).

Chatbots are widely utilized AI technology in various areas – among them being E-learning. Chatbots are essentially AI-based computer programs that imitate natural language conversations with humans via apps, messaging services, and websites. Chatbot provides administrative information, helps students to get answers to problems, and even conduct evaluation of students' knowledge (El Azhari et al., 2023).

In summation, this seems to be the beginning of an AI era based on the tremendous degree of interest organizations today are devoting to AI. AI is employed to aid in resolving complex problems encountered by humans – particularly problems that lend themselves to being automated. This chapter examined the types of AI - narrow and general and looked at how AI is already being utilized in various facets of our lives as organizations use AI to advantage. However, the question remains, does AI have any bearing on the management aspects of organizations? Later in this chapter information will be provided on succinct ways in which AI is impacting other business areas as it relates to the management function of organizations.

Human Resources

A variety of systems work together to strategically manage people in organizations, including the values and guiding principles that have been adopted by the founders/ owners and leaders, establishing a culture across the organization, guidelines identifying how the values and principles impact procedures and policies, hiring and evaluation practices, and training and benefit programs within the organization. This combination of systems establishes the field of human resources, confirming the need for a perspective that employees are more than a variable cost, they are assets. If organizations recognize these human assets can impact organizational performance and success, both individually and collectively, they will establish methods and structures to elicit the best from those assets, using both management and development strategies.

Human Resource Management

The actions that affect the nature of the relationship between the organization and its employees are generally referred to as management decisions. These decisions are operational in nature, aiming to improve employee efficiency to fundamentally ensure the competitive advantage of the organization. The field of human resource management (HRM) grew out the need to address the people side of these management decisions in the early 20th century and was initially called personnel management. These departments were responsible for the administrative side of record keeping and compliance with labor laws. As the responsibilities within organizations expanded to specialized job duties of benefits (forms of non-cash rewards), compensation (the cash return employees receive in the form of salaries or wages), and staffing, a gap between the intentions of organizational policies and the outcomes developed. To study this phenomenon, theorists developed two models to describe and define the functions of HRM within organizations: hard and soft (Guest, 1987).

Soft HRM

The soft approach to HRM is associated with the Harvard School Model (Beer et al., 1984) and McGregor's Theory Y perspective (1960), utilizing individual talents and equating employee behavior as self-regulated rather than controlled by external policies and pressures. These models are based on a high level of trust as both the organizations and employee's needs are acknowledged above compliance. Storey's (1992) model made a clear distinction between the aspect of managing humans and administrative-only functions by suggesting that employees be selected, compensated, and trained with detailed forethought: "it is human capability and commitment which distinguishes successful organizations…the human resource ought to be nurtured" (p. 26).

This approach is often seen as less strategic because the results are not expressed as easily in quantitative metrics like productivity. However, it can feature a strong communication structure, competitive pay, rewards, and appraisal systems, less turnover, and a long-term staffing plan.

Hard HRM

The hard approach to HRM is based on notions of tight strategic control (Devanna et al., 1984) and the economic model of man according to Theory X (McGregor, 1960). It is related to the quantitative aspects of work in which the policies are closely linked to performance systems and strategic and competitive goals of the organization. Employees are viewed as a cost of doing business and are to be positioned within the organization as numbers and skills, at the right time and place (Legge, 1995). This approach results in increased productivity and profit. It also results in high turnover, little empowerment, pay structures that recruit and retain adequate employees, and untapped employee potential.

An early model designed with a hard approach for managing personnel presented selection, appraisal, development, and rewards as the key components (Fombrun & Tichy 1984). In their cycle, interconnected processes focused on selecting employees who could perform the tasks needed by the organization. An assessment of employee performance impacted the distribution of compensation and incentives. Training was implemented to improve workforce talent. The model emphasized the interdependence of the four processes and their impact on the overall effectiveness of the organization, acclimating the structure of the organization and policies to a human resources system.

Summary. To remain successful, organizations must integrate human resource practices into business policies and corporate strategy. However, the conflicting foundations of managerial control and human nature in the two HRM models make it difficult to incorporate them into one comprehensive HRM approach. Hard models are built on the premise that employees dislike work and need tight control and direction while soft models assume employees are motivated to work in pursuit of self-fulfillment. Cardon and Stevens (2004) found that merging the two models by integrating HRM policy with business strategy provided little evidence that, while employment practices were changing, the changes lacked strategic focus. Thus, a new discipline emerged to establish a common ground for a system that provides employee development, training, bi-directional trust, and cultural change in performance because of commitment: human resource development.

Human Resource Development

Unlike other resources, human resources have unrestricted capabilities and potential. This can be nurtured by creating a climate that continuously identifies those aptitudes. Human resource development (HRD) systems aim to create a culture within organizations to foster that potential, assisting employees as they develop knowledge, skills, and abilities for both personal growth and organizational effectiveness. HRD was first introduced by Nadler (1969) in the United States by defining it as those learning experience which are organized, for a specific time, and designed to bring about the possibility of behavioral change. Initially, the focus was to select and retain the right employee for the job. Development programs were one-size-fits-all approaches to maintain the workforce's job skills. However, a shift in the HRD discipline moved toward matching the employee needs with those of the organization and to provide support within the organization so both can accomplish their goals, creating a culture of growth with programs and policies that promoted individualized employee development.

As the discipline grew across the globe, the definition expanded. McLagan and Bedrick (1983) defined HRD as the "integrated use of training and development, career development, and organization development to improve individual and organizational performance" (p. 7), and Gilley et al. (2002) stated the mission of HRD was to:

Provide individual development focused on performance improvement related to current job; provide career development focused on performance improvement for future jobs; develop performance management systems used to enhance organizational performance capacity and capability; provide organizational development that results in both optimal utilization of human potential; improved human performance, enhancing the culture and therefore its effectiveness. (p. 12)

Swanson and Holton (2022) viewed HRD as a process used to engage different people at different times and locating HRD in different places both inside and outside the organization, reviewing the context in which it occurs and the content it supports. They emphasized that organizations are human-made and rely on that human expertise to establish and achieve goals.

The components of HRD such as performance appraisals, counselling, training, and organization development interventions are used to initiate, facilitate, and promote this process in a continuous way. Because the process of developing human resources has no limit, the methods of implementing these initiatives should be examined periodically determine if they are fostering or impeding the process. Organizations can facilitate the process of development by systematically planning each initiative, allocating appropriate organizational resources, and embodying a philosophy of development that values human beings and promotes their continuous growth.

HRD initiatives help build a more active and reliable workforce that can adapt to an ever-changing work environment, but organizations that fail to allow employees to meet their individual needs will see valued employees exiting. These initiatives incorporate both formal (classroom training; a planned change effort) and informal (coaching; mentoring) opportunities that may represent the company's effort to contribute to the development of the individual and the organization. Career Development programs match the needs of the employee with those of the organization with the major components being counseling and training. Through a process of defining career goals and creating plans within the context of organizational realities, organizations can identify internal promotional opportunities and develop talent management strategies such as succession plans to ensure those individuals are ready to assume their new roles. These efforts can be combined with the organization's mission to design organizational development interventions (McLean & McLean, 2001).

Training and Learning

The need for employee development occurs at several different levels within an organization. While new employees have been selected based on their prior knowledge and skill levels, they may need to learn additional information at the beginning of their tenure with the organization. Other developmental needs may surface after an employee's performance review or through the observation of a supervisor. The introduction of new technology, equipment, or a change in vendor may demand skill development. Behavioral changes may need to be addressed. Employees identified for potential promotions could require additional skills or knowledge. All these issues can be addressed with training and learning activities. They are designed to focus on individual growth and development and to produce results quickly.

Delivery methods for training and learning activities can include structured, instructor-led learning in a formal classroom, planned, guided, and created by subject experts with defined learning objectives (Marsick & Watkins, 2001). When the content of the training will impact the success of the organization, such as onboarding new employees or compliance training, formal training is the most suitable option. However, employees are drawn away from their work to attend. Online training delivers a formalized learning strategy that can be completed with less time restrictions or location boundaries but requires a self-directed learner to be successful. Informal learning activities do not involve lesson plans or learning outcomes and could occur at any time and at different locations. Informal learning is often unplanned. Knowledge can be shared between employees during day-to-day work activities, initiated by either the employee providing the knowledge or the employee wanting to learn (Colley et al., 2002). Because informal learning happens casually, it does not induce tension or stress for the employee.

Performance Management

Performance management is a systemwide approach used to improve organizational performance, studying where performance breaks down within the organization and interventions that are put in place to achieve performance results (Gilley et al., 2002). It plays a crucial role in aligning individual and team efforts with overall business objectives by ensuring employees have the knowledge, skills, motivation, and support to do their job. The primary goal of performance management is to create an environment where employees can perform at their full potential and align with the overall goals of the organization. It involves various processes such as goal setting, evaluation, feedback, improvement strategies, motivation tactics, and performance appraisal systems (Richard & McCray., 2023).

A formal performance management system ensures everyone within the organization understands expectations, goals, and career progress, including how an individual employee's work aligns with the organization's overall vision. By implementing effective performance management systems, organizations can enhance employee performance, productivity, and ultimately drive organizational success. This is achieved by providing clarity in roles and expectations, facilitating skill development, and enabling informed decisions on promotions and rewards, all short-term gains. Performance management also strives to improve overall organizational capability with continuous improvement by turning every interaction with employees into opportunities to learn and develop. Properly structured systems can also direct the allocation of funds into the organization's performance budget to address developmental needs.

Career Development

Career development has evolved from a solitary tool for individual growth to a key strategic asset for many far-sighted organizations. Organizations use career development initiatives to "identify, develop, and prepare the appropriate employees for future positions, including initiatives at the individual (career planning and awareness) and organizational level (coaching, succession planning, human resource planning)" (Gilley et al., 2002, p. 15). These are long-term initiatives because they provide continuous development opportunities and encourage ever-increasing levels of competency, preparing the employee for future opportunities and ensures the organization's ability to fill current and future staffing needs. Career development matches the needs of the employee with those of the organization. If they are planned and designed correctly, with the focus on the relationship between the employee and their work as well as the employee and the organization, they will bring out the best an individual can be and finding a place in an organization where they can express excellence and contribute to the goals of the organization (Garavan & Coolahan, 1996).

While some career development initiatives focus on vertical development for those who want upward mobility, others focus on lateral transfers when an employee identifies a position that better fits their skills and values. Attention should be given to alternative paths that reflect more personal aspirations and not necessarily the traditional organizational needs. Super (1990) conceptualized career development in terms of life stages whereby employees and their abilities, interests, and qualifications for jobs change over time. As they age chronologically, their saliency in a work role may remain high, but it also could diminish. Their ability to measure their saliency is referred to career maturity, which allows them to make career decisions (stay in a position or search for a new opportunity). Fitz-Enz and Mattox (2014) found the longer an employee stayed in a position without a promotion or challenge, the more likely they were to become disengaged or leave the organization. At the employee level, individuals may be dissatisfied with their career, which can be detrimental to their well-being as well as impact the overall success of their employer. They must be able to reflect on their own interests, skills, and qualifications (Kononiuka et al., 2020).

However, this construct of maturity was envisioned only in a stable work environment, not one in which employees were forced to make a post-career choice work adjustment (such as being displaced due to the use of AI). Super et al, (1996) proffered the construct of adaptability as the central process in adult career development. Adaptability refers to an employee's willingness and readiness to engage in developmental measures that are necessary to alter their career path. Employees do not express change readiness similarly, and so organizations must be prepared to provide support and resources at different levels. This may include psychosocial support to deal with the trauma of job loss and occupational transition as well as career counseling to identify new career paths. Employees may need training to develop new skills or may need to pursue formal educational programs and certificates at the post-secondary level.

Coaching and Mentoring. Coaching is a collaborative, reflective, developmental interface used to empower employees through structured, focused interactions with another individual who does not have formal supervisory authority over the coachee to achieve professional outcomes. It facilitates professional learning and uses a goal-focused relationship to develop and grow the employee's capacity in the workplace. It has primarily been focused on effective leadership roles and responsibilities; however, coaching can be used in the development of any employee within an organization through personal, on-the job training for skills and competence and can serve as a developmental intervention to reflect the intended outcomes of coaching in an organizational context.

Coaching has the capacity to influence and transform organizational values, ethics, and policies, so the proper selection of a coach is vital to the organization. The use of appropriate strategies, tools, and technology can promote desirable and sustainable change for the benefit of the coachee and potentially the other stakeholders (Bachkirova et al., 2017). Coaches can be selected from within the organization or can be brought in from outside. Large organizations have the option of selecting a coach from within the organization who will have prior knowledge of the coachee and an awareness of the organizational culture, allowing for a quicker building of mutual trust and respect. However, smaller organizations may need to solicit the help of an external coach, providing an individual who would come to the relationship without bias but could need additional time to build a trusting relationship with the coachee.

The similarity between coaching and mentoring is that they both provide a one-on-one relationship that is designed to enhance an employee's career development. Mentoring also involves receiving guidance on improvement from a more experienced person, but the mentor can peer, a supervisor, or someone else within the organization. Mentoring varies from personal and professional growth to the socialization of new employee (Joo, 2005). Mentors generally provide advice on navigating the organization and identifying future opportunities while assisting with the creation of a professional network. Long-term development is usually part of mentoring, and coaching generally has a finite timeline, more aligned with developing goals and skills needed for a specific position or job (Nguyen et al., 2019).

Organizational Development

HRD is primarily about organized and self-directed activities that are tailored towards increasing knowledge, skills, and competencies to ultimately improve behavior of persons within an organization. These activities, entailing learning, performance, and change that work in unison to bring to fruition the envisaged organizational effectiveness by developing new and innovative solutions to problems and self-renewing capacity, are referred to as organizational development (OD) (Gilley et al., 2002).

Each organization must perform a deep introspection, discover problems and weaknesses, and direct resources toward those improvements. Leaders must develop the ability to establish a viable vision and then have the communication skills to move primary stakeholders into action based on their comprehensive analysis of the factors impacting results. The interventions may require a variety of techniques to improve the overall efficiency and performance of the organization. According to Raina (2018):

OD is planned long-term effort aimed at improving functional efficiency of the organization. The process is supported and guided by top management and aims to improving an organizational vision and problem-solving capacity and developing a positive work culture to help an organization to improve its performance in the prevailing business environment. (p.106)

This would be accomplished through flexible options provided by policies and programs at institutions as well as a change in climate.

RELATIONSHIP BETWEEN AI AND HRD

The integration of AI in the workplace has become a significant topic of interest in the last decade. Coordinating AI into different parts of business activities offers numerous benefits for different industries. From developing efficiency and proficiency to upgrading the dynamic interaction, simulated intelligence has changed the working environment. Human Resource Development (HRD) is an area where AI advancements are being utilized to upgrade productivity and exactness. With advancements in AI, machine learning algorithms and natural language processing, is reforming the way that organizations enroll, locally available, train workers and pursue vital HRD related choices. Vital reasoning assumes an urgent part in growing long haul objectives and adjusting them to an association's goals. It included dissecting informational collections, understanding business sector patterns and understanding labor force needs from now on. This capacity to think decisively permits HRD expertly to contribute in a critical manner in various regions.

Anderson (2023) explained how different organizations are leveraging AI algorithms to understand and analyze large amounts of employee data in a short period of time. This data could include performance metrics, employee feedback and engagement levels. By analyzing this information with AI techniques, organizations can correctly predict trends related to attrition rates, identify factors contributing positively or negatively towards productivity and even recommend personalized career development plans for employees based on patterns observed across similar profiles. The use of AI in such complex analysis enables HRD professionals to make informed decisions regarding talent management strategies ultimately leading towards increased retention rate of high-performing employees.

A huge viewpoint that makes the compromise of simulated intelligence into HRD exceptionally successful is its capacity to mechanize dreary errands. These tasks were for the most part finished by individuals anyway the robotization pushes HR specialists to focus on fundamental drives like capacity on the board, laborer improvement, etc. Man-made reasoning has additionally helped upgrade precision in navigation. By separating data from various sources, for instance, laborer studies, execution organizations and reviews, it can help with recognizing models and examples. This approach considers the relationship to go with informed decisions.

Notwithstanding, a worry that is many times raised about the coordination of simulated intelligence in HRD is work removal. There is a trepidation that AI will robotize undertakings customarily performed by people, prompting a diminished requirement for human contribution in HRD capabilities.

Moreover, HRD incorporates managing individual workers and their requirements. It requires figuring out private inspirations and offering help custom-fitted to every situation. While simulated intelligence can break down a lot of information rapidly and give specific proposals, it misses the mark on capacity to interface on a profound level. While there might be concerns, Zielinski (2023) argued that it will lead to a shift in job roles rather than complete elimination. HRD professionals will have more time to focus on labor force planning and representative commitment rather than expending excessive energy on administrative tasks for CEOs. They can use their skill in grasping the one-of-a-kind requirements of representatives, cultivating a positive workplace, and executing ability maintenance techniques. The potential benefits offered by AI in HRD are immense, but there are some challenges that come with integration of AI in HRD. One focal issue is the potential for bias within AI algorithms. In the recent years, there has been an increase in the importance of aligning HRD strategies with organizational objectives. By incorporating the 'Big Picture' thinking into HRD and following the trends of AI, it has become easier to stay ahead of the curve in a dynamic business landscape.

Despite efforts to reduce bias through automation, there is still a risk that AI could be acting based on previous data. If they are not examined during the development process, it may result in unfair practices that neglect certain populations and create unequal opportunities. For example, a gender imbalance within the dataset may reinforce pre-existing workforce stereotypes. To address consequences arising from the use of their machine learning-based applications, organizations must regularly audit their process to reduce the risks associated with higher exposure.

Resistance from employees related to concerns about job adequacy is another obstacle faced by businesses implementing AI in HRD. Although automation streamlines several processes, such as recruitment and talent acquisition, there are times when employees' tasks may be automated, raising concerns about job loss. Such worries can be settled by featuring the cooperative nature among computer-based intelligence and the laborers in the work environment. The benefits of simulated intelligence with regards to saving time for errands that are more significant, upgrading pursuing decisions through experiences in view of information, and advancing worker improvement potential open doors that should be conveyed by HRD divisions.

While carrying out AI in HRD practices, variety and consideration are extremely urgent variables to consider. Organizations should ensure their calculations don't build up specific arrangements of predispositions, and maintaining diverse teams throughout the algorithm design process can help reduce risks since different viewpoints help improve potential biases. Adherence to moral guidelines, which incorporate guaranteeing straightforwardness regarding how choices have been made following examination and reception, assumes a pivotal part in addressing these concerns. Furthermore, leaders who create an environment of continuous development and learning help themselves and their employees recognize the value of investing time and effort into their own professional growth alongside advancements brought about by AI technology (Yorks et al., 2022). This section aims to explore the current applications of AI in HRD while highlighting their benefits and challenges.

Training and Learning With AI

Training and learning are areas where AI has had a significant impact. Traditional methods within this area have relied on the one size fits all approach (Ali et al., 2023). However, AI has introduced personalized training programs that cater to employees' learning styles, needs, and preferences, including the sensory modalities of visual, auditory, and kinesthetic (Lujan & DiCarlo, 2006). Integrating AI algorithms into internal communication platforms enables the automatic analysis of employees' preferences and behaviors, allowing for tailored content delivery that aligns with their individual needs and interests. Machine learning algorithms can analyze vast amounts of data to identify patterns and trends, allowing organizations to personalize training programs based on employees' specific needs and learning styles. This personalization enhances the effectiveness of training and allows employees to learn at their own pace and in a way that resonates with them, resulting in improved knowledge retention and skill development (Malik et al., 2023)

One example of AI in training and learning is the case of Kiehl, a skincare company. Kiehl developed a personalized learning platform that leverages AI-based recommendations to provide custom training content to employees based on their individual needs (Green, 2023). This approach mirrors the personalized skincare recommendations provided to customers. By tailoring the learning experience, employees can elevate their knowledge of Kiehl's products and the science of skincare, ultimately improving their performance in their roles. This demonstrates how AI can be used to create personalized learning experiences that address specific skill gaps and maximize employee development (Korzynski et al., 2023). These initiatives allow organizations to improve employee performance and productivity by providing personalized learning experiences that address individual skill gaps and needs. It also enables continuous monitoring of employees during training sessions, allowing for intervention if additional support is necessary, resulting in maximum engagement and effectiveness (Dutta et al., 2023). This ultimately leads to enhanced knowledge and expertise among employees, benefiting the organization.

Training and learning are also delivered through electronic devices without the presence of an instructor. This includes gaming software in which employees compete in a series of decision-making schemes while exploring strategic solutions that impact other players in the game as well as the overall organization. Silva et al. (2021) found the competitive nature of the game can attract individuals that thrive in a competitive environment and serve as a motivating factor for employees Simulation training provides employees repeated practice of a multisensory experience by imitated conditions within the workplace. While these simulation systems can be costly, they do provide a risk-free environment without the danger of injury or lost time due to equipment difficulties (Aati et al., 2020).

These examples showcase the potential of AI in transforming traditional approaches to training and development. By providing personalized content and recommendations, AI enhances the learning experience for employees, improves knowledge retention, and facilitates its application in the workplace. Moreover, organizations must carefully examine the ethics involved in the implementation of AI, including matters such as data privacy and preventing unintended negative outcomes.

Performance Management With AI

The integration of AI technology in performance management offers several benefits, including data-driven evaluations and intelligent performance analytics. With AI, organizations can gather and analyze large amounts of data to gain valuable insights into employee performance (Su et al., 2021). This data-driven approach helps identify areas for improvement, informs decision-making processes, and provides the capacity to evaluate the system after the implementation is complete. Hancock et al. (2023) reported that some organizations have implemented generative language models within their HRD functions that produce reasonable responses during simulations where they answer convincingly while creating authentic responses. This advancement grants HRD specialists to replicate conversations and circumstances with employees, for instance, during training or performance review sessions. The positive side of this recreated knowledge application is that it gives a safeguarded environment to practice inconvenient conversations, surveying different outcomes, and enhancing interpersonal skills.

Tools such as Workday Performance Management, Oracle HCM, Reflektive, Engagedley, etc. provide personalized feedback based on employees. By using predictive analytics, these tools can help analyze patterns in employee behavior and address the need for tailored development plans. This allows for better employee engagement and organizational performance. Additionally, by reducing the biases included in standard assessment methods, objectivity is enhanced. AI systems produce unbiased assessments because they concentrate on information analysis rather than making subjective decisions.

Buck and Morrow (2018) highlighted AI-powered real-time monitoring provides ongoing feedback loops between management and staff. Before these technologies were developed, businesses would have to wait for quarterly or annual reviews or check in to identify results. They now have the capability to do both while easily resolving any issues that may impact employee performance. In addition, through different forms of interactions, AI-powered sentiment analysis employs language analysis to spot early indications of employee disengagement. This gives businesses an insight to take preventative action before something wrong happens thus lowering the risk of turnover and ultimately promoting a productive workplace.

Career Development With AI

While staffing is typically viewed as an HRM function, career development is essential to the success of developing employees once they are within the organization. Wilson et al. (2022) stated digital technologies designed for career guidance have a role in helping manage the transformation of AI into the workplace. The use of AI algorithms for staffing can be used to predict attributes of candidates or employees and the relationship between those attributes and predictive performance within the position. Organizations can use technology and work machines to analyze internal data to track high performing employees, those who are not performing well, trends in staffing needs (higher productivity periods), turnover patterns, and retirement timelines. Organizations that have struggled developing succession plans in the past can utilize AI to foster the process by providing career roadmaps when promising employees require guidance and advise on the appropriate direction for their goals.

A key benefit of utilizing AI to support workers in becoming career adaptable is that coaching and mentoring can yield a better outcome than an employee trying on their own. Both coaching and mentoring can be accessed in a virtual arena, presenting accessibility and flexibility. In less-developed or lower-populated geographic areas, identifying mentors can be difficult when attempting to suit a particular need (e.g., female, BIPOC, etc.) (Knouse, 2001). Opening the search to technology-based relationships provides alternatives to locating mentors and allows the technology to connect the pair across geography regions, time zones, and multinational organizations. Grosso, et al. (2022) studied an employability support toolkit with a web-based platform and found that it provided a personalized services for career change, guiding users through a journey with personalized conversation with the AI coach.

Lee et al. (2019) found that AI-powered experiences with chatbots can be used to initiate career development conversations and then will conduct a series of psychometric tests that suggest job categories or promotional opportunities to the employee. Because the chatbot has access to all data available on the web, including critical labor market information and stats, it can provide personalized career recommendations and feedback in real time, making it a convenient and effective tool for career planning. Employees can build an electronic portfolio, and the chatbot can monitor an employee's progress and remind them of unmet goals. This system can be made accessible to supervisors within the organization who need to track their existing employees or may want to scan the data when identifying candidates for internal hiring.

Chatbots are programed to use either voice or text input, so they can begin mentoring employees through career planning activities. They can ask questions about career goals and potential new roles and make recommendations on courses or certifications to complete. After consulting an organization's website, a chatbot will understand what employer's value. They can assess an employee's skills and competence levels and then match the results to job profiles that require the same level of competency and skills (D'Silva et al., 2020). Through writing programs, chatbots can make suggestions on how employees can tailor their resumes and applications for those open positions and create an action plan. These processes can reduce the amount of time employees need to increase skill sets or search for jobs, and it can decrease the amount of time an employer needs to identify the appropriate personnel to fulfil an open position. Compared to human career counselors, chatbots can provide more unbiased advice to each employee.

It is essential that organizations create a work environment which fosters employee growth. This can be accomplished by implementing AI-enhanced career development in the workplace, allowing employees to fulfill their career needs. Thus, enhancing organizational loyalty. Organizations will benefit by retaining a greater number of their competent and qualified employees with higher levels of job satisfaction, lower employee turnover, and fewer complaints (Werther & Davis, 1996). However, organizations that fail to allow employees to meet their individual needs may lose valued employees.

Organizational Development With AI

When OD is merged with the uses of AI, a link between the two exists, and by extension, a link with HRD. Schein and Schein (2018) recognized that one of our new realities today is an increasing interaction with AI. This is evident as software is boosted by intelligent data-assimilating devices that substitute some types of work or develop entirely new types of jobs. By virtue of AI being utilized to enhance the efficiency of software, technology, and other aspects of an organization to bring about change and development for efficiency, it is indicative of synchronization between HRD and AI. A case in point is the use of ChatGPT and Bing Chat, if used in Wikipedia for example, would not only consume what Wikipedia covers, but would also go further and organize what it covers (Booth, 2023). Such utilization of new technology (AI) would therefore improve the performance of that organization.

Additionally, Booth (2023) further noted that if ChatGPT and Bing Chat, for instance, were directed to U.S tax codes and regulations, they would learn the codes and regulations therein. Hence, if prompted, an appropriate response would ensue, demonstrating the use of AI in this example can foster organizational development and bring about change for the optimal functioning of the organization. This is categorized as an intervention aimed at improving the organization (Raina, 2018). With the environment being such that use of AI is fast becoming part and parcel of the workplace, for organizations to continue operating and remaining competitive, it is incumbent they seek ways of taking advantage of the added efficiency AI can bring in solving problems to stay ahead of the competition.

In many firms, the use of AI technology for efficient business administration is becoming more commonplace. The use of AI to assist in the resolution of various control issues is one of the most cutting-edge and contemporary methodologies. Chen et al. (2022) revealed how various businesses deployed AI-driven chatbots to serve as customer service reps during the outbreak while eliminating any potential biases frequently present in customer service personnel. All clients are treated equally because of the constant replies these chatbots deliver that are unaffected by the users' emotions or personal convictions. Conscious or unconscious biases of people can have a negative effect on how decisions are made inside an organization. AI systems base choices on objective data analysis rather than personal judgments or biases. This promotes the abolition of discriminatory behaviors and guarantees equity in all areas within the organization. In conclusion, AI applications in HRD have a remarkable ability to transform routine cycles into ones that are more competent, objective, and thorough. Modernized screening devices are used in selection methods to lessen inclination, and chatbots provide modified joint efforts often through capacity gaining. Motorization also helps in evaluation, when a lot of data needs to be handled to support different levels of deftness. Using generative language models reproduces conversations for testing and fosters social skills. The difficulties encountered mostly revolve around estimations that are skewed and worker concerns over the viability of the company.

FUTURE ADVANCEMENTS IN AI THAT WILL IMPACT HUMAN RESOURCES

With the rising advancement of computer-based intelligence innovations, HRD professionals are encountering massive changes that might reshape the way they work. This section investigates future headways in simulated intelligence that will affect HR, examining both their positive and negative implications.

Conversational AI

Gilmurray (2023) discussed how conversational AI insights stages address another exciting movement shaping the destiny of HRD. Platforms like Google Dialogflow, Microsoft Bot Framework, etc., impact natural language processing which allow future employees / candidates to interact in a better way with recruiters. These interactions take place through chatbots and respect HR-related demands. Conversational AI enables fast and correct responses about HR methodologies, preferences, or common information around the affiliation. This advancement in technology helps employees get essential information at any given point without wasting time.

Generative AI

Generative AI's intelligence's capacity to analyze vast amounts of data moreover stresses almost all security and ethical consequences. As affiliations amass wide information around their laborers for examination purposes, questions might develop regarding consent, data security measures, and likely manhandling of personal information. It is principal for HRD specialists to discover a few kinds of agreement between utilizing generative computer-based insights encounters whereas with respect to people's security benefits.

Generative AI includes technologies such as ChatGPT, Image synthesis, etc. and is a powerful tool that can transform the field of HR (Bedard et al., 2023). These technologies can help analyze vast amounts of data related to past employee performance reviews and feedback. This data will help provide valuable insights for shaping future workforce strategies. The positive impact of these movements can't be denied; in any case, it is noteworthy also to think about their related negatives. One concern develops from biases that are embedded within historical data used by machine learning programs to better resume. There is a risk that such biases may extend within AI driven systems without proper oversight or interventions measures considered.

Talent Analytics

As businesses are growing, it is becoming more important to recognize the benefits that talent analytics brings. It is an essential component of strategic HRD in businesses. It gives businesses the ability to forecast employment requirements, plan their personnel more effectively, and promote diversity and inclusion programs. With technological improvements enabling more advanced analysis and predictive modeling methods, the future of talent analytics is bright. However, businesses must address challenges involving confidentiality of information, improving analytical capabilities, moral considerations, and biases existing in the statistics and models used. To successfully adopt talent analytics practices, Yorks et al. (2022) suggested linking talent analytics practices with organizational goals, encouraging collaboration between HR, data analysts, and IT specialists, and developing a learning culture that encourages proficiency in using cutting-edge analytic tools.

The capability of measuring the impact of diverse HR initiatives on business outcomes was emphasized by Polzer (2022). By examining the data connected with them, organizations may more accurately gauge the effectiveness of training initiatives, workforce diversity initiatives, and employee engagement activities. It encourages evidence-based initiatives by providing unbiased insights into crucial HRD metrics like attrition rates, time-to-hire ratios, or cost-per-hire figures. HRD practitioners may more easily defend investments in initiatives for human capital management thanks to these metrics.

While AI has succeeded in eradicating human biases and accelerating commercial operations, there are biases inherent in AI technologies that may be problematic. Varsha (2023) emphasized the need to establish efficient policies and methods for managing biases in artificial intelligence systems. When developing AI models from scratch, a variety of useful datasets should be used to prevent biased findings. Algorithms must also be regularly checked and inspected to detect any potential biases that may emerge over time or because of changes in data sources. Openness and comprehensibility should also be given top importance by developing techniques that allow humans to understand how decisions are made by AI systems. Collaboration amongst diverse groups, including ethicists, psychologists, politicians, and technologists, is essential for effective efforts to reduce bias in AI systems.

Future advancements in AI are expected to fundamentally alter several aspects of HRD processes; however, caution should be exercised regarding the negative effects that may result from them perhaps not being used as intended. The use of continuous screening devices powered by AI computations increases efficiency but necessitates careful inspection to prevent the spread of tendencies to show internal genuine information. Conversational artificial intelligence systems support fostering openness but must be improved to replace human partnerships regarding sensitive subjects that call for sensitivity. While generative computer-based insights provide crucial information for ways of capacity augmentation, there should be strict adherence to security guidelines and ethical standards to protect employees' extremely proprietary information.

False insights movements might theoretically disrupt HRD methods by streamlining procedures, improving employee experiences, and providing crucial experiences to crucial free heading. This is true in broad terms with genuine implementation and control. In any event, it is important to be aware of any potential drawbacks associated with these advancements and take proactive steps to reduce risks. The unavoidable future of HRD may fully profit from its outstanding capabilities by sensibly reining in simulated intelligence.

Conclusion

Organizations grow only through the efforts and competencies of their human resources. Personnel policies can keep the morale and motivation of employees high, but these efforts are not enough to make the organization dynamic and take it in new directions. Employee capabilities must continuously be developed and sharpened. When employees use their initiative, take risks, experiment, innovate, and make things happen, the organization must promote a supportive organizational culture. Even an organization that has reached its limit of growth, needs to adapt to the changing environment and technological advancements. No organization is immune to the need for processes that help to acquire and increase its capabilities for stability and renewal.

The differences between HRD and HRM can be difficult to summarize because they share overlapping objectives and methods. Both can be essential constituents within organizations, but the difference between managing people and developing them is far more than one letter. Those who are dedicated to development require a different skillset and spend their time solving challenges that are embedded in multiple layers of the organization. HRM generally operates as its own entity, involving the people who work in that department. The purpose of HRM is to maintain the functions of an organization: processing compensation, employee records, and benefits packages. In comparison, HRD involves members from several departments to foster growth in employees, and their success continually refines the structure of an organization.

Job tasks in HRM are administrative in nature and are more day-to-day oriented. They focus on identifying and hiring quality employees and utilize employee-level systems to motivate employees with incentives and rewards. HRD job tasks are more related to strategic planning and are focused on organizational-, community-, and societal-level initiatives. They motivate employees by improving workplace culture by demonstrating ways to grow professionally through career development, training, and organization development interventions.

Organizations will always experience turnover. Formal succession planning and informal career coaching are effective future-proof planning strategies that can be predicted with AI-based systems to ensure organizations will always have a resilient workforce with the knowledge and skills to perform critical tasks. Effective employee development can improve the performance level for the entire organization because HRD fosters employee commitment and alters their attitude towards change with their new enhanced capabilities.

REFERENCES

Aati, K., Chang, D., Edara, P., & Sun, C. (2020). Immersive work zone inspection training using virtual reality. *Transportation Research Record: Journal of the Transportation Research Board*, *2674*(12), 224–232. doi:10.1177/0361198120953146

Ali, N. A. A., Hamdan, A., Alareeni, B., & Dahlan, M. (2023). Artificial intelligence in the process of training and developing employees. In *International Conference on Business and Technology* (pp. 558-568). Cham: Springer International Publishing. 10.1007/978-3-031-26953-0_50

Anderson, K. (2023, June 20). *How AI is transforming HR*. International Association for Human Resources Information Management. https://www.ihrim.org/2020/02/how-artificial-intelligence-is-transforming-hr/

Bachkirova, T., Spence, G., & Drake, D. (Eds.). (2017). *The SAGE handbook of coaching*. Sage.

Banks, D., & Liu, Y. (2023). Statistics, AI, and autonomous vehicles. *Amstat News*, *555*, 10–15.

Bedard, J., Lavoie, K., Laverdiere, R., Bailey, A., Beauchene, V., & Baier, J. (2023, August 25). How generative AI will transform HR. *BCG Global*. https://www.bcg.com/publications/ 2023/transforming-human-resources-using-generative-ai

Beer, M., Spector, B., Lawrence, P., Quinn Mills, D., & Walton, R. (1984). *Managing human assets*. The Free Press.

Booth, D. (2023). Build capacity with generative artificial intelligence. *Journal of Environmental Health*, *86*(2), 26–28.

Buck, B., & Morrow, J. (2018). AI, performance management and engagement: Keeping your best their best. *Strategic HR Review*, *17*(5), 261–262. doi:10.1108/SHR-10-2018-145

Cardon, M., & Stevens, C. (2004). Managing human resources in small organizations: What do we know? *Human Resource Management Review*, *14*(3), 295–323. doi:10.1016/j.hrmr.2004.06.001

Carson, B., & Hruska, M. (2023). Practical and pragmatic AI application. *TD: Talent Development*, *77*(1), 32–37.

Chen, Y., Biswas, M., & Talukder, M. S. (2022). The role of artificial intelligence in effective business operations during COVID-19. *International Journal of Emerging Markets*, *18*(12), 6368–6387. doi:10.1108/IJOEM-11-2021-1666

Colley, H., Hodkinson, P., & Malcolm, J. (2002). *Non-formal learning: Mapping the conceptual terrain: A consultation report*. University of Leeds Lifelong Learning Institute.

D'Silva, G., Jani, M., Jadhav, V., Bhoir, A., & Amin, P. (2020). Career counselling chatbot using cognitive science and artificial intelligence. In *Advanced Computing Technologies and Applications: Proceedings of 2nd International Conference on Advanced Computing Technologies and Applications—ICACTA 2020* (pp. 1-9). Springer Singapore. 10.1007/978-981-15-3242-9_1

Devanna, M. A., Fombrun, C. J., & Tichy, N. M. (1984). A framework for strategic human resource management. In *Strategic Human Resource Management*. Wiley.

Dutta, D., Mishra, S. K., & Tyagi, D. (2023). Augmented employee voice and employee engagement using artificial intelligence-enabled chatbots: A field study. *International Journal of Human Resource Management*, *34*(12), 2451–2480. doi:10.1080/09585192.2022.2085525

El Azhari, K., Hilal, I., Daoride, N., & Ajhoun, R. (2023). SMART chatbots in the E-learning domain: A systematic literature review. *International Journal of Interactive Mobile Technologies*, *17*(15), 4–37. doi:10.3991/ijim.v17i15.40315

EverestLabs uses AI, robotic arms for more efficient cycling. (2023). *Waste 360.*

Fitz-Enz, J., & Mattox, J. (2014). *Predictive analytics for human resources*. John Wiley and Sons. doi:10.1002/9781118915042

Fombrun, C. J., & Tichy, N. M. (1984). A framework for strategic human resource management. In *Strategic Human Resource Management*. John Wiley and Sons.

Garavan, T. N., & Coolahan, M. (1996). Career mobility in organizations: Implications for career development - Part I. *Journal of European Industrial Training*, *20*(4), 30–40. doi:10.1108/03090599610117063

Gilley, J. W., Eggland, S. A., & Gilley, A. M. (2002). *Principles of human resource development* (2nd ed.). Basic Books.

Gilmurray, K. (2023) *The A-Z organizational digital transformation*. Independently Published.

Green, N. (2023). *How artificial intelligence will impact and transform HR and L&D*. Academic Press.

Grosso, C., Sazen, N., & Boselli, R. (2022, September). AI-implemented toolkit to assist users with career “configuration”: The case of create your own future. In *Proceedings of the 26th ACM International Systems and Software Product Line Conference-Volume B* (pp. 158-165). 10.1145/3503229.3547043

Guest, D. (1987). Human resource management and industrial relations. *Journal of Management Studies*, *24*(5), 503–521. doi:10.1111/j.1467-6486.1987.tb00460.x

Hancock, B., Schaninger, B., & Yee, L. (2023, June 5). Generative AI and the future of HR. *McKinsey & Company*. https://www.mckinsey.com/capabilities/people-and-organizational performance/our-insights/generative-ai-and-the-future-of-hr

Hole, K. J., & Ahmad, S. (2021). A thousand brains: Toward biologically constrained AI. *SN Applied Sciences*, *3*(8), 743–757. doi:10.1007/s42452-021-04715-0

HR Innovation and Tech Fest. (n.d.). https://www.techfestconf.com/aus/hr-blog/ai-mean-humans-human-resources

Ketter, P. (2017). Artificial intelligence creeps into talent development. *TD: Talent Development*, *71*(4), 22–25.

Kinney, S. (2023). AI-driven robots handle high-speed logistics sorting and depalletizing: The robotic system from plus one robotics incorporates a robot, AI-based software, and remote supervisor software. *Vision Systems Design*, *28*(2), 12–15.

Knouse, S. B. (2001). Virtual mentors: Mentoring on the internet. *Journal of Employment Counseling*, *38*(4), 162–169. doi:10.1002/j.2161-1920.2001.tb00498.x

Kononiuka, A., Pająkb, A., Gudanowskaa, A. E., Magruka, A., Kozłowskaa, J., & Sacio-Szymańskab, A. (2020). Foresight for career development. *Foresight and STI Governance*, *14*(2), 88–104. doi:10.17323/2500-2597.2020.2.88.104

Korzynski, P., Mazurek, G., Altmann, A., Ejdys, J., Kazlauskaite, R., Paliszkiewicz, J., Wach, K., & Ziemba, E. (2023). Generative artificial intelligence as a new context for management theories: Analysis of ChatGPT. *Central European Management Journal*, *31*(1), 3–13. doi:10.1108/CEMJ-02-2023-0091

Larkin, C., Drummond Otten, C., & Arva, J. (2022). Paging Dr. JARVIS! Will people accept advice from artificial intelligence for consequential risk management decisions? *Journal of Risk Research*, *25*(4), 407–422. doi:10.1080/13669877.2021.1958047

Lee, H., Chatterjee, I., & Cho, G. (2023). A systematic review of computer vision and AI in parking space allocation in a seaport. *Applied Sciences (2076-3417)*, *13*(18), 10254-10271.

Lee, J. D., Jheng, E. S., Kuo, C. C., Chen, H. H., & Hung, Y. H. (2023). Novel robotic arm Working area AI protection system. *Sensors (Basel)*, *23*(5), 2765–2779. doi:10.3390/s23052765 PMID:36904969

Lee, T., Jagannath, K., Aggarwal, N., Sridar, R., Wilde, S., Hill, T., & Chen, Y. (2019). Intelligent career advisers in your pocket? A need assessment study of chatbots for student career advising. *Twenty-fifth Americas Conference on Information Systems*, Cancun, Mexico.

Legge, K. (1995). *Human resource management: Rhetorics and realities*. Macmillan. doi:10.1007/978-1-349-24156-9

Lujan, H. L., & DiCarlo, S. E. (2006). First-year medical students prefer multiple learning styles. *Advances in Physiology Education*, *30*(1), 13–16. doi:10.1152/advan.00045.2005 PMID:16481603

Malik, A., Budhwar, P., Mohan, H., & Srikanth, N. R. (2023). Employee experience –the missing link for engaging employees: Insights from an MNE's AI-based HR ecosystem. *Human Resource Management*, *62*(1), 97–115. doi:10.1002/hrm.22133

Marsick, V. J., & Watkins, K. E. (2001). Informal and incidental learning. *New Directions for Adult and Continuing Education*, *89*(89), 25–34. doi:10.1002/ace.5

Martinez, R. (2019). Artificial intelligence: Distinguishing between types & definitions. *Nevada Law Journal*, *19*(3), 1015–1042.

McGregor, D. (1960). Theory x and theory y. In D. S. Pugh (Ed.), *Organization Theory: Selected Readings*. Penguin Books.

McLagan, P. A., & Bedrick, D. (1983). Models for excellence: The results of the ASTD training and development competency study. *Training and Development Journal*, *37*(6), 16–20.

McLean, G. N., & McLean, L. (2001). If we can't define HRD in one country, how can we define it in an international context? *Human Resource Development International*, *4*(3), 313–326. doi:10.1080/13678860110059339

Nadler, L. (1969). The variety of training roles. *Industrial and Commercial Training*, *1*(1), 33–37. doi:10.1108/eb003030

Nguyen, C. A., Artis, A. B., Plank, R. E., & Solomon, P. J. (2019). Dimensions of effective sales coaching: Scale development and validation. *Journal of Personal Selling & Sales Management*, *39*(3), 299–315. doi:10.1080/08853134.2019.1621758

Polzer, J. T. (2022). The rise of people analytics and the future of organizational research. *Research in Organizational Behavior*, *42*, 1–13. doi:10.1016/j.riob.2023.100181

Raina, R. (2018). Change management and organizational development. *Sage (Atlanta, Ga.)*.

Rajakishore, N., & Vineet, S. (2020). The problem of machine ethics in artificial intelligence. *AI & Society*, *35*(1), 103–111. doi:10.1007/s00146-017-0768-6

Richard, P. J., & McCray, J. (2023). Evaluating leadership development in a changing world? Alternative models and approaches for healthcare organisations. *Human Resource Development International*, *26*(2), 114–150. doi:10.1080/13678868.2022.2043085

Schein, E. H., & Schein, P. A. (2018). What is new in OD? Nothing, yet everything. *OD Practitioner*, *50*(4), 6–8.

Silva, R., Rodrigues, R., & Leal, C. (2021). Games-based learning in accounting education–which dimensions are the most relevant? *Accounting Education*, *30*(2), 159–187. doi:10.1080/09639284.2021.1891107

Storey, J. (1992). *Developments in the management of human resources*. Blackwell.

Su, Z., Togay, G., & Côté, A. M. (2021). Artificial intelligence: A destructive and yet creative force in the skilled labour market. *Human Resource Development International*, *24*(3), 341–352. doi:10.1080/13678868.2020.1818513

Super, D. E., Savickas, M. L., & Super, C. M. (1996). The life-span, life-space approach to careers. In D. Brown & L. Brooks (Eds.), *Career choice and development* (3rd ed., pp. 121–178). Jossey-Bass.

Swanson, R. A., & Holton, E. F. (2022). *Foundations of human resource development* (3rd ed.). Berrett-Koehler Publishers, Inc.

Thomas, P., & Busenhart, S. (2021). Narrow artificial intelligence is latest disrupter to insurance industry: NAI, just like the industrial revolution is going to result in new government programs, as well as new theories of contract law and injury law. *Best's Reviews*, *122*(5), 16–17.

Varsha, P. S. (2023). How can we manage biases in artificial intelligence systems – A systematic literature review. *International Journal of Information Management Data Insights*, *3*(1), 100165–100174. doi:10.1016/j.jjimei.2023.100165

Werther, W. B., & Davis, K. (1996). *Human resources and personnel management* (5th ed.). McGraw-Hill.

Wilson, M., Robertson, P., Cruickshank, P., & Gkatzia, D. (2022). Opportunities and risks in the use of AI in career development practice. *Journal of the National Institute for Career Education and Counselling*, *48*(1), 48–57. doi:10.20856/jnicec.4807

Yorks, L., Abel, A. L., & Rotatori, D. (2022). *Strategic human resource development in Practice. Management for Professionals*. Springer. doi:10.1007/978-3-030-95775-9

Zielinski, D. (2023). Is technology the answer to hr's growing burnout problem? *Society of Human Resource Management.* https://www.shrm.org/hr-today/news/hr-magazine/fall-2023/pages/can-artificial-intelligence-solve-hrs-burnout-problem.aspx

KEY TERMS AND DEFINITIONS

Artificial Intelligence: The theory and development of computer systems that are geared towards the performance of tasks that require the intelligence of humans under normal circumstances (Ketter, 2017).

Human Resource Development: Any process or activity that either initially or over the long term, has the potential to develop adults' work-based knowledge, expertise, productivity, and satisfaction, whether for person or group/team gain, or for the benefit of an organization, community, nation, or ultimately, the whole of humanity (McLean & McLean, 2001, p. 322).

Chapter 3
Reskilling in the Artificial Intelligence Era

Paula Cristina Nunes Figueiredo
https://orcid.org/0000-0002-5267-546X
Universidade Lusófona, Portugal

Maria João Justino Alves
https://orcid.org/0009-0007-4717-7574
Universidade Lusófona, Portugal

José Carlos Rouco
https://orcid.org/0000-0002-8710-0367
Universidade Lusófona, Portugal

ABSTRACT

The rise of artificial intelligence (AI) is having a profound impact on the workforce. As AI automates more and more tasks, it becomes increasingly important for employees to reskill and upskill to stay relevant and competitive. There are several assumptions about the impact of AI on the workforce. This chapter focuses on the technological impact of AI on skills management and learning and development, that is, how these management practices contribute to meeting the reskilling needs of human resources. Furthermore, the way we learn and develop is also changing in the age of AI. Traditional learning methods are being complemented with new, more engaging, and interactive methods. AI is also creating new opportunities for lifelong learning. Other dimensions must be studied in relation to the impacts of AI, which will be suggested in the final considerations.

DOI: 10.4018/979-8-3693-0712-0.ch003

INTRODUCTION

Concerns about the future of work, the jobs and skills of the future are highlighted by international studies (WEF, 2020, 2023) and researchers (Itam & Warrier, 2023; Lynn et al., 2023; Singh et al., 2022; Zachariah et al., 2022). They all share concerns about the impact of technology on the workforce, particularly artificial intelligence (AI).

AI is a broad term that encompasses a wide range of technologies, from machine learning to natural language processing. AI is still in its early stages of development, but it is rapidly evolving and is expected to have a major impact on the workforce in the coming years. The implementation of AI systems is causing very significant changes at an accelerated pace in the workforce, from a strong probability of job elimination and job displacement to layoffs, new positions, and types of work, i.e., new jobs opportunities, emergence of new work profiles, monitored and aligned with the greater complexity that tends to characterize current work processes (Ekuma, 2023; Lloyd & Payne, 2019; Morandini et al., 2023).

According to The Future of Jobs Report 2023, employers estimate that 44% of employees' skills will be affected in the next 5 years and 6 out of 10 employees will need training before 2027. However, only half of employees currently have access to adequate training opportunities. The priority skills that need to be developed between 2023-2027 are: - analytical thinking, which is expected to account for 10% of training initiatives on average; creative thinking, which will be the subject of 8% of skills improvement initiatives; training to use AI and big data is considered a priority by 42% of the companies surveyed; and, leadership and social influence (40% of companies); resilience, flexibility and agility (32%); and curiosity and lifelong learning (30%). The report's conclusion reinforces that the skills that companies say are rapidly increasing in importance are not always reflected in their skills improvement strategies (WEF, 2023).

Accepting this reality means recognizing that increased attention is needed towards the issue of workforce skills and competences. Learning and development it is a strategic and operational area, focused on behavioral performance to attain both organizational and personal needs and objectives. As an example, post COVID-19 and with the growth of remote working, challenges and opportunities have been created to improve skills and reskill employees (Itam & Warrier, 2023). Organizations need to be proactive in promoting training and development programmes that address digital literacy, soft skills and the changing skills requirements caused by remote working (Sharma et al., 2022). Through upskilling and reskilling opportunities, organizations can promote employee development, improve retention rates, and improve overall organizational performance (Yarberry & Sims, 2021). Upskilling has been the main process, and now reskilling appears to be a principal strategy to endorse the maintenance, the relevance, and the competitiveness of employees in a context of growing integration of IA systems in work processes, in a paradigm that is directing societies towards new and distinct realities, the industry 4.0 paradigm.

In this context, this essay looks at recent developments on the importance of reskilling in an organizational context where artificial intelligence is increasingly present. Specifically, we will discuss the challenges and opportunities in terms of competences management and learning and development. These considerations provide the backdrop for further research into the importance of competency-based human resource management in responding to the demands of implementing AI in organizations. The chapter is structured in 4 parts. First, some concepts and assumptions of IA are presented. Then we look at the importance of reskilling in the current context and, how learning and development also must fit in with AI. Finally, we present the conclusions, implications, and recommendations for future studies in the final considerations.

THE ARTIFICIAL INTELLIGENCE ERA: CONCEPTS AND ASSUMPTIONS

Artificial intelligence (AI) is the ability of machines to mimic or enhance human intelligence, such as reasoning and acquiring knowledge through experience (Afzal et al., 2023). According to Kaplan & Haenlein (2019), AI is "a system's ability to interpret external data correctly, to learn from such data, and to use those learnings to achieve specific goals and tasks through flexible adaptation." These abilities are impacting the nature of work and of organizational models (Morandini et al. 2023), challenging, namely, management politics, processes and practices on actual and future skills needed to face its related challenges (Ekuma, 2023; Hancock et al., 2020; Jaiswal et al., 2022; Morandini et al., 2023).

AI has an exponential capacity for automating intelligence, tending to lead to increased productivity and organizational efficiency, to processing activities related to intangible content, data processing, scenario projection, among others intellectual activities, affecting all kinds of jobs and employees (Dwivedi et al., 2021; Hancock et al., 2020; Leinen et al., 2020) (Global Deal, 2023). The management of artificial intelligence (AI) introduces in a new era of information technology management. Managing AI includes communicating, leading, coordinating, and controlling an ever-changing frontier of computational advancements that refer to human intelligence in addressing increasingly complex decision-making problems (Berente et al., 2021).

There are numerous concepts of IA in the literature, and by analyzing the challenges and opportunities of IA for HRM, some authors even recommend a unified definition of IA (Pan & Froese, 2023). Thus, in this research, it is assumed that IA is the capacity for robots to learn, reason, comprehend, and act rationally and intelligently, rather like humans do (Sousa et al., 2023). According to these authors, the machine's ability to understand its environment and make choices that maximize its chances of successfully achieving its goals is how AI is defined in today's context.

In the AI age and automation, the role of managers is gradually replaced by algorithms (Alahmad & Robert, 2020). One significant challenge is the breakdown of the interpersonal relationship between managers and employees, which is frequently based on identification. The degree to which a employee identifies with his or her manager, or the extent to which the manager is included in the employee's sense of self, has been shown to be especially important in establishing trust and rapport. Other challenges that have also begun to be studied and concern researchers have to do with issues of organizational justice (Robert et al., 2020) and the role of humans in the future of leadership (Quaquebeke & Gerpott, 2023). The latter has strong implications for leadership education and development.

AI has already greatly improved the quality and effectiveness of knowledge acquisition, problem-solving strategies, knowledgeable tutors, optimal solution systems, organization, modeling, and other aspects of knowledge management (KM) (Taherdoost & Madanchian, 2023). However, there are more advanced potential AI applications in the context of KM that could have a significant impact and help groups and businesses.

Effective KM also involves managing employees' skills, so the importance of upskilling and reskilling in the AI era is indisputable.

Upskilling and Reskilling in Today's Context

Upskilling processes translates into learning new skills or developing existing ones in current job, a continuous education to respond to professional gaps; reskilling processes configures learning oriented towards new skills for a new role or/and task, in a new area. Reskilling is critical to providing employees with the ability to adapt to changes, to develop new and/or different skills and competencies, to take a new career, to be effective and efficient in their roles (Kilag et al., 2023; L. Li, 2022; Morandini et al., 2023). The literature identifies these two processes as being capable of responding to the needs of adaptation and/or transformation of the workforce, i.e., professional development, to meet the demands and requirements of current organizational productive activity (Ekuma, 2023; Jaiswal et al., 2022; Kilag et al., 2023; L. Li, 2022; Morandini et al., 2023), which have "become crucial for individuals and organizations to remain competitive and relevant" (Kilag et al., 2023), for managers and leaders as well as for operational and technical employees.

The complex reality is that, according with the World Economic Forum (WEF) (2020), "The workforce is automating faster than expected, displacing 85 million jobs in next five years; The robot revolution will create 97 million new jobs, but communities most at risk from disruption will need support from businesses and governments; In 2025, analytical thinking, creativity and flexibility are among the top skills needed; with data and artificial intelligence, content creation and cloud computing the top emerging professions; [and] The most competitive businesses will be those that choose to reskill and upskill current employees". In the aforementioned WEF report (2020), it can be read that, "On average, respondents to the Future of Jobs Survey estimate that around 40% of workers will require reskilling of six months or less [...]" (p.5), and that "For those workers set to remain in their roles, the share of core skills that will change in the next five years is 40%, and 50% of all employees will need reskilling" (p.6). These estimates refer to the employed population, therefore not including people in a situation of unemployment, whose number is 208 million (corresponding to a global unemployment rate of 5.8% percent), according to the International Labor Organization (ILO/OIT, 2023). At last, European Commission (2020) states that "Learning throughout life, including at an older age, is what will make the difference. Yet less than two in five adults participate in learning every year" and defends that "Each person in the EU should be empowered and rewarded to up- and reskill" (p.4).

In other words, societies and organizations face the need of mass upskill and reskill the workforce, to proceed with the new paradigm, one that values human capital and intellectual resources – society and industry 4.0; that is, all jobs will change, and most today's people and employees will have to learn new skills. (Li, 2022). International Labor Organization (ILO, 2021) "found that investing in the development of human capital, including through upskilling and reskilling, can lead to improved productivity and economic growth" (Kilag et al., 2023:51). Researchers concluded in their study on the importance of upskilling and reskilling initiatives that communication, time management, work organization and prioritization of tasks, the construction of collaborative interpersonal relationships, critical thinking, problem solving and continuous learning are personal and organizational key skills, as their development contributes to improving one's own performance and that of employees, to a more effective talent retention strategy and to enhancing a culture of continuous learning (Kilag et al., 2023).

Soft competences such as critical and strategic though, active learning, creativity, or complex problem solving (in addition to those mentioned) complement hard skills and, are at the central core of the new kind of skills demands for everyone (Ekuma, 2023; Kilag et al., 2023; L. Li, 2022). Cognitive and conceptual skills become essential to the competitiveness of employees, both internally and externally, and allow them to deal with potential negative consequences of the widespread use of AI, such as "cognitive complacency or disqualification" (Jarrahi, 2019; Tredinnick, 2017).

Using data from OECD Skills for Jobs 2022, Global Deal (2023) confirm the centrality of soft skills nowadays, "In most countries, skill shortages relate to high-level cognitive skills, such as creativity and problem solving; complex social interaction skills, such as social awareness and empathy; soft skills, such as autonomy, leadership, collaboration, and communication skills; and science, technology, engineering, and mathematics skills, including ICT skills. Surpluses, on the other hand, relate mainly to physical skills such as stamina and strength, fine motor skills such as dexterity, and knowledge related to sectors that have been subject to heavy automation" (p.8).

Organizations must prepare the work of the future and be prepared for the future of work, for changes, some very profound, in its nature and the respective skills required, an example of which are traditionally labor-intensive sectors. For instance, according to Ellingrug et al. (2020), employees in traditionally labor-intensive sectors (e.g., retail, manufacturing, agriculture, or food suppliers) will need most probably more reskilling than those with higher education training. They estimated that 39 to 58 percent of global work activities in operationally labor-intensive sectors could be automated due to the predictability and repetitive nature of the tasks (p.2). In 2017, the results of a questionnaire carried out by McKinsey with 116 executives from large organizations reported that for a third of those interviewed the topic of skills was among the top ten, but only 7% considered that their organizations were fully prepared to overcome the predictable gaps within the scope of competencies (Ellingrug et al., 2020). Respondents also mentioned three important constraints on the ability to deal with this problem - poor clarification on the impacts of automation and digitalization; they do not have the tools and knowledge to quantify the retraining needs of their employees; the respective HR structures did not have the capacity to implement strategies aimed at the imperative of retraining employees (Ellingrug et al., 2020).

However, these executives also considered that it is up to their organizations to lead the development of the new skills required by society and industry 4.0, and that at least half of their workforce should be reskilled so that they can remain in the organization and fille new roles. From some works and WEF & PWC (2021), the idea remains that organizations, by providing their employees with the appropriate skills to respond to AI challenges, are ensuring, in a technologically disruptive context, their own survival, becoming more attractive and better able to retain talent, aligning with a culture of continuous learning, innovation and adaptability (Chui et al., 2016; Ekuma, 2023).

Some organizations are already promoting reskilling processes at a large scale – "global retailer Walmart, for example, is investing $4 billion over four years to help staff in frontline and back-office jobs transition to new customer service-oriented roles (Ellingrug et al., 2020). E-commerce giant Amazon has pledged to spend $700 million on technology training by 2025 to help employees move to higher-skill jobs" (p.4), being this shift "to higher-skilled jobs", an orientation towards high-value work, a strategic principle in the management and development of people, respectively on social and professional contexts.

The growing demand for multi-talented and highly qualified employees is leading multiple organizations to invest in different innovative approaches that focus on the integration of skills training sets, focused on intelligent collaboration strategies between humans and machines (Li, 2022). An organizational reskilling or upskilling program must be aimed at employees, clearly illustrating what its offers are and what is expected, so that everyone understands the value proposition of it, so that this investment in professional and personal development as success. Also, these programs "must be tailored to the specific needs and context[s] (…)" (Kilag et al., 2023, 55).

Industry 4.0 intelligent systems highlight the need to build an intelligent relationship between humans and machines, incorporating this relationship into the central core of workforce development and continuous learning processes, based on reskilling and up skilling programs that promote this intelligent cooperation (Li, 2022; Morandini et al., 2023).

Based on a PwC report from 2018, Ekuma (2023) states that upskilling and reskilling initiatives have a major impact on organizations success because are keys to foster the adaptability to technological challenges, to attract and retain talent, and to pursue a culture of innovation. These initiatives, if succeed, are also linked, for instance, to employee satisfaction, to motivation, to professional growth and, as already pointed out, to retention.

Implement upskilling and reskilling programs is, nowadays, a huge challenge – the vast skills set is changing in an unlimited way, almost all the employees need to be retrained in a upskilling or reskilling logic, the costs of these retraining programs are incommensurable, these programs must be flexible, adaptable, interchangeable and scalable, efficacious, and efficient, and they demands time availability, and the involvement of all key actors, governments, organizations, social partners, educative and formative system (Global Deal, 2023).

The up or reskilling options are diverse and can/should be used simultaneously, depending on the demands and urgency of the organizational context. Thus, organizations can invest internally in skills development, supporting and retaining their employees with continuous learning strategies, paying fees for specialized external training, or inviting specialists; They can also recruit new employees with the necessary skills, avoiding possibly more time-consuming reskilling processes in the short term (Li, 2022).

Learning and Development in the Artificial Intelligence Era

Human resource management (HRM) faces significant obstacles in creating and preserving a competitive edge in the face of volatility, uncertainty, complexity, and ambiguity (VUCA) (Achoki, 2023). The four pillars of the VUCA environment are becoming increasingly deeply rooted in the organizational context. Recent technology developments have resulted in new employment, needs, goods, procedures, work arrangements, and ways of providing services, all of which have significantly changed workplaces and required the development of new workplace competences.

Lifelong learning must be assumed, by organizations and people, as a strategic dimension, so that both, in interaction and collaboration, are able to adapt, adjust and respond appropriately to the talent demands required by the society 4.0 (Ekuma, 2023; Li, 2022). The continuous learning strategy has become and remains an organizational and societal requirement to face the complexity of work and production processes.

Employers must strategically build employees' skill sets in accordance with company goals. It is imperative to continually invest in the training and development of people, ensuring a workforce equipped with the skills that allow them to remain competitive and employable, at a time where the nature of interactions between employees and technical and technological equipment is changing disruptively, by the action of AI and automation (Morandini et al., 2023). People require skills in many different areas to function well in such a dynamic society. These skills include, but are not limited to, technology skills, self-management skills, social and intercultural skills, cognitive skills, entrepreneurial skills, and knowledge of 21st century transdisciplinary issues. In order to survive in the face of ongoing disruption, the future of employment will likely center on retraining individuals and continuously enhancing their skill sets (Achoki, 2023).

Covid-19 pandemic situation created unprecedented challenges for human resource managers (i.e., recruitment, onboarding, and training) that have expedited AI application's adoption in HRM (Prikshat, Islam, et al., 2023). However, the academic literature has not yet offered a strategic framework to guide HR managers in adopting and implementing it (Malik et al., 2023). Researchers are trying to develop these frameworks. Because of its interdisciplinary nature, some researchers refer that AI-HRM is a topic that extends beyond the field of HRM (Pan & Froese, 2023). For example, the development of AI-based HR tools is dependent on progress in technical fields, whereas implementations of such AI tools and the consequences of AI implementations are dependent on knowledge from social science.

AI is automating an increasing number of tasks and, consequently, questioning the profile of skills needed for them, a situation that requires a careful look at skills development processes to keep employees relevant, employable, and competitive. As a result, some researchers even propose an Intelligent Human Resource Management model where the HR function can be firmly positioned to generate sustainable strategic advantages for organizations (Kaur & Gandolfi, 2023b). In addition, it develops a value creation model, which articulates how the integration of AI technologies into HRM creates organizational value.

According to some researchers, AI-augmented HRM refers to the HRM function's ability to integrate AI techniques within an organization's existing business intelligence systems to aid problem-solving and decision-making for positive HRM-specific operational, relational, and transformational outcomes (Prikshat, Malik, et al., 2023).

In short, many others researchers are concerned about the impact of AI on human resource management, seeking to understand which practices will be most influenced by the implementation of AI systems (Afzal et al., 2023; Jiaping, 2022; Johansson & Herranen, 2019; Johnson et al., 2022; Kaur et al., 2023; Kaur & Gandolfi, 2023a, 2023b; Palos-Sánchez et al., 2022; Shaddiq et al., 2023; Vrontis et al., 2022), even with integration with green human resource management (GHRM) (Garg et al., 2018). There is a consensus that people management practices should absorb AI systems to make processes more effective and adapted to work models and environments. Future advancements in artificial intelligence will expand personalization, mechanization, and data-based decisions in human resource management; and HR managers should likewise know about the challenges they might experience (Menaka, 2023).

The integration of AI and its impact on HRM in organizations has been the subject of study in recent years. Artificial intelligence is at first utilized in recruiting (to find the best contender for open positions); this cycle includes figuring out candidates considering range of abilities, experience, capabilities, and social fit (Menaka, 2023). In addition to the impacts on employee recruitment and employee selection (Johnson et al., 2020), some research points to direct impacts on learning and development (L&D) (Li et al., 2023), and more specifically on digital learning (Gubbins et al., 2023). These researchers focus on the factors, opportunities and challenges associated with digital learning as an approach to achieving learning objectives and organizational development at the same time.

Because of artificial intelligence, which is reforming the entire learning and development process, these experts can convey better and truly captivating learning. Learning and development solutions powered by artificial intelligence can provide employees with flexible growth opportunities on demand (Menaka, 2023). Using information, simulated intelligence-driven calculations can also assess each employee's knowledge, abilities, and experiences and deliver individualized learning materials that are tailored to their needs, inclinations, and learning preferences. Individualized training can keep employees confident in their own and professional development while also assisting them in effectively developing their abilities and achieving their vocation goals (Menaka, 2023).

The findings show that AI innovations such as natural language processing, artificial neural networks, interactive voice response and text to speech, speech to text, technology-enhanced learning, and robots can improve the efficiency of the learning and development process (Bhatt & Muduli, 2022). Furthermore, the findings show that AI can be used to evaluate learning aptitude, test learners' memory, track learning progress, measure learning effectiveness, aid learners in identifying mistakes, and suggest corrections. Finally, L&D professionals can use AI to facilitate a faster, more accurate, and less expensive learning process that is suitable for a large learning audience at the same time, flexible, efficient, convenient, and less expensive for learners.

A recent study shows the impact of AI on learning in the workplace and concludes that: - AI significantly reduces people's on-the-job learning; AI makes employees more pessimistic about the future, leading to burnout and less motivation for on-the-job learning; AI's replacement, mismatch, and deskilling effects reduce people's income while extending working hours, reducing their available financial resources and disposable time for further learning; AI's impact on on-the-job learning is more pronounced for older, female, and less-educated employees (Li et al., 2023). The inhibitory effect of AI on further learning is more pronounced in countries with more intense human-AI competition, more labor-management conflicts, and poorer labor protection.

AI provides capabilities that support three areas of business functioning (Davenport et al., 2018): - AI can enhance business process automation by providing cognitive capabilities within the software; AI can provide cognitive insights that facilitates decision-making; and, using intelligent agents and chatbots, AI can support cognitive engagement. In this sense, it is imperative that, on the one hand, employees develop skills so that organizations make use of technology and optimize their internal processes and, on the other hand, that the training and development process itself makes use of AI to boost learning and contribute to the reskilling of employees.

FINAL CONSIDERATIONS

The future is uncertain. Employees have experienced a series of setbacks in recent years, and more tumultuous times may be on the way, with the possibility of a global recession, geopolitical conflicts in the works, the shadow of the COVID-19, and the impact (positive or negative) of artificial intelligence (AI) and greater automation of work.

In this context of uncertainty, the employability of companies' human resources takes on greater importance in strategic business management. It is essential to promote learning and development as a way of reducing the gap between existing skills and those that employees need to develop in the face of future challenges. Upskilling and reskilling are therefore two current trends of extreme importance for companies. Employees themselves believe that management skills will be the most important in their jobs in the future, followed by interpersonal skills and data analysis skills. However, 67% of employees believe that future skill sets will include technological skills that are not yet considered mandatory, which will necessitate that employers and employees prioritize skill development and training in preparation for the coming years (Richardson & Antonello, 2023).

As part of the continued essential efforts to operationalize skills requirements (soft and hard) in the current and future context, training strategies and offers are available and have the conditions and resources to take place. It is essential that the stakeholders present (businesspeople, organizations, and governments) work together to facilitate, promote and encourage everyone to seek ways of being and doing that benefit and empower people, both in the professional and social context.

From the top to the organizational base, it urges the recognition of the value of people development processes. Investments in 4.0 technology must necessarily be accompanied by technically, cognitively, socially, and emotionally mature employees, and by an organizational culture shaped by values of lifelong learning, as well as flexibility and collaboration, all so relevant and necessary in dynamic, innovation, and demanding contexts.

In this way, this essay has implications both at an individual level, making employees aware of the need to invest in lifelong learning, and at an organizational level, alerting them to the impacts of technology and the need to promote upskilling and reskilling as a way of guaranteeing the company's competitiveness and sustainability. A people management policy based on competency-based learning and development is fundamental to facing future challenges.

Research on these topics is thus essential for organizations to better understand employees' behaviors and promote the acquisition of new skills to achieve better collaboration between humans and AI. This study focused on the technological impact of AI on reskilling, however, other dimensions should be studied, namely the socio-cultural, psychological, and ethical issues associated with AI. In the organizational context, it is also important to explore how leadership styles and management strategies should adapt to promote an environment conducive to continuous learning and innovation in the face of AI advances. The roles and skills required of leaders and managers need to evolve in the age of AI, so these are topics that need to be developed, if possible with case studies.

REFERENCES

Achoki, P. M. (2023). Upskilling and Reskilling for a VUCA World. *GiLE Journal of Skills Development*, *3*(2), 34–52. doi:10.52398/gjsd.2023.v3.i2.pp34-52

Afzal, M. N. I., Shohan, A. H. N., Siddiqui, S., & Tasnim, N. (2023). Application of AI on Human Resource Management: A Review. *Journal of Human Resource Management - HR Advances and Developments, 2023*(1), 1–11. doi:10.46287/FHEV4889

Alahmad, R., & Robert, L. (2020). Artificial Intelligence (AI) and IT identity: Antecedents identifying with AI applications. *26th Americas Conference on Information Systems, AMCIS 2020*, 1–10.

Berente, N., Gu, B., Recker, J., & Santhanam, R. (2021). Managing artificial intelligence. *Management Information Systems Quarterly*, *45*(3), 1433–1450. doi:10.25300/MISQ/2021/16274

Bhatt, P., & Muduli, A. (2022). Artificial intelligence in learning and development: a systematic literature review. In *European Journal of Training and Development*. Emerald Group Holdings Ltd. doi:10.1108/EJTD-09-2021-0143

Chui, M., Manyika, J., & Miremadi, M. (2016). Where machines could replace humans-and where they can't (yet) The technical potential for automation differs dramatically across sectors and activities. *The McKinsey Quarterly*.

Davenport, T. H., Ronanki, R., Wheaton, J., & Nguyen, A. (2018). Artificial Intelligence for the real world. *Harvard Business Review*, 108–116.

Dwivedi, Y. K., Hughes, L., Ismagilova, E., Aarts, G., Coombs, C., Crick, T., Duan, Y., Dwivedi, R., Edwards, J., Eirug, A., Galanos, V., Ilavarasan, P. V., Janssen, M., Jones, P., Kar, A. K., Kizgin, H., Kronemann, B., Lal, B., Lucini, B., ... Williams, M. D. (2021). Artificial Intelligence (AI): Multidisciplinary perspectives on emerging challenges, opportunities, and agenda for research, practice and policy. *International Journal of Information Management*, *57*, 101994. Advance online publication. doi:10.1016/j.ijinfomgt.2019.08.002

EkumaK. (2023). *Rethinking Upskilling and Reskilling in the Age of AI and Automation: A fsQCA Approach*. doi:10.20944/preprints202309.0055.v1

Ellingrug, K., Gupta, R., & Salguero, J. (2020). *Building the vital skills for the future of work in operations*. McKinsey and Company.

European Commission. (2020). *European Skills Agenda for Sustainable Competitiveness, Social fairness and resilience.* European Commission. https://ec.europa.eu/migrant-integration/sites/default/files/2020-07/SkillsAgenda.pdf

Garg, V., Srivastav, S., & Gupta, A. (2018). Application of Artificial Intelligence for Sustaining Green Human Resource Management. *2018 International Conference on Automation and Computational Engineering, ICACE 2018*, 113–116. 10.1109/ICACE.2018.8686988

Global Deal. (2023). *Upskilling and reskilling for the twin transition: The role of social dialogue.* Thematic Brief. https://www.theglobaldeal.com/resources/Upskilling-and-reskilling-for-the-twin-transition.pdf

Gubbins, C., Garavan, T. N., & Bennett, E. E. (2023). Digital Learning: A Bright New Dawn for Learning and Development. In T. Lynn, P. Rosati, E. Conway, & L. van der Werff (Eds.), *The Future of Work - Challenges and Prospects for Organisations, Jobs and Workers* (pp. 127–149). Palgrave Macmillan. doi:10.1007/978-3-031-31494-0_9

Hancock, J. T., Naaman, M., & Levy, K. (2020). AI-Mediated Communication: Definition, Research Agenda, and Ethical Considerations. *Journal of Computer-Mediated Communication, 25*(1), 89–100. doi:10.1093/jcmc/zmz022

Itam, U. J., & Warrier, U. (2023). Future of work from everywhere: A systematic review. *International Journal of Manpower*. Advance online publication. doi:10.1108/IJM-06-2022-0288

Jaiswal, A., Arun, C. J., & Varma, A. (2022). Rebooting employees: Upskilling for artificial intelligence in multinational corporations. *International Journal of Human Resource Management, 33*(6), 1179–1208. doi:10.1080/09585192.2021.1891114

Jarrahi, M. H. (2019). In the age of the smart artificial intelligence: AI's dual capacities for automating and informating work. *Business Information Review, 36*(4), 178–187. doi:10.1177/0266382119883999

Jiaping, Y. (2022). Enterprise Human Resource Management Model by Artificial Intelligence Digital Technology. *Computational Intelligence and Neuroscience, 2022*, 1–9. doi:10.1155/2022/6186811 PMID:36479021

Johansson, J., & Herranen, S. (2019). *The application of Artificial Intelligence (AI) in Human Resource Management: Current state of AI and its impact on the traditional recruitment process.* Academic Press.

Johnson, B. A. M., Coggburn, J. D., & Llorens, J. J. (2022). Artificial Intelligence and Public Human Resource Management: Questions for Research and Practice. *Public Personnel Management*, *51*(4), 538–562. doi:10.1177/00910260221126498

Johnson, R. D., Stone, D. L., & Lukaszewski, K. M. (2020). The benefits of eHRM and AI for talent acquisition. *Journal of Tourism Futures*, *7*(1), 40–52. doi:10.1108/JTF-02-2020-0013

Kaur, M., & Gandolfi, F. (2023a). Artificial Intelligence in Human Resource Management-Challenges and Future Research Recommendations. *Review of International Comparative Management*, *24*(3). Advance online publication. doi:10.24818/RMCI.2023.3.382

Kaur, M., & Gandolfi, F. (2023b). "Intelligent"-Human Resource Management (I-HRM) in the Era of Disruptions: A Value Creation Model. *Empirical Economics Letters*, *22*(1), 73–93. doi:10.5281/zenodo.8312953

Kaur, M., Gandolfi, F., Ag, R., & Resmi, A. G. (2023). Research on Artificial Intelligence in Human Resource Management: Trends and Prospects. *Global Journal of Management and Business Research, Administrative Management*, *23*(5), 30–46. https://www.researchgate.net/publication/371691941

Kilag, O. K. T., Padilla, K., Yorong, F., & Merabedes, J. (2023). Importance of Upskilling and Reskilling in Educational Leadership and Management. *European Journal of Learning on History and Social Sciences*, *1*(1), 49–57. https://orcid.org/0000-0003-0845-3373

Leinen, P., Esders, M., Schütt, K. T., Wagner, C., Müller, K.-R., & Stefan Tautz, F. (2020). Autonomous robotic nanofabrication with reinforcement learning. *Science Advances*, *6*(36), 1–8. doi:10.1126/sciadv.abb6987 PMID:32917594

Li, C., Zhang, Y., Niu, X., Chen, F., & Zhou, H. (2023). Does Artificial Intelligence Promote or Inhibit On-the-Job Learning? Human Reactions to AI at Work. *Systems*, *11*(3), 114. Advance online publication. doi:10.3390/systems11030114

Li, L. (2022). Reskilling and Upskilling the Future-ready Workforce for Industry 4.0 and Beyond. *Information Systems Frontiers*. Advance online publication. doi:10.1007/s10796-022-10308-y PMID:35855776

Lloyd, C., & Payne, J. (2019). Rethinking country effects: Robotics, AI and work futures in Norway and the UK. *New Technology, Work and Employment*, *34*(3), 208–225. doi:10.1111/ntwe.12149

Lynn, T., Rosati, P., Conway, E., & Van Der Werff, L. (2023). *The Future of Work - Challenges and Prospects for Organisations, Jobs and Workers*. Palgrave Macmillan. http://www.palgrave.com/gp/series/16004

Malik, A., Budhwar, P., & Kazmi, B. A. (2023). Artificial intelligence (AI)-assisted HRM: Towards an extended strategic framework. In Human Resource Management Review (Vol. 33, Issue 1). Elsevier Ltd. doi:10.1016/j.hrmr.2022.100940

Menaka, R. (2023). Role of Artificial Intelligence (AI) in Human Resource Management (HRM) in Recent Era. *Shanlax International Journal of Management*, *11*(2), 32–38. doi:10.34293/management.v11i2.6664

Morandini, S., Fraboni, F., De Angelis, M., Puzzo, G., Giusino, D., & Pietrantoni, L. (2023). The Impact of Artificial Intelligence on Workers' Skills: Upskilling and Reskilling in Organisations. *Informing Science*, *26*, 39–68. doi:10.28945/5078

Organização Internacional do Trabalho (ILO). (2023). *Desaceleração económica poderá forçar os trabalhadores a aceitar empregos de menor qualidade*. Imprensa. OIT. https://www.ilo.org/lisbon/sala-de-imprensa/WCMS_865482/lang--pt/index.htm

Palos-Sánchez, P. R., Baena-Luna, P., Badicu, A., & Infante-Moro, J. C. (2022). Artificial Intelligence and Human Resources Management: A Bibliometric Analysis. In Applied Artificial Intelligence (Vol. 36, Issue 1). Taylor and Francis Ltd. doi:10.1080/08839514.2022.2145631

Pan, Y., & Froese, F. J. (2023). An interdisciplinary review of AI and HRM: Challenges and future directions. *Human Resource Management Review*, *33*(1), 100924. Advance online publication. doi:10.1016/j.hrmr.2022.100924

Prikshat, V., Islam, M., Patel, P., Malik, A., Budhwar, P., & Gupta, S. (2023). AI-Augmented HRM: Literature review and a proposed multilevel framework for future research. *Technological Forecasting and Social Change*, *193*, 122645. Advance online publication. doi:10.1016/j.techfore.2023.122645

Prikshat, V., Malik, A., & Budhwar, P. (2023). AI-augmented HRM: Antecedents, assimilation and multilevel consequences. *Human Resource Management Review*, *33*(1), 100860. Advance online publication. doi:10.1016/j.hrmr.2021.100860

Richardson, N., & Antonello, M. (2023). *People at Work 2023: A Global Workforce View*. Academic Press.

Robert, L. P., Pierce, C., Marquis, L., Kim, S., & Alahmad, R. (2020). Designing fair AI for managing employees in organizations: A review, critique, and design agenda. *Human-Computer Interaction*, *35*(5–6), 545–575. doi:10.1080/07370024.2020.1735391

Shaddiq, S., Khuzaini, & Irpan. (2023). Governance of Human Resources Management in the Digital Era. *Journal of Business and Management Studies*, *5*(3), 80–96. doi:10.32996/jbms.2023.5.3.8

Sharma, M., Luthra, S., Joshi, S., & Kumar, A. (2022). Analysing the impact of sustainable human resource management practices and industry 4.0 technologies adoption on employability skills. *International Journal of Manpower*, *43*(2), 463–485. doi:10.1108/IJM-02-2021-0085

Singh, A., Jha, S., Srivastava, D. K., & Somarajan, A. (2022). Future of work: a systematic literature review and evolution of themes. In Foresight (Vol. 24, Issue 1, pp. 99–125). Emerald Group Holdings Ltd. doi:10.1108/FS-09-2020-0093

Sousa, M. J., Sousa, M., Rocha, Á., & Di Virgilio, F. (2023). Scoping Review on AI as a Driver for Industry. In R. Pereira, I. Bianchi, & Á. Rocha (Eds.), Digital Technologies and Transformation in Business, Industry and Organizations (Springer, Vol. 2, pp. 235–243). doi:10.1007/978-3-031-40710-9_13

Taherdoost, H., & Madanchian, M. (2023). Artificial Intelligence and Knowledge Management: Impacts, Benefits, and Implementation. In Computers (Vol. 12, Issue 4). MDPI. doi:10.3390/computers12040072

Tredinnick, L. (2017). Out-of-the-Box: Artificial Intelligence and professional roles. *Business Information Review*, *34*(1), 37–41. doi:10.1177/0266382117692621

Van Quaquebeke, N., & Gerpott, F. H. (2023). The Now, New, and Next of Digital Leadership: How Artificial Intelligence (AI) Will Take Over and Change Leadership as We Know It. In *Journal of Leadership and Organizational Studies*. SAGE Publications Inc. doi:10.1177/15480518231181731

Vrontis, D., Christofi, M., Pereira, V., Tarba, S., Makrides, A., & Trichina, E. (2022). Artificial intelligence, robotics, advanced technologies and human resource management: A systematic review. *International Journal of Human Resource Management*, *33*(6), 1237–1266. doi:10.1080/09585192.2020.1871398

World Economic Forum. (2020). *The Future of Jobs Report 2020*. WEF. https://www.weforum.org/press/2020/10/recession-and-automation-changes-our-future-of-work-but-there-are-jobs-coming-report-says-52c5162fce/

World Economic Forum. (2023). *The Future of Jobs Report 2023*. WEF. https://www3.weforum.org/docs/WEF_Future_of_Jobs_2023.pdf

World Economic Forum & PwC. (2021). *Upskilling for shared prosperity*. Insight Report. https://www.pwc.com/gx/en/issues/upskilling.html

Yarberry, S., & Sims, C. (2021). The Impact of COVID-19-Prompted Virtual/Remote Work Environments on Employees' Career Development: Social Learning Theory, Belongingness, and Self-Empowerment. *Advances in Developing Human Resources*, *23*(3), 237–252. doi:10.1177/15234223211017850

Zachariah, M., Avanesh, N. M., & Arjunan, S. N. (2022). Future of Work Places. In P. Figueiredo, E. Tomé, & J. Rouco (Eds.), *Handbook of Research on Challenges for Human Resource Management in the COVID-19 Era* (pp. 1–22). IGI Publisher. doi:10.4018/978-1-7998-9840-5.ch001

KEY TERMS AND DEFINITIONS

Artificial Intelligence: Refers to a robot's ability to learn, reason, comprehend, and behave intelligently and rationally, much like humans.

Learning and Development: Is a people management practice that consists of a continuous process of acquiring new skills and competences needed to perform effectively at work in an environment of rapid technological change.

Reskilling: Is the process of acquiring new skills and competences to work in a new area.

Upskilling: Is the process of acquiring new skills and competences related to the employee's current area of work.

Chapter 4
Art of Leading in the AI Age:
Portrait of a Leader

R. Alamelu
https://orcid.org/0000-0003-0539-2480
SASTRA University, India

ABSTRACT

The usage of cyber-physical systems in manufacturing settings and the proliferation of connected IT systems have both contributed to a rise in the volume of available data. Artificial intelligence (AI) is being used more and more by businesses to sift through this mountain of data and draw meaningful insights. The widespread adoption and implementation of AI has far-reaching implications for socio-technical work systems. Distinct leadership needs and challenges might be identified. Effective AI deployment and use necessitates strong leadership. Considering the scenario and the rapid development of AI to give organisations with practical instructions and ideas, more research is needed into AI's influence on leaders and leadership. This chapter analyses the various strategic transformation through creating a better AI culture by improvising skills and competencies required in the AI arena.

INTRODUCTION

The ongoing progress in incorporating artificial intelligence into the workplace necessitates that leaders adapt their tactics and approaches in order to proficiently address the developing challenges and exploit the possible advantages linked to this technology. The integration of artificial intelligence technologies in the workplace has led to a notable restructuring of the workforce by automating certain procedures and tasks. There is a considerable population that has reservations about the

DOI: 10.4018/979-8-3693-0712-0.ch004

current trend, as they express apprehensions surrounding the possibility of robots replacing human employment, leading to potential job layoffs and leaving humans vulnerable. Conversely, there is a group of individuals that exhibit enthusiasm regarding the rise of artificial intelligence owing to its potential to create new employment opportunities and avenues for economic expansion. Within corporate environments, the introduction of artificial intelligence automation is anticipated to make certain vocations vulnerable to displacement, while simultaneously creating novel employment prospects. Nevertheless, it is undeniable that the required skill sets in the upcoming labour market are currently undergoing a significant transition. It is crucial for leaders in the sector to anticipate future changes and develop methods to enhance the skills of their employees, so enabling them to adapt efficiently to altering job requirements.

LEADERSHIP TODAY -BASICS

The notion of leadership, both as a topic of academic investigation and as a term, can be comprehended and expressed in several manners. Within a leadership eco system, the notions of leadership and responsibility exhibit a strong interconnection. A leader assumes the responsibility for multiple domains, ranging from the overall functioning of the company to the well-being and management of its employees. Relevant elements for employees may include domains such as information, qualification, and communication. The notion of employee leadership might be open to several interpretations. The manifestation of this phenomena is evident through the wide range of leadership behaviours that have been developed in academic research. Leadership demonstrates discernible behaviours along the course of value creation (Gao, 2020). The process encompasses the conceptualization, establishment, and articulation of specific goals and strategies. Concurrently, leadership undertakes the obligation of producing and organising activity. As a result, it creates a favourable environment for the achievement of goals. Leadership assumes the responsibility of providing guidance and management through the utilisation of crucial communication (Yannick Peifer, 2022). Within this context, there exists a notable degree of diversity in the various forms and approaches to leadership. Leaders have the capacity to demonstrate both task-oriented and employee-oriented behaviours. The understanding of the combo of both that aligns with a certain scenario dependent on the circumstances. The level of both task orientation and staff orientation might exhibit variability. Nevertheless, it is widely recognised in scholarly literature that the existence of both components is essential for effective leadership (Gatziu Grivas, 2023). The phenomenon of employees being guided by leaders is a perpetual facet of leadership. During the duration of adopting a leadership position, the leader demonstrates certain behavioural patterns that are indicative of effective leadership. The primary objective of leadership is to influence subordinates by demonstrating successful leadership characteristics (Surji, K. M. S, 2015). The current study is centred on the topic of Artificial Intelligence and leadership, drawing from existing reviews in the research fields. It specifically examines four main areas: strategic transformation, skills and competences, culture creation and the development self of a leader in the AI arena.

STRATEGIC TRANSFORMATION

The concept of strategic transformation refers to the process of implementing significant changes within an organization's overall strategy to adapt to evolving market. The integration and application of artificial intelligence into enterprises requires a thorough analysis of strategic factors. The effective integration and usage of artificial intelligence heavily rely on the strategic planning and implementation of the change process (Chen, 2022). The primary factor to be considered is the acknowledgement by leaders that the execution of a strategic change process is a task that encompasses a substantial time period. Leaders frequently exhibit a collective understanding of artificial intelligence. Having a well-defined objective that outlines the future potential of artificial intelligence is of utmost importance. The selection and articulation of objectives play a pivotal role in the strategic transformation process. To enhance this process, it is beneficial to employ a well-defined vision as a starting point of reference. A vision functions as a initial idea that offers guidance and establishes a sense of direction and orientation. It serves as a foundational structure for the implementation of strategic initiatives. Furthermore, the successful execution of the projected modification requires adequate communication. In the given context, leaders bear the obligation of proficiently conveying and embodying the overarching vision and strategic orientation. The inclusion of relevant stakeholders throughout the change process, coupled with a dedication to transparency, are essential elements that contribute to the attainment of success (Mayfield 2014). Nevertheless, it is crucial to recognise that human leadership continues to be essential in offering strategic guidance, envisioning future goals, and demonstrating empathy, as evidenced by the following strategies:

THE REDISTRIBUTION OF CAPITAL RESOURCES

This research report offers an analysis of the projected implications of artificial intelligence in work environments, with a particular emphasis on the restructuring and reorientation of different professions. An analysis was undertaken by the researchers at the MIT-IBM Watson AI Lab, wherein they examined 170 million online job listings spanning the years 2010 to 2017. The study employed artificial intelligence and machine learning techniques in its approaches. The study's primary finding is that while jobs experience incremental changes over long periods, the restructuring of activities happens at a considerably accelerated pace. Moreover, employment positions encompass a multitude of tasks. The generation of value throughout many professions and businesses is mostly ascribed to the actions conducted by individuals in the workforce. The advancement of technology will lead to the replacement of specific tasks by artificial intelligence and machine learning. Nevertheless, the results of the research suggest that just a small proportion, specifically 2.5%, of job roles involve a substantial quantity of activities that are considered appropriate for the use of machine learning techniques.

RESOURCES, INITIATIVES IN DEVELOPING THE WORKFORCE

In the realm of modern business practices, corporations are not only accountable for creating profits for shareholders; rather, but they are also anticipated to have a positive impact on various stakeholders, encompassing consumers, suppliers, communities, and employees. Moreover, the recognition of the significance of allocating resources towards the development and nurturing of competent individuals and other pertinent stakeholders is increasingly acknowledged as a pivotal determinant in attaining sustainable economic outcomes. The revised declaration on corporate governance issued by the Business Roundtable underscores the emerging expectations that prioritise the obligation of companies to offer assistance to their workforce by means of training and educational endeavours. These efforts are designed to enable the acquisition of new skills that are crucial in a constantly changing global environment. Based on a recent study carried out by the IBM Institute for Business Value, a considerable proportion of employees will necessitate retraining or reskilling within the upcoming three years because of the influence of artificial intelligence (Goldstein, 2023). The incorporation of technical training is unquestionably a crucial component. With the rising need for employment opportunities that require intellectual acuity, judgement, and other uniquely human attributes, it is crucial for leaders and managers to place emphasis on fostering the future-oriented capabilities of their workforce. The cultivation and enhancement of "people skills" like critical thinking, innovation, and proficient communication might facilitate the attainment of this objective. Through the implementation of these initiatives, leaders within organisations may effectively support the process of transitioning their workforce to engage in collaboration with intelligent machines. This is particularly relevant as various activities within the business undergo transformation and experience changes in their perceived value.

THE ENHANCEMENT OF LEARNING FOR FORTHCOMING GENERATIONS

As the prevalence of artificial intelligence grows across many industries and institutions, it becomes imperative for innovators and corporate executives to not only understand the impact of AI on business operations but also its wider implications for society. In conjunction with the necessity of allocating resources towards reskilling endeavours within enterprises, it is vital for CEOs to engage in collaborative efforts with policymakers and other stakeholders from the public and private spheres. The objective of this collaboration is to provide significant support for educational and vocational training, thereby promoting investment in inclusive training and reskilling programmes that are available to all employees.

Based on empirical study, it has been observed that the impact of technology on the demand for and earning capacity of mid-wage workers exhibits a disproportionate effect, ultimately leading to a contraction of the middle class. During investigation, it was found that in the context of occupational transitions, a ratio of four tasks shifting to low-wage professions and one task moving to a high-wage occupation was observed for every five activities that moved away from mid-wage occupations. As a result, there is a discernible trend of more pronounced salary growth in both the lower and higher income brackets as opposed to the middle wage bracket. The potential of emerging educational models and avenues for lifelong learning to address the growing skills gap is significant. These models provide opportunities for persons from all backgrounds, including middle-class individuals, students, and mid-career professionals, to acquire in-demand competencies. The prioritisation of resource distribution among different educational pathways, including community college, online learning, apprenticeships, and a collaborative endeavour involving public and private entities that seeks to equip high school students with the essential competencies for emerging technical careers such as cloud computing and cybersecurity, artificial intelligence etc., This skill gap needs to be mapped with strategic move of the leader.

CREATING AI CULTURE

The effective implementation and usage of artificial intelligence are reliant on the importance of leadership and organisational culture. The necessary participation of stakeholders is dependent on an appropriate organisational culture (Fleming, 2020).

The development of a corporate culture is an essential requirement for promoting acceptance among stakeholders. In the contemporary context, it is crucial for the corporate culture to adopt and adapt errors and setbacks that may occur during the process of organisational change (Yohn, 2021). In the present context, the corporate culture might be further delineated. The formation of an appropriate culture of leadership, prevention, work, and communication is deemed necessary by the firm. The integration and application of artificial intelligence are inherently connected to substantial transformational changes. Artificial intelligence is anticipated to become a crucial element within the leadership dynamic between employees and their superiors, owing to its intrinsic characteristics. Enterprises are faced with a wide range of unique opportunities as they navigate the shift into the era of artificial intelligence. One option that can be considered involves the establishment of a culture that is propelled by artificial intelligence. The establishment of a technological framework is an essential component, nonetheless, there is an additional variable that has the capacity to ascertain the triumph or downfall of a traditional organisation. Attaining success in the era of artificial intelligence encompasses more than mere financial resources and technological expenditures. It requires leaders to undergo a paradigm change in their perception of culture as a medium of communication (Vinuesa, 2020).

The effectiveness of developing and designing an AI-driven culture relies on the senior management's capacity to implement a prompt technology transition effort. There exists an urgent imperative to prioritise the optimisation of artificial intelligence development and to commence a project focused on fostering a culture that is in harmony with this technology. The objective of this undertaking is to develop and establish a new type of organisational culture known as an AI-powered culture. Culture refers to a collective set of ideas and distinct patterns of behaviour that hold significance within a certain organisation framework. Culture often centres on participation in centralised meetings, collaborative endeavours, the cultivation of trust, and the advancement of learning. Organisational involvement refers to the active participation of individuals inside a collective entity, wherein they engage in a coordinated and cooperative manner to achieve a shared objective.

The objective is to promote team cohesion and facilitate efficient information sharing within an organisation through the cultivation of increased collaboration. Organisational learning is widely acknowledged and embraced as a core tenet inside the firm, placing emphasis on professional growth that is aided by external suppliers and subject matter experts. These endeavours aim to cultivate a setting that is favourable for ongoing development and progress.

Once the cultural framework has been built based on these four fundamental principles, it becomes imperative to actively promote activities and notable accomplishments in a comprehensive manner. The newsletter or communication platform incorporates the accomplishments not only of current employees but also of those who have moved on to more advanced positions, leveraging the expertise gained, training and development earned, and their length of service within the business. The commendable proposal to retain all employees must consider the phenomenon of natural attrition and upward mobility within the organisational hierarchy. Neglecting to do so may heighten the probability of individuals seeking better employment prospects elsewhere. Hence, it is crucial that an organisational culture functions as the unifying element that brings together members of an organisation, while simultaneously demonstrating the capacity to adjust and harmonise with pragmatic factors. Trust is a multifaceted phenomenon that encompasses both benefits and drawbacks, as it involves a mutually dependent connection between leaders and their team members. Most of the research endeavours aim to identify individuals who have aspirations for upward mobility within the organisational hierarchy, those who are motivated to engage in continuous learning and development within their current roles, and those who display a temporary inclination and may consider career changes based on personal inclinations.

Organisations can effectively incentivize employees to adapt to the rapid evolution of technology by prioritising the well-being and needs of individuals, and subsequently providing the required technological resources to keep up with advancements in artificial intelligence. Team leaders proactively encourage and cultivate a culture of embracing risks within their teams, while also endeavouring to uphold a positive perspective on innovation. This new viewpoint offers improved flexibility and agility and the discussion inferred that the development of a cultural environment that promotes the incorporation of artificial intelligence carries substantial consequences for attaining business prosperity within organisations. The effective realisation and conceptualization of a culture powered by artificial intelligence require the resilience and guidance of senior-level executives. A culture powered by artificial intelligence (AI) should proactively involve all stakeholders within the organisation, promoting trust, continuous learning and development, collaborative initiatives, and a collective sense of camaraderie throughout the entire organisation (Ransbotham, 2021). Organisations possess the capacity to obtain benefits from cultural shifts, so achieving prosperity and augmenting their effectiveness within the era of artificial intelligence (AI). This includes developing their employees to the tune of recent changes.

COMPETENCIES AND SKILLS

Leaders possess the ability to employ artificial intelligence (AI) as a mechanism for improving their repertoire of skills and amplifying their aptitude for proficient decision-making. Artificial intelligence possesses the capacity to provide customised feedback and direction, thereby aiding leaders in the identification of areas for improvement and the enhancement of their leadership skills. Leaders has the capacity to employ artificial intelligence (AI) as a mechanism for assessing data and identifying patterns that may enhance their decision-making procedures (Hohenstein, 2023). This feedback possesses the capacity to aid leaders in discerning areas necessitating improvement and devising precise methods to enhance their leadership capabilities. Moreover, artificial intelligence (AI) possesses the capacity to support leaders in formulating well-informed judgements grounded in empirical facts. The objective is accomplished by conducting an examination of comprehensive datasets, in which artificial intelligence algorithms has the capability to identify and differentiate patterns and trends (Mikalef,, 2021).

This can aid leaders in making informed decisions and developing plans that are based on empirical evidence and intelligent analysis. Artificial intelligence (AI) possesses the capacity to facilitate talent management endeavours by discerning individuals' talents and potential. AI-enabled exams possess the capacity to analyse many facets of individuals, including their aptitudes, personality characteristics, and employment background. This facilitates executives in acquiring crucial insights pertaining to the potential and career development needs of their workforce. This technique enhances leaders' ability to identify individuals with significant potential, so enabling them to provide them with opportunities for personal and professional advancement. Strategic decisions have significant consequences; therefore, it is important to consider the transparent use of artificial intelligence. This involves understanding the underlying reasoning behind the prediction results and the deductions it makes based on certain data sources. The incorporation of artificial intelligence (AI) is anticipated to have a substantial impact on the acquisition and development of crucial skills and competences. This behaviour can be ascribed, to some extent, to the autonomous characteristics of AI systems, which empower them to produce inferences and exercise autonomous decision-making. Over the course of time, the integration of artificial intelligence (AI) will facilitate the transfer of diverse responsibilities that have conventionally been carried out by human leaders. The result involves a reallocation of duties between human leaders and artificial intelligence. The anticipated alteration in leadership needs and competencies are projected to be substantial (Dennison, 2023). Observable alterations can be identified in various areas of competence, including professional competences, methodological competencies, personal competencies, and social competencies.

It is crucial for humans to actively participate in the collaborative process of developing their roles in relation to artificial intelligence (AI). In addition, it is crucial for employees to possess a thorough comprehension of their distinct significance within the broader framework (Wilson, 2019). Trust can be conceptualised as a comprehensive framework that covers both the subjective experience of happiness and the objective sense of safety. It is crucial for individuals to have confidence that they will encounter lucrative career prospects upon waking up in the morning. Leaders must also consider the implications of artificial intelligence on their customers, partners, and the wider society. Prejudice emerges as a salient ethical concern within the realm of artificial intelligence (AI). The utilisation of artificial intelligence algorithms has the capacity to exhibit the biases that are inherent in its creators, hence leading to outcomes that perpetuate discriminatory practises. It is crucial for leaders to place a high priority on the advancement of AI technologies, giving significant attention to diversity and inclusivity. This approach guarantees that these technologies effectively depict and address the varied requirements of the individuals they are designed to serve. Another ethical question relates to the implications of artificial intelligence on the areas of privacy and security. Artificial intelligence systems possess the capacity to amass significant volumes of personal data, hence augmenting the likelihood of unauthorised access, misuse, and theft of this information. Leaders must place significant emphasis on prioritising the advancement and application of artificial intelligence technology while concurrently ensuring the protection of the privacy and security of their employees, customers, and stakeholders.

SELF DEVELOPMENT OF LEADERS IN THE AI ARENA

The fourth aspect of interest is the relationship between artificial intelligence and the self-development of leaders. This section addresses the requisite components. Emotional intelligence, commonly referred to as EQ, encompasses the cognitive capacity to perceive, comprehend, and effectively regulate one's own emotions. Additionally, it encompasses the ability to discern and manage the emotions of others, with the ultimate objective of reducing conflicts and cultivating improved interpersonal connections. The learning of this particular set of skills holds significant importance in the contemporary period characterised by the prevalence of artificial intelligence. Leaders that exhibit a heightened degree of emotional intelligence (EI) possess the ability to engage with others in a proficient manner, while also exemplifying attributes such as empathy and comprehension.

The notions of agility and innovation hold considerable significance across diverse fields. Both agility and innovation are essential for firms to effectively respond to dynamic and complex surroundings, as well as to maintain a competitive edge.

The demonstration of agility and flexibility by leaders is of utmost importance in effectively adapting to changing circumstances and successfully navigating the intricacies of decision-making, especially when using contemporary technologies. The capacity to promptly adjust and acquire novel proficiencies in response to rising technological breakthroughs is an essential attribute for effective leadership. This will enhance the involvement of both leaders and workers in the usage of emerging technologies. The rapid expansion of the Internet of Things has resulted in the production of around 2.5 quintillion bytes of data. Without a question, machines possess significant potential and demonstrate superior ability in identifying patterns from data as compared to humans. Therefore, it is crucial for leaders to develop a complete data vision that allows them to see significant patterns from the large volume of data at their disposal. This objective can be accomplished by employing dashboards, which function as valuable instruments for establishing an effective business strategy, vision, and organisational comprehension. The process described above includes several distinct stages, including mining, preparation, mapping, modelling, analysis, and deployment. These stages are crucial for the creation and execution of data solutions. The subject matter pertaining to critical and creative thinking holds considerable significance within the realm of scholarly discussion. The importance of possessing the capacity to actively participate in critical and creative thinking is widely acknowledged across diverse academic disciplines.

Although artificial intelligence (AI) has the ability to rapidly generate well-informed decisions using up-to-date information, it is important to recognise that the fundamental element of critical thinking remains within human leaders. Critical thinking is a cognitive process characterised by the thorough examination of events from several angles, utilising unbiased information, acquired expertise, empirical evidence, and previous experiential understanding. The present incapacity of Artificial Intelligence to execute this aspect of logical reasoning is a significant constraint. To maintain relevance, firms must continually engage in the process of producing innovative solutions and business concepts. Nevertheless, it is crucial to acknowledge that the current state of artificial intelligence (AI) does not possess the requisite capacity to adequately tackle this undertaking.

Ethical judgement pertains to the cognitive process of assessing and formulating conclusions grounded in moral principles and values. The process entails evaluating activities. Artificial intelligence (AI) possesses the ability to produce cost-efficient options and tactics; but it lacks the ethical competence to appropriately address the ensuing implications. When faced with business difficulties, executives bear the responsibility of assessing the extent to which the solutions produced by Artificial Intelligence are congruent with the values, objectives, and mission of the organisation. To effectively lead in the context of machine learning, it is imperative for a leader to prioritise the exploitation of impartial data and to do thorough validation of the resulting outcomes before deploying the model. The need to safeguard data privacy has become increasingly crucial due to the rising prevalence of fraudulent activities. The forthcoming leaders of society will have the responsibility of handling cyber threats, hence requiring the development of comprehensive organisational regulations that incorporate both employee behaviour and technological security measures.

Empathy is an essential attribute that a leader must possess, as it encompasses the ability to perceive and comprehend the viewpoints of individuals. This enables a leader to effectively foster trust among their employees and develop positive relationships, ultimately resulting in increased productivity for the firm. It is imperative for a manager or leader to embrace the principles of unity and collective viewpoints. What are the key attributes that contribute to the cultivation of an exemplary leader? In customary parlance, individuals may refer to the qualities of assertiveness, assurance, or decisiveness. This phenomenon can be ascribed to the enduring practice of organisations providing incentives and placing value on those who demonstrate confidence.

As human beings, we collectively recognise the presence of uncertainty in diverse facets of existence. Every situation has a variety of possible results that can be characterised in relation to their likelihoods. Nevertheless, in the context of conducting business, the act of expressing any type of reluctance often leads to additional inquiry or, in a less desirable situation, raises doubts over the level of ability. The primary aim of a learning approach is to develop proficiency in the ability to exude confidence and certainty on a specific outcome. Nevertheless, it is not uncommon for those in positions of leadership, possessing significant levels of authority, to heavily depend on conjecture when confronted with decision-making scenarios (Kjellström, 2020) . However, as artificial intelligence becomes more integrated into multiple sectors, many leaders are seeing the need for a new leadership paradigm. Artificial intelligence (AI) systems predominantly engage in the generation of mathematical probabilities for particular events or offer advisory recommendations. In light of this condition, it is imperative for leaders to modify their communication techniques and decision-making processes.

As firms integrate artificial intelligence (AI) technologies, it becomes crucial for leaders to recognise and embrace the existence of uncertainty, understand the constraints of AI, and cultivate a mentality that fosters innovative thinking. The fundamental basis of this unique methodology resides in probabilistic decision-making, which entails considering the potential manifestation of diverse outcomes. Individuals that adopt a leadership style that is congruent with and facilitates the use of this technology will gain a notable edge in the era of artificial intelligence. Organisations that neglect this aspect may potentially possess substantial quantities of data with significant monetary value yet struggle to successfully capitalise on its potential (Provitera, 2023).

THE UNDERSTANDING OF PROBABILISTIC DECISION MAKING

The dominant framework in current business practises is marked by a deterministic perspective, aiming to reduce or eliminate uncertainty. Decisions are frequently evaluated based on their moral or ethical propriety. By whom was the final decision rendered? Is it appropriate for them to hold that position?

AI and Machine Learning (ML) models require a certain set of questions. AI models do not just evaluate the dichotomy between "correct" and "incorrect". Conversely, these systems function based on a probabilistic framework, providing valuable perspectives on the mathematical probability of encountering uncertainty. When the incorporation of human intuition and experience is taken into account, a debate gains increased intrigue and becomes more well-informed, providing valuable practical insights from the outset. This is in opposition to the customary practise of retrospectively analysing factual information.

Fundamentally, the present circumstances no longer centre on the identification of the individual accountable for the "erroneous" decision and the scrutiny of their aptness for the corresponding position. This chance enables us to engage in proactive inquiry into things preceding an event, enhance our understanding of problems, and detect any erroneous assumptions. Moreover, it wields a substantial impact on team empowerment. Probabilistic systems that are efficient can assist leaders in recognising and accepting their personal biases, as well as the biases of their teams, when formulating assumptions on certain outcomes. Teams are currently provided with a notable opportunity to thoroughly analyse the process and apply improvements that will successfully contribute to the attainment of company objectives. The participants possess prior knowledge, which eliminates the need to retrospectively justify an intuition or subjective judgement that did not produce the expected result. Probabilistic thinking refers to a cognitive approach that involves reasoning and decision-making based on probabilities. It involves acknowledging and incorporating uncertainty and the implementation of data for probabilistic decision-making in organisations is now under progress; yet, a considerable number of organisations struggle to properly harness its potential. A restricted subset of companies has adopted a probabilistic decision-making methodology across all of its operational domains. Nevertheless, significant progress has been made in certain domains, including the fields of forecasting, asset maintenance, and failure prediction.

CHALLENGING ROLE OF AI AND LEADER INTEGRATION

It is imperative to recognize that people engaged in data-related tasks are integral members of one's own team. Within the domain of artificial intelligence, it is common for cross-functional teams to consistently exhibit a greater level of achievement and accelerated advancement. The effective implementation of influential artificial intelligence (AI) initiatives in business environments requires the collective effort of a broad workforce with a wide array of capabilities. The team is required to demonstrate the capacity to integrate commercial acumen, discernment, and knowledge when developing AI models. In addition, it is imperative for the team to incorporate personnel in authoritative roles who possess the competence to make prompt and resolute decisions grounded in the outcomes produced by these models.

The building of the model requires a joint effort involving individuals who possess technical expertise, while the understanding of its predictions and the subsequent execution of suitable actions required those with commercial acumen. When any component of this approach takes place in isolation, the resulting consequences tend to be of substandard quality, prone to delays, and often lacking in relevance. This issue is one of the contributing reasons that lead to the failure of multiple machine learning programmes in reaching the production level.

The incorporation of artificial intelligence (AI) into corporates is swiftly approaching, necessitating the guidance of visionary leaders to support this process of change. The CEOs who attain the highest level of success in an organisation powered by artificial intelligence are those that exhibit a profound dedication to fostering curiosity and actively endeavour to obtain a thorough comprehension of the subject matter, rather than depending solely on external sources for their knowledge and experience. Expertise is not always a prerequisite; rather, a fundamental aspect is in cultivating a spirit of curiosity.

The concept of artificial intelligence being regarded as a potential threat to human supremacy is an enticing proposition. The basic goal of artificial intelligence (AI) is to augment, improve, and maybe replace human intelligence, a widely recognised and accepted source of competitive advantage within the human population. There is a lack of empirical evidence to substantiate the claim that the impact of artificial intelligence will not encompass the realm of leadership. It is highly likely that artificial intelligence (AI) will replace many aspects of the cognitive processing and absorption of factual material, which are integral components of leadership. Concurrently, our hypothesis suggests that artificial intelligence will also prompt an increased emphasis on the "soft" aspects of leadership, which encompass personality traits, attitudes, and behaviours that enable individuals to assist others in achieving a common goal or shared purpose.

The shift from rigid leadership elements to more adaptable ones extends beyond the era of artificial intelligence. Based on a thorough examination of numerous studies conducted over a period of five decades, it has been determined that personality traits, such as curiosity, extraversion, and emotional stability, possess twice the level of importance compared to IQ, which is widely accepted as the conventional metric for assessing reasoning capabilities, when it comes to predicting the effectiveness of leadership.

According to a research viewpoint, the concept of leadership has had tremendous evolution across the span of thousands of years, so indicating that its core principles are unlikely to undergo major modification. Nevertheless, it is indisputable that alterations in the environment can exert a substantial influence on the formation of essential skills and behaviours that ultimately shape the efficacy, or lack thereof, of leaders. During a specific period in human history, which is believed to have occurred alongside the development of language, the criteria for effective leadership underwent a transformation. This shift entailed a transition from primarily valuing physical attributes to placing greater emphasis on cognitive capabilities. Consequently, intelligence and expertise gained prominence, while the importance of force and physical power diminished. Likewise, it is foreseeable that the current revolution in artificial intelligence (AI) will result in the commercialization and mechanisation of the data-centric elements of leadership, while delegating the more intricate facets of leadership to human individuals.

The present study continually demonstrates that in a period characterised by artificial intelligence, which brings about substantial disruption and quick, uncertain development, it is crucial to reevaluate the core essence of effective leadership. The perceived worth of certain traits, such as a deep understanding of a specific domain, the ability to make timely judgements, possessing leadership skills, and prioritising immediate goals, is declining. On the other hand, leadership styles that prioritise agility are anticipated to assign significant importance to attributes such as humility, flexibility, imaginative thinking, and ongoing involvement. The subsequent section offers a comprehensive examination of these competencies.

The notion of humility is a virtue that holds significant importance within diverse cultural and philosophical frameworks. In a period marked by rapid changes, it is equally important to be cognizant of one's areas of lacking knowledge as it is to be aware of one's current knowledge. Unfortunately, leaders often face obstacles in their quest for knowledge pertaining to current achievements as a result of the vast and heterogeneous nature of the information that is amassed on a daily basis. In the current era of artificial intelligence, it is crucial for leaders to display a strong inclination towards acquiring knowledge and demonstrate openness to seeking insights from both internal and external sources within their enterprises. Furthermore, it is vital for individuals to possess the ability to establish trust in persons who hold a greater level of expertise than themselves. This information may be derived from an individual who is 20 years junior or holds a position three tiers lower within the organisational structure. In the context of the artificial intelligence era, a competent leader recognises that an individual's subordinate position within a hierarchy or their restricted professional experience should not be seen as a barrier to their potential to make a substantial impact.

Nestlé and other comparable firms have effectively implemented comprehensive reverse mentorship schemes. The primary objective of these initiatives is to build a comprehensive structure that facilitates the integration, recognition, and effective utilisation of the knowledge and skills possessed by team members, colleagues, and staff members. The final purpose is to improve the overall performance and achievement of the organisation. The notion of humility may seem paradoxical when contemplating the imperative of projecting an appearance of self-assurance and knowledge. Nevertheless, it is commonly acknowledged that there is a constant lack of strong association between confidence and real performance. Indeed, individuals who possess authentic expertise tend to demonstrate a higher degree of humility in contrast to those who have limited or no experience.

The notion of adaptability pertains to the capacity of persons or systems to make adjustments or alterations. At the organisational level, adaptability denotes the readiness to partake in innovation and adequately address both favourable circumstances and potential risks as they emerge. At the individual level, it involves exhibiting openness to new ideas, showing a readiness to adjust one's perspective even if it causes personal discomfort or challenges one's ego, and effectively communicating the revised viewpoint to relevant stakeholders, including colleagues, teams, and clients. In the context of the artificial intelligence era, it is important to recognise the desirable nature of adopting a flexible mindset, which is frequently perceived as vulnerable or indicative of fluctuating commitment. This quality becomes particularly valuable when it contributes to the improvement of decision-making through the acquisition of informed options. Leaders that exhibit flexibility showcase a readiness to adopt novel techniques in response to changing conditions. Their ability to adapt enables them to efficiently overcome challenges, prioritising the acquisition of knowledge over the need to prove their own correctness. Carlos Torres Vila, the Chief Executive Officer (CEO) of BBVA, a major Spanish financial organisation, played a pivotal role in transforming the corporation from a traditional brick-and-mortar banking institution into a very successful financial services entity in the digital era (Carlos Torres, 2018). In light of the transformation occurring within the industry, he introduced a groundbreaking organisational culture that fosters adaptability, versatility, cooperation, an enterprising attitude, and ingenuity. (https://www.bbva.com/en/carlos-torres-vila-digital-revolution-proving-success/).

The notion of vision pertains to an individual's capacity to perceive and comprehend visual stimuli. The relevance of vision has continually played a crucial role in the domain of effective leadership. Nevertheless, in an epoch characterised by rapid technical progress and transformative changes in corporate frameworks, the importance of possessing a clearly articulated vision becomes increasingly imperative. This phenomenon can be attributed to a growing lack of clarity experienced by persons who are followers, subordinates, or employees of leaders. This lack of clarity pertains to the desired course of action, the specific actions to be taken, and the underlying reasoning that informs these decisions. Leaders that possess a clearly defined vision demonstrate the capacity to offer persuasive and meaningful solutions to these concerns, thereby showcasing exceptional skill in effectively communicating their thoughts. Furthermore, the capacity to foresee empowers a leader to proficiently implement crucial organisational transformations without submitting to current, transient considerations.

Several current chief executive officers (CEOs) of well-known digital corporations, such as Amazon, Tesla, Facebook, Tencent, Alibaba, and Google, have successfully conveyed their organisational concepts, although facing notable immediate risks.

The notion of engagement holds substantial importance when examining many academic areas. In order to effectively navigate the era of artificial intelligence, it is crucial for a leader to maintain a persistent and engaged connection with their immediate environment. This allows individuals to accurately notice and respond to significant stimuli, rather than being distracted by irrelevant factors. These indications can present either obstacles to their goals or offer support in achieving their aspirations. In order to effectively lead in an agile manner, it is crucial for leaders to actively participate and simultaneously develop methods to encourage team participation, especially during challenging times and when faced with difficult conditions.

In the contemporary era of artificial intelligence, the process of interacting with others can be more conveniently accomplished by utilising digital platforms and technologies. An example of this phenomenon can be witnessed in the context of Zalando, a major German e-commerce company, which has effectively incorporated a wide array of digital technologies into its operational structure. These tools have been purposefully developed to facilitate the ability of the organization's senior management to efficiently capture and handle a wide range of significant topics that are brought up by all employees. The aforementioned solutions include zTalk, an interactive chat programme; zLive, a social intranet platform intended for enterprise-wide use; and zBeat, a survey tool that regularly collects feedback from employees regarding their continuing work experiences (Zendesk, 2023). Does the facts provided above suggest that leadership experiences substantial transformations in the era of artificial intelligence? However, it is imperative to acknowledge that there are two notable distinctions.

At the outset, it is expected that the competence of leaders in technical aptitude will be eclipsed by the capabilities of intelligent robots, although their interpersonal qualities will assume greater importance. Moreover, within the context of the artificial intelligence era, it becomes apparent that enduring leadership attributes, such as integrity and emotional intelligence, will retain their value. Nevertheless, it is imperative for leaders to display humility by recognising and appreciating the contributions made by others. Additionally, they should demonstrate adaptability in effectively addressing unanticipated obstacles. Furthermore, leaders must uphold a steadfast dedication to their overarching goals and actively engage with the ever-changing external environment. The artificial intelligence (AI) business is currently undergoing significant expansion, leading to noteworthy ramifications for leadership roles. Artificial intelligence (AI) utilises several technologies, including machine learning (ML), object identification, and advanced data analytics, in order to optimise the decision-making process. In numerous organisational scenarios, the utilisation of robust artificial intelligence (AI) models can be leveraged to offer recommendations for the most advantageous course of action.

LEADERSHIP ABILITIES

Do individuals in the workforce possess sufficient leadership abilities to effectively lead a company towards success in the era of artificial intelligence (AI)?

Let us initiate the discussion by analysing the dynamic attributes of leadership. With the advancement of technological intelligence, leaders will no longer bear exclusive responsibility for making regular judgements. Undoubtedly, it is crucial for the upcoming generation of leaders, including team managers, business unit heads, and C-level executives, to prioritise the human factor in the decision-making process. This is of utmost importance given the increasing dominance of artificial intelligence in data-driven and context-based decision-making. It is important to acknowledge that corporate executives are actually reaping advantages from the advent of artificial intelligence. The findings of a study done by Infosys indicate that a substantial majority of the executives in top-level management, comprising 90% of the respondents, have reported observing real benefits arising from the implementation of artificial intelligence (AI) technology (Infosys report, 2018). Moreover, a significant percentage of individuals responsible for making IT decisions, namely 77%, have demonstrated a sense of assurance over the ability of employees to acquire the essential competencies required to effectively adjust to new positions facilitated by artificial intelligence. Therefore, to effectively harness the advantages of artificial intelligence (AI) and minimise any potential disruptive outcomes, it is crucial for the current workforce to actively develop competent leadership skills, with a particular focus on readiness for AI and automation.

SPECIFIC SET OF SKILLS FOR AI LEADER

Considering the forthcoming era of artificial intelligence (AI), it is crucial to cultivate a range of leadership qualities that are widely recognised as successful. This article emphasises three abilities that are particularly crucial in preparation for the aforementioned era. In the foreseeable future, it is anticipated that artificial intelligence (AI) will replace specific traditional aspects of leadership. An example will be shown to illustrate the application of automated analysis of historical facts in extracting data for informed decision-making in the business context. The potential of artificial intelligence to accurately anticipate future events will enable the workforce to be adequately prepared and equipped. Hence, what are the implications for leaders within organisations? As previously mentioned, it is crucial for individuals to reevaluate their approach to leadership from a humanistic perspective and incorporate the following skill sets: The objective of this study is to examine the significance of leadership in the context of artificial intelligence, a period characterised by the swift evolution of technology and business frameworks. This suggests that the knowledge obtained through direct personal experience will rapidly become outdated. Leadership necessitates a willingness to abandon antiquated ideologies and actively participate in the process of "unlearning." This involves letting go of preconceived notions, even if they are substantiated by substantial practical knowledge, and actively seeking out information in unknown areas. It is imperative to substitute conventional approaches with inventive alternatives, which may entail some degrees of uncertainty. Furthermore, it is imperative to cultivate a mindset of openness, where leaders demonstrate a willingness to embrace and acknowledge valuable insights and inputs from individuals within the organisation as well as external collaborators, regardless of their position within the hierarchical structure.

The attribute of possessing foresight has long been regarded as a significant quality within the domain of leadership, with its importance being further amplified in the current period characterised by the presence of artificial intelligence (AI). Having a comprehensive comprehension of the trajectory in which a team or organisation is advancing is of utmost importance. Nevertheless, it is imperative that the roadmap maintains its adaptability and is open to frequent revisions. The future leaders will exhibit the attributes of agility and imaginative cognition, enabling them to formulate strategies that can adeptly address the ever-changing dynamics in the domains of commerce, socioeconomics, and politics.

The increasing prevalence of advanced technological systems, particularly artificial intelligence (AI), has amplified the need of soft skills. The introduction of automation in positions that are centred around processes will unavoidably result in a shift in the roles and dynamics of leaders as they engage with their staff. Within the realm of human resources, a pivotal responsibility involves the facilitation of mitigating employees' concerns pertaining to artificial intelligence (AI). In order to efficiently manage larger volumes of data and cultivate a more strategic attitude, it will be necessary for line managers to possess the requisite capacity to deliver training to people. Proficiency in mediating interpersonal interactions, resolving disagreements, and eliciting optimal performance from individuals will be a vital skillset in the realm of leadership.

Moreover, this phenomenon is not limited to a single labour classification or horizontal categorization. It is crucial for executives at the C-level to maintain regular communication with both frontline employees and department heads with extensive tenure, as the latter will be tasked with supervising a sizable contingent workforce. Therefore, it is crucial for effective leadership to maintain ongoing engagement with both individuals and the surrounding environment.

METHODS FOR FORMULATING AN ARTIFICIAL INTELLIGENCE-PREPARED SUCCESSION STRATEGY

Various tactics can be employed to effectively equip the workforce with the necessary skills and competencies to meet the leadership requirements of the future driven by artificial intelligence (AI). The aforementioned items include:

- Reverse mentoring is a practise that seeks to cultivate empathy and promote a desire to welcome change.
- Leadership coaching is a distinct and specialised approach to enhancing professional growth that places particular attention on the development of soft skills, such as creativity, communication, and foresight.
- The employment of AI screening techniques to assess candidate personalities is a method employed in the selection of leaders.
- The practise of crowdsourcing ideas, whether through physical forums or utilising software, is widely popular in current society.
- The possession of data literacy is of utmost importance for leaders as it enables them to comprehensively understand the ramifications of artificial intelligence (AI) and skilfully guide the workforce towards the attainment of desired objectives.

The growing presence of artificial intelligence (AI) as a disruptive force across several industries necessitates the recognition and attentiveness of present-day leaders. Based on estimations, a diverse array of sectors, such as the public sector (56%) and retail and consumer packaged products (85%), are employing artificial intelligence (AI) to automate a variety of operations. In the foreseeable future, this phenomenon will surpass its current focus on operational efficiency and adopt a more strategic form.

IMPROVED COLLABORATION BETWEEN HUMAN LEADERS AND ARTIFICIAL INTELLIGENCE

It is crucial to underscore that artificial intelligence (AI) will not replace the need for human leaders at every level of the organisational hierarchy. Within the context of a highly competitive corporate environment, the role of an entity is mostly limited to that of a collaborator and facilitator, working towards the attainment of success. The revaluation of leadership abilities holds significant significance in facilitating efficient functioning throughout the period characterised by the presence of artificial intelligence. To effectively respond to the advent of artificial intelligence, it is crucial to comprehensively overhaul many aspects of your workforce, encompassing the processes of employee recruiting and training, as well as the strategic considerations for future leadership transitions.

The emergence of artificial intelligence and automation is anticipated to profoundly alter the nature of work. The recognition and resolution of the ongoing revolution in artificial intelligence and data-driven technologies, commonly known as the "intelligence revolution," hold paramount importance for leaders. They must not disregard this transformative process and should also ensure that their counterparts within the organisation do not overlook it. Contemporary and future business leaders are required to take into account a range of significant factors. These include acquiring a comprehensive comprehension of artificial intelligence (AI), tackling challenges related to human interaction, alleviating ethical dilemmas associated with AI, guaranteeing the establishment of suitable technological infrastructure, and considering other pertinent aspects. The main inference derived from this analysis suggests that the relevance of leadership skills in relation to human beings will endure in the upcoming intelligence revolution, possibly exceeding their current level of importance. Individuals are, and will persistently remain, the primary and indispensable asset for every given organisation. Nevertheless, it is important to note that the leadership traits that will be highly esteemed in the future may exhibit substantial differences from the conventional leadership talents that are today held in high regard. There is an expectation that in forthcoming times, there will be a heightened emphasis on specific interpersonal attributes, like humility and emotional intelligence.

The emergence of artificial intelligence (AI) as a result of the digitalization process is expected to have a substantial influence on the corporate working landscape. This involves both the activities conducted by persons in positions of authority, as well as the notion and practise of leadership as a whole. Leaders will face substantial obstacles while also being required to fulfil several expectations. The core theme of this discourse centres on the following clusters: Strategic Transformation Process, Qualification, Culture, and the interconnectedness between a leader and their self. In the course of undergoing change, it is crucial for individuals to adopt the role of active agents in shaping the outcomes. This necessitates their proactive engagement in the formulation of objectives and visions, as well as the facilitation of the strategic process's progress. The engagement of stakeholders and the implementation of transparency hold considerable significance within this particular setting. Additionally, individuals encounter modified requirements in relation to their unique skill sets. Therefore, it is crucial to acquire supplementary credentials. As a leader, there will be an increased focus on social competencies. The effective integration of artificial intelligence (AI) requires an organisational culture that is progressively more conducive to its application. The establishment of this culture will be the task of leaders. Concurrently, the domain of leadership will experience a process of evolution and broadening as a result of the incorporation of artificial intelligence as an additional element. The operations they engage in will experience a gradual shift. The manifestation of this phenomena will mostly occur through the influential role of leaders in shaping the relationship between employees and artificial intelligence. The actions and conduct of individuals will be of utmost importance in guaranteeing the efficient implementation and usage of artificial intelligence. When contemplating the implementation and utilisation of artificial intelligence (AI), it is crucial to embrace a holistic viewpoint. The improvements involve both potential strategies for leaders to mitigate their burden and potential difficulties linked with the adoption of artificial intelligence in leading staff. However, it is important to acknowledge that leaders also have the power to take on the role of AI users. This phenomenon could result in persons assuming a second role, thereby exacerbating the intricacies they encounter. Furthermore, leadership can be demonstrated across several levels of hierarchy within an institution. This suggests that the challenges and requirements associated with artificial intelligence are anticipated to possess unique attributes. One could hypothesise that the changes will depend on the particular leadership style demonstrated by an individual, which may differ in terms of being focused on tasks or focused on employees.

During periods of significant economic change, there are considerable problems associated with the process of changing skills and work techniques for workers. Additionally, leaders are required to reevaluate resource allocation and workforce training, further adding to these challenges. For the optimal realisation of artificial intelligence (AI)'s capacity to improve our professional endeavours and advance societal welfare, it is crucial for organisational leaders to exhibit readiness in addressing the imminent challenges.

THE AI BASED LEADERSHIP IN VUCA AND BANI WORLD

The technology sector is well acquainted with the concept of change. Indeed, technological advancements have a reputation for fundamentally altering the established norms and regulations that govern businesses and society. This holds paramount importance considering the requirements of our evolving era. Driven by fundamental changes resulting from digitization, regulation and compliance, globalisation, ethical consumerism, consolidation, environmental sustainability, and similar factors, businesses are actively seeking to not only navigate but also exploit the opportunities arising from a VUCA (volatility, uncertainty, complexity, ambiguity) world. Each of these parameters is producing a distinct outcome. The presence of volatility necessitates the ability to make quick and decisive decisions while maintaining clarity. Uncertainty necessitates the transformation of risk into a competitive advantage. The increasing intricacy of the interconnections and impacts among various components of the value chain necessitates a global perspective and a continuous focus on diverse and specialised knowledge. Ambiguity requires thorough contemplation, understanding, adaptability, and above all, modesty. Conventional leadership skills have limitations when it comes to addressing these exceptional challenges. Upgrading leadership styles is essential for navigating through challenging situations.

Leaders in various sectors are required to engage in innovation. The majority of industries are currently experiencing disruptions caused by smaller entities and non-traditional sources. Innovation is a crucial catalyst for distinguishing oneself from competitors, and businesses are progressively more inclined to assume risks in order to provide enhanced value. With the transformation of technology, businesses that effectively adopt and exploit technology are gaining a competitive advantage in the business world. Contemporary leaders must incorporate innovation as an integral part of their organisations' fundamental structure. One way to achieve this is by creating suitable risk-and-reward systems and providing employees with opportunities to utilise various resources and collaborate with different teams within the organisation. Encouraging individuals to investigate alternative approaches for addressing intricate business challenges stimulates innovation.

There is no indication that the business environment will become less intricate and uncertain over time. However, this does not imply that organisations subject themselves to the unpredictable forces of change. Adaptive leaders possess the ability to relinquish previous biases and embrace novel approaches to guaranteeing business success. In order to thrive in a VUCA (volatile, uncertain, complex, and ambiguous) environment (VUCA, 2023), it is crucial to embrace a proactive rather than reactive approach. This entails making strategic investments in the business during challenging times, potentially even with greater intensity, in order to reap the rewards when stability is restored. Leaders and organisations that can effectively navigate these inherent contradictions and embrace the VUCA elements will be able to establish and maintain market leadership.

The VUCA (Volatile, Uncertain, Complex, Ambiguous) concept has become a guiding principle for many leaders in our fast-paced and increasingly intricate world. Previously, the SPOD (Simple, Predictable, Orderly, Deterministic) world was widely regarded as the standard for business and organisational leadership. Nevertheless, with the increasing interconnectivity and complexity of the world, the VUCA framework has become the standard in the business realm. This framework predominantly mirrored the period following the Cold War, characterised by swift technological progress and geopolitical changes.

In the present time, the COVID-19 pandemic and the Ukraine war have additionally altered our comprehension of the world. The BANI (Brittle, Anxious, Nonlinear, Incomprehensible) framework, developed by anthropologist, author, and futurist Jamais Cascio, has emerged as a more suitable approach for understanding the complexities of our global environment (Stefan F.Dieffenbacher, 2023). The world is constantly evolving, and the transition from SPOD to VUCA and now BANI is evidence of the dynamic nature of our global environment. As leaders, it is imperative to remain knowledgeable about emerging trends, as they exert a substantial influence on our ability to navigate and comprehend the world.

CONCLUSION

Leaders are required to maintain a careful balance between the utilisation of artificial intelligence technology and the necessity for human judgement and intuition. It is imperative for organisations to give utmost importance to the development of a work environment that nurtures a sense of worth and active participation among their employees, especially considering the growing prevalence of artificial intelligence (AI) technology in the workplace. The development of a proficient human leadership framework requires the growth of a company culture that promotes employee proactivity and the generation of new ideas. Moreover, it involves the recognition and resolution of employees' concerns and needs, including the provision of support for their emotional and psychological well-being. Leaders must prioritise the establishment and maintenance of communication channels that exhibit qualities of openness and transparency. This approach facilitates an environment where employees feel comfortable expressing their concerns and actively contributing their ideas. Efficient information management is crucial for ensuring the transparency and accountability of AI systems. With the increasing prevalence of AI, it is crucial to establish a comprehensive comprehension of the decision-making process and data sources employed by these systems. Implementing these measures can foster confidence in AI systems and guarantee their ethical utilisation. Furthermore, effective information management is essential for the continuous upkeep and enhancement of AI systems. As additional data becomes accessible and the requirements of the system evolve, it is necessary to update and enhance the data utilised by the AI. Robust information management techniques are necessary to ensure optimal efficiency of the AI system. To summarise, efficient information management is crucial for the successful integration and utilisation of AI. Ensuring the quality, transparency, and accountability of these systems is essential. It is a continual process that is vital for the continuous maintenance and enhancement of AI. The utilisation of AI decision-making is transforming the field of business intelligence through the analysis of extensive datasets, leading to enhanced decision-making procedures. Machine learning, natural language processing, and computer vision are integral elements of artificial intelligence that enhance the speed and precision of decision-making. AI provides many levels of support, ranging from automating simple activities to enabling fully independent decision-making, depending on the complexity of the scenario. Organisations are utilising artificial intelligence (AI) skills in several domains such as marketing, sales, product development, and strategy to improve operational efficiency and produce financial profits. Nevertheless, organisations must overcome the problem of handling the dangers connected with AI adoption in order to fully exploit its benefits. Furthermore, the existence of human leadership plays a critical role in fostering innovation, which is an essential element for the long-term viability of any organisation in the age of artificial intelligence. Leaders must prioritise the establishment of an atmosphere that nurtures creativity and innovation within their workforce, thereby creating a culture that values experimentation and the inclination to undertake risks. It is imperative for organisations to prioritise the allocation of sufficient resources and infrastructure to facilitate their employees' involvement in the investigation of innovative concepts and technologies.

REFERENCES

Chen, D., Esperança, J. P., & Wang, S. (2022). The Impact of Artificial intelligence on Firm Performance: An application of the Resource-Based View to E-Commerce Firms. *Frontiers in Psychology*, *13*, 884830. Advance online publication. doi:10.3389/fpsyg.2022.884830 PMID:35465474

Communications. (2018, April 4). *Carlos Torres Vila: "The digital revolution is proving a success."* NEWS BBVA. https://www.bbva.com/en/carlos-torres-vila-digital-revolution-proving-success/

Dennison, K. (2023, March 14). The Impact Of Artificial Intelligence On Leadership: How To Leverage AI To Improve Decision-Making. *Forbes*. https://www.forbes.com/sites/karadennison/2023/03/14/the-impact-of-artificial-intelligence-on-leadership-how-to-leverage-ai-to-improve-decision-making/

Dieffenbacher, S. F. (2023). https://digitalleadership.com/blog/bani-world/

Fleming, M. (2020, March 24). AI is changing work — and leaders need to adapt. *Harvard Business Review*. https://hbr.org/2020/03/ai-is-changing-work-and-leaders-need-to-adapt

Gao, Z., Wanyama, T., Singh, I., Gadhrri, A., & Schimdt, R. (2020). From Industry 4.0 to Robotics 4.0 - A Conceptual Framework for Collaborative and Intelligent Robotic Systems. *Procedia Manufacturing*, *46*, 591–599. doi:10.1016/j.promfg.2020.03.085

Gatziu Grivas, S., Imhof, D., & Gachnang, P. (2023). Correction to: Position Paper - Hybrid Artificial Intelligence for Realizing a Leadership Assistant for Platform-Based Leadership Consulting. In M. Ruiz & P. Soffer (Eds.), *Advanced Information Systems Engineering Workshops. CAiSE 2023. Lecture Notes in Business Information Processing* (Vol. 482). Springer. doi:10.1007/978-3-031-34985-0_20

Goldstein, J., & Goldstein, J. (2023). *New IBM study reveals how AI is changing work and what HR leaders should do about it.* IBM Blog. https://www.ibm.com/blog/new-ibm-study-reveals-how-ai-is-changing-work-and-what-hr-leaders-should-do-about-it/

Hohenstein, J., DiFranzo, D., Kizilcec, R. F., Aghajari, Z., Mieczkowski, H., Levy, K., Naaman, M., Hancock, J., & Jung, M. (2023). Artificial intelligence in communication impacts language and social relationships. *Scientific Reports*, *13*(1), 5487. Advance online publication. doi:10.1038/s41598-023-30938-9 PMID:37015964

Infosys Report. (n.d.). https://www.infosys.com/age-of-ai/Documents/age-of-ai-infosys-research-report.pdf

Kjellström, S., Stålne, K., & Törnblom, O. (2020). Six ways of understanding leadership development: An exploration of increasing complexity. *Leadership*, *16*(4), 434–460. doi:10.1177/1742715020926731

Mayfield, P. (2014). Engaging with stakeholders is critical when leading change. *Industrial and Commercial Training*, *46*(2), 6872. doi:10.1108/ICT-10-2013-0064

Mikalef, P., & Gupta, M. (2021). Artificial intelligence capability: Conceptualization, measurement calibration, and empirical study on its impact on organizational creativity and firm performance. *Information & Management*, *58*(3), 103434. doi:10.1016/j.im.2021.103434

Peifer, Y., Jeske, T., & Hille, S. (2022). Artificial Intelligence and its Impact on Leaders and Leadership. *Procedia Computer Science*, *200*, 1024–1103. doi:10.1016/j.procs.2022.01.301

Provitera, M. S. M. (2023, August 23). *Creating an AI-powered culture demands a change in how people managers and leaders think*. https://www.peoplemanagement.co.uk/article/1834909/creating-ai-powered-culture-demands-change-people-managers-leaders-think

Ramsbotham, S. (2021, November 2). The cultural benefits of artificial intelligence in the enterprise. *MIT Sloan Management Review*. https://sloanreview.mit.edu/projects/the-cultural-benefits-of-artificial-intelligence-in-the-enterprise/

Surji, K. M. S. (2015). Understanding Leadership and Factors that Influence Leaders' Effectiveness. *European Journal of Business and Management*, *7*(33). Advance online publication. doi:10.7176/EJBM/7-33-2015-03

Vinuesa, R., Azizpour, H., Leite, I., Balaam, M., Dignum, V., Domisch, S., Felländer, A., Langhans, S. D., Tegmark, M., & Nerini, F. F. (2020). The role of artificial intelligence in achieving the Sustainable Development Goals. *Nature Communications*, *11*(1), 233. Advance online publication. doi:10.1038/s41467-019-14108-y PMID:31932590

VUCA. (n.d.). https://www.vuca-world.org/

Wilson, H. J. (2019, November 19). How humans and AI are working together in 1,500 companies. *Harvard Business Review*. https://hbr.org/2018/07/collaborative-intelligence-humans-and-ai-are-joining-forces

Yohn, D. L. (2021, February 9). Company culture is everyone's responsibility. *Harvard Business Review*. https://hbr.org/2021/02/company-culture-is-everyones-responsibility

Zendesk. (2023, June 13). *14 Best Live Chat Software And Apps for 2023*. Zendesk India. https://www.zendesk.com/in/service/messaging/live-chat/

Chapter 5
Investing in Artificial Intelligence (AI) for Business Leaders to Enhance Decision-Making

Ahmed Sedky
https://orcid.org/0000-0002-8087-4175
Walden University, USA

ABSTRACT

Decision-making is a high-risk process for businesses' life cycle worldwide. Wrong decisions by business leaders may lead to business closure in critical situations for all firms, including small and medium-sized enterprises. Leaders invest in artificial intelligence to improve their decision-making capabilities and contribute to their businesses' sustainability. Grounded in Herbert Simon's decision-making theory, the purpose of this chapter's multiple case study was to explore why artificial intelligence may enhance business leaders' decision-making. Three business leaders from different organizations in the United States and UAE's real estate properties industry participated in this research. Data were collected through semi-structured interviews and from a review of previous literature. A key recommendation for firms is to invest in artificial intelligence. Artificial intelligence may allow business leaders to improve decision-making, reduce the potential risk of closure, extend business opportunities, and positively contribute to communities' stability and growth.

DOI: 10.4018/979-8-3693-0712-0.ch005

INTRODUCTION

Mouzas and Bauer (2022) stated that businesses, including small and medium-sized enterprises (SMEs), face the potential risk of closure because of the exposure to severe market competition every year. Also, Kharlamova et al. (2019) pinpointed that business closure negatively affects countries' Gross Domestic Product (GDP) and the employment rates of global communities. The disappointment of the labor showcase to assimilate the existing work constraint leads to an increase in the unemployment rates with an impact on hardship and influences the individual's physical and mental well-being. Unemployment leads to weak aggregate demand, and the global economy is more likely to experience a negative gap, with the actual GDPs becoming less than the potential ones. Therefore, analyzing the reasons behind businesses closure gained significant importance to aid economies and communities to continue growing.

Many reasons could lead to business closure. Through exploring a case, Mayr et al. (2020) expressed that researchers analyzed the reasons behind the closure of many businesses and found that the most significant reasons are (a) financial-related reasons, such as struggling cash flow and wrong investment and (b) management-related reasons, such as lack of planning and weak leadership skills. However, the leadership effect might drive the success and failure of the provided reasons. Leaders could not make decisions that help their firms survive the challenging business environments. Decision-making is one of the essential reasons and a critical process that impacts the existence of firms and the continuity of their operations. Lack of persistent efforts, prioritization, and shortage of skilled resources represent critical challenges to firms. Sedky (2021) confirmed that small and medium-sized enterprises (SMEs) are extremely important for economic growth and employment. The European Commission (2019) endorsed the importance of SMEs, demonstrating through its report that SMEs comprise 99.8% of businesses and employ 66.6% of the workforce in Europe. Therefore, decision-making is critical to driving every organization's direction and development.

Leaders should possess the confidence to make decisions that determine organizations' paths. The process of making decisions is not an easy task for business leaders. Leaders need the tools and sufficient data to eliminate risks and assure success, especially when making complex decisions (Newman & Ford, 2020). Artificial Intelligence (AI) could be the tool business leaders need to access firms' data, allowing for a superior view of situations before making decisions. AI has become the technology of choice to spot and solve complex business problems in various industrial sectors where organizations are present (Allal-Cherif et al., 2021; Vrontis et al., 2021). Leaders use AI to collect data, analyze data, and make beneficial decisions that lead their organizations to success through building assumptions and developing business scenarios. However, the lack of knowledge about AI could represent a milestone for leaders to decide to invest in AI. At the same time, the increased risks in critical situations could be the enabler for such an investment. From this perspective, investing in AI could allow organizational leaders to become more capable of making better decisions that enable their firms to succeed and continue operating. Therefore, investing in AI is extremely important to solve organizational problems by enhancing decision-making to ensure firms' success.

In this chapter, the researcher explored the importance of investing in AI for business leaders to enhance their decision-making. The researcher explored previous literature and conducted a qualitative multiple case study that involved the participation of real estate property industry leaders from the United States and the United Arab Emirates (U.A.E.). The researcher relied on Herbert Simon's decision-making conceptual framework to bridge research gaps (Saunders et al., 2020). The purpose of this chapter is to explore why investing in AI may enhance business leaders' decisions and enable sustaining their firms.

HERBERT SIMON'S DECISION-MAKING CONCEPTUAL FRAMEWORK

Herbert Simon (1959) introduced the decision-making framework through which he focused on the decision-makers' interests that influenced their decisions. According to Humphreys (2021) and Maung (2020), Simon emphasized that leaders made decisions under the influence of the notion bounded rationality, where decisions were built on acceptable solutions rather than systematic choices and best solutions. Those solutions are based on parameters such as priorities, values, and objectives. Researchers use Simon's decision-making conceptual framework to discover the best practices of planning and controlling within organizations by employing psychological concepts such as human thinking. Thus, the decision-making framework has three factors: (a) the concept of bounded rationality influences decisions, (b) the leader's expertise plays a significant role in the quality of decisions, and (c) studying the cognitive limitation is essential for understanding the decision-making process.

Researchers find the decision-making framework a valuable framework in organizational performance research. The framework allows researchers to understand business leaders deeply. The framework provides researchers with the needed guidance to understand leaders' capabilities and the quality of their decisions. Like many researchers, Whittaker (2018) used Simon's framework to understand human behavior's influence on decision-making. Leaders' understanding of historical and existing circumstances is a lengthy data exploration task that could be accelerated using AI tools. AI access to relevant data allows leaders to eliminate personal biases that could influence human decisions, make systematic choices, and apply best practices (Cummins et al., 2022). Thus, decisions are made faster in sophisticated situations. From such a perspective, the researcher relied on Simon's decision-making framework to explore why investing in AI may enhance business leaders' decision-making and drive sustainability for their firms.

LITERATURE REVIEW

Artificial Intelligence (AI)

AI applications are important for various fields in life as they help enhance leaders' decisions by studying their business-related data. Aldosari (2020) emphasized that AI represents modern applications of information systems to accomplish many tasks that require the ability of inference, deduction, and perception while studying the nature of human intelligence. During research, Lin et al. (2021) concluded that business leaders relying on AI gain access to intelligent methods that enhance their transformational leadership capabilities and the quality of their decisions. Instead of the manual processes of gathering data, data context, cleansing, and proceeding to data analysis, with few predefined steps. Business leaders could make faster decisions based on the AI applications adopted in the workplace (Leff & Lim, 2023; Petrin, 2019). AI is essential for business leaders to increase the speed of decision-making, which may influence their response rate to critical business situations. Therefore, adopting AI applications is important for enhancing business operations.

The digital era enabled business leaders to create new high-value products and services through machine learning, a sort of AI. With machine learning techniques, Gregory et al. (2020) and Schrettenbrunnner (2020) spotted that leaders adopted a novel approach to solving their businesses' operational problems through better decision-making. Also, Duan et al. (2019) stated that leaders reshaped traditional industries' methods and analyzed big data in a shorter time by implementing AI applications that significantly reflected business processes' efficiency. When leaders gain access to and analyze their firms' data, they can innovate and add more value to their firms' operations. Therefore, leaders' decisions became faster and more effective with the implementation of AI.

Business Leaders

Business organizations need leaders to lead their operations and guide their employees. Organizations may take the form of a corporate, large-sized, medium-sized, small business, or micro-business. According to Gilbert and Kelloway (2018) and Northouse (2018), all organizations need business leaders to lead the business toward their anticipated organizational goals. Leaders' responsibilities may vary from strategic to tactical or operational, and some leaders may combine the three types of responsibilities depending on the firm's structure and chart. In all cases, the leadership role is significant for businesses' existence.

As Bonsu and Kuofie (2019) stated, researchers through modern research highlighted that business leaders might possess different leadership styles. Avolio and Bass (1991) developed the full range leadership theory and classified the leadership styles into three: (a) transformational, (b) transactional, and (c) passive-avoidant leadership styles. There is no leader who possesses a single leadership style. However, a leader may possess more attributes of a leadership style than the other and tend to act according to such a style. Therefore, all leadership styles may exist within firms, and leaders need to develop styles that support their firms' success.

Transformational leaders are the leaders who drive change within their firms by developing new methods and inspiring a group of followers. According to Curtis (2018), the attributes of transformational leaders are (a) idealized influence through which also Johnson and Bullard (2020) highlighted that leaders used to lead by example and act like role models to their group of followers, (b) individualized consideration which reflects what extent leaders interact with their followers' needs, (c) inspirational motivation which reflects how the leader inspires followers and keep them motivated, and (d) intellectual stimulation which Donkor and Dongmei (2018) defined as the leader's role to encourage followers to develop innovative ideas. Transformational leaders significantly impact business sustainability and organizational development (Guhr et al., 2018; Mohtady Ali et al., 2023). When a leader is transformational, the transformational leadership style's attributes represent most characteristics expressed in addressing organizational situations. Therefore, firms need to ensure that they have plenty of those leaders to reach and occasionally exceed their organizational goals.

Transactional leaders exist within all businesses. Transactional leaders use their organizational roles and entitled authorities by the organizational policies to influence their teams to achieve firms' goals (Abdelwahed et al., 2022; Barnett, 2019). The attributes of transactional leaders are (a) active management by exception, where the leaders' duty is to solve organizational problems, (b) contingent reward, which leaders would announce to their teams for the business goals they need to achieve, and (c) passive management by exception through which the leader interferes with solving an existing problem (Northouse, 2018; Pratama et al., 2018). Various research from around the globe investigated the role of transactional leaders in organizational success and sustainability. In some cases, their role positively contributed, and in others, their provided contribution was minor.

While the transformational and transactional leadership styles have contributed to organizational sustainability, the passive-avoidant leadership style failed to contribute properly. The passive management by exception attribute represents the highest ranking within passive-avoidant leadership. Passive-avoidant leaders avoided interfering in leading their teams and did not contribute to solving organizational problems even when problems existed (Adeel et al., 2018; Zhou et al., 2020). Passive-avoidant leaders failed to add value to their firms, and on some occasions, they had a negative impact on organizational success. Passive-avoidant leaders represented a lack of leadership and caused a loss of business opportunities (Parra et al., 2022). As this leadership style exists widely in organizations, the People and Culture Departments need to work with passive-avoidant leaders to develop their skills for the sake of their businesses' sustainability.

AI AND BUSINESS LEADERS' DECISION-MAKING

The competition between firms has been fierce and rapidly growing. A miscalculated decision might lead to unwanted consequences ranging from losing opportunities and market-share and leading to business closure. Business leaders try to avoid decision-making when the risks are high. Liu and Zhu (2022) confirmed that the solution to such a problem was implementing supporting technology to mitigate risks and seize opportunities. The recent digitization trend has been growing worldwide in various fields and changing how firms used to do business (Brock & von Wangenheim, 2019). Leaders invested in AI to effectively use their organizational resources for the benefit of the business (Sedky, 2023; Wee et al., 2022). AI led to enhanced processes and efficient time management, which spared more time for leaders to plan and set strategies. As a result, businesses found opportunities to gain a comparative advantage and maximize their firms' market share by implementing AI tools.

Leaders rely on AI tools to access and use the gathered data throughout the journey of leading their businesses. The strategic role of leadership implies that business leaders create contexts to develop scenarios and assumptions that enable them by the end to make decisions (Smith & Green, 2018; Tienken et al., 2022). For example, a leader needs to gather data about a new market before deciding to enter such a market. The surrounding uncertainty challenges the leaders while they make decisions. Therefore, leaders need to be rational and develop means that aid in reaching beneficial decisions to ensure business continuity.

Also, during disruptions, the business-related risks increase dramatically, which may lead to business closure. Business leaders need to make decisions to ensure their firms' safety and mitigate such risks during these crucial times (Unhelkar & Gonsalves, 2020). However, the decision-making process becomes challenging with the business disruption's uncertainty. Without access to such data and the uncertainty connected to critical situations, a leader may make harmful decisions for the organization and expose it to increased risks. AI enables leaders to automate processes and operate their businesses at minimum risks. Therefore, Leaders need AI to gain access to a significant amount of data to make the right decisions that their firms need.

As the leaders gain the needed access, they need to analyze the collected data. Leaders need to gear with tools and the right technology that enable the rightful use of such data. The AI-based tools enable leaders to ensure high-quality processing of such data, so the generated information drives quality decisions (Forscher et al., 2022). In addition, AI enables business leaders to deal with high volumes of data at a maximized speed, reflecting on the speed of decision-making. Jones (2018) highlighted that some firms understood the need to possess the proper technology and implemented advanced AI tools to fuel quality leadership experience that enables leaders' decision-making engine. Leaders combining AI-based analysis and leadership experience were able to formulate business resilience and recovery plans that enable their businesses to survive in challenging times. With such technology implementation, AI proves to be an important tool that allows leaders to enhance their scenarios for better decisions. Therefore, there is an increased probability that leaders will make the right decisions that serve their firms.

In serving their firms, it is the leaders' responsibility to predict and anticipate business trends before they exist. Peifer et al. (2022) warned that depending on human capabilities might not drive leaders to build relevant scenarios and accordingly make correct decisions. Leaders turn unknown circumstances into known and identified ones using developed AI systems (Simon, 1991). In such cases, leaders use AI to analyze big data gathered by the business internally and externally to predict the business possibilities to enhance their decisions in expanding business or avoiding business disruptions. For example, leaders may predict the success of a product in one region over another, which creates opportunities and allows innovation. Also, leaders may overcome a security-related situation by relying on systemized intelligence. Therefore, AI is increasingly important in enabling leaders to access broader data.

Implementing AI improved organizations' performances and allowed them to optimize operations. The AI's reflection on operations started by adding machine learning tools, decision tree learning, neural networks, multilevel insights, robotics, and customer interaction to replace the human efforts in these sections based on developed algorithms. For example, training machine learning algorithms to analyze broader data ranges allowed the development of prediction models. The prediction models contributed to the decision-making process by providing numerous decision options to the leaders based on the analyzed data. Thus, leaders were able to make better decisions.

Leaders using AI tools in the process of making decisions are more likely to achieve their organizational goals. Douer and Meyer (2020) emphasized that the employed intelligent systems allowed the leaders to work on different processes in series. For example, on many occasions, AI software worked on collecting the relevant data while the leader narrowed such data down to filter to the most relevant ones. Another example that confirmed what Jones (2018) expressed was that a leader might decide in a situation, and AI technology executed the decision. The importance of AI technology increases every day and should be used properly to achieve the anticipated goals. Leaders understood that AI had become an essential part of the decision support systems in numerous fields of life.

Examples of AI Solutions for Businesses

Human needs and expectations are in continuous growth. Many organizations have decided to invest in AI technology-based solutions to meet expectations and enhance human lives (Ciuffetti, 2019). According to Amazon (2022), the purpose was to solve sophisticated situations such as the slow decision-making process, low-quality customer experience, and inefficient use of firms' resources. Such organizations realized that depending on ordinary and manual means will not sort their problems, and such problems might increase as their databases increase daily. Therefore, leaders decided to use AI to facilitate operations by partnering with AI solution providers.

Amazon Web Services, Inc. (AWS) invested in AI solutions that allow business leaders to decide and perform their tasks better through machine learning and deep learning. For example, AWS's tools allowed Disney's DTCI Technology group leaders to tag content with descriptive metadata, which made Disney writers and animators identify characters easily. In this case, the AI tool enabled the functional leaders and their teams to avoid redundancy by building algorithms that look up specific characters at every production stage for the leaders to approve before tagging with the Disney knowledge base. The tool improved the accuracy of searches within the base, freed up human resources to focus on other development areas, and supported the automation of metadata creation.

Another example relates to the healthcare industry, specifically Cambia Healthcare Solutions (Cambia). Cambia is committed to granting access to decision-making criteria related to critical healthcare information. However, large organizations face the challenge of managing their data because of the sophisticated electronic health record systems. The problem impacted individuals as there was a challenge in understanding the provided information other than billing, which Cambia realized and looked to solve. Cambia partnered with AWS to provide AI and machine learning solutions to solve such a problem. The collaboration with AWS extended to using multiple services such as Jouni, which provides health-related solutions for health plan members and their families. Also, Gambia used Amazon Comprehend Medical, which extracts medical information from unstructured text, and Amazon SageMaker, which provided Cambia's developers and data scientists features to use machine learning models quickly. Thus, when Cambia relied on AWS's SageMaker to shift up to 40% of the data science resources from operations support to operate in developing solutions instead. The impact was significant for the business and consumer.

3M is a well-known multinational conglomerate that operates in various fields, including industry, worker safety, U.S. health care, and consumer goods. Specifically, the management faced a serious quality problem at 3M's St. Paul sandpaper factory that could have affected their business continuity. The solution was to invest in improving the quality of their products, such as Scotch tape and Post-it notes. 3M management decided to invest in AI and machine learning through the partnership with AWS. The ultimate purpose was to improve their products' quality and support innovation in the healthcare field. 3M, with the use of AWS's SageMaker solution, was able to improve the quality of their products through an improved testing process that does not take a long period. Also, the company was able to process an increased amount of data generated by scanning and testing. In addition, machine learning enabled 3M to process the billing codes of 3M products at no time.

As AWS provides AI solutions, other firms have a great share in providing AI-supporting solutions to businesses worldwide, with Microsoft leading the line. The Met Office, the UK's national weather service, supports businesses ranging from agencies to governments. Two of the main roles of The Met Office are to predict the effects of climate change and provide means to a net zero future. The Met Office needs to handle the big data available on the platform, which is not an easy task. The management decided to implement an AI solution that enables The Met Office to use the data better to achieve the anticipated results. The Met Office partnered with Microsoft (Microsoft, 2018). Such a partnership enabled The Met Office to drive innovation and better use of resources through The Met Office's mission. Thus, The Met Office's management could use the resources efficiently with better decision-making capabilities through the proper use of big data.

Another case of significant AI success enabling businesses' sustainability is the case of the Spanish bank Ibercaja. The bank has provided financial services to firms and farmers across the Spanish region for more than 140 years. The management took the initiative to invest in technological means to help farmers use water and energy better and manage the crops. The choice was to partner with Microsoft to use AI and provide the farmers with cloud-based technology. The bank implemented a digital transformation, allowing Spanish farmers to manage their farming businesses. The farmers could make better decisions in managing their fields' water and energy consumption and handling their crops.

DEHN's management, a German firm operating since 1918, decided to invest in AI. DEHN provides lightning protection systems that safeguard buildings, public institutions, and critical infrastructure facilities. With the amount of data that DEHN possessed, the challenge of managing the firm's business increased, and the firm needed to use the available resources better. DEHN partnered with Microsoft for AI and a cloud-based solution that accelerated the data calculations and the flexibility needed to run the daily operations. Thus, DEHN leaders gained access to more data that enabled efficient operations and resource allocation.

From the examples, AI machine learning technology provided business leaders significant support to fix real business problems. Such problems could have affected those firms on different scales, starting from increased operation costs, loss of time, unmet customers' needs, loss of opportunities, lack of innovation, and ultimately business continuity. Therefore, investing in AI brought business success to organizations in various fields.

METHOD AND DISCUSSION

In addition to exploring previous literature on investing in AI, the researcher conducted a qualitative multiple case study. The case study focused on business leaders' investment in AI to enhance decision-making in the United States and U.A.E. The researcher conducted semi-structured interviews with business leaders from the real estate property industry. The researcher targeted market-leaders firms that managed a sizable portfolio in the real estate industry to understand the influence of AI on their success. The purpose of the multiple case study was to explore why AI may enhance business leaders' decision-making.

Qualitative Methodology and Multiple Case Study Design

Research methodology has three types. According to Taguchi (2018), researchers could use (a) qualitative, (b) quantitative, and (c) mixed-methods in conducting research. In qualitative research, researchers intend to explore the reasons and insight behind a phenomenon (Saunders et al., 2020). Researchers in quantitative research examine hypotheses by analyzing surveys and represent findings numerically (Miller et al., 2020). In mixed methods, a researcher combines the qualitative and quantitative to validate the results of each method (Taguchi, 2018). The researcher used a qualitative method to answer the research question: Why may AI enhance business leaders' decision-making?

Researchers use different designs in qualitative research. According to Taguchi (2018), qualitative research design can be (a) a case study, (b) phenomenological, (c) narrative, and (d) ethnographic. The researcher used a multiple case study to explore similarities and differences among cases based on semi-structured interviews with leaders from various functions related to the real estate property industry. The leaders represented businesses from the United States and U.A.E. The multiple case study design enabled the researcher to reveal an in-depth understanding of why business leaders invest in AI. Following are the observations from the conducted interviews.

The Interviews

The researcher used semi-structured interviews to explore why AI may enhance business leaders' decision-making and enable business sustainability. The targeted sample belonged to leading firms in the real estate property industry in the United States and the U.A.E. The researcher focused on market-leading firms with sizable portfolios to explore if AI implementations had an impact on their business success and sustainability. The researcher conducted three interviews: (a) an interview with a business leader from a leading firm in the United States and (b) interviews with two business leaders from two leading firms in the United Arab Emirates. The interview questions ranged from generic questions about firm structure, governance, and internal procedures to narrowed-down questions that focused on decision-making processes within the targeted firms and the leaders' understanding of AI technologies' importance.

Observations From the U.S. Business Leader Interview

Most organizations lack knowledge of the IT leaders' capabilities and support applications. AI applications may enhance businesses' decisions. There is a lack of knowledge of AI capabilities from the business side. Also, there is a gap in research in spotting such knowledge lack. Business leaders need to consider the growing importance of AI solutions implementation for the future growth of their firms. Machine learning will perform repetitive and redundant tasks, while business resources could focus on many important tasks related to driving business strategies and direction. AI allows for numerous benefits to the business by emphasizing data-driven decisions. Thus, creating AI awareness will encourage business leaders to implement such solutions and enhance business decisions.

When large organizations purchase buildings worth tens or hundreds of millions of dollars, the business analysis becomes critical and needs to be accurate to help with the decision-making. Many U.S. real estate businesses need help managing properties by tracking large subsidiaries, loans, and commercial real estate in the U.S. Northeast and, occasionally, in Western European countries. As the business possesses massive amounts of data on the population and actual income of that area to invest in and check the inflation impact, enhancing the underwriting process allows leaders to decide on making real estate loans based on demographic data. Some organizations use the GEMS operating system as a backbone for the leadership to make loan decisions on higher-value transactions by defining priorities and focusing on opportunities.

Decision-making is extremely critical in delivering on the business needs. One of the tools used and approaches is the Agile Scrum methodology to promote staff harmony from two perspectives: (a) externally through communication with the business analysts on being clear on the decision we need to make and (b) internally within the team on how to deliver business requirements. A lack of consistent information could represent a setback to the overall business performance. Thus, managing data and the firm's expectations are critical aspects that influence the entire business performance.

AI contributes to several different areas of the business in managing big data. The need for machine learning became critical because machine learning helps identify aspects to make better decisions and approach business requirements more efficiently with agile scrum. For example, in the agile scrum approach, decision-making involves voting on story points. Machine learning allows a better understanding of business requirements through an illustrated view of what actions to make better decisions and respond to organizational needs. In addition, implementing machine learning models helps expedite processes, allows for more measurable accuracy, and adds value to the business. Accordingly, the business leaders decided to implement AI machine learning software to support the firm's operations and decision-making.

One of the main benefits of using artificial intelligence is related to long-term benefits. Implementing AI tools improves the quality of operations in large organizations. A firm can deliver better content based on efficient systems connected to AI. AI-based tools shorten long processes and eliminate systems constraints. For example, the AI tool bridges organizational gaps in large organizations that employ thousands of employees to enable enhanced business decisions. AI allows for long-term efficiency in intelligent data search within the firm's departments, which allows data refining to improve the organization's decision-making process. In addition, the AI tool expedites and enables leaders to make better and faster decisions to achieve organizational goals. Organizational strategies should support the implementation of AI tools to enhance decision-making based on data analysis. Organizations should have a continuous development plan to comply with the changing needs of organizations over time, and leaders' training is necessary to create awareness of implementing AI within organizations. Thus, AI machine learning will improve short- and long-term business performance, eliminate redundancy, and improve staffing efficiency to avoid excess hiring.

Observations From the Emirati Market: The First Interview

Leaders need to identify the organizational needs that require fulfillment to deploy the proper AI solution. By all means, such needs should be customer-centric to contribute to business growth. Leaders add value by prioritizing how to satisfy customers when implementing machine learning to solve organizational problems by fulfilling firms' needs. However, customer satisfaction and meeting organizational goals are always challenged if the business lacks control over several aspects. First, many organizations lack the proper investment in storing business data to build on analytics that may include AI. Before adopting AI and mainly machine learning within an organization, such an organization needs the proper infrastructure to maximize the benefits of implementing the AI solution. Once the business has the data and data analytics bond, the embedded impact would be artificial intelligence and machine learning, which would trigger data-based decisions for better results for the business. Successful businesses should have the right setup, data storage, and AI technology. Therefore, implementing the right data-driven technology is a survival-related need for all firms.

In addition, a lack of proper insights when dealing with data negatively affects decision-making. Mostly, the focus goes on historical experiences rather than using the historical experience to build on for the future. Such firms keep reporting monthly and yearly experiences while analyzing data to predict the future should be a target for well-organized firms to control their costs and spot opportunities. For example, with data analysis, firms can avoid previous mistakes in real estate properties, leading to losing leasing opportunities and leasing more apartments. The impact could be increased revenues based on understanding and fulfilling customers' needs. Another example relates to optimization when firms implement customer-centric approaches to collecting more data from the market to attract more potential tenants based on analyzing their needs. Firms should not focus on the past but use the experience to gain comparative advantages over the competition. In order to analyze broader data, firms need to implement AI solutions since depending on basic software will not facilitate analyzing big data. Therefore, businesses need to focus on adding value by using all the accessible data to analyze and remodel decisions to maximize profit.

Also, firms lose consistency in decision-making as access to the necessary information to make the correct decision does not exist. Leaders need to possess perfect data to develop decision scenarios and achieve organizational goals. Investing in AI provides a proper solution that enables leaders to access the relevant information to business cases. AI machine learning learns the developed algorithms and analyzes business data. The technology provides business leaders with accurate information by gathering broader data, creating context, and focusing on the relevant data for specific business cases. Such a process prevents leaders from making bad decisions for the business. Future-focused firms understood the importance of data and did not rely on internal data but purchased external data to support better AI analysis and make better decisions.

Further, many businesses lose opportunities to profit because of leadership absence and underestimating business ideas from followers. Leaders need to set priorities and involve their followers in the decision-making process. Leaders should adopt a creative environment, apply change management concepts to involve followers, and set targets per horizon to adjust staff focus. Therefore, developing leadership, positive mindsets, and target prioritization criteria are essential for optimizing firms' functions and business growth.

Another aspect for further assessment is that the classic hierarchical decision-making method is no longer valid for facing the continuous changes occurring worldwide and the challenging business environment. Leaders who involve their teams are more likely to find means to succeed in transforming organizational vision and managing change within their organizations by breaking hierarchical barriers. Business leaders and their teams need to understand internal and external factors influencing decision-making. With the leader and the team accessing the available firm data through AI, finding solutions to organizational problems could be achievable and enhance the relationships within firms. Thus, the collaboration between leaders and members of their teams allows for enhanced solutions to organizational challenges based on bringing different perspectives into internal communications.

Modern business implies that business leaders should be forward-thinkers to stay relevant to the circumstances surrounding their markets. Leaders relying on AI gain access to valuable information and foresee their firms' opportunities from the broader information obtained from the AI data analysis. A clear example from the real estate property industry is collecting data from proposed tenants for leased apartments may drive broader knowledge of customers' preferences and promote customized products to turn those customers from proposed to real tenants. Another example would be managing the apartments' periodic maintenance by possessing the data and using machine learning to understand when maintenance is required. Such action may reduce reactive and redundant maintenance to minimized levels and support having all apartments ready to lease. In addition, the operational leaders will understand the assets' behavior and models to plan their maintenance activities with targeted zero breakdowns in the apartments and avoid massive spending on breakdowns. Such controls supported by AI machine learning provide potential tenants with various options with increased levels to seal leasing agreements.

The growing importance of AI implies that business leaders and all involved members attend AI training. Members' lack of understanding of machine learning will lead to losing opportunities that will tackle innovation and the needed change initiatives within businesses. Many views may argue such a point by only considering leaders to attend the AI training. However, offering AI training to organizational staff is beneficial for understanding how to maximize the AI solution's benefits. Proper training should also be provided to team members who are supposed to use the AI software daily.

Improved decision quality is the outcome of the collaboration between leaders and their teams. Every related member should be involved in decision-making as, on several occasions, team members were able to bring insightful opinions with increased values to their firms. For example, startups have faced the threat of closure several times by focusing on their leaders and neglecting their other staff. In contrast, the leader might face the challenge of knowing every new trend in the market. Involving team members along the way enables firms to observe the other options through market intelligence and may promote solutions for existing organizational problems.

At last, managers should look to the broader image when implementing technology by adopting an open approach to multiple technology sources. Pure focus on a specific solution might harm the business by losing opportunities. Instead, managers should be open to implementing a variety of software so that, collaterally, the technology better serves the business. Thus, partnerships could involve more than a technology brand as long as the business has the proper architecture that enables the technology to work for the benefit of the business.

More Observations From the Emirati Market: The Second Interview

Decision-making is critical and requires leaders with relevant experience and knowledge to add value to their firms. Business leaders combine professional experience with emotional intelligence when making decisions. However, leaders need to understand the parameters of authority, starting from the business environment and sustainability to governance. In addition, leaders need to define activities, goals, roles, and reverse engineering before implementing AI to identify how the AI software will work with the existing system and the access to the firms' data.

Organizations have an ethical obligation to enrich employees' knowledge and skills. Upskill staff should be part of the business development plan, as training brings deeper knowledge and reflects on real-time learning and experience. From such a perspective, AI knowledge and training are essential to staying relevant to the worldwide business changes. AI-knowledgeable firm members will understand and accept implementing AI solutions in their business with proper execution to achieve goals and expand the business. Leaders with AI knowledge could trust and easily accept using AI technology to process, optimize, and design business frameworks. AI is new knowledge that whoever implements it leads the market through innovation and better decisions. Thus, AI-driven organizational members could be the fit for future leaders who drive business success.

Sophisticated projects need time to complete. Team members might feel stressed because of workloads and strict commitment to achieve project goals within the indicated timeframe to execute projects. In more resolution, some organizations may lose business if their teams do not complete projects through the approved timeline. AI software provides leaders and their team members with the needed support by executing repetitive and time-consuming project tasks, allowing the team to focus on developing solutions based on the processed information by the AI tool. Leaders gain trust and enjoy enhanced relationships with employees when they use AI to optimize their firms' processes by eliminating human interference in unnecessary tasks. In such a scenario, project timelines become achievable as the team invests the efforts to execute nonredundant tasks that require decision-making rather than admin-related work. Therefore, AI allows leaders to manage time by investing teams' efforts in important business aspects such as engagement in decision-making.

AI is the future of business, and business leaders need to understand how to leverage AI solutions to develop their firms as fit for the future. Leaders solve business problems using AI tools to validate, relate, and analyze data to optimize processes. AI software allows businesses to understand and improve the response rates to customers' needs to enhance customer experience (CX). AI machine learning improves over time and enhances communications with business clients from audio to mobile chatting platforms. Thus, AI machine learning needs proper implementation and algorithms to perform accurately.

AI tools need time to understand and improve performance. Machine learning requires time to advance and understand, most likely similar to humans. However, there are advantages and disadvantages to relying on AI solutions. Unlike humans, the most obvious advantage is that machine learning can learn to do decision-support tasks efficiently and accurately. However, the disadvantage of machine learning is that machine learning lacks emotional intelligence, unlike humans. From such a perspective, leaders use AI in decision-making support activities and rely on the human factor to choose the best option through emotional intelligence after exhausting the machine intelligence.

RECOMMENDATIONS

Reviewing the literature and the observations of the multiple case study through this chapter, the researcher recommends that firms need to invest in AI solutions. The need for AI tools is increasing daily because of the circumstances surrounding the business environment and the severe competition over market shares. However, before firms invest in AI tools, business leaders need to identify their needs for proper technology deployment. The idea is not about implementing AI solutions but what support AI can provide business leaders. Thus, leaders must understand their organizational needs to implement the right tools per the business needs.

After identifying firms' needs, the leaders and their teams need to attend AI training and fully comprehend AI literature. Research proved that when individuals gain knowledge, they are more likely to build constructive implementations based on such knowledge. So, when a firm invests in training team members, implementing and using the technology daily becomes easier and faster. Team members also need to understand that implementing the technology correlates with the better use of human resources. For example, AI machine learning software can learn to tackle repetitive tasks that occupy firm members' time. Rather, the employees should focus on business tasks with increased value to the business, such as their participation in the decision-making process. With such participation in decision-making, teams' capabilities are more likely to uplift and, after time, may handle higher roles within their firms.

Leaders also need to use AI tools in a proper manner to bring benefits to their firms, relying on machine learning's speed in processing big data to develop decision scenarios. Big data exceeds traditional data within an organization as it is the biggest portion of data. With a click using the AI tool, the tool accesses large amounts of data and starts to analyze the data to determine if they correlate to the topic subject to the decision. Then, the tool relates patterns used to develop future state scenarios. In addition to machine learning, AI relies on natural language to detect and treat data errors that could be duplicated, outliers that mislead, and irrelevant data. Then, the tool identifies and develops data formats relevant to the assigned task. There could be as many scenarios as the AI tool is defined before starting the process, accompanied by justifications to enable leaders to narrow down the results per each scenario. When business leaders look to choose from the developed data-driven scenarios, leaders should not base their decisions only on the outcomes of the AI-developed scenarios. Conversely, business leaders need to employ their emotional intelligence besides the AI-calculated algorithmic results. In the end, business leaders are entitled to make the decision, and relying on artificial intelligence will not factor areas beyond the data analyzed. Business leaders need to select the best scenario out of the selection options provided by the AI tool to ensure the maximum benefits for their firms (see Figure 1). At this point, firms will likely achieve increased benefits, create more opportunities, and better serve their communities. Thus, AI adds value to the decision-making processes within operating firms.

Figure 1. The process of AI-based decision-making

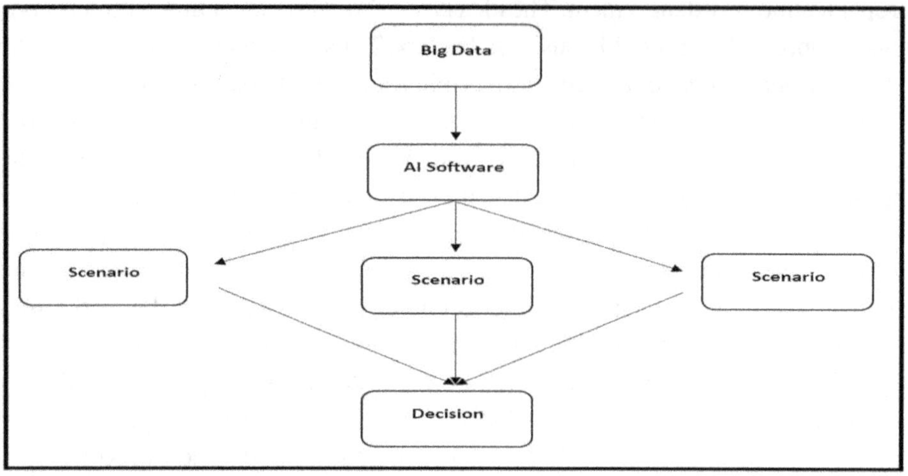

FUTURE RESEARCH DIRECTIONS

Through this chapter, the researcher focused on answering why business leaders invest in AI and the impact of such investment on decision-making. Besides reviewing the literature, the research adopted the qualitative multiple case study in exploring why AI may enhance business leaders' decision-making through semi-structured interviews with real estate properties business leaders from the United States and U.A.E. The Researcher suggests that future chapters may explore the topic by conducting a quantitative approach to increase the sample size and generalize the results. Also, for future chapters, researchers could explore other regions to compare the results to this chapter's results.

Another approach for future chapters is to explore the impact of AI on analyzing data provided to business leaders to drive innovation and entrepreneurship. Also, researchers may assess future investments in AI to support decision-making by comparing different AI models. According to Gartner (2019), the investment in decision support is expected to surpass all other AI initiatives by 2030 (see Figure 2). Decision support might reach 44% of the world business value, and decision automation might reach 19%.

As for this chapter's limitations, accessing a broader sample, especially in the United States, was a limitation that may not influence the generalization of the results. In addition, through this chapter, the researcher focused on the U.S. and U.A.E. business, while in future chapters, researchers may include other regions or participants from other industries.

Figure 2. Worldwide business value by AI type in millions of dollars (Gartner, 2019)

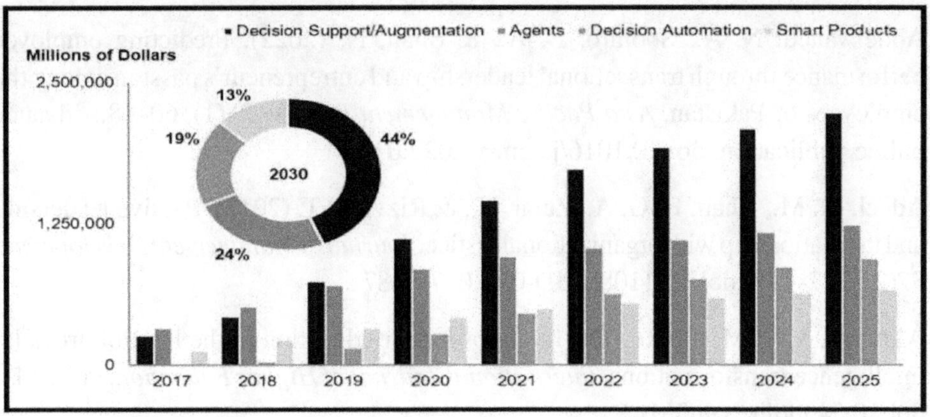

CONCLUSION

Firms' increased risks through daily operations imply that business leaders take further precautions while making decisions. Wrong decisions may cost businesses severely, leading to the stoppage of operations and business closure. Leaders need to achieve business sustainability by improving their decision-making. AI could be a powerful tool that enables leaders to improve their decisions and organizational performance. Proper AI implementation will help collect relevant data for each business problem and provide well-tailored scenarios for business leaders' choices that serve their firms. The leaders and their teams need to maximize the use of AI to improve their performance, participate in brainstorming business cases, and make rightful decisions that enable business sustainability. Leaders with better decisions may allow their firms to survive the severe market competition and label them fit for the future, bringing extended business growth opportunities. Therefore, AI allows for better decision-making that may drastically decrease business closure rates, continuous contribution to the GDP, and a stable employment market, which serves communities' stability and growth.

ACKNOWLEDGMENT

The researcher appreciates the interviewees' valuable time and dedicated efforts in attending and responding to the interview questions.

This research received no specific grant from any funding agency in the public, commercial, or not-for-profit sectors.

REFERENCES

Abdelwahed, N. A., Soomro, B. A., & Shah, N. (2022). Predicting employee performance through transactional leadership and entrepreneur's passion among the employees of Pakistan. *Asia Pacific Management Review*, *28*(1), 60–68. Advance online publication. doi:10.1016/j.apmrv.2022.03.001

Adeel, M. M., Khan, H. G. A., Zafar, N., & Rizvi, S. T. (2018). Passive leadership and its relationship with organizational justice. *Journal of Management Development*, *37*(2), 212–223. doi:10.1108/JMD-05-2017-0187

Aldosari, S. A. M. (2020). The future of higher education in the light of artificial intelligence transformations. *International Journal of Higher Education*, *9*(3), 145. doi:10.5430/ijhe.v9n3p145

Allal-Cherif, O., Simon-Moya, V., & Ballester, A. C. C. (2021). Intelligent purchasing: How artificial intelligence can redefine the purchasing function. *Journal of Business Research*, *124*(1), 69–76. doi:10.1016/j.jbusres.2020.11.050

Amazon. (2022). *Amazon Web Services (AWS) - AI with AWS Machine Learning*. Amazon Web Services, Inc. https://aws.amazon.com/ai/

Avolio, B. J., & Bass, B. M. (1991). *The full range leadership development programs: Basic and advanced manuals*. Bass, Avolio Associates.

Barnett, D. (2019). Full range leadership as a predictor of extra effort in online higher education: The mediating effect of job satisfaction. *Journal of Leadership Education*, *18*(1), 86–101. doi:10.12806/V18/I1/R6

Bonsu, S., & Kuofie, M. (2019). Small business survival. *Journal of Marketing Management*, *10*(1), 51–63.

Brock, J. K.-U., & von Wangenheim, F. (2019). Demystifying AI: What digital transformation leaders can teach you about realistic artificial intelligence. *California Management Review*, *61*(4), 110–134. doi:10.1177/1536504219865226

Ciuffetti, P. (2019). Opportunities for non-data scientists to apply machine learning technology. *Information Services & Use*, 1–7. doi:10.3233/ISU-190067

Cummins, N. M., Barry, L. A., Garavan, C., Devlin, C., Corey, G., Cummins, F., Ryan, D., Cronin, S., Wallace, E., McCarthy, G., & Galvin, R. (2022). The better data, better planning census: A cross-sectional, multi-centre study investigating the factors influencing patient attendance at the emergency department in Ireland. *BMC Health Services Research*, *22*(1), 471. Advance online publication. doi:10.1186/s12913-022-07841-6 PMID:35397588

Curtis, G. J. (2018). Connecting influence tactics with full-range leadership styles. *Leadership and Organization Development Journal, 39*(1), 2–13. doi:10.1108/LODJ-09-2016-0221

Donkor, F., & Dongmei, Z. (2018). Leadership styles: A decade after the economic recession and lessons for businesses in developing economies. *Management Research and Practice, 10*(3), 1-20. http://www.mrp.ase.ro

Douer, N., & Meyer, J. (2020). The responsibility quantification model of human interaction with automation. *IEEE Transactions on Automation Science and Engineering, 17*(2), 1044–1060. doi:10.1109/TASE.2020.2965466

Duan, Y., Edwards, J. S., & Dwivedi, Y. K. (2019). Artificial intelligence for decision making in the era of Big Data – evolution, challenges and research agenda. *International Journal of Information Management, 48*, 63–71. doi:10.1016/j.ijinfomgt.2019.01.021

European Commission. (2019). *SME performance review.* https://ec.europa.eu/growth/smes/business-friendly-environment/performance-review_en

Forscher, P. S., Wagenmakers, E.-J., Coles, N. A., Silan, M. A., Dutra, N., Basnight-Brown, D., & IJzerman, H. (2022). The benefits, barriers, and risks of big-team science. *Perspectives on Psychological Science*. Advance online publication. doi:10.1177/17456916221082970 PMID:36190899

Gartner. (2019). *Gartner says AI augmentation will create $2.9 trillion of business value in 2021.* https://www.gartner.com/en/newsroom/press-releases/2019-08-05-gartner-says-ai-augmentation-will-create-2point9-trillion-of-business-value-in-2021

Gilbert, S., & Kelloway, E. K. (2018). Self-determined leader motivation and follower perceptions of leadership. *Leadership and Organization Development Journal, 39*(5), 608–619. doi:10.1108/LODJ-09-2017-0262

Gregory, R. W., Henfridsson, O., Kaganer, E., & Kyriakou, H. (2020). The role of artificial intelligence and data network effects for creating user value. *Academy of Management Review*. Advance online publication. doi:10.5465/amr.2019.0178

Guhr, N., Lebek, B., & Breitner, M. H. (2018). The impact of leadership on employees' intended information security behaviour: An examination of the full-range leadership theory. *Information Systems Journal, 29*(2), 340–362. doi:10.1111/isj.12202

Humphreys, P. (2021). Socialising the decision-making process: Transaction provenance decision support. *Journal of Decision Systems*, 1–15. doi:10.1080/12460125.2020.1868653

Johnson, M. R., & Bullard, A. J. (2020). Creation of a structured performance-based assessment tool in a clinical research center setting. *The Journal of Research Administration, 51*(1), 73–89.

Jones, W. A. (2018). Artificial intelligence and leadership: A few thoughts, a few questions. *Journal of Leadership Studies, 12*(3), 60–62. doi:10.1002/jls.21597

Kharlamova, G., Stavytskyy, A., Chernyak, O., Giedraitis, V., & Komendant, O. (2019). Economic modeling of the GDP gap in Ukraine and worldwide. *Problems and Perspectives in Management, 17*(2), 493 509. doi:10.21511/ppm.17(2).2019.38

Leff, D., & Lim, K. T. K. (2023). The key to leveraging AI at scale. *Journal of Revenue and Pricing Management, 20*(3), 376–380. doi:10.1057/s41272-021-00320-3

Lin, K., Liu, J., & Gao, J. (2021). AI-driven decision making for auxiliary diagnosis of epidemic diseases. *IEEE Transactions on Molecular, Biological, and Multi-Scale Communications*, 1–1. doi:10.1109/TMBMC.2021.3120646

Liu, H., & Zhu, X. (2022). Design of the physical fitness evaluation information management system of sports athletes based on artificial intelligence. *Computational Intelligence and Neuroscience, 2022*, 1–10. doi:10.1155/2022/1925757 PMID:35814574

Maung, A. M. (2020). Administrative reform in the Myanmar police force: Decision-making and community-based policing. *Journal of Current Southeast Asian Affairs, 39*(3), 428–443. doi:10.1177/1868103420942781

Mayr, S., Mitter, C., Kücher, A., & Duller, C. (2020). Entrepreneur characteristics and differences in reasons for business failure: Evidence from bankrupt Austrian SMEs. *Journal of Small Business and Entrepreneurship, 33*(5), 539–558. doi:10.1080/08276331.2020.1786647

Men, F., Yaqub, R. M. S., Yan, R., Irfan, M., & Fatima, M. e. (2022). Resource-based theory perspective in the textile industry: The impact of the digital supply chain on operational performance. *Frontiers in Environmental Science, 10*, 1017297. Advance online publication. doi:10.3389/fenvs.2022.1017297

Microsoft. (2018). *Microsoft - Artificial Intelligence in Business.* Microsoft. https://www.microsoft.com/en-us/ai/industry/ai-in-business

Miller, C. J., Smith, S. N., & Pugatch, M. (2020). Experimental and quasi-experimental designs in implementation research. *Psychiatry Research, 283*, 112452. doi:10.1016/j.psychres.2019.06.027 PMID:31255320

Mohtady Ali, H. M., Ranse, J., Roiko, A., & Desha, C. (2023). Enabling transformational leadership to foster disaster-resilient hospitals. *International Journal of Environmental Research and Public Health*, *20*(3), 2022. doi:10.3390/ijerph20032022 PMID:36767388

Mouzas, S., & Bauer, F. (2022). Rethinking business performance in global value chains. *Journal of Business Research*, *144*, 679–689. doi:10.1016/j.jbusres.2022.02.012

Newman, S. A., & Ford, R. C. (2020). Five steps to leading your team in the virtual COVID-19 workplace. *Organizational Dynamics*, *50*(1), 100802. doi:10.1016/j.orgdyn.2020.100802 PMID:36536689

Northouse, P. G. (2018). *Leadership: Theory and practice*. Sage Publications.

Parra, E., García Delgado, A., Carrasco-Ribelles, L. A., Chicchi Giglioli, I. A., Marin-Morales, J., Giglio, C., & Alcaniz Raya, M. (2022). Combining virtual reality and machine learning for leadership styles recognition. *Frontiers in Psychology*, *13*, 864266. Advance online publication. doi:10.3389/fpsyg.2022.864266 PMID:35712148

Peifer, Y., Jeske, T., & Hille, S. (2022). Artificial intelligence and its impact on leaders and leadership. *Procedia Computer Science*, *200*, 1024–1030. doi:10.1016/j.procs.2022.01.301

Petrin, M. (2019). Corporate management in the age of AI. SSRN *Electronic Journal*. doi:10.2139/ssrn.3346722

Pratama, A., Mustika, M. D., & Sjabadhyni, B. (2018). Coaching as intervention to increase leaders' contingent reward behavior. *Journal of Workplace Learning*, *30*(3), 150–161. doi:10.1108/JWL-07-2017-0061

Saunders, M. N. K., Lewis, P., & Thornhill, A. (2020). *Research methods for business students* (8th ed.). Pearson Education Limited.

Schrettenbrunnner, M. B. (2020). Artificial-intelligence-driven management. *IEEE Engineering Management Review*, *48*(2), 15–19. doi:10.1109/EMR.2020.2990933

Sedky, A. (2023). Digital supply chain: A proposed solution to the global supply chain disruption impact on business sustainability. In *Digital Supply Chain, Disruptive Environments, and the Impact on Retailers* (pp. 160-177). IGI Global. doi:10.4018/978-1-6684-7298-9.ch009

Sedky, A. M. (2021). *The relationship between transformational, transactional, and passive-avoidant leadership styles and small business sustainability* [Doctoral dissertation]. ProQuest Dissertations and Theses Global.

Simon, H. A. (1959). Theories of decision-making in economics and behavioral science. *The American Economic Review*, *49*(3), 253–283.

Simon, H. A. (1991). Bounded rationality and organizational learning. *Organization Science*, *2*(1), 125–134. doi:10.1287/orsc.2.1.125

Smith, A. M., & Green, M. (2018). Artificial intelligence and the role of leadership. *Journal of Leadership Studies*, *12*(3), 85–87. Advance online publication. doi:10.1002/jls.21605

Taguchi, N. (2018). Description and explanation of pragmatic development: Quantitative, qualitative, and mixed methods research. *System*, *75*(4), 23–32. doi:10.1016/j.system.2018.03.010

Taylor, B., & Whittaker, A. (2018). Professional judgement and decision-making in social work. *Journal of Social Work Practice*, *32*(2), 105–109. doi:10.1080/02650533.2018.1462780

Tienken, C., Classen, M., & Friedli, T. (2022). Engaging the sales force in digital solution selling: How sales control systems resolve agency problems to create and capture superior value. *European Journal of Marketing*. Advance online publication. doi:10.1108/EJM-11-2021-0918

Unhelkar, B., & Gonsalves, T. (2020). Enhancing artificial intelligence decision making frameworks to support leadership during business disruptions. *IT Professional*, *22*(6), 59–66. doi:10.1109/MITP.2020.3031312

Vrontis, D., Christofi, M., Pereira, V., Tarba, S., Makrides, A., & Trichina, E. (2021). Artificial intelligence, robotics, advanced technologies and human resource management: A systematic review. *International Journal of Human Resource Management*, *33*(6), 1–30. doi:10.1080/09585192.2020.1871398

Wee, M., Scheepers, H., & Tian, X. (2022). The role of leadership skills in the adoption of business intelligence and analytics by SMEs. *Information Technology & People*. Advance online publication. doi:10.1108/ITP-09-2021-0669

Zhou, Z. E., Eatough, E. M., & Che, X. X. (2020). Effect of illegitimate tasks on work-to-family conflict through psychological detachment: Passive leadership as a moderator. *Journal of Vocational Behavior*, *121*, 103463. doi:10.1016/j.jvb.2020.103463

KEY TERMS AND DEFINITIONS

Artificial Intelligence: A demonstrated Intelligence by machines to perform human tasks and ease organizational processes, which helps individuals achieve their organizational goals.

Decision-Making: A process through which an individual can make choices by gathering information and assessing resolutions

Machine Learning: A type of artificial intelligence (AI) that allows applications to learn by practice and predict outcomes with accuracy.

Passive-Avoidant Leadership: A state of absence of leadership that might cause organizational losses.

SageMaker: One of Amazon Web Services (AWS) products that enables users to leverage machine learning features.

Transactional Leadership: A leadership style through which a leader uses the designation powers to achieve organizational goals.

Transformational Leadership: A leadership style through which the leader inspires and influences a group of followers.

Chapter 6
Data Science in the Employee Recruitment Process

João Farinha
https://orcid.org/0000-0002-4193-8914
ISLA Santarém, Portugal

Maria Fatima Pina
https://orcid.org/0000-0003-3738-1153
ISLA Santarém, Portugal

ABSTRACT

In the information age, organizations are more powerful as they have more information. However, having information is not enough. It needs to be compiled and organized so that it can be used. This compiled information can be used in many areas of an organization, including the recruitment of new employees. Organizations are always looking for ways to improve productivity and profitability. The COVID-19 pandemic has made this even more important. To do this, they need employees with the right skills for the job. This is where data science comes in. Data science is the field of study that analyses and processes data so that it can be used to make and create informed decisions. This study aims to investigate how data science can be used to help organizations hire new employees. The project will explore how data science can be used to identify the skills and qualifications that are most important for a particular role, screen candidates more effectively, and make better hiring decisions.

DOI: 10.4018/979-8-3693-0712-0.ch006

INTRODUCTION

In the realm of the job market, there exists a duality: permanent contracts (job-led market) and temporary contracts (candidate-led market). Currently, due to factors such as low employability, the pursuit of new skills, economic uncertainty, and the more recent Covid-19 pandemic, we have witnessed a transformation in the job market, with a shift towards temporary contracts. Not too long ago, those entering the job market had a mindset of securing employment with a reputable company and staying there until the end of their careers. Employees didn't plan frequent job or company changes, and there was suspicion towards those who did. Companies only parted ways with employees in truly dire circumstances, and employees received benefits based on their tenure and salary. Today, the situation is different. Employees change jobs and employers more frequently due to increased opportunities and a greater need for skill development. Layoffs are more common, employees view themselves as more temporary, and employers as more like customers. Part-time work is more prevalent, and employees take greater responsibility for their retirement plans. External factors also exert significant influence on the job market. This shift in mindset and the job market has been further exacerbated by the recent Covid-19 pandemic, which forced many individuals to change careers and leave their previous industries. High-quality candidates are a valuable commodity, so it's no surprise that recruitment leaders are constantly vigilant and on the lookout for new technologies to help them find the best candidates for their roles. This leads to the need for organizations to hire employees with specific skill sets to fulfill their requirements. This necessity has given rise to roles such as "Talent Analytics" and "People Science," which represent a more technological approach to work. These new roles are part of a field known as Data Science. As modern technology has evolved, the creation and storage of vast amounts of data have become possible. However, often these data remain dormant in databases and are not used. The use and interpretation of this data bring significant benefits to organizations and societies worldwide as it aids in making more informed and thoughtful decisions. This is where the benefits of Data Science come into play, as it involves studying this data and creating data banks. Data Science uncovers trends and generates insights that companies can use to make better decisions, particularly in understanding and distinguishing each candidate to ultimately select the best fit for the company's needs. Indeed,

"As a vast amount of data is currently available, organizations across various industries are focused on exploring them to gain a competitive advantage" (Provost & Fawcett, 2013a, p. 1).

The Role of Data Science on Recruitment Processes: Benefits and Challenges

As mentioned by various authors as Justenhoven, R., & Edenborough, R. (2011), Cappelli, P. (2015), Boudreau, J., & Rice, S. (2016) or O'Neil, C. (2016) and Strohmeier, S., & Piazza, F. (2014) among others, Data Science can greatly aid in the employee recruitment process. It accomplishes this through various means, such as resume analysis, where algorithms pinpoint candidates with the most relevant qualifications, saving time in initial screening. Additionally, Natural Language Processing (NLP) assists in keyword matching to quickly identify suitable applicants. Automated assessments, based on Data Science algorithms, evaluate technical skills, especially vital in skill-specific fields. Furthermore, predictive models use historical employee performance data to forecast success in specific roles. Indeed, for example, prediction models can be used to prevent excessive production and machine failure in product sales and maintenance. This approach has been successfully employed by Netflix and Amazon to predict customer preferences, leading to increased sales and growth (Quan, T. Z., & Raheem, M., 2023). Data Science also contributes to diversity and inclusion efforts by identifying potential biases in recruitment and recommends corrective actions. Social media and online profile analysis provide deeper insights into cultural and professional alignment with the organization. Moreover, the continuous collection and analysis of recruitment data enable ongoing process enhancements, pinpointing effective hiring sources and areas needing improvement. In essence, Data Science offers invaluable insights, streamlines screening, enhances accuracy in candidate selection, and bolsters overall recruitment efficiency, provided ethical and transparent use of algorithms to ensure equal opportunities for all candidates.

Despite the numerous benefits of using Data Science techniques to perform the recruitment process, there are challenges that must be consider when implementing Data Science in the recruitment process. Indeed, one of the primary concerns is data privacy and security. Protecting candidate information is crucial, and employers must ensure compliance with data protection regulations to safeguard their reputation and avoid potential legal consequences.

According with Wu, J.X.S., Liu, S. (2019), for instance, business digitization has aggravated the existing security and privacy concerns of customers, resulting in new challenges on organizational security and privacy protection. Therefore, by examining the interaction between security objects, these authors provided some suggestions for the research and industry communities, based on the Information Security Model of IBM.

Another challenge is ensuring data quality and accuracy. Clean and consistent data is vital for effective data-driven decision-making, and employers must address potential biases in the data to ensure fair and unbiased hiring practices. This may involve regular data audits and cleansing, as well as incorporating feedback from hiring managers and candidates to continuously improve data quality.

Finally, it is also important to balance data-driven decision-making with human intuition. Indeed, while data analytics can provide valuable insights and streamline the hiring process, human judgment remains an essential component. Furthermore, employers should avoid over-reliance on data analytics and foster collaboration between recruiters and data scientists, implementing checks and balances in the decision-making process in order to ensure the best possible hiring outcomes.

Another challenge is related with cultural, diversity, equity, and inclusion factors, since organizations that prioritize cultural, diversity, equity, and inclusion in their teams often experience better financial performance and business growth. A diverse and inclusive workforce drives innovation, improves decision-making, and contributes to better market understanding, all of which positively impact a company's bottom line. Furthermore, a strong focus on these values helps attract top talent, leading to a more competitive advantage.

Creating an environment that fosters cultural, diversity, equity, and inclusion within teams requires a strategic approach. This involves building an inclusive culture, implementing unbiased recruitment, and hiring processes, providing equal opportunities for growth, and encouraging collaboration and open communication among team members. By adopting these strategies, organizations can develop high-performing teams that excel in innovation and problem-solving.

Establishing a culture that values and respects diversity is paramount in promoting cultural, diversity, equity, and inclusion. Organizations should create an environment where individuals from diverse backgrounds feel welcome, included, and valued. This involves implementing policies and practices that encourage equity and inclusivity, as well as offering training and resources to raise awareness of unconscious bias and promote cultural competence. When team members feel a sense of belonging, they are more likely to contribute their unique perspectives and skills, leading to improved collaboration and innovation and these goals are challenges that must be faced and support the relevance of this study.

Main Objectives

In this study, the primary goals are:

To assess the role of Data Science teams in supporting organizations in the process of hiring new employees: The main focus is on understanding whether Data Science teams can effectively contribute to the recruitment process within organizations. This involves evaluating their ability to transform stored data into actionable knowledge that aids in identifying suitable candidates for various roles.

To investigate the impact of Data Science on organizational productivity and profitability: The study aims to explore how the utilization of Data Science techniques can positively affect an organization's overall productivity and financial performance. This includes examining whether the insights derived from data analysis can lead to better decision-making and, consequently, improved profitability.

Secondary Objectives Include

To analyse the current state of information management within organizations: This involves assessing the extent to which organizations are equipped to handle and leverage the information they possess. It explores the challenges associated with managing databases and the need for effective data organization.

To explore the relevance of Data Science in the context of the COVID-19 pandemic: Given the adverse effects of the ongoing COVID-19 pandemic, the study may investigate how Data Science can play a crucial role in helping organizations adapt to changing circumstances and economic challenges.

To identify the key competencies required for different roles within organizations: The research may aim to identify and categorize the specific skills and qualifications needed for various positions within an organization, with a focus on how Data Science can assist in matching candidates with the right skill sets to job vacancies.

To assess the potential for continuous knowledge generation through data analysis: This objective involves examining how Data Science can contribute to the ongoing accumulation of knowledge within an organization by extracting valuable insights from data sources.

Overall, the primary objective is to evaluate the role of Data Science in the hiring process, while the secondary objectives encompass broader aspects related to information management, pandemic resilience, competency mapping, and knowledge generation within organizations.

Research question: *"What is the impact of Data Science in the New Employee Recruitment Process?"*

THEORY

Management and Brief Historical Evolution

Companies rely on those in management positions. In addition to directing and overseeing employees, a manager must communicate with senior professionals to ensure that the team they are overseeing meets the goals and promotes the company's mission.

In terms of responsibilities, managers fulfil basic duties, although their roles may vary depending on the industry, they are in (Indeed, Editorial Team, 2021). The term "Management" can be defined in various ways, as evidenced by the definitions given by some scholarly authors on the subject. For example, Fayol, in 1954, stated that management involves forecasting and planning, organizing, commanding, coordinating, and controlling. Years later, Terry, in 1972, defined management as a distinct process that includes planning, organizing, action, and control carried out to determine and achieve objectives through the use of people and resources. Subsequently, in 1986, Drucker defined management as a versatile organ that manages a company, manages managers, and manages the worker and the work. More recently, Das and Mishra (2019, p. 8) provide a definition of management. The authors state that the essence of management boils down to the technique of extracting work from others in an integrated and coordinated manner to achieve specific objectives through the productive use of material resources. The mobilization of physical, human, and financial resources and the planning of their utilization for business purposes to achieve objectives can be enhanced through management. "Management is a universal process in all organized, social, and economic activities. Wherever there is human activity, there is management" (Das & Mishra, 2019, p. 8). Taking these definitions into account, management can be defined as the coordination and administration of tasks with the aim of achieving an objective. This administration of activities includes establishing organizational strategies and coordinating the efforts of employees to achieve these objectives through the application of available resources.

Functions of Management

The functions of management aim to keep managers informed about what is happening in the organization, what needs to be done, and how to do it. Initially, it was Fayol (1954) who defined what would be the five functions of management, which were accepted for decades: Planning, Organization, Staffing, Leading, and Controlling. Currently, in general, and according to Schermerhorn and Bachrach (2020, p. 9), and Griffin (2021), four functions are accepted: Planning, Organization, Leadership, and Control. Griffin (2021) defines Planning as the process of setting performance objectives and the actions that need to be taken to achieve them. In this stage, methods and strategies are evaluated to determine how progress should be made towards the goal. Griffin (2021) defines Organization as the process of task distribution, resource allocation, and coordination of individual or group activities. In this phase, the plan is put into action by establishing a hierarchical system that serves as the foundation for the organization's mission and plans to move forward. Griffin (2021) defines Leadership as the process of inspiring enthusiasm and motivating people to work hard to fulfil the organizational plans and objectives. This stage involves stimulating individuals to increase their performance in order to achieve all proposed organizational goals. Griffin (2021) defines Control as the process of measuring the performance of the work done, comparing the results to the objectives, and taking corrective measures if necessary. This is the stage where progress toward each established objective is measured in relation to organizational goals, requiring coordination between managers and employees to ensure that the organization is moving in the right direction. These four management functions highlight the essential skills that a manager must possess to effectively supervise, coordinate, and communicate with employees.

Management by Objectives (MBO)

In 1974, Drucker introduced the Management by Objectives (MBO) approach. This management model aims to improve organizational performance through the effective definition of management and employee objectives. According to this theory, including the opinions and objectives of all employees and management in goal-setting and action plans encourages participation and commitment among employees, as well as alignment of objectives throughout the organization (Hayes, 2021b). Management by Objectives, MBO, is the establishment of a Management Information System (MIS) designed to compare actual performance with defined objectives.

Like any theory, MBO has its advantages and disadvantages. The main advantages and benefits include: Increased employee motivation and commitment. Improved communication between employees and management. Opportunities for employees to work to their strengths, skills, and educational experiences. Setting goals that guide the organization toward success. The main disadvantages are: A strong focus on organizational objectives and goals can sometimes lead to the neglect of other aspects of the organization, such as culture, ethical conduct, and areas of engagement and contribution. Pressure on employees to meet goals within a specific timeframe. In Management by Objectives, MBO, Drucker defines six points to be considered: Objectives are determined in collaboration with employees. Objectives are formulated both quantitatively and qualitatively. Objectives should be challenging and motivating.

There should be daily feedback on the situation, in terms of coaching and development, rather than static management reports. Rewards (recognition, appreciation, and/or compensation for performance) for achieving desired objectives. The basic principle is based on growth and development, not punishment. By increasing commitment, managers have the opportunity to focus on new ideas and innovations that contribute to organizational development and goals (Mulder, 2010). To implement this management technique, organizations should follow five steps, summarized by Mulder (2010) and Hayes (2021b) as follows: Determine or review organizational objectives throughout the company. This overview should result from the organization's mission and vision.

Translate organizational objectives for employees. These objectives should be measurable for employees and managers. Encourage employee participation in defining individual objectives. After sharing the organization's objectives with employees, they should be encouraged to define their own objectives to achieve organizational goals. Monitor employees' progress. Evaluate and reward employee progress.

Operations Management

All organizations, including non-profit organizations, provide services or products. To ensure their survival, organizations must stay competitive and focus on the consumer, business relationships, innovation, quality, time-based competition, efficiency, costs, and diverse international perspectives. With significant technological advancements, intense global competition among organizations, and the prevalence of e-business, flexibility and responsiveness have become essential. It is crucial to ensure that the products or services offered are of the highest quality and offer benefits that attract consumers. The increasing financial pressure necessitates that organizations be agile and eliminate any waste, adopting a lean management approach. This is where Operations Management comes into play. Operations Management is the specialty that concerns itself with administering business models to maximize organizational efficiency. Operations Management involves the planning, scheduling, and supervision of processes with the aim of transforming inputs into finished products or services. Reid and Sanders (2019), initially in 2002 and updated in 2019, defined Operations Management as the business plan that plans, organizes, coordinates, and controls the resources needed to produce the organization's goods and services. According to the authors, Operations Management is a management function that involves the management of people, technologies, equipment, information, and many other resources, making this specialty the core of an organization. They also argue that without operations, there would be no products or services to sell. According to Barnes (2018), Operations Management is crucial in our daily lives because it is responsible for creating and distributing all the products and services we need daily, such as the food we eat, the clothes we wear, the transportation we use, the healthcare we receive, and more. Barnes (2018) also contends that virtually all aspects of our daily lives are dependent on Operations Management. More recently, Hayes (2021c) defined Operations Management as the management of business models with the aim of creating the highest level of efficiency within the organization. The primary concern is the conversion of materials and labour into goods or services as efficiently as possible, thereby maximizing the organization's profit. The author further notes that operations management teams always strive to balance costs with revenue to achieve the highest possible net operating profit.

Process Management and Business Process Management (BPM)

Process Management is a systematic approach that ensures the effectiveness and efficiency of the business. It is a methodology used to align business processes with strategic objectives. It is a long-term strategy that continually monitors business processes to maintain optimal efficiency (KissFlow, 2021a).

Business Process Management involves the execution of work. Processes form the core of any business and permeate all departments and staff, playing a crucial role in the outcome of operations. It is these processes that define the pathways and flows of activities executed within and between different aspects of the business. According to Ferreira (2020), BPM is defined as the practice of creating, executing, monitoring, and optimizing business processes. It's worth noting that BPM is a methodology, not a product, capable of transforming an organization into a well-oiled machine. When used correctly, this methodology aligns with the aim of Continuous Improvement.

Hayes (2021b) succinctly summarizes BPM as a concept focused on analysing and creating workflows and business processes within the organization. BPM holds significant importance in the business world because it guides the business to operate as efficiently as possible, delivering the best results, whether in terms of quality, service, response time, customer experience, or satisfaction. Hayes (2021b) further states that the primary objective is to assist organizations in their drastic restructuring by designing business processes from scratch. This restructuring enables systems to quickly adapt to the capacity to continue production and the efficiency with which they respond to market changes or inherent system alterations. Ferreira (2020) also points out that BPM operates in a continuous cycle, with four steps:

Design (Project): Identification of existing processes as well as areas for improvement. Mapping of work methods between people and systems and evaluation of any dependencies or transfers.

Execute (Execution): Implementation of the processes identified and planned in the planning phase.

Monitor (Monitoring): Tracking of processes to stay updated on their status and performance. Identification of areas with low performance or potential bottlenecks.

Optimize (Optimize): Utilization of the information gathered in the monitoring phase to make process improvements for greater efficiency or cost savings.

In 2021, there is an update to the BPM cycle (Figure 1), this time by the KissFlow website (2021b), which describes that the BPM cycle comprises not 4, but 5 steps: Design (Project), Model, Execute, Monitor, and Optimize.

Design (Project): Most processes include a form for data collection and working methods to process them.

Model: Representation of the process in a visual layout. Correcting details such as deadlines and conditions to provide a clear sequence of events and data flow throughout the process.

Execute: Implementation of the process by testing it with a small group first and then expanding it to all users. In this step, there should be restricted access to confidential information.

Monitor: Monitoring the process as it goes through the working method. Using metrics to track progress, measure efficiency, and identify bottlenecks.

Figure 1. Illustration of the BPM cycle updated by KissFlow website (2021b).
Source: Authors' own elaboration.

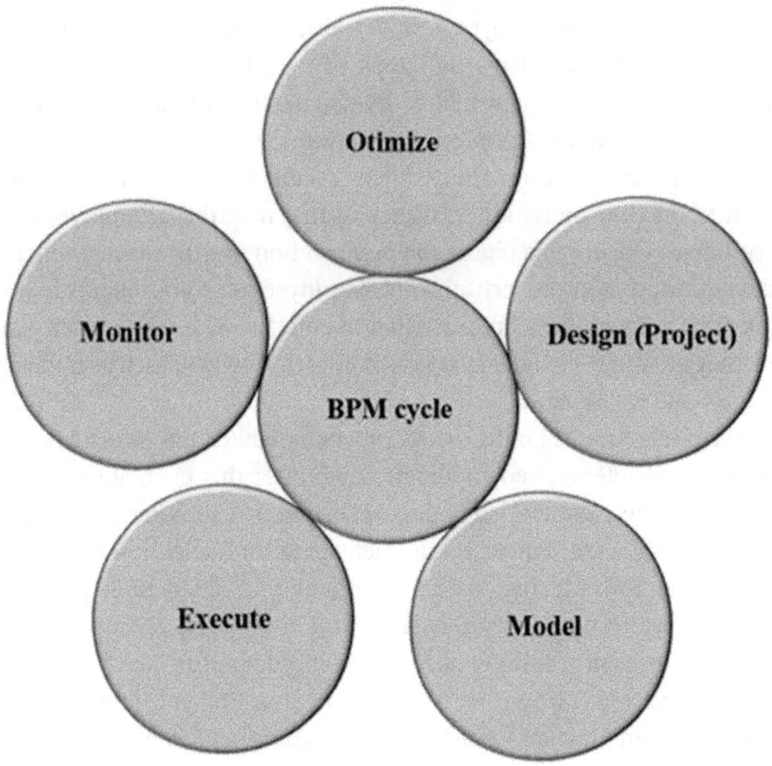

Optimize: After analysis, identifying the changes that need to be made to the form or working method to make them more efficient. Considering steps for improving the business process.

Studying the benefits, Ferreira (2020) also provides examples of the benefits that effective BPM implementation can bring to an organization, such as: Cost efficiency, derived from simplifying operations and collaborations, and reducing duplicated efforts. Thus, organizations can lower costs and increase productivity. Increased productivity through the automation of repetitive tasks, removing obstacles, and reducing the number of unnecessary tasks. Enhanced employee and customer satisfaction. A stronger corporate strategy due to BPM alignment with business outcomes. This way, organizations improve their overall performance and resource optimization.

Recruitment Processes and Historical Evolution of Recruitment

Finding and retaining talent is a vital part of a successful organization. However, it is challenging to find qualified personnel, and it is even more difficult to retain them. Replacing a salaried employee costs, on average, 6 to 9 months worth of salaries. Through a well-structured, organized, and efficient recruitment process, organizations can reduce employee turnover and the cost of replacing them (Perucci, 2020). Doyle (2021) elucidates the steps of a formal recruitment process that organizations follow to find new talent, divided into three phases: Human Resource Planning, Recruitment, and Employee Selection.

Human Resource Planning: The company establishes the number of employees it wishes to hire, the characteristics, and the skills they need these employees to possess.

Recruitment: During this phase, the organization tries to reach a specific group of candidates through job advertisements, employee referrals, job postings, campus recruitment at universities, among other methods. When interested candidates respond, they are interviewed and assessed in various ways, such as reviewing their backgrounds and references.

Employee Selection: Finally, the employer evaluates the information gathered about each of the interviewed candidates and, after this evaluation, selects those who possess all the characteristics the organization is looking for. Regarding the benefits of having an effective recruitment plan and selection process, Perucci (2020) highlights lower hiring costs, higher quality of newly hired employees, and increased employee productivity. Lower Hiring Costs: Being proactive in hiring new employees increases profitability and organizational performance. This is because it ensures that various departments of the organization are provided with ideal human resources and talents for the functions required of them. Higher Quality of New Employees: By screening high-quality candidates, there is a higher chance of retaining their interest. Prolonged processes can diminish interest in the organization and force candidates to seek other alternatives. Increased Employee Productivity: An effective recruitment process allows Human Resources teams to invest more time in training and developing both new and existing employees. When it comes to finding new candidates, depending on the requirements, resources, and immediate needs, organizations have several ways to do so, according to Doyle (2021), through:

Recruiters: Employees working for Human Resources departments or recruitment agencies, whose main function is to study potential candidates' profiles.

Career Pages: Job offers posted on organizations' websites, giving candidates the opportunity to search and review job listings and apply online.

Job Websites: Organizations with active recruitment and a constant search for new employees not only post offers on their own websites but also use other job websites to reach a larger audience.

Social Media: Nowadays, organizations have exponentially increased the use of social media in recruitment. Platforms such as LinkedIn, Facebook, Twitter, among others, are used for recruiting purposes.

An effective and well-developed recruitment process can bring enormous benefits to any organization. To ensure that this process is done correctly to extract the best results, it is essential to first identify the organization's needs. After this identification, a good job description must be prepared, determining the duties and responsibilities of the role, thus helping to communicate the organization's needs and expectations to potential candidates, so they know exactly what is expected of them. Next, recruitment plans are created. These plans aim to create a strategy for more effective job promotion. During this phase, the employees who will review resumes, schedule interviews, and make decisions about the best candidate are also determined.

Following this is the beginning of the search for new candidates using the "keyword" search tool. This technique reduces search time during the recruitment process by eliminating unqualified candidates. With this research done and the targets defined, the recruitment process itself follows. For this phase to be effective, timely and continuous communication is crucial because the best candidates always have several options and can quickly move on to other opportunities if they are not shown the due interest. Next are the interviews with candidates, which can be face-to-face or online. Once the interviews have been conducted, it is up to the employer to formalize an offer that the candidate will not want to pass up. The final step, following confirmation that the offer has been accepted, is the implementation of an integration process that allows new employees to start their experience with the organization positively. The goal is for them to adapt and acclimatize more easily to the new job, workspace, and colleagues (Perucci, 2020).

Technology

Technology is a vital force in this modern era of globalization. It has revolutionized the global economy and become a critical part of competitive strategy. Technology has helped us overcome major obstacles in globalization and international trade, such as trade barriers, the absence of a common ethical standard, transportation costs, and delays in information exchange. Technological advances have played a significant role in creating and expanding the global market, and Multinational Companies are now viewed as key players in globalization. The market has globalized at an extremely accelerated pace, and innovations from countries are often carried out by Multinational Corporations. Significant technological advancements have also enabled many companies to expand across borders, facilitating research and development (Lamba, 2009). For Buchanan (2020), technology is the systematic development over time of techniques used to create and make things. Buchanan (2020) also provides a brief and concise piece of history on how this term, which holds so much weight today, came into existence. Buchanan mentions that the term "technology" is a combination of two Greek words, "technē," which means technique, and the word "logos," which means reason. In Greece, the combination of these two words meant a discourse on fine and applied arts. This expression began to appear in English only in the 17th century and was then used to express a discussion solely about applied arts. In the early 20th century, this term encompassed an enormous and constantly growing range of means, processes, ideas, tools, and machines. In the mid-20th century, the term "technology" began to be defined as "the means or activity by which man seeks to change or manipulate his environment."

Another more recent definition of technology comes from the Editors of the Encyclopaedia Britannica (2021), who define technology as "the application of scientific knowledge to the practical aims of human life or as the change and manipulation of the human environment." Regarding technological advancements and developments, Davret (2020) identifies four phases of this manifestation of scientific progress:

Emerging Technology: In this stage, the acquisition of the production process, infrastructure, skilled labor, mastery of management systems, and product quality is carried out. This stage is marked by a high level of risk because there are no previous experiences to support it, making the risk and failure rate quite high, which makes this stage time-consuming.

Adaptation: In this phase, the process of adapting to more sophisticated technologies that allow the commercialization of products tailored to local or external demand takes place. This stage is also called rapid technology due to its rapid progress and dissemination.

First Degree of Innovation: This stage witnesses the most significant technological developments and introduces the first degrees of innovation, allowing organizations to improve their productivity and competitiveness. Organizations begin to have their research laboratories and produce their own licenses. Basic Technology: In this stage, technology becomes one of the main pillars on which organizations depend, and without it, the production and competitive process collapse. In terms of the advantages of technological development, Dravet (2020) identifies the following:

Business Efficiency: Practically everything can be done instantly using technology. Manufacturing tools have been greatly simplified, leading to a significant reduction in waste and costs for consumers.

More Jobs: Technology has created a large number of new jobs.

Better Communication: Staying in touch is easier than ever. One can communicate anywhere in the world almost instantly.

Healthcare: The emergence of new and varied forms of technology in the healthcare field allows for better care of the population.

In terms of disadvantages, Dravet (2020) again identifies the following:

Social Gaps: Technology is quite expensive, and keeping up with the latest trends is nearly impossible for the population not belonging to the upper class.

A Generation of Laziness: As everything has become easier to do, people tend to become complacent more easily and have forgotten how to get their hands dirty.

Technologies Become Obsolete: Since technological development is happening so rapidly, what is considered top-of-the-line today will be obsolete tomorrow. Technologies are constantly changing, so they are quickly replaced.

The modern era is so dependent on technology that it is very challenging to do without it in our lives. It is present and essential in various aspects of our lives, such as education, healthcare, communication, entertainment, and agriculture. Technological development occurs every moment, continuously, with the aim of continually assisting the population.

The technology and data-driven revolution are marked by high-speed and large-volume of data that affect almost all industries and internal operations of businesses, and where companies implement digital transformations to enhance their operational efficiency, effectiveness, and maintainability (Sindhu, V., Anitha, G. & Geetha, R., 2021). In this process, usually, a collaborative data ecosystem is developed to integrate different stakeholders such as customers, suppliers, production, and technical support to achieve a common organizational or business goal. An example of this process is the optimization of manufacturing by using data to identify potential ways of improving specific manufacturing processes or collaborating with other departments.

Data and Types of Data

Since the invention of computers, the term "data" has been used to refer to computerized information, whether it's transmitted or stored. This data can be text or numbers written on paper, facts present in a person's mind, or bytes or bits within the memory of one or more electronic devices. According to Vaughan (2019), data is information that has been efficiently formatted for movement or processing. In an article by SimpliLearn (2021), data is defined as different types of information that are formatted in a specific way. Beal (2021), in an article originally published in 1996 and updated at the end of 2021, also defines data as "referring to distinct pieces of information, usually formatted and stored in a manner consistent with a specific purpose." The expansion of big data has led to a significant demand to transform these data into useful information.

Data is the fuel that can steer an organization in the right direction or, in the simplest of situations, provide actionable insights that can help with current campaign strategies, easily organize the launch of new products, or create new and different experiences. In this digital age, data holds immense importance, and it's crucial to store and process it properly and without errors. When dealing with data sets (datasets), the category plays a significant role in determining the pre-processing strategy that works for each set or the type of statistical analysis that should be applied to achieve the best results. Therefore, Sharma (2020) divides data into two major categories: Qualitative Data and Quantitative Data (see, for instance, Figure 2).

Qualitative Data

According to Sharma (2020), qualitative data, or categorical data, describe the object under consideration using a finite set of discrete classes. In other words, this type of data cannot be easily counted or measured using numbers and is therefore divided into categories. Within this category, there are two subcategories of data:

Nominal: Data sets that do not have a natural order. A good example of this type of data is the colour of a mobile phone. Colours cannot be compared.

Ordinal: Data sets that have a natural order, maintaining their class of values. An example of this type of data could be a test score. "Very Good" is undoubtedly better than "Good."

This coding of data into qualitative data is crucial because machine learning models cannot directly handle these values, which need to be converted into numerical types since the models are mathematical in nature.

Quantitative Data

Sharma (2020) indicates that this type of data attempts to quantify things and does so by considering numerical values that make them inherently countable. Within this category, there are again two subcategories of data:

Discrete: Numerical values that fall into this category are integers or whole numbers. For example, the number of cameras, processors, etc.

Continuous: This subcategory includes real numbers, as they are continuous values. An example of this type of data could be the lifetime of an electronic component.

Figure 2. Types of data
Source: Authors' own elaboration.

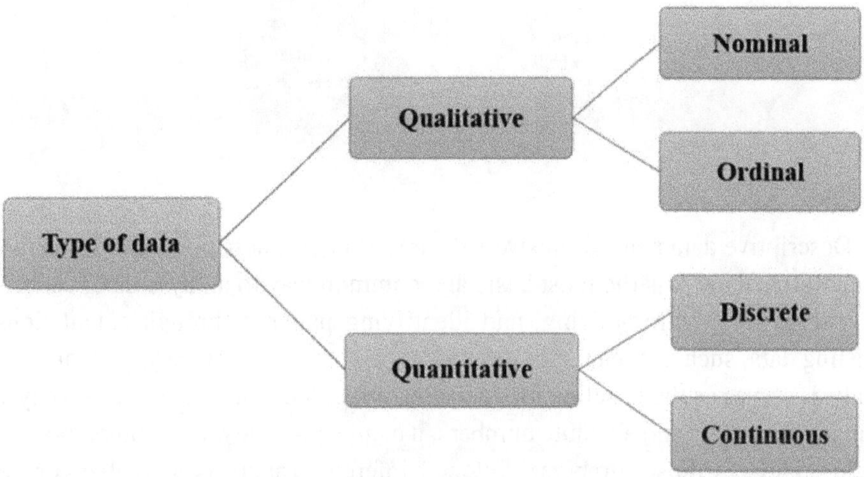

Methods of Data Analysis

Data analysis is how valuable insights are obtained, keeping the entire structure informed for decision-making and helping to better understand customer needs. Roldós (2021) introduces and explains the 6 methods of data analysis: Text Analysis, Descriptive Analysis, Inferential Analysis, Diagnostic Analysis, Predictive Analysis and Prescriptive Analysis (see, for instance, Figure 3).

Text analysis uses machine learning with natural language processing (NLP) to organize unstructured text data for analysis, extracting knowledge. This is a qualitative analysis that goes beyond just statistics and numerical values, providing deeper and targeted insights into why something might be happening or why it happened.

Figure 3. Methods of data analysis

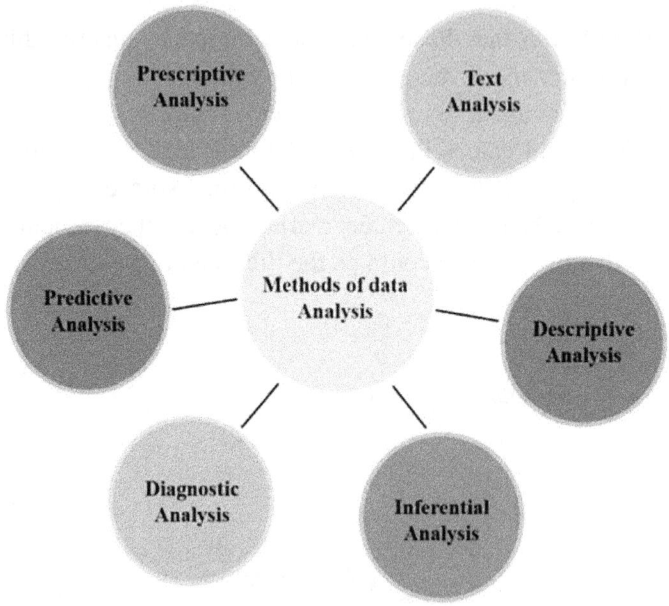

Descriptive data analysis answers the question "What happened?" by analysing quantitative data. It is the most basic and common way to analyse data, concerned with describing, summarizing, and identifying patterns through calculations of existing data, such as mean, median, mode, percentage, frequency, and range. This analysis serves as the baseline for analysing other data, but since it deals only with statistical analysis and absolute numbers, it cannot provide the reason or motivation for how and why those numbers developed. Inferential analysis generalizes or makes hypotheses about "What happened?" by comparing statistics from groups within an entire population. The most common methods for conducting this type of analysis are hypothesis testing and estimation theories. Diagnostic analysis, also known as root cause analysis, aims to answer "Why did X happen?" This analysis uses knowledge of statistical analysis to try to understand the cause or reason behind the statistics by identifying patterns or deviations within the data. Predictive analysis uses known data to make assumptions about future events. It is concerned with "What is likely to happen." Widely used in sales analysis, this analysis combines demographic and purchase data with other data to predict customer actions. Prescriptive analysis is the most advanced form of analysis, as it combines all your data and analyses, producing a model prescription: "What action should be taken?" This analysis works to analyse multiple scenarios, predict the outcome of each, and decide the best course of action based on those results.

Data Science

Currently, Data Science is an essential part of the industry, primarily because the massive amount of data generated daily needs to be analysed and processed to extract knowledge from it. Over the years, organizations have begun to implement Data Science techniques to grow their businesses and enhance customer satisfaction. According to an article by IBM (2020), Data Science is defined as a multidisciplinary approach used to extract knowledge from the vast and constantly growing volumes of data collected and generated by organizations. This science encompasses data preparation for analysis and processing, conducting advanced data analytics, and presenting results to reveal patterns, enabling stakeholders to draw informed conclusions. Techopedia (2021) also defines Data Science as a broad field that refers to the collective processes, theories, concepts, tools, and technologies that enable the review, analysis, and extraction of knowledge and information from raw data. It is oriented toward helping individuals and organizations make the best decisions based on stored, consumed, and managed data. Additionally, SimpliLearn (2021) provides its definition of Data Science. According to them, Data Science is the domain of study that deals with large volumes of data using modern tools and techniques to uncover invisible patterns, gain meaningful insights, and make business decisions. Data Science employs complex machine learning algorithms to build predictive models. This field is, therefore, crucial for Artificial Intelligence (AI) and machine learning.

Recently, Quan, T. Z., & Raheem, M. (2023) enumerate and presented a detailed description of the top 10 most currently demanded Data Science jobs, and performed an extensive analysis and salary prediction, specifically, for the data science employment domain with a specialized skill set, which produced outcomes that can effectively resolve real problems, providing insights into demanding data science skill sets and technical or soft knowledge that leads to higher salaries and employment opportunities.

In the past, Provost, F., & Fawcett, T. (2013b) introduces the fundamental principles of data science for business, and "data-analytic thinking" necessary for extracting useful knowledge and business value from the collected data. In this reference is also possible to find information that helps to understand many data-mining techniques, since it provides examples of real-world business problems to illustrate these principles.

Regardless of the industry an organization is in or its size, companies looking to remain competitive in the era of information and Big Data must efficiently develop and implement Data Science techniques. Indeed, "The power of Data Science comes from a deep understanding of statistics, programming, hacking, and communication." (Bandyopadhyay, 2017).

Data Science in the Recruitment Process (Recruitment Analytics)

In today's world, a data-driven approach is an absolute necessity in the recruitment process of any organization. It is essential to understand and study the talent market to be more consistent and efficient in hiring new employees (McConnell, 2021). Companies like Google, Cisco, Deloitte, and others all use Recruitment Analytics to strengthen their decision-making processes and employee hiring, making them leaders in this industry. More case studies with real-world examples demonstrating the successful application of Data Science in the digital business and covering interdisciplinary aspects of Data Science can be founded, for instance, in Márquez, F., & Lev, B. (2019). Also, an evidence-based review using an integrative synthesis of published peer-reviewed literature on Human Resource Analytics is available in Marler, J. H., & Boudreau, J. W. (2017).

Recruitment Analytics

According to Aviahire (2020), a company founded in 2018 to help organizations improve their teams in terms of talent and teamwork, Recruitment Analytics is defined as the detection, interpretation, and simplification of significant patterns for recruiting, selecting, and hiring employees. The benefits of this analysis compared to traditional hiring methods, as per McConnell (2021), include:

Provides objective visibility into the effectiveness and value of recruitment activities.

Helps maintain a record of high-potential candidates, actively feeding future hires.

Allows the creation of a robust talent pipeline or a permanent record of all candidates or hires that can be consistently reviewed. Provides potential for learning and process improvement. Enables more proactive recruitment for better decision-making and timing.

Helps predict which candidates are likely to perform well and which may be poor hires.

Levels of Recruitment Analytics. Van Vulpen (2022) distinguishes three levels in Recruitment Analytics: operational reports as level 1, advanced reports as level 2, and analysis as level 3.

Operational Reports: This is a descriptive analysis and represents the primary metric of recruitment.

Advanced Reports: Creating these reports requires combining multiple data sources, such as candidate experience.

Analysis: This level represents strategic and predictive analysis in the recruitment process. Strategic analysis includes segmentation, statistical analysis, and the development of people models, while predictive analysis encompasses the development of predictive models, and strategic and scenario planning.

Data Science encompasses a wide range of methods for data collection and analysis. In the recruitment sector, there are numerous ways to collect and study data to profile the desired candidate for a new position. Two effective methods for conducting this analysis are Talent Analytics (or People Analytics) and People Science. These concepts are used for data collection to increase the effectiveness and efficiency of recruitment processes.

Talent Analytics (People Analytics)

According to Rosie (2019), in an article on the "harver" website, talent analytics is the analysis of employee data with the aim of making better business decisions. It produces information about the type of person who should be hired based on existing personnel. This knowledge is used to understand the strengths and weaknesses of both existing and potential employees. Rosie (2019) identifies the main benefits of this method:

Provides better hiring insights; Develops recruitment process tracking metrics; Continuously collects feedback; Applies predictive analysis; Improves employee retention rates; Increases profits. Saves time; Promotes transparency; Enhances brand awareness; In conclusion, this method provides significant benefits for optimizing employee performance. It not only allows recruiters and hiring managers to select more qualified and engaged personnel, but also provides data that supports their decision-making processes. In a recent paper, Yoon, S. W., Han, S., & Chae, C. (2023) provide a comprehensive examination of the current research landscape of People Analytics from Human Resource Development perspectives, by leveraging the methodologies of bibliometrics and topic modeling, and revealing a convergence particularly evident in areas such as workforce planning and management, data-informed decision-making, applying analytics to various Human Resource functions, and emphasizing the ethical and societal implications of data analytics in Human Resource.

People Science

Black (2020) and the entire People Science team at Glint define this method as the study of what makes people happy and successful at work and how to create environments and habits that promote happiness and success. In other words, it uses data, analyses, and employee insights to understand how employees work and interact with their work environment. This provides information about how employees interact with the workplace and how it affects their environment and performance. This method integrates fields of study such as industrial-organizational psychology, organizational development, and occupational psychology with increasingly relevant fields like Data Science, product management, and design. According to Jason and Glint (2020), this method creates value for the customer in three ways: Helps customers shape and gain buy-in for a people success strategy that combines engagement, performance, and learning; Helps customers become successful practitioners, elevating them in their roles and ensuring partnership success.

"People Science is the practice of collecting feedback about employees' experiences at work and using that data to inform and understand how to make the workplace better for everyone." - Cullen, as quoted by McPherson (2022).

Critical Literature Review

Effective organizational management relies on individuals in leadership roles who guide and oversee employees to achieve goals and uphold the mission. Management encompasses the mobilization of physical, human, and financial resources and strategic planning, as highlighted by Das et al. (2019), who state that "management is a universal process inherent in all organized, social, and economic activities." At the pinnacle of management sits the CEO (Chief Executive Officer), responsible for defining the company's strategy and vision. While the CEO, in collaboration with the Administrative Board, defines the organization's strategy broadly, its specifics emerge at the operational level. Operations Management and Process Management play pivotal roles in translating this strategy into tangible actions. Operations Management, focusing on planning, scheduling, and supervising processes, ensures inputs are efficiently transformed into outputs, i.e., finished products and services. The Chief Operating Officer (COO) oversees this, often termed the CEO's "right-hand." Processes are vital, ensuring an organization's efficiency and effectiveness. Poorly defined processes risk profitability. Business Process Management (BPM) is key, with stages including process projection, modelling, execution, monitoring, and optimization. Crucially, people are at the heart of organizations. Talent acquisition and retention are essential, but in today's competitive landscape, recruitment has become more challenging. A well-defined and efficient recruitment process is necessary to prevent candidates from losing interest due to lengthy or unengaging procedures. To achieve this, organizations must identify their needs, craft comprehensive job descriptions, create recruitment plans, and leverage technology.

Technology, a force in globalization, impacts communication, economies, and information exchange. Information technologies build networks and manage databases. Data Science, essential in the modern era, analyses, processes, and extracts knowledge from vast data, offering a competitive edge. In recruitment, data-driven insights help attract and retain talent. Data Science collaborates with Human

Resources to study talent markets effectively. The Data Science process involves six phases, including problem framing, data collection, processing, exploration, in-depth analysis, and crucially, result communication. As technology permeates daily life, it becomes increasingly indispensable in recruitment. Attracting, retaining, and developing talent is essential for organizational success. It's not just about recruiting talent; it's about nurturing and evolving it.

Methods

The methodology to be used for studying this subject will be quantitative methodology, through the examination of data collected in a questionnaire.

Quantitative Methodology

Quantitative Research Methodology, according to Bhandari (2021), is the process of collecting numerical data with the aim of identifying patterns and averages, making predictions, testing causal relationships, and generalizing results to broader populations. This methodology is widely employed in natural and social sciences, such as biology, psychology, economics, marketing, sociology, etc. Bhandari (2021) also states that this methodology is the opposite of qualitative research methodology, as it involves the collection and analysis of non-numerical data (such as text, videos, or audio).

Advantages and Disadvantages

"Quantitative research is often used to standardize data collection and generalize results" (Bhandari, 2021). Thus, Bhandari (2021) highlights the primary advantages and disadvantages of this methodology. The advantages include: Replication: The study can be repeated due to standardized data collection protocols and tangible definitions of abstract concepts. Direct Result Comparisons: Results can be statistically compared. Large Sample Groups: Data from large sample groups can be processed and analyzed using reliable and consistent procedures through quantitative analysis. Hypothesis Testing: The use of formalized and established hypothesis testing procedures means that research variables, predictions, data collection, and testing methods must be carefully considered and reported before reaching a conclusion. Having defined the advantages, Bhandari (2021) subsequently identifies the disadvantages, which include: Superficiality: The use of precise and restrictive operational definitions can inaccurately represent complex concepts. Limited Focus: Predefined variables and measurement procedures may result in the neglect of other relevant information. Structural Bias: Despite structured procedures, structural biases can still affect quantitative research. Missing data, imprecise measurements, or inadequate sampling methods are biases that can lead to incorrect conclusions.

Lack of Context: Quantitative research sometimes uses non-natural environments, such as laboratories, or does not consider historical and cultural contexts that can influence data collection and its results.

The Background of the Study and the Methods Used to Obtain Data

There are several methods used for the collection of quantitative data, including Questionnaires, Correlational Research, Causal-Comparative Research, and Experimental Research. According to QuestionPro (2022), a web-based software company for creating and distributing surveys, these tools are characterized as follows:

Questionnaires (I) serve as the fundamental tool for all methodologies and studies involving quantitative research outcomes. Any organization, whether small or large, wishing to understand what their customers think about their products or services can use questionnaires for this purpose. Through questionnaires, an organization can pose multiple questions, gather and analyse data from a group of customers, and, following this analysis, produce numerical results. This type of research can be conducted with a specific target group or multiple groups for comparative analyses. An essential prerequisite for the effectiveness of this research is the use of a randomly selected sample to maintain the accuracy of the results. Correlational Research (II) is conducted to establish a relationship between two closely related entities, determining how one affects the other and identifying any observed changes. This research method aims to add value to naturally occurring relationships. It requires at least two different groups to be successful. Researchers in this type of study often manipulate one of the variables to achieve desired outcomes. Causal-Comparative Research (III) primarily relies on comparison. Researchers use this method to establish a cause-and-effect relationship between two or more variables, where one variable is dependent on another independent variable. The independent variable is established but not manipulated, and its impact on the dependent variable is observable. These variables or groups should also be formed as they naturally exist. This method extends beyond the statistical analysis of two variables to examine how several variables or groups change under the influence of the same factors. It is a versatile method that does not depend on the type of relationship between variables, and statistical analysis is used to present the results distinctly. Experimental Research (IV) involves verifying or refuting a statement. There can be multiple theories in experimental research, with a theory being a statement that can be tested and confirmed or disproved. Once a statement is established, efforts are made to understand its validity. This method is primarily used in the natural sciences, as there are many statements that need to be proven as true or false (QuestionPro, 2022). These various research methods provide organizations and researchers with a range of tools for conducting quantitative research and obtaining valuable insights into different aspects of their subjects of interest.

Sampling Method and Sample Calculation

According to the study conducted above, it can be inferred that this project will use the quantitative methodology. To conduct a quantitative study, questionnaires will be used. Specifically, a questionnaire will be created and distributed to several Portuguese companies to assess employees' perceptions of the impact of Data Science on the recruitment process. Therefore, the research question to which an answer is expected is: *"What is the impact of Data Science in the New Employee Recruitment Process?"*.

In order to conduct the study on the subject, it is necessary to determine the sample size for the study. To calculate this sample size, the tool provided by Santos (2017) will be used. This tool will allow the calculation of the study's sample from the Portuguese working population. To use this tool, it is necessary to define the sampling error, confidence level, and population.

We trust that the act of studying a portion of the observed population does not alter the inherent characteristics of the population under investigation. Therefore, we employ sampling to uncover these population characteristics in their unaltered state (Thompson, 2012). An ideal sample should faithfully mirror the characteristics of interest within the population, aiming to replicate them as closely as practically possible. It should be representative, with each sampled unit reflecting a known proportion of individuals in the population (Lohr, 1999). Within the context of the present research, which is structured around finite populations, various sampling methods are applied based on the specific characteristics of these populations. The determination of the sample size was statistically derived, considering a finite population of approximately 4,320,492 potential workers, as outlined below:

$$n = Z_\alpha^2 \frac{N.p.q}{i^2 \left(N-1\right) + Z_\alpha^2 .p.q}$$

In this equation, 'n' represents the anticipated sample size from a population of size 'N,' 'Z_α' corresponds to the value associated with the Gaussian distribution, 'p' is the expected prevalence of the parameter under evaluation, 'q' is derived as 1 minus 'p' and 'i' represents the sampling error.

With a 90% confidence level and a 5% margin of error, the projected representative sample size is 271. In practice, 123 responses were collected (approximately 45%) through a questionnaire survey, which was distributed via email and social media channels. Notably, all respondents were required to answer all questions, ensuring that the database does not contain any missing values.

Sample Error and Confidence Level

Santos (2017) defines sampling error as the difference between the survey's estimated value and the true value. It must be entered the maximum sampling error allowed by the study in the calculator. In most cases, the researcher determines this value. Typically, the configured value is 5%.

The probability that the actual sampling error falls below the accepted sampling error defined by the survey is termed the confidence level. When a 5% sampling error is specified, the confidence level indicates the probability that the survey's error will remain within the range of 5%. In other words, the confidence level is a measure of the reliability of a result, and it indicates the probability with which the estimation of the location of a statistical parameter in a sample survey is also true for the entire population from which it was sampled (Santos, 2017).

Population

The total count of items within the research scope is known as the population. It represents the quantity of elements designated for examination. When the researcher lacks exact knowledge of the total number of elements in the universe, it is advisable to err on the side of caution and select a sufficiently large figure to prevent the effective population from expanding (Santos, 2017).

Characterization of the Sample

In this subtopic, we will analyse the demographic data collected through the administered questionnaire to conduct a sample study.

The demographic data analysis provides valuable insights into the sample of respondents. In terms of gender, 58.5% of respondents are female, while 41.5% are male. Regarding age, the majority fall into the 45 years or older category (54.5%), with the 18 to 24 years age group representing the smallest percentage (9.8%). When considering the sector of activity, the tertiary sector, encompassing services, prevails, with 62.6% of respondents. Meanwhile, only 9.8% work in the primary sector, linked to nature-based activities, and 27.6% in the secondary sector, which includes manufacturing and construction. Professions among respondents are diverse, encompassing administrative, commercial, teaching, engineering, military, and other roles. Educational backgrounds reveal that a significant portion holds a bachelor's degree (44.7%), with 24.4% having a master's degree or higher, and 20.3% completing secondary education (12th grade). Regarding years of professional experience, 35% have 21 to 30 years, with 18.7% having less than 5 or 11 to 20 years of experience each, and 13% having more than 30 years. The majority of respondents work in Santarém (46.3%) or Lisbon (38.2%), while other locations like Leiria, Porto, and Setúbal also have representation, indicating geographical diversity within the sample.

Data Collection tool and Composition of the Questionnaire

The chosen research approach focuses on collecting primary data. Data collection started with an anonymous questionnaire administered through a Google Form, which was distributed via email and social media platforms. Respondents accessed the Google platform using the provided questionnaire link, and they were restricted to submitting their responses once. To ensure that all questionnaires were completed and suitable for information analysis, all questions were mandatory. The questionnaire consists of closed-ended, multiple-choice questions where respondents can select only one response. This limitation in responses was implemented to enhance the precision and reliability of the data obtained.

The questionnaire developed was adapted from a survey launched in 2018 by DICE. The questionnaire consists of 19 questions, with the first 8 questions being demographic in nature. These questions inquire about gender, age, sector of activity, profession, current position, academic background, years of professional experience, and workplace location. The remaining 11 questions encompass knowledge about technology (Data Science, Machine Learning, and Artificial Intelligence) and the recruitment process.

Results Analysis

In this section, we delve into the demographic data gathered through our questionnaire survey. Our findings reveal a diverse profile of respondents.

Firstly, regarding gender, we observe that a significant majority of participants are female, accounting for 58.5% of the sample. In terms of age, our respondents span a wide range, yet a substantial portion, approximately 54.5%, falls into the 45 and older category. Conversely, the youngest demographic, aged 18 to 24, comprises a smaller segment, constituting just 9.8% of the total.

When examining the sectors of activity, the tertiary sector, primarily encompassing services, stands out as the dominant field, with 62.6% of respondents engaged in this sector. In the professional realm, our survey captures a diverse array of occupations and positions. Academically, the majority of participants hold a bachelor's degree, constituting 44.7% of the respondents, while a significant 24.4% possess a master's degree or higher qualification.

In terms of professional experience, a substantial 35% of respondents boast between 21 to 30 years of work experience, demonstrating a wealth of knowledge and expertise within our sample. Finally, concerning workplace location, our data indicates that a notable proportion of participants, around 46.3%, are based in Santarém, with a significant presence also found in Lisbon, where 38.2% of respondents are employed. These demographic insights provide a comprehensive profile of our study's sample population, offering valuable context for our subsequent analyses and conclusions.

Quantitative Data Analysis

In this section, we delve into the analysis of the demographic data collected through a questionnaire survey to explore the potential of Data Science in improving the recruitment process for new employees. The data analysis encompasses various aspects, including respondents' satisfaction with current recruitment methods, the need for improvements in existing recruitment processes, their knowledge of Data Science, and their perception of the impact and utility of Data Science techniques in the recruitment domain.

Satisfaction with Current Recruitment Methods: The analysis reveals that 40.65% of respondents are content with their companies' current recruitment methods, while 34.15% remain undecided. Additionally, 17.07% express dissatisfaction with the existing recruitment approaches.

Need for Improvement in Current Recruitment Processes: Over 50% of the respondents believe that there is room for improvement in their companies' recruitment methods, with 34.6% strongly agreeing with this notion.

Knowledge of Data Science: A substantial majority of the respondents (75.61%) lack any knowledge of Data Science techniques, while only 24.39% claim some degree of familiarity with the subject.

Use of Data Science Techniques in the Company: Approximately half of the respondents (50.41%) state that their companies do not employ Data Science techniques, whereas only 12.20% confirm their companies' usage of such techniques. The remaining 37.40% are uncertain about their companies' use of Data Science techniques.

Importance of Data Science for the Future of Recruitment: Respondents' opinions on the significance of Data Science technologies for the future of recruitment vary. While 0.81% believe these technologies will have little to no importance, 1.63% consider them to be of minor importance, 26.02% regard them as moderately important,

42.28% see them as crucial, and 29.27% anticipate a high level of importance in the future of the recruitment process.

Incorporation of Data Science Techniques: Respondents are generally optimistic about the potential of Data Science techniques and technologies in facilitating the recruitment process. A considerable proportion (44.72%) believes these tools will be very useful, with an additional 21.14% considering them extremely useful. Only 5.69% anticipate limited usefulness.

Probability of Implementation in the Future: Regarding the likelihood of implementing Data Science techniques in their companies, opinions vary. While 8.13% deem it highly unlikely, 21.14% consider it unlikely, 21.95% believe it could go either way, 34.15% see a likelihood of implementation, and 14.63% expect a high probability of adoption.

These insights provide a comprehensive profile of the study's sample population, shedding light on their perceptions of Data Science's role in the recruitment process.

Critical Discussion of Results

Through the analysis of the results obtained from questionnaire responses and the relationships established between variables, it becomes evident that a significant portion of employees currently believes that recruitment processes need improvement. In a society that is constantly evolving, staying at the forefront of human resources in organizations is imperative. Furthermore, it is clear that knowledge about Data Science, one of the ways to enhance the recruitment process, is not widespread. This is exemplified by the fact that 75% of the sample lacks knowledge in this area. The scarcity of studies in the field, limited knowledge dissemination, and a dearth of practical cases for reference and analysis contribute to this knowledge gap.

Given that Data Science requires a high level of expertise and substantial investment for implementation, it is apparent that, despite some organizational openness towards its adoption, there is still a lack of readiness to fully embrace it.

Through data analysis, it is also discernible that the absence of Data Science techniques, regardless of one's knowledge about Data Science, is perceived to result in more inadequate hires, missed opportunities, and a prolonged and protracted recruitment process. Similarly, when it comes to the impact of Data Science techniques, respondents, whether knowledgeable about these techniques or not, believe that their use reduces turnover, enhances candidate quality, and makes the process more efficient and less time-consuming. According to the analyses conducted, background verification and organization and scheduling are tasks that respondents believe would benefit the most from the implementation of Data Science techniques.

Furthermore, there is a prevailing neutral opinion regarding the displacement of employees due to the implementation of Data Science techniques, with "displacement" referring to employee layoffs or role changes within the organization.

It is worth noting that despite some existing knowledge about Data Science, the younger age group, specifically those aged 18 to 24, demonstrates the least familiarity with Data Science. This suggests that this crucial field, which holds immense potential for the future, may not be sufficiently promoted among younger individuals who stand to gain significant benefits from its application.

Pre-Conclusion

The quantitative data analysis presented in this section offers a valuable glimpse into the attitudes and perspectives of our survey respondents regarding the integration of Data Science into the realm of recruitment. Through a thorough examination of demographic data, we have unveiled significant insights. A substantial portion of the workforce, while generally satisfied with current recruitment methods, acknowledges the potential for improvement. Interestingly, the majority of respondents possess little to no knowledge of Data Science, highlighting a potential knowledge gap within the workforce. Despite this, there is a prevailing optimism about the transformative power of Data Science in recruitment, with many recognizing its importance and utility for the future. The varying opinions on the likelihood of implementation in their respective companies reflect the evolving landscape of recruitment practices. These findings collectively shape a comprehensive profile of our study's sample population and provide valuable context for our concluding remarks on the role of Data Science in revolutionizing recruitment.

CONCLUSION

Secondary Findings

Through this study on the implementation of Data Science techniques and technologies in the recruitment process, several conclusions can be drawn. Firstly, it becomes evident that a data-driven approach is increasingly crucial for the future of organizations, particularly in the context of recruitment. In an era marked by heightened competitiveness and rivalry, understanding the talent market is paramount for efficient and consistent hiring of new employees. Given the rapid technological advancements and increased specialization of individuals, having insights into factors influencing candidate choices and aligning them with organizational goals is fundamental. Data Science, therefore, emerges as an indispensable tool for shaping the future of organizations. In a world where knowledge and information are pivotal for informed decision-making and maximizing benefits, Data Science holds significant promise.

Primary Findings

As evaluated in the literature review, a quantitative study was conducted to address the question: "*What is the impact of Data Science in the New Employee Recruitment Process?*" This study analysed various data collected through questionnaires and unveiled that Data Science is a field that is yet to gain widespread recognition among the general public. While it remains relatively less discussed in daily conversations, it is a domain that carries immense benefits for organizations, as information is indeed power. Even with some ambiguity surrounding the techniques and technologies employed in Data Science, individuals generally believe in the advantages it brings. In the context of recruitment, it is evident that employees, on the whole, perceive Data Science as having the potential to significantly enhance the quality of candidates and streamline the recruitment process, making it more efficient and objective.

Final Conclusion

In conclusion, it can be asserted that a more technology-driven approach to the recruitment process is increasingly indispensable for the future of organizations. Although the realm of Data Science demands substantial investment and a wealth of knowledge for its implementation, the substantial benefits it offers cannot be understated. Despite the limited availability of studies and knowledge about this field in Portugal, employees recognize that this approach brings significant improvements to the recruitment processes of organizations.

Limitations and Future Studies

During the course of this research, we encountered several limitations, primarily revolving around time constraints and the responsiveness of the study's participants. Concerning time limitations, it is worth highlighting that this encompasses both the available time for conducting the research and the time required by respondents to provide their feedback. As for the responsiveness of the participant pool, we must consider various factors, including the daily influx of survey invitations, the impending peak season, and the prevalence of remote work. These variables can significantly impact individuals' willingness to engage with electronic devices, as some may prioritize leisure activities over functional tasks once their workday concludes. Looking ahead to future research opportunities upon the conclusion of this study, there are several intriguing avenues to explore. One compelling direction involves replicating a similar study with a more extensive and diverse sample, thereby gaining a more comprehensive understanding of the subject matter. Additionally, delving into the practical application of Data Science techniques and technologies to produce actionable insights and quantifiable outcomes holds significant promise. Indeed, further research endeavours in this field have the potential to substantially contribute to its advancement and reveal additional benefits and practical applications.

ACKNOWLEDGMENT

The authors acknowledge the financial support of ISLA Santarém. The second author also acknowledge Fundação para a Ciência e a Tecnologia (FCT) and COMPETE 2020 program for financial support to project UIDB/00048/2020.

REFERENCES

Aviahire. (2020, junho 23). *What is Recruitment Analytics? Recruitment analytics plays an...* Medium. https://medium.com/aviahire/what-is-recruitment-analytics-how-is-it-beneficial-fb5bc9be1f0b

Bandyopadhyay, R. (2017, January 9). *The Data Science Process: What a data scientist actually does day-to-day.* Springboard. https://medium.springboard.com/the-data-science-process-the-complete-laymans-guide-to-what-a-data-scientist-actually-does-ca3e166b7c67

Bansal, S. (2021). *What Is Data Science Process and Its Significance?* AnalytixLabs. https://www.analytixlabs.co.in/blog/data-science-process/

Barnes, D. (2018). *Operations management: an international perspective*. Thomson. https://books.google.com/books/about/Operations_Management.html?hl=pt-PT&id=5tHxzQEACAAJ

Beal, V. (2021, December 17). *What is Data?* Webopedia. https://www.webopedia.com/definitions/data/

Bhandari, P. (2021, December 8). *What Is Quantitative Research? Definition, Uses and Methods*. Scribbr. https://www.scribbr.com/methodology/quantitative-research/

Black, J. (2020, April 9). *What Is People Science? Think modern organizational development*. Glint. https://www.glintinc.com/blog/what-is-people-science/

Bloomenthal, A. (2021, July 21). *Chief Operating Officer (COO) Definition*. Investopedia. https://www.investopedia.com/terms/c/coo.asp

Boudreau, J., & Rice, S. (2016). *Predictive HR Analytics: Mastering the HR Metric*. Harvard Business Press.

Buchanan, R. A. (2020, November 18). *history of technology*. Encyclopaedia Britannica. https://www.britannica.com/technology/history-of-technology

Cappelli, P. (2015). Why We Love to Hate HR... and What HR Can Do About It. *Harvard Business Review*, *93*(7-8), 54–61.

Chatterjee, M. (2022, January 13). *Top 9 Job Roles in the World of Data Science for 2022*. GreatLearning. https://www.mygreatlearning.com/blog/different-data-science-jobs-roles-industry/

Cloud Education. I. (2020, May 15). *What is Data Science*. IBM. https://www.ibm.com/cloud/learn/data-science-introduction

Colorado State University. (2021, September 27). *What Do IT Professionals Actually Do? Roles & Responsibilities*. CSU Global. https://csuglobal.edu/blog/what-does-an-information-technology-professional-really-do

ComputerScience. (2021, September 27). *Information Security Analyst Careers*. ComputerScience.Org. https://www.computerscience.org/careers/information-security-analyst/

Das, U. C., & Mishra, A. K. (2019). *Management Concepts and Practices*. www.ddceutkal.ac.in

Davenport, T. H., & Patil, D. J. (2012, October). *Data Scientist: The Sexiest Job of the 21st Century*. Harvard Business Review. https://hbr.org/2012/10/data-scientist-the-sexiest-job-of-the-21st-century

Davret, J. (2020, July 29). *The Stages of Technology Development*. LivePositively. https://www.livepositively.com/the-stages-of-technology-development/

de Feo, J. A., & Barnard, W. (2005). Six sigma: La feuille de route 6 sigma du Juran institute. formation Green et Master Black Belt. In *The Juran Institute*. Mc Graw Hill. https://www.piloter.org/six-sigma/juran-six-sigma.htm

Debois, S. (2022, March 8). *10 Advantages and Disadvantages of Questionnaires - Survey Anyplace*. SurveyAnyplace Blog. https://surveyanyplace.com/blog/questionnaire-pros-and-cons/

Doyle, A. (2021, December 2). *The Recruitment and Hiring Process*. TheBalanceCareers. https://www.thebalancecareers.com/recruitment-and-hiring-process-2062875

Encyclopaedia Britannica. (2021, April 15). *Technology*. Encyclopaedia Britannica. https://www.britannica.com/technology/technology

Ferreira, S. (2020, November 18). *Business Process Management: What Is BPM and Why You Need It*. Outsystems. https://www.outsystems.com/blog/posts/business-process-management/

Frankenfield, J. (2020, July 28). *Cloud Computing Definition*. Investopedia. https://www.investopedia.com/terms/c/cloud-computing.asp

Gageiro, J. N., & Pestana, M. H. (2013). *Alpha de Cronbach para a análise da consistência interna*. Análise Estatística. https://analise-estatistica.pt/2013/09/alpha-de-cronbach-para-a-analise-da-consistencia-interna.html

Gordon, J. (2021, June 27). *Business Process Redesign - Explained - The Business Professor, LLC*. The Business Professor. https://thebusinessprofessor.com/en_US/mgmt-operations/business-process-redesign

Gourley, L. (2020, May 21). *The 7 Wastes of Lean Production*. PTC - Digital Transforms Physical. https://www.ptc.com/en/blogs/iiot/7-wastes-of-lean-production

Griffin, R. W. (2021). *Fundamentals of Management*. https://books.google.pt/books?hl=pt-PT&lr=&id=IhQcEAAAQBAJ&oi=fnd&pg=PP1&dq=management&ots=on2-srv2N0&sig=LJ0Iz6kzEumc8AZKP5id7nTCKTA&redir_esc=y#v=onepage&q=management&f=false

Hammer, M. (1990, August). *Reengineering Work: Don't Automate, Obliterate*. Harvard Business Review. https://hbr.org/1990/07/reengineering-work-dont-automate-obliterate

Hayes, A. (2021a, August 19). *Business Process Redesign (BPR) Definition*. Investopedia. https://www.investopedia.com/terms/b/business-process-redesign.asp

Hayes, A. (2021b, September 5). *Management by Objectives (MBO) Definition*. Investopedia. https://www.investopedia.com/terms/m/management-by-objectives.asp

Hayes, A. (2021c, October 29). *Operations Management (OM) Definition*. Investopedia. https://www.investopedia.com/terms/o/operations-management.asp

Hayes, A. (2022, March 5). *Blockchain Definition: What You Need to Know*. Investopedia. https://www.investopedia.com/terms/b/blockchain.asp

Indeed Editorial Team. (2021, December 8). *What Is Management? Definitions and Functions*. Indeed. https://www.indeed.com/career-advice/career-development/what-is-management

Justenhoven, R., & Edenborough, R. (2011). *Assessment and Development Centres: Strategies for Success in HR and Business Performance*. Gower Publishing, Ltd.

KissFlow. (2021a, February 21). *What is Process Management?* KissFlow. https://kissflow.com/workflow/bpm/what-is-process-management/

KissFlow. (2021b, November 21). *Business Process Management (BPM) - Definition, Steps, and Benefits*. KissFlow. https://kissflow.com/workflow/bpm/business-process-management-overview/

Koren, Y. (2021, December 15). *Reconfigurable Manufacturing Systems*. University of Michigan. Retrieved December 15, 2021, from https://ykoren.engin.umich.edu/research/rms/

Kumari, R. (2020, October 30). *What is Information Technology? Definition, Types, and Examples*. AnalyticSteps. https://www.analyticssteps.com/blogs/what-information-technology-definition-types-and-examples

Landau, P. (2021, November 15). *What Is Lean Manufacturing?* ProjectManager. https://www.projectmanager.com/blog/what-is-lean-manufacturing

Lohr, S. L. (1999). *Sampling Design and Analysis*. Duxbury Press.

Marler, J. H., & Boudreau, J. W. (2017). An evidence-based review of HR Analytics. *International Journal of Human Resource Management*, *28*(1), 3–26. doi:10.1080/09585192.2016.1244699

Márquez, F., & Lev, B. (2019). *Data Science and Digital Business*. Springer., doi:10.1007/978-3-319-95651-0

Mason, H., & Wiggins, C. (2010, September 25). *A Taxonomy of Data Science*. Datists. https://web.archive.org/web/20211219192027/http://www.dataists.com/2010/09/a-taxonomy-of-data-science/

McConnell, B. (2021, July 22). *Data analytics in recruitment: How to apply predictive analytics*. RecruiteeBlog. https://recruitee.com/articles/analytics-in-recruitment

Mckay, D. R. (2019, April 22). *Chief Operating Officer Job Description: Salary, Skills, & More*. The Balance Careers. https://www.thebalancecareers.com/what-is-a-coo-4172823

McKay, D. R. (2019a, September 23). *Computer and Information Systems (CIS) Manager Job Description: Salary, Skills, & More*. TheBalanceCareers. https://www.thebalancecareers.com/computer-and-information-systems-manager-525998

McKay, D. R. (2019b, September 27). *Computer Systems Analyst Job Description: Salary, Skills, & More*. TheBalanceCareers. https://www.thebalancecareers.com/computer-systems-analyst-526001

McPherson, J. (2022, January 22). *Introducing our People Science team*. Culture Amp. Retrieved January 22, 2022, from https://www.cultureamp.com/blog/introducing-our-people-science-team

Monroe. (2017, April 13). *What is a Reconfigurable Manufacturing System?* MonroeEngeneering. https://monroeengineering.com/blog/what-is-a-reconfigurable-manufacturing-system/

Mulder, P. (2010). *What is Management By Objectives (MBO)*. Toolshero. https://www.toolshero.com/management/management-by-objectives-drucker/

Nantasenamat, C. (2020, July 27). *The Data Science Process. A Visual Guide to Standard Procedures...* TowardsDataScience. https://towardsdatascience.com/the-data-science-process-a19eb7ebc41b

O'Neil, C. (2016). *Weapons of Math Destruction: How Big Data Increases Inequality and Threatens Democracy*. Crown Publishing Group.

Pathak, R. (2021a, May 21). *Information Technology - functions, applications & Importance*. AnalyticSteps. https://www.analyticssteps.com/blogs/information-technology-its-functions-and-why-it-important

Pathak, R. (2021b, October 27). *What is the role of technology in business?* AnalyticSteps. https://www.analyticssteps.com/blogs/what-role-technology-business

Perucci, D. (2020, April 23). *The Quick Guide to an Effective Recruitment Process*. BambooHR. https://www.bamboohr.com/blog/guide-effective-recruitment-process/

Pinto, J. P. (2006). *João Pinto Introdução Ao Lean Thinking*. Cadeia de Abastecimento. https://pt.scribd.com/document/52886880/Joao-Pinto-Introducao-ao-Lean-Thinking

Profita, M. (2020, September 17). *Top 10 Computer Science Jobs*. TheBalanceCareers. https://www.thebalancecareers.com/top-jobs-for-computer-science-majors-2059634

Provost, F., & Fawcett, T. (2013a). Data Science and its Relationship to Big Data and Data-Driven Decision Making. *Big Data*, *1*(1), 51–59. doi:10.1089/big.2013.1508 PMID:27447038

Provost, F., & Fawcett, T. (2013b). *Data Science for Business: What You Need to Know about Data Mining and Data-Analytic Thinking*. O'Reilly Media.

Quan, T. Z., & Raheem, M. (2023). Human Resource Analytics on Data Science Employment Based on Specialized Skill Sets with Salary Prediction. *International Journal of Data Science*, *4*(1), 40–59. doi:10.18517/ijods.4.1.40-59.2023

QuestionPro. (2022, March 21). *Quantitative Research: Definition, Methods, Types and Examples*. Retrieved March 21, 2022, from https://www.questionpro.com/blog/quantitative-research/

Reddy, L. S., & Kulshrestha, P. (2019). Performing the KMO and Bartlett's Test for Factors Estimating the Warehouse Efficiency, Inventory and Customer Contentment for E-retail Supply Chain. *International Journal for Research in Engineering Application & Management*, *05*, 2454–9150. doi:10.35291/2454-9150.2019.0531

Reid, R. D., & Sanders, N. R. (2019). *Operations Management: An Integrated Approach* (7th ed.). Wiley. https://books.google.pt/books?hl=pt-PT&lr=&id=c8-8DwAAQBAJ&oi=fnd&pg=PA1&dq=Operations+Management:+An+Integrated+Approach,+7th+Edition+pdf&ots=5p2VjwGoFx&sig=Vb9CW33zYft9tcmxR9dDwb5bbrE&redir_esc=y#v=onepage&q&f=false

Roldós, I. (2021, January 9). *What Is Data Analysis? Examples & Why It Matters*. MonkeyLearn. https://monkeylearn.com/blog/data-analysis-examples/#inferential

Rosie. (2019, September 25). *9 Benefits of Talent Analytics and How to Use It*. Harver. https://harver.com/blog/talent-analytics/

Santos. (2017). *Cálculo Amostral*. https://praticaclinica.com.br/anexos/ccolaborativa-calculo-amostral/ccolaborativa-calculo-amostral.php

Schermerhorn, J. R., Jr., & Bachrach, D. G. (2020). *Exploring Management*. Wiley. https://books.google.pt/books?hl=pt-PT&lr=&id=zw8IEAAAQBAJ&oi=fnd&pg=PA1&dq=what+are+the+functions+of+management&ots=ExEhCGtMY2&sig=zA6E3NslNLLbfgDQbQaqvBNDcIs&redir_esc=y#v=onepage&q&f=false

Sharma, R. (2020, December 1). *4 Types of Data: Nominal, Ordinal, Discrete, Continuous*. UpGrad. https://www.upgrad.com/blog/types-of-data/

Shen, S. (2020, February 9). *What is the Data Architecture We Need?* Towards Data Science. https://towardsdatascience.com/what-is-the-data-architecture-we-need-72606e71ba0c

SimpliLearn. (2021a, December 30). *What is Data Science? Prerequisites, Lifecycle and Applications*. SimpliLearn. https://www.simplilearn.com/tutorials/data-science-tutorial/what-is-data-science

SimpliLearn. (2021b, December 16). *What Is Data: Types of Data, and How to Analyze Data* [Updated]. Simplilearn. https://www.simplilearn.com/what-is-data-article

Sindhu, V., Anitha, G., & Geetha, R. (2021). Industry 4.0-A Breakthrough in Artificial Intelligence the Internet of Things and Big Data towards the next digital revolution for high business outcome and delivery. *Journal of Physics: Conference Series*, *1937*(1), 1–7. doi:10.1088/1742-6596/1937/1/012030

Six Sigma Daily. (2020a, January 9). *What is Six Sigma? Definition, Methodology and Tools*. Six Sigma Daily. https://www.sixsigmadaily.com/what-is-six-sigma/

Six Sigma Daily. (2020b, May 7). *Why Was Six Sigma Created and Why Is It Important?* Six Sigma Daily. https://www.sixsigmadaily.com/why-was-six-sigma-created/

Slyther, K. (2019, February 25). *What Is Information Technology? A Beginner's Guide to the World of IT*. Rasmussen University. https://www.rasmussen.edu/degrees/technology/blog/what-is-information-technology/

Stokdyk, D. (2019, October 29). *What is Information Technology (IT)?* Southern New Hampshire University. https://www.snhu.edu/about-us/newsroom/stem/what-is-information-technology

Strohmeier, S., & Piazza, F. (2014). Detecting Deceptive Opinions in Online Restaurant Reviews. *ACM Transactions on Intelligent Systems and Technology*, *5*(4), 1–30.

Techopedia. (2020, April 30). *What is a Programmer?* Techopedia. https://www.techopedia.com/definition/4813/programmer

Techopedia. (2021, June 1). *What is Data Science?* Techopedia. https://www.techopedia.com/definition/30202/data-science

Thompson, S. K. (2012). *Sampling. Wiley Series in Probability and Statistics* (3rd ed.). John Wiley & Sons, Inc.

University, B. (2018). *What is Data Science?* Berkeley School of Information. https://ischoolonline.berkeley.edu/data-science/what-is-data-science/

Van Vulpen, E. (2022, January 22). *Recruitment Analytics: The 3 Levels to Optimize Recruiting*. AIHR. Retrieved janeiro 22, 2022, from https://www.aihr.com/blog/recruitment-analytics/

Vaughan, J. (2019, July). *What is Data?* TechTarget. https://www.techtarget.com/searchdatamanagement/definition/data

Vennam, S. (2020, August 18). *What is Cloud Computing?* IBM. https://www.ibm.com/cloud/learn/cloud-computing

von Rosing, M., von Scheel, H., & Scheer, A.-W. (2014). *The complete business process handbook: body of knowledge from process modeling to bpm* (Vol. I). Elsevier.

White, S. K. (2018, June 12). *What is Six Sigma? Streamlining quality management.* CIO. https://www.cio.com/article/227977/six-sigma-quality-management-methodology.html

Wu, J. X. S., & Liu, S. (2019). Information Security Research Challenges in the Process of Digitizing Business: A Review Based on the Information Security Model of IBM. In F. García Márquez & B. Lev (Eds.), *Data Science and Digital Business.* Springer. doi:10.1007/978-3-319-95651-0_6

Yoon, S. W., Han, S., & Chae, C. (2023). People Analytics and Human Resource Development – Research Landscape and Future Needs Based on Bibliometrics and Scoping Review. *Human Resource Development Review*, *0*(0). Advance online publication. doi:10.1177/15344843231209362

Chapter 7
Happiness Management:
How Artificial Intelligence Can Help Managers

Natália Costa
https://orcid.org/0000-0002-7569-6482
ISLA-IPGT, Portugal

Marisol Guadalupe Moreira Costa
ISLA-IPGT, Portugal

ABSTRACT

Uncertainty, innovation, competitive advantage, globalization, and digitalization are some of the changes that have forced managers to rethink the way they manage their organizations. So, management models are beginning to emerge, focusing on human capital (employees). Happiness management arose as a new form of organizational culture, and the main objective is to ensure the well-being of employees by promoting positive experiences/emotions in the workplace. Artificial intelligence combines the ability to learn similarly to humans, with an even more extensive capacity than humans. Although its effects on employees still divide opinions, what is certain is that innovation in this area is increasingly common in organizations in a broad field.

INTRODUCTION

Globalization, digitalization, and COVID-19, among other changes, are affecting the way that managers look at their organizations and how to manage them (Costa, Neto, et al., 2022; Costa, Oliveira, et al., 2022; Costa & Oliveira, 2022a, 2022b; Meister, 2023).

DOI: 10.4018/979-8-3693-0712-0.ch007

This chapter proposes to develop a conceptual study about the happiness management culture and how can artificial intelligence (AI) help managers in the promotion of happiness at work. First, the concepts will be explored separately to provide a broad overview of the topic under analysis. Subsequently, a section on the interconnection of the two themes will be developed. This last section is developed using ChatGPT, as there is still little analysis of this topic. The main objective is to associate this new perspective of management with de AI, presenting some of the possibilities suggested by AI and how they can be implemented in organizations.

COVID-19 was the biggest crisis in a recent period bring the necessity to rethink the ways how things are done and how can organizations survive this (Castro-Martinez et al., 2022; Castro-Martínez, Díaz-Morilla, & Pérez-Ordoñez, 2022; Castro-Martínez, Díaz-Morilla, & Torres-Martín, 2022; Castro-Martínez & Díaz-Morilla, 2021; Qin & Men, 2022).

For AI, the pandemic has been a positive factor that has helped the development of this area in organizations (Rožman et al., 2022). The lockdown measures introduced by most governments around the world forced organizations to adapt. These adaptations included remote working as a way of minimizing productivity losses, but also to avoid contamination and the propagation of the virus. It should be understood that the concept of remote working is associated with "organizational personnel performing their job responsibilities outside of traditional office environments" (Aleem et al., 2023, p. 1). It can therefore be said that "the development and diffusion of digital technologies (especially those supporting communication, collaboration, and social networking), along with the pervasive dissemination of powerful and easy-to-use mobile devices, are supporting businesses and employers in their quest to develop a smart working system." (Aleem et al., 2023, p. 1).

Happiness management it's a new management model that appears. This new perspective of the management model emerged in an era where innovation, competition, but also uncertainty, and employee insecurity are improving feelings like anxiety, disorientation, and mental stress (Castro-Martinez et al., 2022; Qin & Men, 2022). If people as a new way to face life, considering "workers prioritize both their work and their personal lives equally" (Kanmani & Fonceca, 2023, p. 361), managers need to face the organizational management considering this ideas. Not least because the concept of happiness cannot be dissociated from personal and professional life (Elpo & Lemos, 2022; Sarkar et al., 2023). This field of investigation it's more recent, but the question that arises is if the new tools with AI can help managers in the promotion of happiness and the process of decision-making.

In the chapter, to meet the objectives that were initially defined will be explored the concept of AI and the possibilities of applications of this. This becomes particularly important at a time when it is estimated that "by 2030 one in two jobs could be significantly transformed by automation, given the tasks involved" (Loureiro et al.,

2023, p. 234). In addition, it is believed that AI has the potential to transform not only the workplace but also how tasks are carried out and even the economy (Mila & Elliott, 2023).

Like all the changes, the introduction of AI in organizations will bring uncertainties and fear because people start to think that AI could replace human labor, but the key is the complementarity between AI and labor, not substitution of labor to the detriment of AI (Loureiro et al., 2023). So, introducing the interaction between AI and employees has some residual problems, but also benefits. The total potential of AI isn't already known, but it's now recognized that "it can also help in developing realistic scenarios about how jobs and skill demand will be redefined in the next decades and how education systems should evolve in response" (Mila & Elliott, 2023, p. 16).

The application of AI can affect employees' happiness and well-being. On the one hand, they can experience high levels of stress (associated with change, but also with everything it entails), feelings of exhaustion, uncertainty, job insecurity, increased levels of anxiety, fear of being replaced and becoming unemployed, fear of change, fear of not being able to acquire the new skills required to work with AI (Liu et al., 2023; Loureiro et al., 2023; Rožman et al., 2022). On the other hand, a huge part of the feelings that the introduction of AI can cause can also be mitigated. This will bring an added challenge for organizations, especially in the way the implementation of "artificial intelligence is changing the enterprise's culture and leadership, acquiring new knowledge and skills, and changing business processes" (Rožman et al., 2022, p. 3). AI "can complement and augment workers' capabilities and, with that, raise productivity, create new jobs, and boost new demand for labor" (Mila & Elliott, 2023, p. 17). So, while the introduction of AI tools can increase negative feelings (such as stress and anxiety), they can also be "balanced with support, they can generate happiness (Nazareno and Schiff, 2021), creating a sense of employee engagement" (Rožman et al., 2022, p. 234). Konovalova et al. (2022) mentioned that AI could be used "in the context of increasing operational efficiency, income and productivity, obsolescence of jobs and replacement of employees, and the need to master new skills in connection with changing professional requirements" (Konovalova et al., 2022, p. 83).

1. HAPPINESS AT WORK

Happiness emerges after a long period of research focused on a negative way (Elpo & Lemos, 2022; Loureiro et al., 2023; Usai et al., 2020). Now, the perspective of the investigation changes, and the search for the factor of promoting happiness, well-being, and positive emotions is more common.

Happiness it's not a new concept but conceptualizing it it's not an easy task. The concept is very variable because depends on individual perception. Because of this, their conceptualization and measurement it's the new focus of recent studies (Castro-Martínez, Díaz-Morilla, & Pérez-Ordoñez, 2022; Galván Vela et al., 2022; Salas-Vallina et al., 2018). In section 1.2. of the present chapter, the authors will explore the main concept and measures used to validate happiness at work.

Nowadays, managers face daily challenges. These challenges require thinking outside the box. For these, managers need to understand that now, more than ever, the necessity of innovation, the competitive advantages, the strong competition, and the environment in the workplace are the new goals for managers. With this scenario, new management models need to be considered (Costa, Oliveira, et al., 2022; Elpo & Lemos, 2022; Meister, 2023). The new management model appears in an attempt to improve the levels of employee motivation (Salas-Vallina et al., 2018) because concern with employees started to emerge. But also, questions like absenteeism, employee burnout, turnover, and the complex task of retaining talent, are waiting for different solutions to be resolved (Elpo & Lemos, 2022; Meister, 2023; Qin & Men, 2022; Salas-Vallina et al., 2018). New management models begin to appear based on a strategy more focused on the internal environment, where people are essential resources for organizational success (Castro-Martínez & Díaz-Morilla, 2020; Elpo & Lemos, 2022; Meister, 2023; Salas-Vallina et al., 2018). These perspectives come from internal marketing and with these, strategies to promote happiness, well-being, and quality of life in the work context of the internal customer (employee) are the focus of these models. The focus on these strategies has begun to capture the attention of managers, since they are associated with the capacity to increase work performance, reduce turnover intentions, and improve levels of happiness and well-being, among others (Qin & Men, 2022).

Happiness as a new management model arises intending to transform the employee experience (Castro-Martínez & Díaz-Morilla, 2020). Happiness management it's capable of improving the employee's performance (Loureiro et al., 2023). Therefore, focusing on the internal customer results in higher levels of customer satisfaction (internal and external). Although a lot still needs to be done for the promotion of happiness in organizations to be seen as a key task for organizational success, we can understand why it is so important (Castro-Martínez, Díaz-Morilla, & Torres-Martín, 2022). So, if we spend an increasing amount of time at work and happiness is one of society's most aspirational desires, we now understand the importance of investigating this construct in this specific context (Elpo & Lemos, 2022). The increase in this topic has led to the creation of some new roles, such as the position of Chief of Happiness who is "responsible for happiness or responsible for quality of life at work" (Castro-Martínez & Díaz-Morilla, 2020, p. 4).

The promotion of happiness in the workplace is important to the "development of highly motivated, dedicated and engaged employees" (Lalić et al., 2020, p. 76), and this brings implications for organizations, the employees, and the work environment. Happiness studies can explore this area from different perspectives, ideologies, or frameworks. Happiness is now considered to be associated with areas like economy, psychology, human resources, marketing, and others (Castro-Martínez & Díaz-Morilla, 2020).

1.1. Definition of the Concept

Defining happiness is an arduous task for which researchers have not yet reached a consensus. The concept of happiness at work depends on understanding, at an early stage, what happiness is and how it can be conceptualized.

Researchers dedicated to the study of happiness, to contribute to the development of this area, have provided different perspectives on how happiness can be understood. In this sense, the most common in these investigations is that the authors associate happiness with other more widely studied constructs. These other constructs are well-being, psychological well-being, the classical perspectives (hedonic and eudaimonic), or considering the concept of happiness from the perspective of positive psychology (Bencsik & Chuluun, 2021; Costa, Oliveira, et al., 2022; Galván Vela et al., 2022; Pathak & Muralidharan, 2021; Usai et al., 2020).

The common idea in the definition of happiness is that it's a subjective construct, as it depends on each individual's overall assessment of their life (Kanmani & Fonceca, 2023; Lalić et al., 2020; Qaiser et al., 2018; Sarkar et al., 2023). Happiness, according to Sarkar et al. (2023), "(...) can be characterized in terms of cognitive judgments of needs and wants and on the other hand in terms of an emotional state of mind." (p. 6901).

In terms of happiness at work, the literature provides indications that this is a multifaceted construct and, therefore, the promotion of happiness in the workplace must consider various factors, such as job satisfaction and commitment to the organization, for example (Castro-Martínez & Díaz-Morilla, 2021). Given that this is a topic that has captured the interest of researchers and organizations (Loureiro et al., 2023), various contributions are beginning to emerge to help develop the study of this area, both in terms of conceptualization and measurement. According to Loureiro et al. (2023), happiness at work is "the experience of energized employees, enthusiastic about their work, finding meaning and purpose in their work, having good relationships at their workplace, and feeling committed to their work" (p.237). Qaiser et al. (2018), define happiness at work as the process of "making the optimum use of resources, overcome the challenges, actively appreciating the highs and preserving the lows that will maximize your performance and achieve the potential" (p. 1671).

Sarkar et al. (2023), on the other hand, state that happiness at work is related to the "pleasant individual decisions (positive attitudes) or pleasant practices (moods, positive feelings, emotions, flow states) at work." (p.6901).

Loureiro et al. (2023) also highlight some of the reasons that have driven the study of this area. In this sense, the authors mention that happy employees produce benefits for the organization (from a holistic perspective), but also influence interpersonal relationships and their own physical and psychological well-being (Castro-Martínez, Díaz-Morilla, & Torres-Martín, 2022; Kanmani & Fonceca, 2023). Thus, it's said that happy employees have a better ability to deal with stressful situations, perform better, and have higher levels of job satisfaction. They are also "more prosocial and cooperative, have greater self-control, better self-regulation, and coping abilities, more satisfying relationships, and lower levels of burnout" (Loureiro et al., 2023, p. 237).

1.2. How to Measure the Impact of Happiness at Work

The implementation of happiness at work culture promotion brings several advantages for the individual, their peers, and their organizations. However, for these, it's necessary some changes and understand how happiness at work can be conceptualized and measured. With this information consolidated it's possible to adjust the activities and the strategies to promote this feeling at the workplace.

As described above, happiness at work it's a complex concept to define. In these ways, several authors compare these to other constructs like well-being, psychological/subjective well-being, the classical perspectives (hedonic and eudaimonic), or considering the concept through the positive psychology perspective (Bencsik & Chuluun, 2021; Costa, Oliveira, et al., 2022; Galván Vela et al., 2022; Pathak & Muralidharan, 2021; Usai et al., 2020). Focus on these, the present section will explore some contributions to conceptualizing these concepts. With the help of the work of the authors Costa, Oliveira, et al. (2022), some scales will be suggested from each of these concepts.

Well-being, according to Wright & Huang (2012), is "considered as positive affect, negative affect, mental health, emotional exhaustion, life satisfaction, domain satisfaction, dispositional affect, and subjective, psychological, and emotional well-being" (p.1188). So, according to these authors, well-being it´s a combination of multiple other constructs. Its definition it's complex, also because this construct is subjective but also multifaceted (García et al., 2022; Meister, 2023). For others, well-being "is a holistic construct encompassing physical, spiritual, emotional, and mental health" (p.336). Considering this, well-being is a positive state on all the levels that encompass everyone's life. The mains scales mentioned to measure well-being as the affective well-being with work by Sevastos (1996) and Watson and Clark (1992).

Psychological or subjective well-being is "related to how people experience the quality of their lives (Diener, 1984) and is concerned with how and why people experience their lives in positive ways" (p.159), according to García et al. (2022). So, this is a construct that depends on everyone's perception and ability to judge the situations they experience throughout their lives. One of the most common scales used for the effect is the Index of psychological well-being.

The hedonic perspective "(...) refers to positive feelings, moods, emotions, and overall life satisfaction." (p.6)" according to Qin & Men (2022). This classic perspective is more related to the search for experiences that produce pleasure and, on the other hand, mechanisms that allow us to escape from emotions that cause suffering or like Sender et al. (2021) say "where happiness is a result of an individual's degree of experience of pleasure versus pain (…)" (p.3). This perspective is also associated with subjective well-being, so the scales used could be the same as mentioned above. Eudaimonic "means having purposeful life experiences that provide directions and values to people's behavior" (Qin & Men, 2022, p. 6). In other words, the individual realizes that their existence/work has meaning. So, it's like thinking like Sender et al. (2021) say that the eudaimonic perspective is "defined as living a complete and virtuous life, using human potential (…)" (p.3). Considering all the mentioned factors, the selection of the scale to this perspective depends on the objective of the investigations. Scales to measure job satisfaction (like the Job Satisfaction Scale), life satisfaction (like the Life Satisfaction Scale, for example), or happiness at work (like the Work-related affective well-being Scale), are the most appropriate.

Positive psychology it's a ramification of psychology that introduces a new way of considering the variables under study. This area brings the idea that investigators could also think of positive variables to study, and not only focus on diseases and prejudicial consequences of work. In this sense, this area considered happiness through the perception of the number of positive experiences/affect lived (García et al., 2022; Graziotin et al., 2017). The scales used in this perspective were related to the effects. The most known scale is the PANAS - Scale of positive and negative effects) and SPANE – Scale of positive and negative experiences, according to the investigation of (Costa, Oliveira, et al., 2022).

2. ARTIFICIAL INTELLIGENCE

As mentioned by Loureiro et al. (2023), "AI is here to stay, inevitably, and a reality for the future" (p. 251), and it's the new challenge for the world (Rožman et al., 2022).

One of the biggest drivers of AI's growth has been the need for digitalization. Innovations at this level, which have allowed the company to have a presence on various digital platforms, as well as to have most of its processes online, have led to an increase in the desire to include AI (Rožman et al., 2022). In addition, the versatility of AI being able to be "incorporated into devices, such as computers or mobiles, or have a form of a more or less anthropomorphized robot (Wirtz et al. 2018) to help in several tasks" (Loureiro et al., 2023, p. 233) benefits its adherence in the organizational context, not forgetting the advantages it can bring.

This is a huge challenge for organizations, as the implementation of AI implies that it "will change the way we work and consequently affect the organization of work and processes in the enterprise" (Rožman et al., 2022, p. 2). This implies that managers assume innovation and success as a primary factor in the organizational culture, and this requires preparing employees for this reality, and providing them with training and the necessary resources so that they feel able to respond to new market needs (Rožman et al., 2022). In addition, training is a way of preparing them for the new reality where the aim is to "improve work by reducing the number of repetitive tasks through automation" (Rožman et al., 2022, p. 6).

In this way, the integration of AI tools in management areas starts to appear. However, the introduction of AI is more common in the service area. But areas like human resources management, marketing, finance, healthcare, logistics, and even the public sector (Arora et al., 2021; Rožman et al., 2022), start to appear associated with the implementation of AI technology (figure 1). However, Liu et al. (2023) believe that AI can be applied in all areas.

Figure 1. Applicability of AI and main areas of implementation

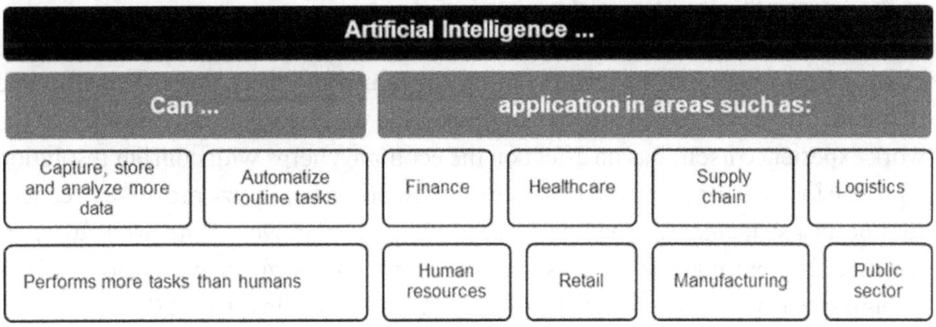

Based on the assumption that "artificial intelligence works similarly to humans and learns similarly to humans" (Rožman et al., 2022, p. 2), it is predictable that there should be some similarities between the tasks performed by both. Figure 1 summarizes what AI can do, and the main areas that apply the AI tools.

However, AI has a higher learning and storage capacity than humans (Rožman et al., 2022), so it will be able to do more tasks, complete human tasks, or even perform "tasks beyond what humans can do" (Loureiro et al., 2023, p. 234). The use of AI can range from performance control, continuous feedback, support systems, motivation, collecting personal information, and managing tasks, among many others (Rožman et al., 2022). Briefly, AI "offers a similar transformational potential to increase and possibly relocate human tasks in social, industrial, and intellectual fields" (Rožman et al., 2022, p. 2).

It is expected that organizations will begin to include "augmented reality and games, big data analytics, simulations, algorithms, social media, machine learning in day-to-day lives which helps to support the decision-making processes" (Arora et al., 2021, p. 288). The inclusion of AI in organizations will allow employees to save time, thus enabling the development of a more innovative, creative climate, and also concentrate on strategic aspects (Arora et al., 2021; Rožman et al., 2022).

One of the most explored specific cases in the literature is probably the use of AI in Human Resources Management. In this sense, some authors mention that AI tools have capabilities in terms of talent management processes (attraction and retention), analysis of HRM indicators, providing virtual assistance, developing appropriate solutions for decision-making in the face of problems experienced in organizations, stimulating employee engagement, as well as employee performance and motivation, optimizing recruitment and selection processes (Arora et al., 2021; Konovalova et al., 2022; Liu et al., 2023). In terms of marketing, Rožman et al. (2022) point out that AI can help to "knowing the customers, their preferences, their behavior, knowledge of the business environment and its changes, and knowledge of the enterprise, strategies and desires" (p. 2).

To conclude this topic and before addressing the concept of AI, it is necessary to start by listing some of the advantages of implementing these tools. This said, the literature offers evidence that AI favors employee well-being; loyalty levels; and the work experience itself; has an effect on the economy; helps with conflict resolution and decision-making; makes it possible to automate and optimize processes; reduces routine tasks; manages schedules/ vacations; list employees who want to leave the organization; manage careers, compensation and performance, among others (Konovalova et al., 2022; Rožman et al., 2022). As Loureiro et al. (2023) point out, "in the end, some tasks will be performed by humans, AI will make others, and both will work as a team, leading to collaborative intelligence" (p.234).

2.1. Definition of the Concept

To understand the concept of AI, it is necessary to take a deep dive to understand why it was given this name and then understand what it means. In this sense, the name AI comes from the association with human intelligence (Mila & Elliott, 2023). In other words, we can say that these machines have some abilities/characteristics associated with humans (Huang & Rust, 2018; Loureiro et al., 2023; Mila & Elliott, 2023). The combination of these human characteristics with the technology capacity is being applied in various areas as a way of improving productivity, and efficiency, and to gain advantage in competitive terms that contribute to the country's economy, like in HRM (Arora et al., 2021).

John McCarthy (1059) is considered the father of AI, stating that it is characterized by a machine with intelligence that uses automation theory, information processing, and cybernetics (Arora et al., 2021). In addition, this AI is composed of "advanced algorithms, high-speed computation large volumes of quality data, which differentiates it from ordinary software" (Arora et al., 2021, p. 288). Compared with humans, AI "recognizes patterns, inclinations, and intentions by combining deep learning and big data" (Rožman et al., 2022, p. 236). AI only has fewer limitations than humans in terms of storage capacity and learning from multiple sources simultaneously.

With the rise of AI, terms such as Machine Learning and Big Data also emerged. The first concept is associated with one of the activities carried out by AI, namely the ability to learn. Big Data "can be referred to as huge, fast flowing, and high-variety data which acts as the fuel essential for advanced predictive analytics and machine learning" (Arora et al., 2021, p. 289).

Loureiro et al. (2023), argue that understanding AI involves dividing it into four types of intelligence (mechanical, analytical, intuitive, and empathetic). The first type of intelligence is usually used for standard tasks or actions. The other types already have the capacity for customization in their implementation. For tasks involving data collection, analytical intelligence is the best choice. When the aim is to provide solutions to a particular problem, intuitive intelligence is required. Finally, when the objective involves communication, based on experience and components related to emotion, empathetic intelligence should be prioritized.

2.2. How to Measure the Impact of Using AI

As described above, the implementation of AI tools has several advantages for organizations, employees, and society itself. However, to gain a better understanding of the level of influence these tools have on these variables, it is necessary to start looking at ways of measuring the impact of their implementation. This could provide relevant input for educational institutions, but also for the government itself (Mila & Elliott, 2023).

This need to evaluate the introduction of AI tools arises, on the one hand, to analyze the impact they have had on the economy/society, but also to begin to establish patterns and scenarios of the changes these tools could cause in society, in ways of working and all the variables that are in some way related to them, to predict what could happen in the future at these levels (Mila & Elliott, 2023).

Five methodological approaches will be presented in table 1 to measure the impact of implementing AI tools. The approaches presented are based on the study by Mila & Elliott (2023). The following methodologies will therefore be explored: "a task-based approach; an approach that draws on information from patents; indicators based on AI-related job postings; measures relying on benchmarks; and a skills-based approach" (Mila & Elliott, 2023, p. 17).

Table 1. AI suggestions for conceptualizing key terms

Key Terms	Suggested Definitions
1. Task-based approach	This methodology is based on analyzing the number of tasks that can be automated. To do this is based on their knowledge of the power of AI tools or that of experts in the field.
2. Approach that draws on information from patents	It is an evaluation methodology that involves analyzing the patent description of other AI tools and aims to identify what kind of tasks these tools can perform in the workplace.
3. Indicators based on AI-related job postings	This approach assumes that companies that use AI tools need employees who master these skills. Therefore, one of the ways to measure this is to analyze the flow of demand for employees with these skills.
4. Measures relying on benchmarks	Benchmarking is a programmed way of evaluating a system's performance. The use of this technique aims to analyze different systems and contrast them to later compare the system with human performance.
5. Skills-based approach	In summary, it establishes a comparison between the capabilities required by AI and humans to perform a determined task.

The implementation of AI-based systems represents an investment for organizations, but also in the training/capture of human capital prepared for this new reality (Babina et al., 2020). In this sense, it is necessary to measure the extent to which the integration of AI is an advantage for organizations, but also "Understanding how AI and robotics impact the workplace is fundamental for understanding the broader impact of these technologies on the economy and society" (Mila & Elliott, 2023, p. 16). The measure of the IA impact also gives information to organizations how it's possible to improve the efficacy, effectiveness, and optimization of their process/tasks/employees (Arora et al., 2021; Babina et al., 2020; Huang & Rust, 2018; Konovalova et al., 2022; Liu et al., 2023; Mila & Elliott, 2023; Rožman et al., 2022).

3. AI AND HAPPINESS MANAGEMENT: WHAT DOES CHATGPT HAVE TO SAY ABOUT THIS?

This topic aims to demonstrate some of the potential that AI can offer to facilitate the work of managers when it comes to managing happiness. To this end, the authors used ChatGPT to see what suggestions it provided for this purpose. The survey was developed using ChatGPT (3.5) and was carried out on 24/09/2023. The question asked was "How can artificial intelligence help managers in happiness promotion?" (the search can be consulted through the link https://chat.openai.com/share/71ce25e1-f190-47d3-ab17-a202be0bb36b).

The answer provided by ChatGPT was positive, in other words, it said that AI can help managers to promote happiness in the workplace. To this end, it suggested twelve possible ways.

Figure 2. AI and the promotion of happiness

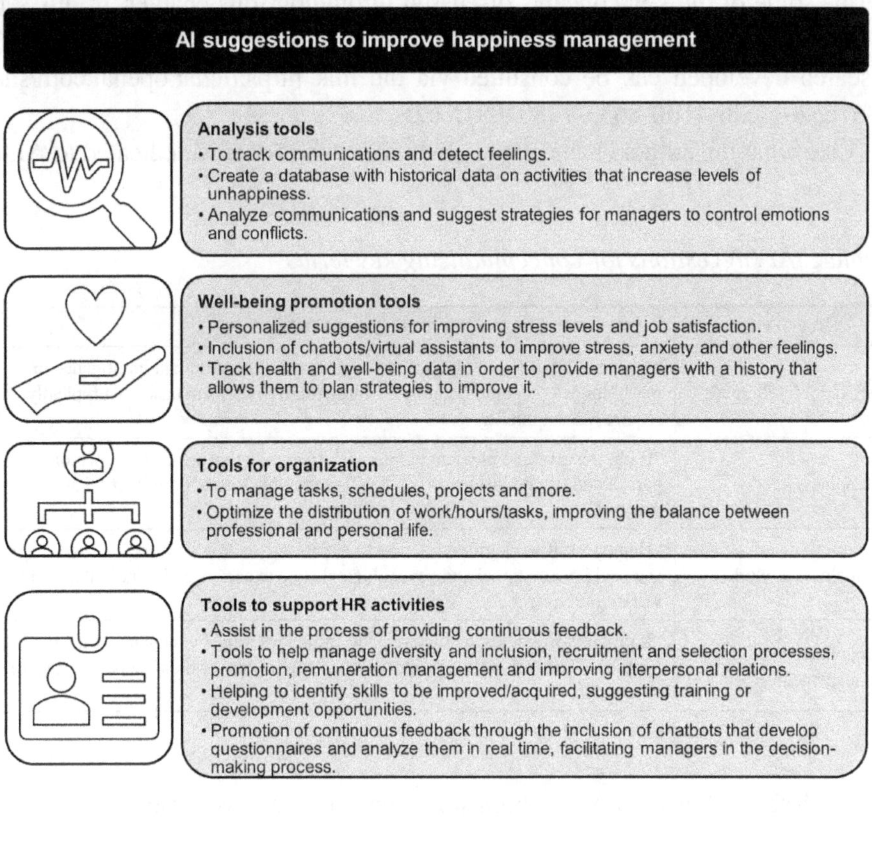

The figure above summarizes the twelve alternatives provided by ChatGPT, which concludes its suggestions with a warning about the use of these tools. It alerts us to ethical issues and to the fact that AI should not be a substitute for the role of manager, but a complement to help them do their job.

Briefly, AI believes that happiness at work can be boosted by using techniques that can detect your emotions, by analyzing communications made by employees and expressions that may show negative feelings. In addition, these tools could also store data that would make it possible to detect, in the long term, which factors are driving negative feelings. At a later stage, AI could be used to develop strategies and provide advice on how to improve well-being and satisfaction at work. Next, it presents a set of solutions that will allow the management of projects/tasks/schedules, among other things, more flexibly and fairly. Finally, it presents some suggestions in terms of tools that can help some of the procedures associated with the HR department, such as performance evaluation, detecting the need for training and development, the recruitment and selection process, and promoting fluid and constant communication (through feedback), among others.

To complement this topic, the authors decided to ask ChatGPT how it would define some of the key concepts discussed throughout this chapter. In this sense, the research carried out on 24/09/2023 made it possible to construct table 2 (the research developed can be consulted via the link https://chat.openai.com/share/a861de20-dcdb-41d6-8633-77804091fec2).

Like what the authors have already mentioned in the topic dedicated to AI, this

Table 2. AI suggestions for conceptualizing key terms

Key Terms	Suggested Definitions
Artificial Intelligence	"Artificial Intelligence (AI) refers to the simulation of human intelligence in machines or computer systems, enabling them to perform tasks that typically require human intelligence."
Happiness	"It is a positive and pleasant emotional experience that varies from person to person and can be influenced by a wide range of factors, both internal and external."
Happiness at work	"Happiness at work, often referred to as job satisfaction or workplace well-being, is a positive emotional and psychological state experienced by individuals in their work environment"
Happiness management	"It involves strategies, techniques, and initiatives aimed at enhancing the overall happiness and satisfaction of individuals, employees, or members of a group or community."

is a multifaceted novelty with a high storage power that has come to revolutionize the most diverse areas. It should be seen as a tool for improving working conditions and as an agent for facilitating these tasks. It can be included in sectors such as "healthcare (diagnosis and drug discovery), finance (fraud detection and algorithmic trading), entertainment (recommendation systems), transportation (self-driving cars), and many others" (OpenAI, 2023).

Happiness is described as a complex, multifaceted construct that fluctuates (meaning it is non-static and non-constant). It predicts the existence of positive emotional states, such as joy, and well-being, among others. In addition, the idea of subjectivity is emphasized, in other words, happiness depends on how each person evaluates their life.

Like happiness, happiness at work refers to the positive feelings experienced in the workplace. It remains a complex, multifaceted, and variable construct for researchers. It is assessed based on personal, organizational, and external factors experienced by individuals. Promoting this is as beneficial for each individual as it is for their peers, but also for organizational success.

As for happiness management, the AI tool mentions that this is still an emerging term, whose work abstracts into promoting the happiness/well-being of employees or organizations (from a holistic perspective). Although it is not considered a formal field, it seeks knowledge from positive psychology, organizational development, and management. This area places special emphasis on the benefits of increasing this state in the organizational context, dedicating itself to proactively developing/powering this state in the contexts in which it operates.

Considering all the information given, it's necessary to understand what factors or variables ChatGPT thinks can promote happiness in the workplace. In this sense, the authors ask "Which variables or factors are capable of promoting happiness at work?" to ChatGPT (consult this research by the link https://chat.openai.com/share/d8ed4a77-3242-4120-b76a-44b94834f9be). In answer to these have been suggested fifteen factors/variables that help in workplace happiness, but we must emphasize that all of this is subjective, meaning that everyone can perceive the relevance of these factors in very different ways. For example, some may value work-life balance more and others the reward system. The variables/factors are divided (table 3), by the authors, into activities that depend on the organization (related to the manager's functions and ways of management), personal perception (that depends on everyone's judgment capacity), and another that combines both perspectives (that means that depends of the ways of management but also the judgment of the of the individual and the proximity of these ways to their values and principles).

Table 3. Factor that improves happiness at the workplace

Organizational Perspective	Personal Perception	A Mix of Organizational and Personal
Positive work environment	Recognition and appreciation	Work-life balance
Skill development and growth	Job security	Meaningful work
Supportive leadership	Autonomy and control	Health and wellness programs
Workplace diversity and inclusion	Fair compensation	Teamwork and social connections
Workplace ethics and values	Workload and stress management	Job design

3.1. Advantages and Disadvantages of Using AI for Happiness Management

According to ChatGPT, the use of AI for happiness management must ensure that it has tools to improve individual and collective well-being, without breaking ethical barriers and data protection.

Figure 3. Advantages vs. disadvantages of AI in happiness management

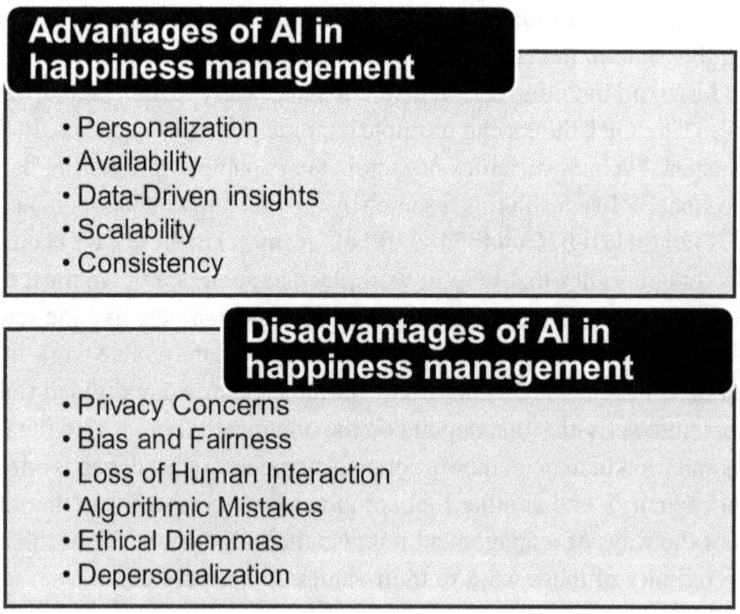

For the development of this topic, the following research was carried out "Advantages and disadvantages of using AI for happiness management", on ChatGPT (3.5), on 5/10/2023 (consult the link https://chat.openai.com/share/b96ab214-0bc9-4e27-bcfe-17a1e98d8a85). The output produced by ChatGPT resulted in a list of five advantages and six disadvantages, which are shown in the figure below.

Personalization, the first advantage mentioned, refers to AI tools being able to filter preferences, behaviors, and other data to offer solutions adapted to the needs. Moreover, these AI tools have the possibility of being available all the time, every day (second advantage mentioned). Then, data-driven insights are a methodology that allows for the collection and analysis of a variety of information, making it possible to highlight possible factors that affect employee happiness. In this way, this information can help in decision-making. The fourth advantage is scalability, which is associated with the ability of these AI tools to cover a huge number of people at the same time, making them cost-effective for organizations. Consistency appears in the last position of the advantages and is related to the fact that these AI tools are free from the effect of emotional influence, meaning that you can offer support without running the risk of having mood alterations after the interaction. Parte superior do formulário

The first huge consequence listed by ChatGPT is the issue of data privacy and confidentiality since AI tools store a lot of personal information. The second disadvantage is associated with the possibility of bias in the processing of the data collected. Bias can interfere in a prejudicial way with the outputs provided. This could result in injustice or lead to discriminatory factors, for example. The third disadvantage is the ideology of exaggerating the use of these tools, in other words, they become the new reality and human interaction begins to be lost. This can lead to an increase in negative feelings, such as loneliness and isolation. AI systems are not infallible and can make mistakes, which may result in recommendations or interventions that are ineffective or even harmful. This is particularly concerning when dealing with mental health issues. In the same line of thought, ethical issues are highlighted as relevant here. AI tools may not have a coherent ability to determine treatment priorities. ChatGPT provides the example that AI may not be able to determine that preserving long-term well-being is more important than promoting a sporadic moment of happiness. The last disadvantage is related to the first advantage identified. While on the one hand, the personalization that these tools can bring to the promotion of happiness can be beneficial, on the other hand, it can lead to the mistake of creating so many specificities that it is no longer suitable for everyone, but only for a specific range of people.

In conclusion, ChatGPT recommends the careful and supervised use of these tools to promote happiness. Not forgetting the need to equally articulate the benefits with the inherent challenges of applying these tools in an organizational context.

CONCLUSION

Digitalization, COVID-19, and other relevant milestones mark the changing trends of classic management models (Costa, Neto, et al., 2022; Costa, Oliveira, et al., 2022; Costa & Oliveira, 2022a, 2022b; Meister, 2023). The objective of the chapter is to develop a conceptual study that associates happiness management with the potential of AI to help managers in the decision-making process and others. In addition, there are presented some suggestions to measure the implementation of a happiness culture and to control the activities done by AI.

Happiness it's a complex and multifaceted construct (Castro-Martínez & Díaz-Morilla, 2021). Its definition is, to this day, one of the huge challenges for researchers in this area. However, happiness could be understood as a subjective construct, that depends on the capacity of judgment and evaluation of everyone's life.

AI is the latest topic that has represented a huge boom in conferences, seminars, articles, and other forms of knowledge dissemination. We are facing a revolutionary new era in the evolution of these tools. AI tools emerged from the combination of human characteristics with technology capacity (Huang & Rust, 2018; Loureiro et al., 2023; Mila & Elliott, 2023).

Happiness management and AI have several advantages, but performance, better competitive advantage, and promoting innovative contexts are essential nowadays. Following this idea emerges the curiosity to understand if AI can help managers in the implementation of a happiness management culture and if these tools are capable of helping managers in other relevant tasks. In this sense, the proposed chapter study suggests developing and presenting theoretical and practical implications. Contributes to the development of happiness management studies and integrate the paper of the AI, as a new reality for the future. Besides this, happiness management has started to be explored by some organizations and the results of this approach have proven to be favorable and differentiating. The association of this new management model with AI it's still very embryonic and pioneering. In this sense, the purpose of this chapter is to provide some inputs as a way of encouraging the study of the themes under analysis.

The study presents some theoretical and practical implications. This study tried to make use of the most recent studies found on these topics to provide a current study on the issues. Also, some measures are suggested for both constructs. At the practical level, both constructs as the power to boost the economy, the market competition, among other variables.

The main limitation is related to the limited information that exists on the subject under analysis. This had repercussions in terms of the research. The authors found some difficulties in finding studies that explored these themes simultaneously, so it became impossible to establish a rigid research protocol, as was intended. In addition, it was not possible to provide more concrete information on what techniques could be used with AI to promote happiness at work.

For future works, the authors, suggest that the studies may analyze specific cases to offer study cases for investigators interested in this area. The second suggestion for future investigation is to create studies that compare the behavior between groups, considering some personal characteristics, such as age. The third place, the association between happiness promotion and AI tools help are lower explorations. In this sense, it will be interesting to develop some studies that investigate the relationship between these two areas. In addition to the suggestions referred to before it will be interesting to develop some qualitative studies to perceive if AI could be a tool to help in happiness promotions. If the answer to this question is positive, it's necessary to know their efficacy and the reason for these results. To conclude, the authors, think that future researchers should conduct more longitudinal studies to verify if the perceptions register changed with time.

REFERENCES

Aleem, M., Sufyan, M., Ameer, I., & Mustak, M. (2023). Remote work and the COVID-19 pandemic: An artificial intelligence-based topic modeling and a future agenda. *Journal of Business Research, 154*(September), 1–16. doi:10.1016/j.jbusres.2022.113303

Arora, M., Prakash, A., Mittal, A., & Singh, S. (2021). HR Analytics and Artificial Intelligence-Transforming Human Resource Management. *2021 International Conference on Decision Aid Sciences and Application, DASA 2021*, 288–293. 10.1109/DASA53625.2021.9682325

Babina, T., Fedyk, A., He, A. X., & Hodson, J. (2020). Artificial Intelligence, Firm Growth, and Industry Concentration. *SSRN*. Advance online publication. doi:10.2139/ssrn.3651052

Bencsik, P., & Chuluun, T. (2021). Comparative well-being of the self-employed and paid employees in the USA. *Small Business Economics, 56*(1), 355–384. doi:10.1007/s11187-019-00221-1

Castro-Martínez, A., & Díaz-Morilla, P. (2020). Comunicación interna y gestión de bienestar y felicidad en la empresa española. *El Profesional de la Información, 29*(3), 1–13. doi:10.3145/epi.2020.may.24

Castro-Martínez, A., & Díaz-Morilla, P. (2021). Internal communication as a strategic area for innovation through change management and organizational happiness. *Obra Digital*, *20*, 131–148. doi:10.25029/od.2021.293.20

Castro-Martínez, A., Díaz-Morilla, P., & Pérez-Ordoñez, C. (2022). Nuevas estrategias de gestión corporativa: La cultura visual como elemento de la comunicación interna y la felicidad laboral. *Methaodos Revista de Ciencias Sociales*, *10*(2), 379–392. doi:10.17502/mrcs.v10i2.605

Castro-Martinez, A., Diaz-Morilla, P., & Torres-Martin, J.-L. (2022). Comunicación interna, bienestar y felicidad organizacional en instituciones hospitalarias españolas durante la crisis de la COVID-19. *Revista Internacional de Relaciones Públicas*, *12*(23), 143–162. doi:10.5783/RIRP-23-2022-08-143-162

Castro-Martínez, A., Díaz-Morilla, P., & Torres-Martín, J. L. (2022). El papel de la comunicación interna en la gestión del teletrabajo durante la crisis de la COVID-19. *Revista de Comunicación de La SEECI*, *55*, 29–51. doi:10.15198/seeci.2022.55.e768

Costa, N., Neto, J. S., Oliveira, C., & Martins, E. (2022). Student's Entrepreneurial Intention in Higher Education at ISLA – Instituto Politécnico de Gestão e Tecnologia. *Procedia Computer Science*, *204*(September), 825–835. doi:10.1016/j.procs.2022.08.100

Costa, N., & Oliveira, C. (2022a). The Psychological Contract of Higher Education Teachers in Portugal - Confirmatory Factor Analysis. *Procedia Computer Science*, *204*, 952–960. doi:10.1016/j.procs.2022.08.116

Costa, N., & Oliveira, C. M. (2022b). The Relationship Between Life Satisfaction, Engagement, and Burnout - Application to Higher Education Teachers in Portugal. In *Lecture Notes in Networks and Systems* (Vol. 315, pp. 221–232). doi:10.1007/978-3-030-85799-8_19

Costa, N., Oliveira, C. M., & Ferreira, P. (2022). How to Measure the Happy-Productive Worker Thesis. In *People Management - Highlighting Futures* (pp. 1–14). doi:10.5772/intechopen.107429

Elpo, P. S., & Lemos, D. D. C. (2022). Felicidade no Trabalho: Conceitos, Elementos Antecessores e Temas Transversais. *Perspectivas Contemporâneas*, *17*(12), 1–19. doi:10.54372/pc.2022.v17.3253

Galván Vela, E., Mercader, V., Arango Herrera, E., & Ruíz Corrales, M. (2022). Empowerment and support of senior management in promoting happiness at work. *Corporate Governance (Bingley)*, *22*(3), 536–545. doi:10.1108/CG-05-2021-0200

García, E. A. H., Galia, F., & Velez-Ocampo, J. (2022). Understanding the impact of well-being on entrepreneurship in the context of emerging economies. *Journal of Entrepreneurship in Emerging Economies*, *14*(1), 158–182. doi:10.1108/JEEE-08-2020-0314

Graziotin, D., Fagerholm, F., Wang, X., & Abrahamsson, P. (2017). Unhappy Developers: Bad for Themselves, Bad for Process, and Bad for Software Product. *2017 IEEE/ACM 39th International Conference on Software Engineering Companion (ICSE-C)*, 362–364. 10.1109/ICSE-C.2017.104

Huang, M.-H., & Rust, R. T. (2018). Artificial Intelligence in Service. *Journal of Service Research*, *21*(2), 155–172. doi:10.1177/1094670517752459

Kanmani, O. J., & Fonceca, C. M. (2023). Employee happiness index and its impact on employee performance. *International Journal of Multidisciplinary Research and Growth Evaluation*, *4*(2), 360–364.

Konovalova, V., Mitrofanova, E., Mitrofanova, A., & Gevorgyan, R. (2022). The impact of Artificial Intelligence on Human Resources Management strategy: Opportunities for the humasation and risks. *Wisdom*, *1*(2), 88–96. doi:10.24234/wisdom.v2i1.763

Lalić, D., Milić, B., & Stanković, J. (2020). Internal Communication and Employee Engagement as the Key Prerequisites of Happiness. In A. T. Verčič, R. Tench, & S. Einwiller (Eds.), *Joy (Advances in Public Relations and Communication Management)* (Vol. 5, pp. 75–91). Emerald Publishing Limited. doi:10.1108/S2398-391420200000005007

Liu, N.-C., Wang, Y.-C., & Lin, Y.-T. (2023). Employees' Adaptation to Technology Uncertainty in the Digital Era: An Exploration Through the Lens of Job Demands–Resources Theory. *IEEE Transactions on Engineering Management*, 1–12. doi:10.1109/TEM.2023.3264293

Loureiro, S. M. C., Bilro, R. G., & Neto, D. (2023). Working with AI: Can stress bring happiness? *Service Business*, *17*(1), 233–255. doi:10.1007/s11628-022-00514-8

Meister, J. (2023). The Future of Work is Employee Well-Being. *OPJU Business Review, 2*(1), 79–88. https://www.opju.ac.in/opjubr/documents/volume2/7.pdf

Mila, S., & Elliott, S. (2023). Measuring the impact of Artificial intelligence and Robotics on the workplace. In *New Digital Work* (pp. 16–30). Springer International Publishing. doi:10.1007/978-3-031-26490-0

Open, A. I. (2023). *How IA conceptualize* ... ChatGPT. https://chat.openai.com/share/a861de20-dcdb-41d6-8633-77804091fec2

Pathak, S., & Muralidharan, E. (2021). Consequences of cross-cultural differences in perceived well-being for entrepreneurship. *Journal of Business Research, 122*(March), 582–596. doi:10.1016/j.jbusres.2020.09.034

Qaiser, S., Abid, G., Arya, B., & Farooqi, S. (2018). Nourishing the bliss: Antecedents and mechanism of happiness at work. *Total Quality Management & Business Excellence*, *31*(15–16), 1669–1683. doi:10.1080/14783363.2018.1493919

Qin, Y. S., & Men, L. R. (2022). Exploring the Impact of Internal Communication on Employee Psychological Well-Being During the COVID-19 Pandemic: The Mediating Role of Employee Organizational Trust. *International Journal of Business Communication*, *00*(0), 1–23. doi:10.1177/23294884221081838

Rožman, M., Oreški, D., & Tominc, P. (2022). Integrating artificial intelligence into a talent management model to increase the work engagement and performance of enterprises. *Frontiers in Psychology*, *13*, 1–16. doi:10.3389/fpsyg.2022.1014434 PMID:36506984

Salas-Vallina, A., Alegre, J., & Fernández Guerrero, R. (2018). Happiness at work in knowledge-intensive contexts: Opening the research agenda. *European Research on Management and Business Economics*, *24*(3), 149–159. doi:10.1016/j.iedeen.2018.05.003

Sarkar, S., Bhubaneswar, P., & Kalita, M. (2023). Association between General Happiness of Employees and Their Performance at Workplace: A Study at a Navaratna Company Background of the Study. *European Journal of Military Studies, 13*(2), 6899–6913. https://www.opju.ac.in/opjubr/documents/volume2/7.pdf

Usai, A., Orlando, B., & Mazzoleni, A. (2020). Happiness as a driver of entrepreneurial initiative and innovation capital. *Journal of Intellectual Capital*, *21*(6), 1229–1255. doi:10.1108/JIC-11-2019-0250

Wright, T. A., & Huang, C.-C. (2012). The many benefits of employee well-being in organizational research. *Journal of Organizational Behavior*, *33*(8), 1188–1192. doi:10.1002/job.1828

ADDITIONAL READING

Abellán-Sevilla, A.-J., & Ortiz-de-Urbina-Criado, M. (2023). Smart human resource analytics for happiness management. *Journal of Management Development*, *42*(6), 514–525. doi:10.1108/JMD-03-2023-0064

Liu, S., Li, G., & Xia, H. (2021). Analysis of Talent Management in the Artificial Intelligence Era. *Proceedings of the 5th Asia-Pacific Conference on Economic Research and Management Innovation (ERMI 2021).* 10.2991/aebmr.k.210218.007

Ravina Ripoll, D. R., Villena Manzanares, D. F., & Gutiérrez Montoya, D. G. A. (2017). Una aproximación teórica para mejorar los resultados de innovación en las empresas desde la perspectiva del "Happiness Management.". *Retos, 7*(14), 113. doi:10.17163/ret.n14.2017.06

Schiessl, D., Dias, H. B. A., & Korelo, J. C. (2022). Inteligência artificial em marketing: Uma análise de rede e agenda futura. *J Mercado Anal, 10*, 207–218. doi:10.1057/s41270-021-00143-6

Sender, G., Nobre, G. C., Armagan, S., & Fleck, D. (2020). In search of the Holy Grail: a 20-year systematic review of the happy-productive worker thesis. *International Journal of Organizational Analysis, 29*(5), 1199–1224. doi:10.1108/IJOA-09-2020-2401

KEY TERMS AND DEFINITIONS

Artificial Intelligence: Artificial intelligence arises from the association between the skills of a machine and human beings. In other words, certain tools can copy human skills or even surpass them.

Eudaimonic Perspective: It corresponds to the need for everyone to understand that what they are and what they do has meaning for others and that their contribution is relevant.

Happiness: Happiness is a subjective concept; in the sense it varies according to everyone's overall perception of their life/experiences. It's a state characterized by a positive mood.

Happiness at Work: It is characterized by a positive feeling that depends on the evaluation of various parameters related to this context (relationship with colleagues/superiors, working conditions, organizational culture, among others).

Happiness Management: It's the process of determining and design strategies to promote happiness at the workplace, developing them to promote a sense of well-being and make interpersonal relationships better.

Hedonic Perspective: It's a way of living life through experiences that bring pleasure, trying to distance oneself from emotions that can lead to feelings of suffering.

Positive Psychology: It's a perspective that aims to see life on the positive side. Therefore, happiness, according to this view, should be understood through the positive emotions/experiences lived.

Well-Being: Well-being depends on each individual's overall assessment of life. In the case of well-being at work, it is associated with the evaluation each employee makes of the job they do, the colleagues they work with, their superiors, and other elements of the environment involved in this context.

Chapter 8
Organizational Psychology and the Impact of Artificial Intelligence on Psychosocial Risks and Technostress Levels

José Baptista
https://orcid.org/0000-0003-4594-5940
Centre for Public Administration and Public Policies, Institute of Social and Political Sciences, Portugal

ABSTRACT

The economic crisis and social changes and the technological advances, including the increase usage of AI, have brought numerous transformations to most workplaces. The pursuit of productivity, combined with the complexity of tasks and time pressures, has led to discussions about possible consequences, not only for workers but also for organizations. This chapter focuses on the psychosocial risks in the workplace as a critical challenge for organizations that aim to ensure the mental and physical well-being and productivity of their workforce. Psychosocial risks encompass a wide range of factors related to work, relationships, and individual well-being, having the potential to impact both mental and physical health. It is critical to recognize that they are not solely a concern of the individual but have far-reaching effects on the organization and society as a whole.

DOI: 10.4018/979-8-3693-0712-0.ch008

INTRODUCTION

Artificial intelligence (AI) presents both opportunities and challenges to organizations. Recently, not only the economic crisis but also the technological advances, including AI, and social changes have brought numerous transformations to most workplaces. The pursuit of productivity, combined with the complexity of tasks and time pressures, has led to discussions about possible consequences, not only for the workers but also for the organizations (Pereira et al., 2023; Ramalho & Costa, 2017). In contrast, although this should be approached with caution, studies also show that AI possesses the potential to enhance individual learning and development in the workplace and, additionally, it has the capacity to aid individual competence development and organizational learning processes (Wilkens, 2020).

In this sense, psychosocial risks in the workplace have been mentioned in the literature, which can be defined as the likelihood of negative effects on the mental, physical, and social well-being of workers due to working conditions that can interfere with their normal mental functioning and psychosocial well-being. Thus, the topic of psychosocial risks in the organizational context has generated a great deal of interest, becoming one of the most relevant and emerging topics of the last three decades, approximately, often being mistakenly equated solely with work-related stress, when it is much more than that (Carvalhais, 2016; Neto, 2015; Ramalho & Costa, 2017).

LITERATURE REVIEW

Work is a fundamental element in the life of any individual, whether as their source of income and survival or due to its regulatory effect on social life, often taking place in an environment with various factors affecting the physical and mental health of the worker (Carvalhais, 2016; Ramalho & Costa, 2017). In this sense, work is a central aspect of life, impacting dimensions such as survival and basic needs, identity, family and familial relationships, social inclusion, health and well-being, and quality of life (Ferreira et al., 2019).

The concept of work can be defined as the almost indirect interaction with a progressive process that involves the handling of information and control of the mechanisms responsible for the direct execution of activities, with each person being responsible for ensuring the compliance with these procedures in their role (Ramalho & Costa, 2017). Related to this term, the concept of work ability represents the current and future (in the relatively near future) capacity to perform the work or function in terms of professional demands, general health, or even their mental resources, in alignment with their abilities to cope with their professional life and the respective ecosystem (Carvalhais, 2016; Fernandes, 2016; Ramalho & Costa, 2017).

Distinguishing between work and employment, the existence of work does not always presuppose the existence of an employment situation, as the concept of employment assumes a legitimizing work activity through a contractual relationship between two parties: the worker and the organization (Andrade, 1989). In this way, not all work is performed in an employment situation, although the opposite is true, and the distinction between these concepts does not affect the tasks performed but only the contractual relationships established. Thus, employment can only be considered a synonym for paid work under certain conditions (Rodrigues et al., 2017).

Hussmanns (2007) distinguishes two types of work: (1) paid work – where people are employed or in an internship situation, and (2) self-employment – where employers or individuals are working for themselves (including producing goods for personal use), belong to production cooperatives, or work as contributing family members. Since work is defined as essential for one's own sustenance and for family support, being not only crucial for subsistence but also a crucial contribution to the sense of dignity and fulfillment throughout life, work should ideally represent a source of financial security, social relationships, personal development, self-esteem, and other determinants of health (Grant et al., 2011).

However, the precarity and insecurity experienced in the job market can impact the health of the working population in the short or long term (Caldbick et al., 2014). The relationships between health and work are quite complex because work can both be detrimental to health and contribute to it as a source. In order for organizations to remain competitive, the pursuit of productivity, coupled with the reduction of the workforce, the complexity of tasks, and various time pressures, has led to the emergence of potential consequences, not only for the working population but also for the organizations, typically derived from psychosocial risks (Carvalhais, 2016; Ramalho & Costa, 2017).

In 1984, the International Labour Organization (ILO) defined psychosocial risk factors in the workplace as all interactions between the work environment and content, organizational conditions, individual capabilities and needs, organizational culture, and personal considerations outside of work that, through individual perceptions and experiences, can influence health, performance, and job satisfaction (ILO, 1984). However, this definition has been widely criticized for being too vague (Vidal-Gomel & Delgoulet, 2022).

In 2010, the World Health Organization (WHO) defined the same concept as all aspects of work planning and management, as well as their respective social and organizational contexts with the potential to cause psychological or physical harm (WHO, 2010). According to more recent definitions, psychosocial risks in the workplace can be defined as the probability of negative effects occurring in the areas of mental or physical health due to working conditions or organizational and relational factors that, in some way, interfere with normal mental functioning or individual psychosocial well-being. In brief, these risks result from a set of conditions and factors intrinsic to the organization of work that need to be identified (Neto, 2015; Ramalho & Costa, 2017).

It is important to make a distinction between risks and risk factors: a risk factor is what underlies the risk itself, representing the intrinsic potential of a particular situation or aspect to cause consequences or harm; on the other hand, risk symbolizes the probability of the realization of that harm (Ramalho & Costa, 2017). Psychosocial risks entail negative consequences, both for individuals and for organizations or society, which can be psychological, physical, or even social in nature. These consequences mostly result from poor organizational management, emphasizing the significant role an organizational psychologist can play in handling such situations. However, risks can also emerge due to socio-economic changes such as globalization, the shift towards a service-based economy, demographic aging, new technological paradigms, new job content and new forms of work organization, changes in workspace and changes in the concept of work and organizational values, among other important aspects associated with the organizational context (Carvalhais, 2016; Fernandes & Pereira, 2016).

Psychosocial risks result from a set of conditions and factors intrinsic to the organization of work that need to be identified (Neto, 2015; Ramalho & Costa, 2017). In general, these risks lead to the deterioration of mental health and psychosocial well-being of the working population, increasing levels of physiological and cognitive stress. This increase can trigger physiological responses (such as neuroendocrine and immune reactions), emotional responses (such as depressive symptoms, anxiety, alienation, and apathy), and cognitive responses (such as decreased concentration, increased difficulties in decision-making processes, and restricted perception). Thus, it is essential to consider that prevention strategies are associated with creating a healthy work environment in which all individuals should feel supported, encouraged, and motivated to develop and achieve a good performance based on their abilities (Carvalhais, 2016; Fernandes, 2016).

The vast majority of these risk factors are related to the nature of labor and social relationships, the pace of work, the definition of job content and organization, emotional demands, the balance between professional and personal spheres, equality in work and employment, or the exercise of leadership. However, the main and most evident psychosocial risks in the workplace include stress, burnout, moral and sexual harassment, bullying and discrimination, cognitive and emotional fatigue, musculoskeletal injuries, work alienation, interference between personal and family life, demotivation and segregation, and finally, contractual precarity (Neto, 2015).

The probability of occurrence of the aforementioned risks depends on the existing hazards and the characteristics they assume. If they indeed occur, this will lead to damage at both the worker level and the level of equipment and organizational functioning. The consequences most frequently mentioned in the literature include absenteeism, turnover, extended sick leaves, contractual insecurity, wage inequality, strikes, lack of engagement and participation, fatigue and sleep disturbances, increased use of psychoactive substances, job dissatisfaction and difficulties in balancing personal and professional life (Carvalhais, 2016; Neto, 2015). The severity of health damage is related to the intensity and duration of exposure to psychosocial risks, and their probability of occurrence depends on the existing hazards and their characteristics (Moreno-Jiménez, 2011).

These risks represent one of the main challenges in the field of occupational safety and health, as they have a significant impact not only on individual health but also on organizations and national economies. This is due to the continuous change and evolution of the nature and organization of work and their impacts on individuals, organizations, societies, and policies. It is increasingly urgent to promote prevention mechanisms implemented at the organizational culture level (Carvalhais, 2016; Fernandes & Pereira, 2016).

Psychosocial risks can be associated with the context or the content of work. In order to combat the risks associated with the work context and professional demands, and in an effort to eliminate them, reduce them, or prevent their recurrence, there are some relevant measures. For example, concerning work schedules, they should allow for a good balance between personal and professional life, enabling all individuals to reconcile the two aspects of life as effectively as possible. Therefore, shift work should also strive to be more fixed and stable, in order to increase the stability and quality of life for the working population. Regarding risks associated with the content, these pertain to the meaning of work and commitment to the workplace, and they should also be reduced or eliminated as effectively as possible by organizations. Examples of this type of risk can include a lack of variety in work and, consequently, the performance of repetitive tasks, short work cycles, and fragmented or meaningless work (Fernandes & Pereira, 2016).

It is important to isolate emerging psychosocial risks within the realm of psychosocial risks, as these risks have a significant impact not only on the work itself but also on the working population. An emerging risk is a new risk, meaning it is unknown, with a high likelihood of spreading within the organization. Typically, they are caused by new processes or new job configurations, new technologies, organizational changes, or social alterations, or even by new scientific knowledge that allows an old problem to be identified as a risk. Other possible causes of the occurrence of emerging psychosocial risks or even unknown risks include social contexts, demographic changes in the population, migratory flows or the global economic crisis. (Carvalhais, 2016; Fernandes & Pereira, 2016).

Concerning new technologies, including the emerging use of AI, this can lead to the phenomenon of technostress, associated with mental fatigue, general discomfort, and anxiety experienced by the working population. This psychosocial risk with such a negative impact can be addressed through appropriate training on the correct use of these new tools (Fernandes & Pereira, 2016).

In the age of technology and information and communication technologies, where they assume such prominence and importance that the entire economy and quality of life seem to depend on them. In this sense, as technostress is associated with the use of new technologies and AI and how people interact with them, it is possible to consider that this specific type of stress, in a highly technology-dependent society, may result from a lack of skills or abilities to work in a healthy way with new technologies or even from simply coexisting with them. Thus, technostress may have a negative (direct or indirect) impact on the attitudes, thoughts, behaviors, and health of the working population, which is often more accustomed to manual work (Silva et al., 2016).

The consequences of technostress at a personal level will manifest in psychophysiological, behavioral, and cognitive dimensions. At the organizational level, the consequences can translate directly into absenteeism, reduced productivity, increased workplace accidents, compensation payments, and an increase in production errors. Indirectly, they may also result in a lack of motivation, job dissatisfaction, decision-making errors, and a deterioration in the work relationships (Silva et al., 2016).

Since AI represents the future of work, literature suggests it may be a factor that could create technostress or negative responses related to the collaboration between humans and AI. The term AI is employed to characterize sophisticated computerized systems and machines that emulate the cognitive functions of the human brain, including learning, reasoning, and planning (Pereira et al., 2023). However, it is important to observe the evolution of AI in a holistic manner and not just consider negative impacts such as the increase in technostress (Xia, 2023).

Among the factors contributing to technostress, the one that are more highlighted in the literature include insecurity in using AI, concerns about misinformation or the credibility of AI itself, overwhelming feelings, and the potential for increased work-family conflict due to increased usage of technology (Cadieux et al., 2021).

To reduce or eliminate psychosocial risks, it is necessary, first and foremost, to conduct a diagnosis using valid instruments and tools that allow the organization to understand the most prevalent risks. Subsequently, strategies for intervention can be designed. In this regard, considering the organization's culture, receptiveness to proposed strategies, and the type of risk identified, organizations can design tasks that make sense to all individuals, enabling the use of their knowledge and clarifying the objectives and the importance of these tasks (Fernandes & Pereira, 2016).

Thus, it will be necessary to take actions to try to reduce or eliminate psychosocial risks, taking into account various aspects, such as: the clear definition of job positions, functions, and responsibilities of each individual; task rotation, enhancing organizational transparency; providing specific training tailored to individual capabilities, resources, and knowledge, leading to a reduction in feelings of uncertainty and insecurity, as well as the acquisition of coping strategies that positively contribute to dealing with various consequences that may arise; or aligning tasks with the needs of each individual, ensuring that they are stimulating and clarifying the importance of their performance at both the organizational and systemic levels in which the organization operates (Fernandes & Pereira, 2016).

DISCUSSION

To address these issues, actions should by ideally take by Organizational Psychologists and the organizations where they work must meet legal and ethical obligations with strategies in place to manage these matters. One of the strategies that Organizational Psychologists can employ to effectively manage psychosocial risks may follow these steps: initiate an action plan that considers objectives, a timeline, and the individuals responsible for different phases, which should be validated by top management to enhance the commitment of all individuals to this issue. Next, ongoing communication of the plan should be carried out, involving all individuals, and a sensitization plan should be developed, including training for leaders and employee representatives to explain the purposes and intervention phases. After completing all these procedures, the first phase of implementing the strategy, mostly related to the conception, communication, and explanation of the action plan, is considered complete (Neto, 2015).

The second phase is related to the evaluation component and the management of exposure to psychosocial risks at work by the Organizational Psychologists. This consists ideally of the following steps: identifying risk factors, estimating their extent, controlling and/or eliminating them, and finally, monitoring the actions that have been implemented. It is also important to emphasize the transparency of the entire process on the part of all parties involved, promoting continuous group improvement (Neto, 2015).

Effective management of psychosocial risks is essential in promoting the health and well-being of the working population, and it should be a significant factor to consider in any organization's strategy. When reflecting on the types of issues organizations have to address regarding psychosocial risks, it is impossible for any to underestimate the importance of these matters for their success. However, the necessary steps to combat these risks are not yet being taken, and there are numerous barriers to overcome in eradicating psychosocial risks and work-related stress, including technostress (Kortum et al., 2010; Neto, 2015).

These barriers include a lack of resources and research, inaction on the part of authorities and employers (lack of political decisions and implementation), lack of enforcement, a lack of understanding of psychosocial risks, workers' fear of unionization, the failure of improvements to reach common workers and address basic needs, a lack of skills regarding new forms of work organization, and a lack of action - often limited to diagnosis with little or no follow-up (Kotrum et al., 2010).

To overcome these barriers, the role of the Organizational Psychologists is vital, given their extensive knowledge of practices aimed at preventing, reducing, or eradicating psychosocial risks. Being Organizational Psychology a specialized field within the broader domain of Psychology that studies human behavior in work settings, it is clear that an Organizational Psychologist is the most suitable and responsible professional for this role. In certain cases, it may also be necessary to appoint one or more active agents to facilitate the process (Riggio, 2018).

In a positive psychosocial environment, work can be highly beneficial for the mental health of the working population, as it provides a better quality of life and higher levels of confidence. This can reflect in organizational success and effectiveness, leading to higher levels of productivity and profits (Carvalhais, 2016). However, it should be considered that a healthy work environment implies that both psychological and cognitive demands are appropriate for each role and the coping abilities of each individual. In other words, one of the strategies is to avoid having a single person responsible for a high number of complex tasks (Carvalhais, 2016).

Having a well-defined role in the organization can indeed be an asset for mental health and personal motivation. In this regard, organizations should be clear and transparent about the roles of each individual, their autonomy and responsibility, while offering transparency and sincerity regarding career development opportunities and avoiding the perception of ambiguity or uncertainty. If possible, promoting learning and training within the organization, as well as employability, should also be encouraged (Fernandes & Pereira, 2016).

Furthermore, another solution to ensure that all individuals feel more motivated, committed, and integrated into their workplace is the guaranty of freedom and autonomy in decision-making regarding their vacations, breaks, and the conditions and characteristics associated with their workplace. It may also be important for tasks to have meaning and purpose, so a possible strategy could involve providing opportunities for all individuals to apply their personal knowledge in their roles (Fernandes & Pereira, 2016).

Since there is an interaction between individual and work-related factors and work and psychosocial risk factors, the exposure of the working population to poor and negative psychosocial environments can influence various levels, from physical to mental health, to the overall work environment and even the quality of leisure and rest time (Fernandes & Pereira, 2016). To combat their occurrence, proper management of psychosocial risks at work will require not only the Organizational Psychologist but also management figures to have a thorough understanding of various aspects related to the organization and the risks that may jeopardize the quality of work life, so that this management is suitable for the context in which it will operate (Carvalhais, 2016).

It's worth mentioning that the health of the working population is not defined solely by its psychological component but also by its physical well-being, and ensuring workplace safety is crucial. To prevent workplace accidents and occupational diseases, organizations should take measures such as providing training on maintaining the correct posture at the workplace, especially when handling heavy loads, if applicable; promoting rest breaks during particularly demanding tasks; and regularly and continuously monitoring the health of all employees through occupational health services (Freitas & Cordeiro, 2013).

In this regard, the adoption of best practices by organizations for promoting health in the workplace and reducing psychosocial risks (including technostress derived from the use of AI) serves as both a protective and health-promoting factor for physical and mental well-being, at both individual and organizational levels, contributing to social justice and inclusivity. The existence of a prevention process for these risks within organizations, with the aim of developing a set of strategies and programs to be implemented, represents a complex process and is one of the main organizational challenges due to the diversity and multitude of existing risks, being a primal responsibility of the Organizational Psychologist (Carvalhais, 2016; Fernandes, 2016).

CONCLUSION

In conclusion, the management of psychosocial risks in the workplace is a critical consideration for organizations aiming to ensure the well-being and productivity of their workforce. Psychosocial risks encompass a wide range of factors related to work, relationships, and individual well-being, and they have the potential to impact both mental and physical health. Identifying, assessing, and addressing these risks is crucial for creating a healthy and supportive work environment, being essential to recognize that psychosocial risks are not solely a concern of the individual but have far-reaching effects on the organization and society as a whole. While various challenges exist, including the increase usage of AI -that the literature refers as the future of work - organizations should not shy away from their responsibilities. They must take proactive steps to create safer and healthier workplaces and the role of Organizational Psychologists is pivotal in guiding this process, as their expertise in human behavior, work environments, and risk mitigation that can help developing effective strategies (Kortum et al., 2010; Riggio, 2018).

REFERENCES

Andrade, M. (1989). *Social - Factores e tipos de pobreza em Portugal*. Celta Editora.

Blustein, D. L., Kenny, M. E., Di Fabio, A., & Guichard, J. (2018). Expanding the impact of the psychology of working: Engaging psychology in the struggle for decent work and human rights. *Journal of Career Assessment*, *27*(1), 3–28. doi:10.1177/1069072718774002

Cadieux, N., Fournier, P., Cadieux, J., & Gingues, M. (2021). New techno-stressors among knowledge professionals: The contribution of artificial intelligence and websites that misinform clients. *International Journal of Electronic Commerce*, *25*(2), 136–153. doi:10.1080/10864415.2021.1887695

Caldbick, S., Labonte, R., Mohindra, K. S., & Ruckert, A. (2014). Globalization and the rise of precarious employment: The new frontier for workplace health promotion. *Global Health Promotion*, *21*(2), 23–31. doi:10.1177/1757975913514781 PMID:24534262

Carvalhais, C. M. (2016). *Gestão dos riscos psicossociais: Caso de estudo no setor das telecomunicações* [Dissertação de mestrado não publicada]. Instituto Superior de Contabilidade e Administração de Coimbra.

Fernandes, C. (2016). *Capacidade para o trabalho: Apreciação dos Riscos Psicossociais na Indústria* [Tese de doutoramento não publicada]. Universidade de Aveiro.

Fernandes, C., & Pereira, A. (2016). Exposição a fatores de risco psicossocial em contexto de trabalho: Revisão sistemática. *Revista de Saude Publica*, *50*(24), 1–15.

Ferreira, J. A., Haase, R. F., Santos, E. R., Rabaça, J. A., Figueiredo, L., Hemami, H. G., & Almeida, L. M. (2019). Decent work in Portugal: Context, conceptualization, and assessment. *Journal of Vocational Behavior*, *112*, 77–91. doi:10.1016/j.jvb.2019.01.009

Freitas, L. C., & Cordeiro, T. C. (2013). *Segurança e saúde do trabalho: guia para micro, pequenas e médias empresas.*

Grant, J. M., Mottet, L. A., Tanis, J., Harrison, J., Herman, J. L., & Keisling, M. (2011). *Injustice at every turn: A report of the national transgender discrimination survey*. National Center for Transgender Equality and National Gay and Lesbian Taskforce.

Hussmanns, R. (2007). Measurement of employment, unemployment and underemployment - Current international standards and issues in their application. *Labor Stat*, *1*, 1–23.

International Labor Organization – ILO. (1984). *Psychosocial factors at work: Recognition and control*. International Labor Office.

Kortum, E., Leka, S., & Cox, T. (2010). Psychosocial risks and work-related stress in developing countries: Health impact, priorities, barriers and solutions. *International Journal of Occupational Medicine and Environmental Health*, *22*(3), 225–238. doi:10.2478/v10001-010-0024-5 PMID:20934955

Moreno-Jiménez, B. (2011). Factores y riesgos laborales psicosociales: Conceptualización, historia y cambios actuales. *Medicina y Seguridad del Trabajo*, *57*(1), 4–19. doi:10.4321/S0465-546X2011000500002

Neto, H. V. (2015). Estratégias organizacionais de gestão e intervenção sobre riscos psicossociais do trabalho. *International Journal on Working Conditions.*, *9*, 1–21.

Pereira, V., Hadjielias, E., Christofi, M., & Vrontis, D. (2023). A systematic literature review on the impact of artificial intelligence on workplace outcomes: A multi-process perspective. *Human Resource Management Review*, *33*(1), 100857. doi:10.1016/j.hrmr.2021.100857

Ramalho, J. F., & Costa, L. S. (2017). Os fatores psicossociais de risco na atividade de técnicos superiores de segurança no trabalho. *Laboreal (Porto)*, *13*(2), 39–49. doi:10.4000/laboreal.359

Riggio, R. E. (2018). *Introduction to industrial/organizational psychology*. Routledge.

Rodrigues, E. V., Samagaio, F., Ferreira, H., Mendes, M. M., & Januário, S. (2017). A pobreza e a exclusão social: Teorias conceitos e políticas sociais em Portugal. *Sociologia: Revista da Faculdade de Letras da Universidade do Porto, 9*. https://ojs.letras.up.pt/index.php/Sociologia/article/view/2566

Silva, M., Queirós, C., & Cameira, M. (2016). Saúde no Trabalho: Tecnostress e Burnout em Enfermeiros. *International Journal on Working Conditions*, *12*(1), 54–70.

Vidal-Gomel, C., & Delgoulet, C. (2022). Analysing relationships between work and training in order to prevent psychosocial risks. *Safety Science*, *145*, 105517. doi:10.1016/j.ssci.2021.105517

Wilkens, U. (2020). Artificial intelligence in the workplace – A double-edged sword. *The International Journal of Information and Learning Technology*, *37*(5), 253–265. doi:10.1108/IJILT-02-2020-0022

Work Health Organization - WHO. (2010). *Health impact of psychosocial hazards at work: An overview*. World Health Organization.

Xia, M. (2023). Co-working with AI is a double-sword in Technostress? An integrative review of Human-AI collaboration from a holistic process of Technostress. *SHS Web of Conferences, 155*, 03022. 10.1051/shsconf/202315503022

Chapter 9
Transformative Power of Artificial Intelligence in Decision-Making, Automation, and Customer Engagement

R. Nalini
SASTRA University, India

ABSTRACT

In the modern business landscape, innovation has become a key driver of success and competitive advantage. To foster innovation within their organizations, leaders play a crucial role in harnessing the synergy between data, technology, design, and people. This integration allows them to effectively address real-world challenges on a large scale, driving transformation and growth. At the heart of AI's contribution to data-driven decision-making lies its ability to process vast datasets with remarkable efficiency. Traditional manual analysis methods are not only time-consuming but also prone to human biases and errors. AI, on the other hand, is driven by data, allowing it to make objective assessments devoid of human preconceptions. This not only enhances decision accuracy but also provides a solid foundation for devising strategies that align with actual market trends and customer preferences.

INTRODUCTION

In the modern business landscape, innovation has become a key driver of success and competitive advantage. To foster innovation within their organizations, leaders play a crucial role in harnessing the synergy between data, technology, design, and

DOI: 10.4018/979-8-3693-0712-0.ch009

people. This integration allows them to effectively address real-world challenges on a large scale, driving transformation and growth. At the heart of AI's contribution to data-driven decision-making lies its ability to process vast datasets with remarkable efficiency. Traditional manual analysis methods are not only time-consuming but also prone to human biases and errors. Artificial Intelligence (AI), on the other hand, is driven by data, allowing it to make objective assessments devoid of human preconceptions. This not only enhances decision accuracy but also provides a solid foundation for devising strategies that align with actual market trends and customer preferences. The concept of digital business transformation (DBT) is receiving increasing recognition, especially as organizations face ongoing pressures to enhance their operational procedures and capacities. DBT encourages novel approaches to collaboration and customer engagement, actively fueling the emergence of fresh business frameworks.

Artificial Intelligence (AI) has emerged as a transformative force across industries, and its impact on business management is profound. This technology, rooted in machine learning and data analysis, holds the promise of reshaping how businesses operate, make decisions, and interact with customers and stakeholders. From data-driven decision-making to process automation and customer insights, AI is revolutionizing the field of business management in unprecedented ways.

INNOVATION IN THE DIGITAL SECTOR: RECENT TRENDS

The definition of digital innovation is continually evolving, with new technological developments emerging almost daily. Keeping pace with these advancements is crucial for organizations seeking to effectively leverage new and emerging technology. However, it's important to note that not every new technology will be suitable for every business. Let's explore some current trends that may impact various industries:

Machine Learning (ML) and Artificial Intelligence (AI) are revolutionizing a wide range of sectors by facilitating improved analytics, automation, and tailored experiences. Businesses can automate processes, enhance decision-making, and extract valuable insights from vast datasets using AI and ML.

As IoT (Internet of Things) devices expand, businesses have numerous options for collecting and analyzing real-time data. Embracing IoT technologies can improve operational efficiency, supply chain management, and customer experiences.

Cloud computing and hybrid infrastructures have fundamentally altered how firms approach infrastructure and application deployment. Cloud platforms' scalability, flexibility, and affordability enable businesses to accelerate innovation and respond to changing market demands.

Data privacy and cybersecurity are closely related issues that gain importance as digital innovation continues to grow. Businesses must prioritize cybersecurity and establish robust defences against ever-evolving threats.

Artificial Intelligence (AI) is a significant driver of change in various industries, profoundly impacting business management. This new technology, rooted in machine learning and data analysis, has the potential to reshape how businesses operate, make decisions, and engage with stakeholders and customers. AI is ushering in dramatic changes in business management, from data-driven decision-making to process automation and customer insights.

Every sector of the economy closely monitors future trends, and discussions about artificial intelligence (AI) inevitably arise in each of these fields. The potential for AI to fundamentally transform work processes is enormous. AI encompasses a broad spectrum of cutting-edge technologies, including automation, machine learning, and cognitive interaction. Businesses are utilizing these technologies to enhance overall efficiency across all industries. In a 2018 survey conducted by Harvard Business Review, which polled 250 CEOs about their companies' use of cognitive technology, three-quarters predicted that AI would have a significant impact on their industries within the next three years.

REVIEW OF LITERATURE

According to Amarasinghe, H. (2023), the incorporation of AI into customer relationship management (CRM) offers contemporary businesses a wide range of benefits and problems. This study explores the probable of AI to transform CRM, highlighting both its many advantages and its inherent disadvantages. Positively, AI streamlines marketing efforts by enhancing client perceptions through sophisticated data analysis. It offers better sales forecasting with predictive analytics and empowers superior customer service by deploying chatbots for common questions.

Shereen Noranee (2023) The researcher utilizing AI technologies, has the potential to enhance consumer satisfaction, market insights, and marketing effectiveness. She makes a significant contribution to a greater understanding of how AI might be realistically applied in the marketing industry and establishes herself as a crucial resource for future research projects. She urges marketers to use AI as a tool to gain an advantage in the dynamic marketing environment.

Castro, S. L. C., Del Pozo Durango Rodrigo Humberto, V., Paúl, A. C., & Estefanía, A. T. P. (2023) Specialists in the marketing industry can gather crucial insights from consumer behavior to improve client segmentation and develop more effective strategies. This study is based on an extensive literature review conducted using numerous reliable databases. Marketing can be customized, customer happiness can be increased, and market shifts can be predicted thanks to AI. Future marketing strategies will be significantly transformed by AI, owing to its competitive edge and enhanced operational efficiency.

Ranković et.al (2023) Due to the rapid development and extensive application of artificial intelligence (AI) across numerous industries, traditional paradigms have experienced substantial alterations. An interesting illustration of this transition is the finance sector. This paper investigates the immediate consequences, possible opportunities, current obstacles, and upcoming prospects of AI in banking, drawing on a thorough investigation of academic literature, industry reports, and real-world case studies. Our analysis demonstrates the significant improvements in productivity, security, and customer happiness that AI has brought to many industries.

Jasmin Praful Bharadiya. (2023) This paper investigates the possibilities that arise from integrating AI and BI to faster business growth.

Kunduru, A. R. (2023) The deployment and management of applications by companies and organizations have undergone significant changes due to the rapid growth of cloud computing.

Soumpenioti, V., & Panagopoulos, A. (2023) The transformative impact of automating repetitive tasks, such as data input and inventory management, on job roles in logistics, leading to streamlined operations and more efficient resource utilization.

Maheswari (2023) S. This study delves into the application of artificial intelligence (AI) in the marketing of fast-moving consumer goods (FMCG). Through an exhaustive examination of pertinent literature, it synthesizes key findings and insights derived from relevant research.

Abrokwah-Larbi, K. and Awuku-Larbi, Y. (2023) The study's findings lend strong credence to the Resource-Based View (RBV) theory, reiterating the significance of recognizing artificial intelligence in marketing (AIM) and personalization—as essential strategic assets for enhancing the performance of small and medium enterprises (SMEs).

Nguyen, D. K., Sermpinis, G., & Stasinakis, C. (2023) This study present a well-defined framework that illustrates the mutually beneficial relationship among these data science concepts in driving fintech innovation. This framework is substantiated by examining their influence on fintech, the financial services industry, and the evolving nature of the data scientist role. Furthermore, we delve into the potential drawbacks of this symbiotic relationship, addressing concerns related to AI ethics, regulatory technology, and the responsible use of smart data as future challenges associated with AI and ML techniques.

Haleem, A., Javaid, M., Qadri, M. A., Singh, R. P., & Suman, R. (2022) Artificial Intelligence (AI) offering benefits such as enhanced data sourcing and management, the creation of sophisticated algorithms, and a transformation in the way brands engage with users. The effectiveness of AI applications largely depends on factors like website nature and business type. Marketers can now prioritize customer-centric approaches in real-time, leveraging AI to swiftly determine the most suitable content and channels based on data-driven insights. This personalized approach not only increases user comfort but also enhances their likelihood of making purchases. Additionally, AI tools can analyze competitor campaign performance and uncover customer prospects. The paper seeks to provide an overview of AI's impact on marketing, explore specific AI applications across various marketing sectors, and assess their transformative potential.

Aw, E. C. X., Tan, G. W. H., Cham, T. H., Raman, R., & Ooi, K. B. (2022) The model incorporates three categories of attributes: human-like attributes, technology attributes and contextual factors. These attributes serve as predictors of continued usage. In turn, they contribute to the formation of perceptual-based outcomes, including parasocial interactions, perceptions of smart shopping, and AI-enabled customer experiences. The study's findings carry both theoretical and practical implications, offering insights into the factors that influence consumers' decisions to use digital voice assistants for shopping and how these choices shape their overall shopping experiences.

Bag, S., Srivastava, G., Bashir, M. M. A., Kumari, S., Giannakis, M., & Chowdhury, A. H. (2022) This study distinguishes itself by investigating essential connections related to user engagement in the midst of the uncertainty brought about by the COVID-19 pandemic and uncovering the underlying mechanisms responsible for driving an upsurge in online sales.

Evelyn Cunningham (2021) The focus of the analysis and evaluation was on the function of IoT sensor networks in cyber-physical system-based manufacturing. The survey data acquired for this study was examined using descriptive statistics.

Saura,J.R, et.al. (2021) The contemporary business challenges within the B2B industry are influenced by interconnected ecosystems, underscoring the critical role that data-driven decision-making plays in crafting successful strategies. Simultaneously, the adoption of digital marketing as a tool for communication and sales highlights the importance and utilization of Customer Relationship Management (CRM) systems for precise company data management.

Wayne D. Hoyer (2020) This paper introduces a novel classification of AI-powered technologies and presents a fresh context for understanding their impact on the customer or shopper journey.

Jain, P., & Aggarwal, K. (2020) The paper includes a dedicated section that covers the implementation of various Artificial Intelligence Marketing strategies. The authors have conducted a thorough analysis of the ramifications of AIM technology across the entire customer lifecycle. Furthermore, the paper provides a detailed analysis, both by sector and region.

Dumitriu, D., & Popescu, M. A. M. (2020) The recent technological advancements have spurred various industries into action. In this era of evolution, marketing has reached a critical juncture where embracing digital trends has become a necessity. While it may appear as a challenging transition for marketers, the truth is that all automated applications and systems driven by artificial intelligence serve to simplify the once complex processes of traditional targeting and customization.

Olson, C., & Levy, J. (2018) Artificial intelligence (AI) is anticipated to be the technology that will experience the most significant growth in the next two years according to marketers. This growth is expected to bring about two primary advantages. Firstly, AI presents an opportunity to save time and enhance efficiency. It will enable marketers to achieve improved business outcomes by offering insights, automation, and execution capabilities, allowing them to allocate more time to strategic planning and creative development. AI provides marketers with a means to expand personalization in their marketing efforts without overloading their teams. It also introduces new avenues for marketers to deliver value to their customers and establish models for lifetime customer relationships, increasing their relevance. This paper explores how marketers can harness AI to enhance their customer relationships through more natural and personalized forms of engagement by leveraging advanced reasoning, comprehension, and interaction capabilities.

Dhanabalan, T., & Sathish, A. (2018). The term "Artificial Intelligence" (AI) has ushered in transformative changes in both our personal and professional lives. Due to its promising potential, the adoption of AI is considered a crucial component of the Industry 4.0 landscape. AI has presented numerous opportunities and challenges across various industries, leading to the development of a multitude of AI-powered technologies that have the potential to significantly enhance the quality of life and bolster the economy.

In India, AI plays a substantial role in various industries and its contributions have a notable impact on GDP growth, and the benefits of AI are expected to have far-reaching effects on these sectors. In an era of globalization, no country can remain unaffected by technological advancements. Therefore, this article examines the current relevance of AI in Indian industries and provides insights into its future potential. Additionally, it offers recommendations for charting a path forward for India in the realm of AI.

OVERVIEW OF BUSINESS MANAGEMENT ARTIFICIAL INTELLIGENCE (AI)

The incorporation of AI into business management has inaugurated a new era filled with opportunities and challenges. Enterprises are leveraging AI technology to automate operations, harness the potential of data, and secure a competitive advantage in an ever-evolving and intricate market.

a. **Decision Making:** AI's capacity to support data-driven decision-making is one of the core features of business management. Businesses generate a substantial amount of information every day in a world where data is abundant. To extract valuable insights, trends, and patterns from this data, AI systems can analyze it. The capability to make decisions based on factual information rather than solely relying on intuition provides managers with greater flexibility. For example, artificial intelligence (AI) can assess sales data to ascertain customer preferences and adapt marketing plans accordingly.

b. **Analytics for Forecasting:** AI algorithms are able to identify trends, foresee changes in the market, and anticipate demand patterns by looking at historical data. Resource allocation, inventory control, and risk evaluation are all aided by this predictive power. For instance, a retailer might utilize AI to forecast demand for particular products over various seasons, improving supply chain operations and minimizing waste.

c. **Automated Processes:** AI's influence on corporate management is typified by process automation. Using AI-powered systems, repetitive and rule-based tasks that waste time and resources can be automated. This improves operational effectiveness while simultaneously decreasing human error. For instance, chatbots powered by AI can deal with common consumer inquiries, freeing up human agents to deal with more intricate conversations.

d. **Customer Insights and Personalized Marketing:** Understanding consumer behaviour is essential for business success, which is why customer insights and personalized marketing are so important. To produce useful insights, AI systems examine client interactions, feedback, and preferences. Customer engagement, loyalty, and conversion rates can all be improved with personalized marketing efforts powered by AI.

e. **Supply Chain Optimization:** AI's prowess in processing and analyzing massive volumes of data in real time is important for enhancing supply chain operations. Businesses may optimize their supply chain procedures and cut costs by anticipating demand variations, spotting possible disruptions, and monitoring inventory levels. Supply networks in sectors with these characteristics are often intricate and intertwined, which is advantageous.

f. **Risk Management:** A powerful tool for risk management, AI has improved data analytic skills. AI may detect potential hazards, vulnerabilities, and threats by analysing a variety of data sources. Businesses are given the ability to manage risks proactively and put mitigation plans in place as a result. Artificial intelligence (AI), for instance, can keep an eye out for irregularities in financial transactions that can point to fraud.

g. **Productivity and Employee Management:** AI is revolutionizing how organizations manage their workforces, resulting in increased productivity and employee management. AI may help with everything from hiring to performance reviews, including finding the best applicants, assessing workers' output, and even recommending new training initiatives. Tools utilizing artificial intelligence (AI) can find skill shortages in an organization and recommend training opportunities for staff to fill those gaps.
h. **Product Development:** AI's influence also extends to encouraging product development. AI can propose creative ideas for fresh goods and services by researching market trends, consumer input, and upcoming technology. The value and relevance of existing products can be increased by using AI to optimize them depending on user behavior and preferences.
i. **Corporate Communication:** The emergence of AI-powered chatbots and virtual assistants is revolutionizing corporate communication and customer service. These tools answer customer questions immediately, walk users through procedures, and provide insightful data. Customer satisfaction is increased and support teams' workload is decreased by their availability around-the-clock.
j. **Competitive Advantage and Ethical Issues:** Companies that successfully implement AI gain a competitive edge by making quicker, data-driven choices, providing individualized experiences, and effectively optimizing their operations. On the other hand, enormous power also carries immense responsibility. It is necessary to address ethical issues including data privacy, algorithmic prejudice, and the effect on employment. For sustaining confidence among stakeholders, it is essential to make sure that AI technologies are implemented ethically and transparently.

The role of artificial intelligence (AI) has emerged as a crucial driving force in utilizing the potential of an excess of data for decision-making in the ever-changing landscape of business management. AI is a crucial ally for managers in the world of business, helping them to navigate the intricacies of an environment that is becoming more and more data-rich. Decision-making processes are catalyzed by the convergence of data and AI, changing them from reactive to proactive. Businesses can detect client preferences, anticipate operational issues, and forecast market trends. Leaders who adopt AI are better equipped to break down conventional barriers and take advantage of opportunities that present themselves in the ever-changing environments of their particular businesses.

Leaders' decision-making processes are being revolutionized by AI's ability to combine vast data sets and offer useful insights. AI has the ability to change sectors, provide durable competitive advantages, and drive innovation that propels enterprises into a bright future if technology, strategy, and ethical awareness are used in the appropriate proportions. The use of AI in company management is a beacon pointing executives toward a new era of knowledgeable, pro-active, and significant decision-making as we stand at the confluence of abundant data and technical innovation.

Organizational structure and success are being radically altered by the use of AI into commercial management. AI is influencing every facet of the corporate landscape, from data analysis and process automation to consumer insights and creativity. Businesses must manage issues with ethical use, transparency, and the impact of AI on people even though the potential benefits are enormous. Businesses may benefit from AI's transformative capacity to generate growth, improve customer experiences, and maintain competitiveness by integrating AI technology intelligently and strategically.

THE EFFECTS OF ARTIFICIAL INTELLIGENCE ON DIGITAL TRANSFORMATION

Automating processes using AI-powered analytics, intelligent data mining, and individualized consumer experiences are among the digital transformation innovators. Automation of repetitive work, reduced human error, and the ability to make proactive decisions are all ways that artificial intelligence (AI) improves productivity and efficiency. Intelligent algorithms analyze large amounts of data, producing useful data that aids decision-makers in making educated decisions. Real-time analytics and predictive modeling enable individualized client interactions, which enhance operations and increase engagement and happiness.

a. **Automation and Efficiency:** By automating repetitive operations, AI-powered automation is transforming businesses and freeing up workers to focus on higher-value jobs. Businesses may improve productivity, save costs, and streamline processes by using machine learning algorithms. AI is being used in sectors including manufacturing, shipping, and customer service to automate repetitive operations and boost accuracy and productivity.
b. **Intelligent Data Analytics:** AI systems have the capacity to instantly evaluate huge datasets and offer insightful information to enterprises. Intelligent decision-making is made possible by AI-powered analytics, which reveals patterns, trends, and correlations. AI is being used by sectors including finance, marketing, and healthcare to obtain useful insights, improve tactics, and spur growth.

c. **Personalization and Customer Experience:** AI is revolutionizing the customer experience by delivering customized interactions and recommendations. By providing individualized product recommendations based on client interests and behavior, firms may increase customer loyalty and boost revenue.

d. **Customer Insights and Personalized Marketing:** Understanding customer behavior is crucial for business success. AI tools analyze customer interactions, feedback, and preferences to generate actionable insights. Personalized marketing campaigns driven by AI can enhance customer engagement, loyalty, and conversion rates.

e. **Supply Chain Optimization:** Supply chain operations can be greatly improved by utilizing AI's capacity to process and analyze massive amounts of data in real-time. Businesses can optimize their supply chain procedures and reduce expenses by anticipating demand variations, spotting potential disruptions, and monitoring inventory levels. This is especially advantageous in sectors with intricate and interwoven supply chains.

f. **Risk Management:** AI's advanced data analysis capabilities make it an effective tool for risk management. By analyzing various data sources, AI can identify potential risks, vulnerabilities, and threats. This empowers businesses to proactively manage risks and implement strategies to mitigate them. For instance, AI can monitor financial transactions for anomalies that might indicate fraudulent activities.

g. **Employee Management and Productivity:** AI is transforming the way businesses manage their workforce. From talent acquisition to performance evaluation, AI can assist in identifying suitable candidates, evaluating employee performance, and even recommending training programs. AI-powered tools can identify skills gaps within the organization and suggest learning opportunities for employees to bridge those gaps.

h. **Innovation and Product Development:** AI's impact extends to fostering innovation and product development. By analyzing market trends, customer feedback, and emerging technologies, AI can suggest innovative ideas for new products and services. Additionally, AI can optimize existing products based on user behavior and preferences, enhancing their value and relevance.

i. **Virtual Assistants and Chatbots:** The rise of AI-powered virtual assistants and chatbots is transforming customer service and internal communication. Their availability 24/7 enhances customer satisfaction and reduces the workload on support teams.

j. **Competitive Advantage and Ethical Considerations:** Ensuring that AI technologies are deployed responsibly and transparently is crucial for maintaining trust among stakeholders.

In the realm of business management, AI serves as an indispensable ally, guiding leaders to navigate the complexities of an increasingly data-rich environment. The convergence of data and AI catalyzes decision-making processes, transforming them from reactive to proactive. Organizations can predict market trends, identify customer preferences, and foresee operational challenges before they arise. By embracing AI, leaders are positioned to transcend traditional boundaries and seize opportunities that arise in the dynamic landscapes of their respective industries.

AI's capacity to synthesize complex data sets and provide actionable insights revolutionizes how leaders approach decision-making. With the right balance of technology, strategy, and ethical mindfulness, AI has the potential to reshape industries, create sustainable competitive advantages, and drive innovation that propels businesses into a promising future. As we stand at the intersection of data abundance and technological innovation, the role of AI in business management stands as a beacon guiding leaders toward a new era of informed, proactive, and impactful decision-making.

The integration of AI into business management is fundamentally reshaping how organizations operate and thrive. From data analysis and process automation to customer insights and innovation, AI is permeating every aspect of the business landscape. While the potential benefits are immense, businesses must also navigate challenges related to ethical use, transparency, and the human impact of AI. By thoughtfully and strategically embracing AI technologies, businesses can harness their transformative power to fuel growth, elevate customer experiences, and maintain competitiveness in an AI-driven world.

AI IMPLEMENTED IN DECISION-MAKING

Organizations may improve decision-making by utilizing AI technology to increase precision, efficiency, and speed, leading to more data-driven, well-informed decisions. Key elements of Artificial intelligence (AI)'s function in decision-making are listed below:

- Using historical data analysis and Artificial intelligence (AI), predictive analytics can forecast future results. AI algorithms produce predictions and probabilities that aid in decision-making by carefully examining historical trends and patterns. AI algorithms, for instance, may estimate default possibilities and assess credit risk within financial institutions, which helps with the loan approval process.

- AI aids businesses in identifying and reducing the risks connected to decision-making. AI models provide risk evaluations and suggest risk-reduction tactics based on an analysis of past data and the identification of risk factors. For instance, AI systems in the insurance sector can evaluate policyholder risks and spot potential fraud, enabling better risk management.
- The decision-making processes are improved by AI technologies, which mix data analysis, machine learning, and human knowledge. For instance, by reviewing patient information and recommending possible treatments, AI can assist clinicians in making diagnoses of diseases.

PROMOTING BETTER CUSTOMER SERVICE BY USE OF AI

Customer service has been changed by artificial intelligence (AI), which has given businesses strong capabilities to improve interactions with customers, increase responsiveness, and offer individualized experiences. Here are a few ways artificial intelligence is advancing service to the customers:

- To manage client enquiries and offer immediate service, AI-powered chatbots and virtual assistants are deployed. These smart systems are able to comprehend and reply in real time to client inquiries, providing answers to frequently asked questions and directing users to self-service options. In order to provide round-the-clock customer care, chatbots can run continuously.
- AI makes use of natural language processing (NLP) strategies to comprehend and decipher human language. As a result, customer support systems are better equipped to understand the attitudes, enquiries, and intent of their clients, resulting in more precise and contextually appropriate responses. Chatbots that are NLP-powered can have discussions with customers that are similar to those of a human.
- To personalize interactions, AI systems analyze customer information. AI can offer customized experiences that enhance customer satisfaction and loyalty by assessing each consumer's distinct requirements and tailoring product recommendations, offers, and communication accordingly.
- AI tools can evaluate consumer sentiments as they are communicated through a variety of channels, including social media, reviews, and direct customer communication. Sentiment research gives businesses the ability to assess customer satisfaction levels, spot impending problems, and proactively respond to client issues, all of which improve service quality.

- AI-powered voice recognition technology empowers users to communicate with devices through voice commands. Speech assistants such as Apple's Siri or Amazon's Alexa utilize artificial intelligence (AI) to understand and respond to spoken requests, providing hands-free customer assistance and facilitating smooth integration with other smart devices.

AI-ENHANCED SUPPLY CHAIN MANAGEMENT

Supply chain management is changing due to artificial intelligence (AI), which is boosting productivity, decision-making, and process optimization. Several significant uses of AI in supply chain management are listed below:

a. **Forecasting Demand:** For accurate demand prediction, AI algorithms can analyze historical sales data and external factors. AI models can generate more precise demand forecasts by considering various factors and complex patterns, enabling businesses to optimize the levels of stock, procurement and planning of production.
b. **Management of Inventory:** Artificial intelligence (AI) solutions assist in lowering stockouts, minimizing excess inventory, and enhancing overall supply chain effectiveness by inevitably altering reorder levels, safety stock levels, and order numbers.
c. **Supply Chain Planning and Optimization:** Using AI, businesses can plan their supply chains more efficiently by taking a variety of aspects into account, such as customer demand, transportation costs, and manufacturing capacity. AI algorithms can design cost-effective, better-performing strategies for production scheduling, routing, and distribution.
d. **Supplier Management:** AI can help with supplier management, including relationship building, evaluation, and supplier selection. AI algorithms can locate the most appropriate suppliers, evaluate their skills, and recommend the best sourcing plans by examining various data. AI can also track the performance of suppliers in real-time, picking up on possible dangers or quality problems.

AI'S REPERCUSSIONS ON BUSINESS OPERATING MODELS

Artificial intelligence (AI) has profound and revolutionary effects on how businesses operate. The following are some significant effects of AI on business operations:

a. **Enhanced Productivity and Efficiency:** AI streamlines repetitive and mundane tasks, liberating staff to focus on more valuable responsibilities. It enhances operational efficiency and productivity, enabling organizations to achieve more in less time through automation and reduced manual labor.
b. **Improved Decision-Making:** AI equips organizations with robust tools to sift through vast amounts of data, derive insights, and make informed decisions. By leveraging AI technologies like machine learning and predictive analytics, businesses can gain deeper insights, identify patterns and trends, and make well-informed choices.
c. **Automation of Processes:** AI enables businesses to automate various administrative tasks. Implementing AI-powered solutions allows organizations to enhance process efficiency, reduce errors, and enhance speed and accuracy.
d. **Customization and Enhancing Customer Experiences:** Artificial intelligence (AI) empowers businesses to deliver personalized experiences to their customers. By analyzing customer data and behavior and using AI algorithms to tailor products, services, and recommendations based on individual preferences, organizations can enhance customer satisfaction and loyalty.

CHALLENGES AND FACTORS TO THINK ABOUT AI

The power of AI is already evident today, especially in the area of decision-making. Indeed, it has made its presence felt in many boardrooms. More than 40% of CEOs report utilizing generative AI to inform their decision-making processes. Numerous benefits are associated with these AI tools, ranging from improved compliance to the promotion of less biased and more inclusive strategic decisions. Concurrently, as AI continues to advance, strategies need to be developed for using these systems in important decision-making. The approach to AI interaction must be carefully considered, and, importantly, decisions that can be wholly delegated to AI need to be identified.

Certain decisions today are exclusively determined by AI. For instance, at Ant Financial, AI is responsible for loan approvals and is set to play an expanding role in wealth management. Additionally, technology giants like Facebook, Microsoft, and Netflix utilize reinforcement learning algorithms to allocate digital content.

Although fully autonomous AI decisions remain relatively rare, AI already plays a significant role in shaping the choices made by executives and consumers. At Amazon, for instance, AI recommendations drive 35% of the company's revenue. Government services are also experiencing a growing influence of this technology. In Singapore, citizens have access to information about government services 24/7 through tools like "Ask Jamie" and the new VICA bot.

The interaction between humans and AI carries significant consequences for the decision-making process. Recent research has revealed that individuals, relying on their distinct decision-making styles, can reach entirely different conclusions when presented with identical AI recommendations. This indicates that simply creating a flawless AI system may not suffice. Even when a human is involved, everybody must consider the psychological factors that influence decision-making.

While numerous obstacles and considerations exist, AI possesses the potential to greatly enhance corporate processes. It is imperative to address ethical concerns associated with AI, such as data privacy, algorithmic biases, and their impact on employment.

Organizations must overcome technological obstacles, invest in infrastructure, and upskill their personnel in order to implement AI technologies. To ensure ethical and accountable use, laws and regulations must also keep up with the quick growth of AI.

FUTURE PROSPECTS FOR ARTIFICIAL INTELLIGENCE (AI) AND MARKET SIZE

The artificial intelligence market, projected to reach a value of $136.55 billion in 2022, is expected to rapidly expand in the coming years due to increased investments in AI technologies, digital disruption, and the need for a competitive edge in a rapidly growing global economy. A Compound Annual Growth Rate (CAGR) of 37.3% is forecasted for the period between 2023 and 2030 for the global artificial intelligence market, with a total value expected to reach $1,811.8 billion by 2030.

The potential impact of AI on the global economy is significant. AI is anticipated to contribute more to the global economy by 2030 than the combined current output of China and India.

The global economy is expected to benefit from AI by a staggering $15.7 trillion by 2030, surpassing the combined economic output of China and India.

In 2020, Baker Hughes introduced a Watson-based application that enabled operators to access real-time well production data. As a result, methodologies have been employed to optimize various operational procedures, improving the forecasting of oil and gas output and delivering positive updates on production rates.

According to 75% of CEOs surveyed by the IBM Institute of Business Value in 2023, the company with the most advanced generative AI will gain a competitive advantage. However, these CEOs are also concerned about managing risks related to discrimination, ethics, and security.

To support clients in implementing generative AI, IBM Consulting has recently established its Center of Excellence (CoE) for Generative AI. This CoE enhances IBM Consulting's existing global expertise in AI and automation, which comprises

21,000 certified data and AI consultants with over 40,000 enterprise engagements. These consultants specialize in assisting businesses across various sectors in implementing and expanding AI to detect and mitigate risks, as well as provide guidance and insights.

By increasing productivity by 1.2 to 2.0 percent, this technology could potentially boost annual sales in the retail and consumer packaged goods (CPG) sector by $400 billion to $660 billion. Generative AI has the potential to automate critical functions such as customer assistance, marketing and sales, as well as inventory and supply chain management, to expedite operations. The retail and CPG industries have long relied on technology, utilizing both traditional AI and cutting-edge analytics solutions to manage extensive data sets encompassing numerous SKUs (Stock keeping unit), extensive supply chains and warehousing networks, and complex product categories such as consumables. Moreover, these industries place a high value on customer engagement, providing opportunities for generative AI to complement existing artificial intelligence initiatives.

CONCLUSION

Professor Marwala highlighted several significant ethical issues associated with AI, including privacy and surveillance, bias and discrimination, transparency and explain ability, job displacement, security, accountability, regulation, and oversight. AI technology undoubtedly offers substantial advantages in various domains, but in the absence of ethical safeguards, it can pose a significant threat to fundamental human rights and freedoms. For instance, the emergence of image generators and video deepfakes presents a formidable challenge to maintaining the integrity of information.

AI plays a crucial role in enhancing the analysis and interpretation of extensive and intricate humanitarian datasets, thereby improving forecasting and decision-making processes. Mobile applications, chatbots, and social media enable real-time interactions with individuals impacted by humanitarian emergencies, creating responsive feedback loops. Chatbots, for example, are employed to comprehend the requirements of refugees across various languages. Digital cash systems offer swift and adaptable assistance, while biometrics aid in establishing digital identities and reuniting families.

Furthermore, AI and automation have the potential to disproportionately affect employment in smaller cities and may exacerbate societal inequalities by automating certain job functions. Addressing these ethical concerns is crucial to harness the full potential of AI while safeguarding individuals and society as a whole.

Undoubtedly, AI has transformed the way business' function and interact with their stakeholders, and this influence on company operations is palpable. It has tremendously increased the efficiency of the task done with very low margin of error and a high profit margin. The present state of AI has already showcased its capacity to enhance decision-making, streamline processes, enhance customer service, and optimize supply chain management. With breakthroughs on the horizon that are poised to revolutionize various facets of organizational operations, the future of AI in corporate functions appears promising. To fully harness AI's capabilities while ensuring responsible and sustainable integration, enterprises must navigate both technical and ethical challenges. Businesses that proactively embrace and leverage AI expertise gain a competitive edge in a world increasingly shaped by advancing AI technologies.

Organizations are now able to achieve new heights of operational effectiveness, client happiness, and company expansion because to the careful and strategic adoption of AI technologies.

REFERENCES

Abrokwah-Larbi, K., & Awuku-Larbi, Y. (2023). The impact of artificial intelligence in marketing on the performance of business organizations: evidence from SMEs in an emerging economy. *Journal of Entrepreneurship in Emerging Economies*. Advance online publication. doi:10.1108/JEEE-07-2022-0207

Adam, M., Wessel, M., & Benlian, A. (2021). AI-based chatbots in customer service and their effects on user compliance. *Electronic Markets, 31*(4), 427–445. doi:10.1007/s12525-020-00414-7

Akter, S., Michael, K., Uddin, M. R., McCarthy, G., & Rahman, M. (2022). Transforming business using digital innovations: The application of AI, blockchain, cloud, and data analytics. *Annals of Operations Research, 308*(1-2), 1–33. doi:10.1007/s10479-020-03620-w PMID:35935743

Allioui, H., & Mourdi, Y. (2023). Unleashing the Potential of AI: Investigating Cutting-Edge Technologies That Are Transforming Businesses. *International Journal of Computer Engineering and Data Science, 3*(2), 1-12.

Amarasinghe, H. (2023). Transformative Power of AI in Customer Relationship Management (CRM): Potential Benefits, Pitfalls, and Best Practices for Modern Enterprises. *International Journal of Social Analytics, 8*(8), 1–10. https://norislab.com/index.php/ijsa/article/view/30

Arora, M., Prakash, A., Mittal, A., & Singh, S. (2021, December). HR analytics and artificial intelligence-transforming human resource management. In *2021 International Conference on Decision Aid Sciences and Application (DASA)* (pp. 288-293). IEEE. 10.1109/DASA53625.2021.9682325

Aw, E. C. X., Tan, G. W. H., Cham, T. H., Raman, R., & Ooi, K. B. (2022). Alexa, what's on my shopping list? Transforming customer experience with digital voice assistants. *Technological Forecasting and Social Change, 180*, 121711.

Bag, S., Srivastava, G., Bashir, M. M. A., Kumari, S., Giannakis, M., & Chowdhury, A. H. (2022). Journey of customers in this digital era: Understanding the role of artificial intelligence technologies in user engagement and conversion. *Benchmarking: An International Journal, 29*(7), 2074-2098.

Bag, S., Wood, L. C., Xu, L., Dhamija, P., & Kayikci, Y. (2020). Big data analytics as an operational excellence approach to enhance sustainable supply chain performance. *Resources, Conservation and Recycling, 153*, 104559.

Brynjolfsson, E., & McAfee, A. (2017). The business of artificial intelligence. *Harvard Business Review, 95*(1), 59-66.

Castro, S. L. C., Del Pozo Durango Rodrigo Humberto, V., Paúl, A. C., & Estefanía, A. T. P. (2023). Impact of Artificial Intelligence on Market Behavior Analysis: A Comprehensive Approach to Marketing. *Remittances Review, 8*(4).

Chandra, S., Verma, S., Lim, W. M., Kumar, S., & Donthu, N. (2022). Personalization in personalized marketing: Trends and ways forward. *Psychology & Marketing, 39*(8), 1529-1562.

Cigerci, M. (2023). Main Effects of Big Data on Supply Chain Management. *Implementation of disruptive technologies in supply chain management*, 27-49.

Cortellazzo, L., Bruni, E., & Zampieri, R. (1938). The Role of Leadership in a Digitalized World: A Review. *Front Psychol, 10*. doi:10.3389/fpsyg.2019.01938

Cunningham, E. (2021). Artificial Intelligence-based Decision-Making Algorithms, Sustainable Organizational Performance, and Automated Production Systems in Big Data-Driven Smart Urban Economy. *Journal of Self-Governance and Management Economics, 9*(1), 31–41. doi:10.22381/jsme9120213

Davenport, T. H., & Ronanki, R. (2018). Artificial intelligence for the real world. *Harvard Business Review, 96*(1), 108-116.

De Bruyn, A., Viswanathan, V., Beh, Y. S., Brock, J. K. U., & Von Wangenheim, F. (2020). Artificial intelligence and marketing: Pitfalls and opportunities. *Journal of Interactive Marketing, 51*(1), 91-105.

Dhanabalan, T., & Sathish, A. (2018). Transforming Indian industries through artificial intelligence and robotics in industry 4.0. *International Journal of Mechanical Engineering and Technology, 9*(10), 835-845.

Dumitriu, D., & Popescu, M. A. M. (2020). Artificial intelligence solutions for digital marketing. *Procedia Manufacturing, 46*, 630-636.

Gupta, S., Leszkiewicz, A., Kumar, V., Bijmolt, T., & Potapov, D. (2020). Digital analytics: Modeling for insights and new methods. *Journal of Interactive Marketing, 51*(1), 26-43.

Haleem, A., Javaid, M., Qadri, M. A., Singh, R. P., & Suman, R. (2022). Artificial intelligence (AI) applications for marketing: A literature-based study. *International Journal of Intelligent Networks*.

Hoyer, W. D., Kroschke, M., Schmitt, B., Kraume, K., & Shankar, V. (2020). Transforming the Customer Experience through New Technologies. *Journal of Interactive Marketing, 51*(1), 57–71. doi:10.1016/j.intmar.2020.04.001

Jain, P., & Aggarwal, K. (2020). Transforming marketing with artificial intelligence. *International Research Journal of Engineering and Technology, 7*(7), 3964-3976.

Jasmin Praful Bharadiya. (2023). Driving Business Growth with Artificial Intelligence and Business Intelligence. *International Journal of Computer Science and Technology, 6*(4), 28-44.

Kunduru, A. R. (2023). Artificial Intelligence Usage in Cloud Application Performance Improvement. *Central Asian Journal of Mathematical Theory and Computer Sciences, 4*(8), 42-47. https://cajmtcs.centralasianstudies

Maheswari, S. (2023). The Transformative Power of AI in Marketing FMCG. *IJFMR-International Journal For Multidisciplinary Research, 5*(3).

Nguyen, D. K., Sermpinis, G., & Stasinakis, C. (2023). Big data, artificial intelligence and machine learning: A transformative symbiosis in favour of financial technology. *European Financial Management, 29*(2), 517-548.

Noranee, S., & bin Othman, A. K. (2023). Understanding Consumer Sentiments: Exploring the Role of Artificial Intelligence in Marketing. *Jurnal Ilmu Ekonomi Dan Manajemen, 10*(1). doi:10.30996/jmm17.v10i1.8690

Olson, C., & Levy, J. (2018). Transforming marketing with artificial intelligence. *Applied Marketing Analytics, 3*(4), 291-297.

Provost, F., & Fawcett, T. (2013). Data science and its relationship to big data and data-driven decision making. *Big Data, 1*(1), 51-59.

Ranković, Gurgu, Martins, & Vukasović. (2023). Artificial intelligence and the evolution of finance: opportunities, challenges, and ethical considerations. *Edtech Journal, 3*(1), 20-23.

Rivas, P., & Zhao, L. (2023). Marketing with chatgpt: Navigating the Ethical Terrain of GPT-Based Chatbot Technology. *AI, 4*(2), 375-384.

Saura, J. R., Ribeiro-Soriano, D., & Palacios-Marqués, D. (2021). Setting B2B digital marketing in artificial intelligence-based CRMs: A review and directions for future research. *Industrial Marketing Management, 98*, 161-178.

Schoemaker, P. J., Heaton, S., & Teece, D. (2018). Innovation, dynamic capabilities, and leadership. *California Management Review, 61*(1), 15-42.

Siau, K. L., & Yang, Y. (2017). *Impact of artificial intelligence, robotics, and machine learning on sales and marketing*. Academic Press.

Soumpenioti, V., & Panagopoulos, A. (2023, September). AI Technology in the Field of Logistics. In *2023 18th International Workshop on Semantic and Social Media Adaptation & Personalization (SMAP)* (pp. 1-6). IEEE. 10.1109/SMAP59435.2023.10255203

Chapter 10
The Effects of Artificial Intelligence (AI) on Marketing

Ana Filipa Vieira Lopes Joaquim
https://orcid.org/0000-0002-3419-1242
ISLA Santarém, Portugal

ABSTRACT

This chapter explores how AI is transforming marketing strategies, customer segmentation, personalized advertising, and customer relationship management (CRM). Additionally, it investigates the ethical considerations and challenges associated with AI implementation in marketing.

INTRODUCTION

Conceptualize Artificial Intelligence (AI) is almost an impossible task, not only because of its range of applications, but mostly because of its technological complexity.

AI can be applied to several fields such as medicine, engineering, education, and marketing to name a few.

For this chapter, the author will focus on the effects of AI on marketing, regarding the innovating strategies, segmentation criteria, advertisement changes, and ethical concerns. In order to do so we need first and foremost to understand the correlations (??) between marketing and the AI definition.

According to Kotler and Armstrong (2016), the simple definition of marketing is based on customer relationships to make companies and brands profitable. Despite the conceptualization of marketing suffering several mutations over time (Kotler et al., 2017), in the present, the main topic of marketing relies on creating a robust emotional bridge between customers and brands (Kotler et al., 2021).

DOI: 10.4018/979-8-3693-0712-0.ch010

Looking back, marketing first conceptualization was entirely focused on production (marketing 1.0), nowadays the epicenter is based on relationships and causes, and society is experiencing marketing 5.0, also known as societal marketing (Kotler et al., 2017, 2021).

This change of paradigm was necessary, because, according to Kotler et al. (2017), the rapid evolution of technology was dehumanizing the applicability of marketing strategies and it was necessary to take a step back in the way marketing viewed its consumers. It doesn't mean that the process is more human than before, but it means that because customers are more informed and the array of selection criteria has increased in terms of items and complexity, the brands need to consider looking at them not as a money machine, but rather as involved partners in the process of buying the products and services.

Before AI, marketeers had to rely on their decisions on market surveys, and purchase behaviors, but most of all on their intuition regarding report sheet analysis, hence and mistakes resulting from bad or insufficient data driven decisions were made (Campbell et al., 2020).

Although according to Deveau et al. (2023) "generative AI promises to disrupt the way B2B[1] and B2C[2] players think about customers experience, productivity, and growth" (2023, p. 1), it seems that is important to conceptualize AI to better understand this claim.

According to McCarthy (2007) AI is "the science and engineering of making intelligent machines, especially intelligent computer programs. It is related to the similar task of using computers to understand human intelligence, but AI does not have to be limited to biologically observable methods" (2007, p. 1).

Nowadays marketeers can understand customers' needs in real-time through large data collection (Haleem et al., 2022), Machine Learning (ML) and linguistic analysis, social media and text mining (Mariani et al., 2022), Task Automation (TA) (Davenport et al., 2021), just to name a few of the AI tools in marketing.

The advent and democratization of social media have indeed provided marketeers with enormous field of personal data almost free of charge and more accurate than market surveys, focus groups, or data collection resulting from questionnaires and surveys, but is it morally ethical to use these personal data without people's knowledge?

Understanding the customer journey brings to the brands a huge advantage to increase their sales and profits, but at what cost?

Despite all AI tools and innovations, several issues must be addressed, such as making the process as humanized as possible, whilst ensuring customers' data secure and private.

Discussing the process humanization with AI may seem contradictory at first, not only because AI tends to have a permanent and systemic penetration of marketing procedures, but because according to Dobrev (2012), it cannot understand human feelings, such as empathy, for Kotler et al. (2017) the analysis of human behavior must be based on understanding their feelings and emotions.

In the past, traditional reports and statistics were based on deductive learning which relies on prior knowledge of the data (Campbell et al., 2020), but with AI technology the process of analyzing big data has become faster and increasingly (more) accurate. According to Campbell et al. (2020), "AI can provide valuable insights about finding the right consumers, engaging with customers, and conducting return-on-investment analysis" (2020, p. 2). with a special focus on Machine Learning, as through this technology, it is possible to identify consumer clusters more precisely. According to Haleem et al. (2022) AI can provide and stratify client profiles, in a more user friendly way, to identify the customer journey process.

Through this process, marketeers can easily understand the customers' needs and, almost, at the same time generate targeted content to satisfy them, creating value and benefits that answer more adequately their expectations. But truth be told that AI technology evolution brings several issues to public debate, such as costumers' privacy concerns (Klockmann et al., 2021; UNESCO/COMEST[3], 2019; UNESCO, 2022).

Addressing the assurance of customer privacy is a complex terrain, as customers willingly share personal information on social media, yet the legality of selling such data to companies remains ambiguous. (Moore, 2019).

Mostly, the use of AI technology has become a mainstream organizational method, but there are several concerns about it, which is why this overview is extremely important for marketing management.

Nevertheless, all the advantages of AI in marketing are essential to understand the evaluation on individuals' perceptions, needs, and behaviors.

Despite UNESCO (2022) having created a document[4] regarding several recommendations on the ethics of AI, effective legislation is still a blurred area in this matter because is unclear, and have little sanction regarding specific uses.

Social Media and text mining are one of the most powerful sources of personal data for marketeers because individuals share their personal information willingly through their publications and engagements with other individuals and companies (Figueiredo & Joaquim, 2023).

In 2015, Harry Davies, a full-time journalist of The Guardian, exposed Cambridge Analytica as a company that used millions of personal data without the knowledge or consent of Facebook users (Fornasier & Beck, 2020). Although, despite all the scandals and public debates regarding privacy policies, according to Wong (2019) Facebook remains, almost, the same in terms of privacy policies.

Through an overview of the literature review regarding articles on AI and on marketing studies which provide a more accurate analysis of this multi-thematic subject, this chapter aims to help integrate and systematize the complexity of marketing with AI technologies, from the perspective of their advantages and disadvantages.

After this introduction, the questions of this work are:

Does AI in marketing bring more proximity between brands and consumers or does it manipulate free choice?

The objectives of this chapter are:

O1 – Conceptualize innovating strategies, segmentation criteria, and advertisement changes regarding AI in marketing.
O2 – Identify the main advantages and disadvantages of AI applications in marketing.
O3 - Systematize the breach of effective legislation on personal data sharing and use.

This chapter is divided into five main sections such as innovation strategies, customer segmentation, personalized advertising, and ethical considerations and challenges regarding AI in marketing.

The first section will conceptualize the evolution of marketing, the second section will presented the innovative strategies regarding the paradigm changes in marketing when AI technology is applied, such as data collection (Haleem et al., 2022), Machine Learning (ML) and linguistic analysis; social media and text mining (Mariani et al., 2022), Task Automation (TA) (Davenport et al., 2021). The third section will focus on segmentation criteria and customer journey analysis, concerning data collection techniques. The changes in personalized advertising will be the topic of the third section, in which the alleged manipulation of free choice will be taken into consideration. In the last section ethical considerations and challenges will be overviewed regarding the implementation of AI in marketing, such as the lack of effective legislation and the gap between the free will data sharing and the business weaponizing use of the personal customer information.

METHODS

The research method of this chapter is based on a qualitative overview of the literature of academic articles, marketing studies, opinion articles, and transnational organizations' websites.

A comprehensive search was conducted in the key databases, namely Scopus, SAGE, Emeralds, Science Direct, and EBSCOhost, following the keywords for article selection presented in Table 1. Studies, reports, and opinion articles on this theme developed by private entities were also considered.

There are several academic studies regarding the advantages of AI on marketing and personal data sharing concerns, but there is a lack of academic literature on the correlation between marketing strategies and AI ethics, implications, and uses regarding the business of sharing and selling Client personal data.

Our main goal was to systematize the effects of artificial intelligence on marketing in contemporaneity, approaching the issue from a global perspective, integrating the benefits and potential hazards AI could bring to consumers, if there is no specific legislation or ethical sense in its use.

Methodological quality and quality of evidence were based on several case studies where AI had been implemented and its results on the effectiveness and efficiency of marketing procedures.

The authors identified, read, and analyzed about one hundred academic articles (97) and twenty research and company studies (20) regarding the marketing and artificial technology effects, and they decided to include opinion online newspaper articles (4) that were about AI's ability to have emotional intelligence to expose its lack of ability.

The multiplicity of research methods aims to be an approach to the investigation of the use of AI in marketing regarding not only the facilitation of the procedure but also to expose several concerns about the free use without appropriate legislation of AI on marketing. Far from being a closed analysis, this chapter's aim is to be the trigger to understand the change of perception regarding privacy in consumers.

THE MARKETING EVALUATION CONCEPT

Marketing conceptualization has suffered several changes, in order to cope with market trends and evolution, the communication and information technologies (ICT), and civil society transformations, as well.

According to Kotler et al. (2017, 2021), marketing can have an evolution process in five stages, being: Product Marketing (marketing 1.0); Consumer-oriented marketing (marketing 2.0); Value-centered Marketing (marketing 3.0) Digital Marketing (marketing 4.0), and more recently to Societal Marketing or Humanity Marketing (marketing 5.0) (Figure 2).

Despite the marketing conceptualization stages pointed out by Kotler et al. (2017, 2021), it's important to understand the genesis of marketing science and its origin.

Back in the 19th century after the Industrial Revolution, marketing was focused entirely on production. In those days the main goal was to transfer factory production to as many buyers as possible (marketing 1.0). It was a standardized type of marketing, with basic products to serve the mass market. Henry Ford's famous phrase about the pseudo possibility of the customer choosing the color of the car, if it was black, greatly characterizes this era of marketing (Mehta, 2022).

Figure 1. Criteria used to select articles

Artificial Intelligence	Segmentation	Personalized	AI ethics
AI technology	Criteria	Advertisement	AI Legislation
Marketing	Customer Journey	Customer behavior	Customer
AI on marketing social media and text mining	Data Collected		Privacy
Machine Learning	Purchase behavior		
Task Automation			

Figure 2. Evaluation of marketing conceptualization

Marketing 1.0	Product Marketing
Marketing 2.0	Consumer-oriented marketing
Marketing 3.0	Value-centered Marketing
Marketing 4.0	Digital Marketing or Relationship Marketing
Marketing 5.0	Societal Marketing or Humanity Marketing

After World World II, society changed, and the Baby Boom phenomenon played a crucial role in transforming individuals into mass consumers, a new era of marketing begun (marketing 2.0), through the invention of television and the democratized evolution of radio (Mehta, 2022).

Nevertheless, according to Neslin and Winer (2023) the report written by the Ford Foundation, in 1959, were the trigger to a "more rigorous approach to research in marketing conducted by faculty in business schools" (2023, p. 2).

Companies and brands adapted their product communication to mass media advertisement while customers became increasingly (more) informed, and the brands felt the need to initiate a segmentation process.

Kotler et al. (2017) allude that customers started to internalize the product's value in their needs and a primary segmentation process became necessary to understand the purchase decision-making process, however, for the authors, customers were still seen as passive targets of marketing campaigns.

The next change in the marketing paradigm was faster than the previous, as there was an urgent need for brands to distinguish themselves and create purchasing needs among consumers, based on differentiation in their values, presenting the intrinsic benefits of the products (marketing 3.0).

Marketing 3.0 Portrays a Values-Driven Era

In this type of society, individuals are seen in addition to consumers, in the case of human beings, who seek to make the world a better place, solving the problems of societies in partnership with companies. These types of people look for companies which represent and address their social, economic, and environmental justice values.

Customers started to gain an active role in marketing strategies, once they felt that their needs were considered by the brands.

The ICT evaluation and its democratization to civil society had transformed the internet into a commodity product (Figueiredo & Joaquim, 2023), so it was natural that the brand's marketing and communication became more accurate and segmentized.

By the end of the 20th century, in the 90s, ICT, the internet in particular, had gained a crucial role in civil society and consequently, there was a need to academically train individuals linked to company marketing, so that brand communication could become digital.

Higher education courses linked to marketing at universities proliferated, in parallel with the rapid evolution of ICT and the need to transform traditional marketing into digital marketing for companies and brands (marketing 4.0) and to create a relationship between them. According to Kotler et al. (2017), Marketing 4.0 is known as relationship-building marketing because of the proximity it created between brands and consumers.-Back then most companies started their digital journey, by creating websites to reach the customer' attention and with the hope of creating needs based on the proximity and differentiation of the perceived values of their products, ultimately aiming for consumers to make purchases.

Nevertheless, the ICT evaluation had become accessible and user-friendly to civil society, consequently consumers become more informed and demanding.

In the beginning of the 21st century, at the end of the first decade, mass media began to be overthrown by new media, with the emergence of social media, like, as for example, Facebook and Instagram.

Social Media users voluntarily provide personal data on social networks through their virtual interactions, whether with their likes on individual or company pages or through their searches and insertion of personal data, such as location, profession, or date of birth. Thus, creating a digital footprint based on a personalized profile of individual characteristics. Marketeers have gained an enormous amount of personal data and insights on their consumer's beliefs, feelings, and engagement with the brands (Deveau et al., 2023).

Although Facebook was not the pioneer in social networks, as there were already others such as MySpace or Hi5, it was, without a doubt, the social network that boosted the emergence of new media. Later on, in the words of Moore (2019), Google and Facebook changed completely the advertisement industry, when they started the online segmentation of paid advertisement.

The author mentioned that companies embraced these new tools with tremendous enthusiasm, without really understanding how the machine worked.

Small companies had finally the opportunity to advertise their products with a small budget alongside big brands and commodity products (Moore, 2019). But there was a caveat, the democratization of the online advertisement industry brought a process of dehumanization of consumers. According to Kotler et al. (2021), individuals were analyzed through algorithms and mechanisms based on report sheets that did little or nothing to identify consumers' emotions or perceptions.

There is no doubt that algorithms cannot empathize with the feelings and emotions of individuals, but they show marketeers the mechanical process of purchasing. Although Kotler et al. (2021) realized that to understand the purchase process of customers, marketeers should understand the customer's perceptions, emotions, beliefs, and behaviors as a whole. In fact, the author points the lack of ability to transform the mechanical and algorithm brand-costumer relationship into an emotional one (marketing 5.0). For that matter, Kotler et al. (2021) realized that marketing should not only rely on the binomial product-costumer paradox but should also include consider humanitarian and sustainable values, like the Sustainable Development Objectives (SDO) (United Nations, 2023).

Marketing 5.0 doesn't neglect ICT technologies, far from that, it embraces it and uses it avidly, but with the necessary acuity to involve three fundamental pillars in contemporary marketing: Sustainable Development Objectives (SDO), products, and consumers.

In the words of Kotler´s et al. (2021) the SDO must be incorporated in marketing considering that costumers want brands and companies committed with the society and the planet.

Nowadays business and society are experiencing a new era of digital innovation, with Artificial Intelligence (AI). Despite AI being a new topic in technology, over recent years it has gained a crucial role in public opinion (Mariani et al., 2022).

Over time, several movies, such as Minority Report (Spielberg, 2002) or books, such as 1984 (Orwell, 1949), just to name a few, had fueled the public imagination in order to understand, conceptualize, and incorporate IA into mainstream daily lives, but fiction has become more or less reality.

The constant and fast innovation in IA technology brought to all fields of business an increase in procedures, and marketing was no exception(Deveau et al., 2023).

Perhaps marketing conceptualization will improve to marketing 6.0, with the incorporation of AI technology regarding ethical topics and recommendations of use.

INNOVATION IN MARKETING STRATEGIES REGARDING AI USES

As mentioned before, AI technology brings to marketing several tools that aim to facilitate marketeers' lives regarding customer behavior analysis (Campbell et al., 2020).

In the past, those studies were based on analogic and digital tools which collected customers' information big data, but it only gave the marketing professionals the past behavior of customers, and they had to rely on their intuition and expertise to create effective marketing strategies (Kotler & Armstrong, 2016). Despite being time consuming, the process was full of human perceptions, interpretations, and, sometimes, errors.

According to Davenport et al. (2021) marketing has been, perhaps, the field that leveraged with AI the most because its core activities rely on understanding and predicting customer's needs to create a desire for acquisition and persuading people into buying. In the words of Deveau et al. (2023) AI implementation in marketing is less expensive, and more effective in procedures.

To conceptualize marketing strategies, the decision-making process has been replaced by the customer journey (Nascimento, 2021), inasmuch as the consumers' approach area became attached to micro strategic brand tasks, conceptualized regarding consumers' feelings and potential brand approaches (Cosgrove, 2012), instead of major campaigns focus on general target.

Machine Learning (ML) processes have changed the strategic marketing framework. According to Mariani et al. (2022), the ML process can provide marketeers with an amount of customer data, in real-time. The authors, quoted by Malter et al., 2020, mentioned that "by embracing theories from psychology and other social sciences, consumer research has increasingly focused on gaining a deeper understanding of the thinking, desires, and experiences of individual consumers" (2022, p. 2), and with integration of AI technology, computers can learn and integrate human capabilities, such as decision making predictions. In the words of Mariani et al. (2022), ML process will be able to learn, understand and interpret human thinking and feelings, through the usage of linguistic analysis, social media data and text mining, of course that has to be programmed for that goal through Task Automation (TA).

Davenport et al. (2021) allude that TA through the use of "AI can streamline the sales process by using extremely detailed data on an individual, including real-time geolocation data, to create highly personalized product or service offers"(2021, p.

4), as AI can provide detailed client profiles allowing to identify and draft dedicated customer journey processes (Haleem et al., 2022).

Through this process, marketeers can easily understand the customers' needs and, almost, at the same time generate content to satisfy them, creating value and benefits that rely on their expectations.

CUSTOMER SEGMENTATION CRITERIA

The customer segmentation criteria used to rely on (Kotler, 2000; Kotler & Armstrong, 2016; Kotler & Keller, 2015) homogeneity among the segment's main needs, uniqueness, and the common reaction of customers to marketing plans and actions. In other words, segmentation criteria refer to the characteristics or variables that organizations use to divide their target market into smaller, more manageable segments.

These criteria help businesses to identify and understand specific groups of customers with similar needs, preferences, and behaviors. Effective segmentation criteria are essential for tailoring marketing strategies, products, and services to meet the distinct requirements of each segment. Until AI technology came along to the marketing field the customer segmentation criteria was e based only on Demographic, Geographic, Psychographic, Behavioral, and Socioeconomic, according to Kotler & Armstrong (2016). However, with the advent of AI, these criteria become almost secondary.

Marketeers made their customer research, to create a target for their products, based on market surveys and information collected through official or nonofficial sources, such as economic and social reports, and purchase behavior after the campaign's implementation and operationalization.

Nowadays, with AI technology and tools, the target analysis became almost obsolete, as companies tend to create buyer personas (Kotler et al., 2021; Mehta, 2022) to provide and simplify client profiles to identify the customer journey process (Haleem et al., 2022).

The customer segmentation criteria became more focused on the individual, despite the larger target. Truth be told that target identification is still very useful in marketing today, but its importance has decreased enormously in the marketing field. The target identification helps the marketeers to create more accurate buyer personas, considering that brands doesn't have only one buyer persona, but in most of the cases marketing managements should conceptualize more than one, in order to have a more notion of costumer's reality needs.

After the advent of the democratization phenomenon of social media, users unconsciously began to provide their data, their preferences, beliefs, tastes, and ideologies and, consequently, showed their involvement with brands and purchasing behaviors. So, marketeers no longer had the necessity to do empirical research about their customers' profiles, as users tend to give them almost free of charge (Chacko, 2023; Conik, 2017).

According to Chacko (2023), "AI marketing combines AI technologies with customer and brand experience data to provide highly precise insights into (...) customer journey and market trends. AI technologies like (...) machine learning (ML), sentiment analysis, and others guide decision-making, so [companies] stay ahead of competitors and are prepared for the challenges of a dynamic marketplace"(2023, p. 1).

The author realizes that the AI algorithms can "listen" to social media users and ML can understand them as well as identify keywords and triggers that can provide marketeers the tools to create personalized social media campaigns.

PERSONALIZED ADVERTISING

When in 2012 Google decided to create, an advertisement system to capitalize the company was far from realizing the way of doing things would be changed forever, according to Moore (2019). Subsequently Facebook followed this system with the added value of personal data, instead of research data provided by costumers on Google browser (Moore, 2019).

At first, the process was unregulated, so every company could create an account and with a minimum budget. In other words, everyone [companies] could through a user-friendly method be a part of Google's advertisement tool without humans, legislative or technical supervision. And the added value was substantial regarding the low budget versus the range of their paid communication (compared to the ones who were required to run advertising (ad) campaigns in traditional media). After all Google as became the most important browser in the internet field.

This advertisement tool performed, an almost, personalize ad campaigns between brands and their potential consumers and clients.

Although the system wasn't free of flaws, not only due the lack of legislation but because users started to feel like they were bombed with ads and companies were no longer getting the expected revenue in the words of Moore (2019), despite their low allocated campaign budgets. By now the Holy Grail of advertisement strategies and campaigns had become a counterproductive investment (Moore, 2019).

The online advertisement process created by Google, in the beginning of the 21st century, was technologic complex and tremendously fallacious.

From 2012 until the last years of that decade, Google bought several small online advertisement companies that had created procedures and technology that the giant Google needed in order to improve their revenues, obliterating the simplification of mechanized advertising processes and making the algorithmic system too cumbersome (Moore, 2019).

Given the growing discredit of the online advertising system created by Google, there was a need for the company to step back and speed up the process, as well as make it more transparent.

Parallelly, Facebook had incorporated, a more or less, similar advertisement tool, but with a major advantage to the brands that can reach their potential buyers in their individuals social pages.

The Google process was based on the individuals research on the internet, but Facebook's created a system that targeting strategies could be more specific based on the choices and preferences of consumers. These preferences were free of charge for companies because there were voluntarily given by the internauts on there social media personal pages.

Google reinvented the entire process but Facebook, by this point had already gained the marketeer's confidence.

Nowadays these two technological giants have conquered the main share of marketing quotes regarding online advertisement (Statistica, 2023).

Social Media and text mining are some of the most powerful sources of personal data for marketeers because individuals share their personal information willingly through their publications and engagements with other individuals and companies (Figueiredo & Joaquim, 2023), as mentioned before.

Based upon algorithms and considering the integration of AI technology, the combination marketeers' professional knowledge and social media data, it is possible to generate personalized advertising.

Regardless the technological innovations, human factors such as privacy or free will tend to be neglected by marketeers. Perhaps neglect is too strong, but it must be considered that there is a very fine line between what users voluntarily provide on social networks and the abusive use of that data.

In 2015, Harry Davies a full-time journalist of The Guardian, exposed Cambridge Analytica as a company that used millions of personal data without the knowledge or consent of Facebook users (Fornasier & Beck, 2020). However, and despite all the scandals and public debates regarding privacy policies, according to Wong (2019) Facebook remains, almost, the same.

ETHICAL CONSIDERATIONS AND CHALLENGES

Ethical considerations regarding the use of AI in marketing are crucial in today's digital landscape. AI technologies offer numerous benefits to marketeers, such as improving targeting, personalization, and efficiency. However, they also raise ethical concerns that must be addressed to ensure responsible and fair use.

The main ethical concern in public debate relies on the Privacy and Data Protection of the users.

The European Parliament and the European Council (2016) created a regulatory document protect General Data, and all European websites must have a Privacy Policy (European Commission, 2018) in which individuals may or may not accept and consent to the use of cookies and personal data.

According to the *Privacy policy for websites managed by the European Commission* (European Comision, 2018):

Consent should be given by a clear affirmative act establishing a freely given, specific, informed, and unambiguous indication of the data subject's agreement to the processing of personal data relating to him or her, such as by a written statement, including by electronic means, or an oral statement. This could include ticking a box when visiting an internet website, choosing technical settings for information society services, or another statement or conduct that indicates in this context the data subject's acceptance of the proposed processing of his or her data. Silence, pre-ticked boxes, or inactivity should not therefore constitute consent. Consent should cover all processing activities carried out for the same purpose or purposes. When the processing has multiple purposes, consent should be given for all of them. If the data subject's consent is to be given following a request by electronic means, the request must be clear, concise, and not unnecessarily disruptive to the use of the service for which it is provided. At the same time, the data subject should have the right to withdraw consent at any time without affecting the lawfulness of processing based on consent before its withdrawal. To ensure that consent is freely given, consent should not provide a valid legal ground for the processing of personal data in a specific case where there is a clear imbalance between the data subject and the controller, and it is, therefore, unlikely that consent was freely given in all the circumstances of that specific situation. It is often not possible to fully identify the purpose of personal data processing for scientific research purposes at the time of data collection. Therefore, data subjects should be allowed to give their consent to certain areas of scientific research in keeping with recognized ethical standards for scientific research. Data subjects should have an opportunity to give their consent only to certain areas of research or parts of research projects to the extent allowed by the intended purpose (2018, pp. 3–4).

However, individuals tend to accept it without reading it. Ibdah et al. (2021) realize that individuals who read privacy policies don´t fully read them or understand the real dimension of acceptance of the terms.

Another concern is the process transparency regarding disclosure and expandability, on one hand, marketeers should be transparent about their use of AI in marketing campaigns, making it clear when AI is involved in decision-making or personalization, on the other hand, AI algorithms should be explainable and there use clear, allowing marketeers to understand how and why certain decisions are made. This helps build trust within the consumers.

According to Mariani et al. (2022) ML based on AI technology can intentionally manipulate the needs of the customers withdrawing their free will of choice. Based on the machine learning system and task automation, the advertisement campaigns become more and more personalized removing a wide range of interpretations by customers to internalize different needs and, consequently, to purchase different types of products. It's true that the marketing genesis is to create needs in costumers, but individuals had the free will perception. Nevertheless, the application and general use of algorithms had became more mainstreamed in marketing strategies, but is this different than subliminal publicity once consumer aren't aware of this application?

In 1957, during the *Picnic* movie, James Vicary, had ad in the projector machine ever five seconds a frame that include the sentences of "drink coke" and "eat popcorns." without viewers knowledge. The sells of these two products increased tremendously at the movie break, according to Vicary (Lindstrom, 2017).

Lindstrom (2017) allude that this experience provoked fear and discomfort in American society because they were living in a Cold War context and there were concerns about this technic regarding subliminal publicity, not only because the people though that this could be used to propagate political propaganda and, but consequently brain wash on their feeling and perceptions. For that matter this technic was forbidden, in 1958.

Marketeers have managed to evolve this procedure into a sub-science of marketing, called neuromarketing. Despite their alleged similarities, neuromarketing does not reach the consumer's subconscious at the moment of advertising, as subliminal advertising does. There is a moment before advertising in which the consumer's subconscious is studied so that the product and the main difference between these two techniques of seducing the consumer.

According to Bhardwaj et al. (2023), neuromarketing "measures human behavior through neuroscientific techniques to observe cognitive processes and identify motivating factors that manipulate responses, such as peer pressure, feelings, and incentive" (2023, p. 1). So, regarding this argument, the use of AI guarantee to marketeers a wide range of performance.

In another words, costumers are no longer able to be guinea pigs with subliminal publicity, but their behavior is understood through brain technics analysis. Nevertheless the ethical use is still a concern in the academic field (Lindstrom, 2017).

Incorporating these ethical considerations into AI-driven marketing strategies can help build trust with consumers, reduce the risk of legal and reputational issues, and promote responsible and sustainable marketing practices.

Marketeers need to stay informed about emerging ethical guidelines and adapt their strategies accordingly as AI technology continues to evolve.

As UNESCO (2022) introduces this topic on their website "Today, artificial intelligence plays a role in billions of people's lives. Sometimes unnoticed but often with profound consequences, it transforms our societies and challenges what it means to be human" (2022). Consequently, UNESCO with COMEST adopted a global agreement on the *Ethics of AI* (UNESCO/COMEST, 2019), that still doesn't answer the urgent need to legislate the use of AI.

In this document institutions recommend the creation of a transnational methodology based on scientific research settled on human rights in order to stablish several tools and procedures to implement best practices related to AI ethical use.

Unfortunately, ethics and legislation aren't the same thing, because on ethics individual can hide themselves in their values, principles, and education, on a micro level, but companies can position themselves, on a macro level, where business culture and national legislation (or lack thereof) could be the perfect excuse to a gray area is created, although legislation is based on common values and principles it seems that common sense isn't the same to all intervenient.

Despite all these concerns, AI brings a crucial advantage to marketeers to do their jobs well and with less effort than before (Campbell et al., 2020).

There is no question that the effects of AI on marketing promote a smooth and easy customer experience between the brands and their target market.

CONCLUSIONS AND IMPLICATIONS

Despite all the advantages of AI in marketing it is essential to understand the consequences of technology on individuals' perceptions, needs, and behaviors.

Innovating marketing strategies such as ML or TA, evaluation of segmentation criteria, and advertisement changes regarding AI in marketing where conceptualized (O1), regarding different academic approaches and their advantages and concerns.

The main advantages of AI applications in marketing are by far, the tend to be more accurate, effective, faster, on costumers' behavior analysis, and less expensive to the brans and companies(O2). The biggest disadvantage and concern in academic and public debate is related to the thin line between the leverage of personal data use by marketeers and the obtrusion in individual lives, more specifically in virtual environments.

Regardless European Parliament and the Europeean Council (2016), UNESCO, (2022) and the European Comision (2018) having created documents to improve the privacy policy and to preserve the integrity and sharing of personal data, there is still a breach of legislation on personal data share and use (O3).

However, there is no right or wrong answer to the main question of this chapter.

It's undeniable, as the literature shows, the increased proximity AI in marketing brings between brands and consumers. One of the biggest advantages is the improved accuracy that the AI use can bring to the process of campaigns. Nevertheless, the disadvantages are also undeniable regarding the (un)ethical use of personal data.

LIMITATIONS AND RECOMMENDATIONS FOR FUTURE RESEARCH

Despite AI technology not being a new topic, nowadays it has gained increasing notoriety because it is a phenomenon that has penetrated the daily lives of individuals and companies. There is no doubt that marketing has gained significant advantages in terms of the personalized suitability of its communication campaigns. As well as the procedures inherent in their operationalization, they tend to be increasingly assertive, faster, and at a lower cost. However, the legislative gap at the national and transnational levels could result in the misuse of privileged personal information.

The European Union has made no effort to educate and warn against the malicious use of AI, and technological evolution has been faster than mentality change or recommended guideline creation.

According to Figueiredo & Joaquim, (2023) "AI Technology isn´t confined to local or national borders, owing its worldwide range, it is extremely difficult to create legislation that is consistent to the specific civil law of the nations. So, for now, society needs to rely on common-sense ethics for the use of AI technology"(2023, p. 82).

This research is intended to become a first-line investigation concerning AI technology and marketing personal data use. It´s urgent to research individuals' feelings regarding the use of technology in marketing. Because to the author there is a thin line between the use of algorithms and subliminal publicity. True be told that in the theoretical field these two topics have different technics, but the goals seem to be the same: manipulate customers behaviour without their knowledge or will.

But this research is far from over and must be acknowledged as one of the most important marketing subjects.

Over the last decades' society has watched the fast evaluation of artificial intelligence, but despite the operational cost reduction, the effectiveness of marketing advertisement campaigns, or the facilitation of communication and data collection, marketeers need to analyse their processes and AI tools regarding costumers' data on an ethical base.

There is a latent, and sometimes truthfully feeling, that robots, computers, and some kind of machines will take away their free will of choice.

Through this research, we were able to establish the strong impacts on AI arising from the correct management marketing processes, strategies, and tools.

Another topic that needs to be explored and understood is the main role of AI technology in Marketing regarding the interaction between companies or brands and their customers, in other words, is important to marketeers are knowledgeable with a sense of educational mission, based on transparency, so that consumers know in advance the purpose of their data.

As important as the subjects above are. There is a need for effective personal data use legislation regarding AI technology to mitigate the abuse of personal data on marketing campaigns. For this technology, ethics need to be clear and pragmatic for everyone, without grey areas.

We understand that these future research directions are too vague to be studied as one, that's why there is a subdivision of the topics, but in the end, the effects of artificial intelligence in marketing are felt by everyone, whether customers or companies and brands.

This literature review intended to fill the gap in literature regarding AI technology in marketing through a catch-all overview of the different items about these topics.

The authors' contribution to academia is related to the identification of different variables that are needed to have more clarity on these nutshell subjects.

REFERENCES

Bhardwaj, S., Rana, G. A., Behl, A., & Gallego de Caceres, S. J. (2023). Exploring the boundaries of Neuromarketing through systematic investigation. *Journal of Business Research*, *154*, 113371. doi:10.1016/j.jbusres.2022.113371

Campbell, C., Sands, S., Ferraro, C., Tsao, H. Y., & Mavrommatis, A. (2020). From data to action: How marketers can leverage AI. *Business Horizons*, *63*(2), 227–243. doi:10.1016/j.bushor.2019.12.002

Chacko, A. (2023). *The role of artificial intelligence in marketing*. Sprout Social. doi:10.1002/9781119506515.ch7

Conik, H. (2017). The Past, Present and Future of AI in Marketing. In *Marketing News* (pp. 1–15). https://www.finextra.com/blogposting/20816/the-past-present-and-future-of-ai-in-financial-services

Cosgrove, K. M. (2012). Political branding in the modern age. In J. Lees-Marshment (Ed.), Routledge Handbook of Political Marketing (pp. 107–123). Routledge - Taylor & Francis Group. doi:10.4324/9780203349908.ch9

Davenport, T. H., Guha, A., & Grewal, D. (2021). *How to Design an AI Marketing Strategy*. Harvard Business Review. https://hbr.org/2021/07/how-to-design-an-ai-marketing-strategy

Deveau, R., Griffin, S. J., & Reis, S. (2023). *AI-powered marketing and sales reach new heights with generative AI*. McKinsey & Company. https://www.mckinsey.com/capabilities/growth-marketing-and-sales/our-insights/ai-powered-marketing-and-sales-reach-new-heights-with-generative-ai

DobrevD. (2012). *A Definition of Artificial Intelligence*. http://arxiv.org/abs/1210.1568

European Comision. (2018). *Privacy policy for websites managed by the European Commission*. Privacy Policy for Websites Managed by the European Commission. https://eur-lex.europa.eu/legal-content/EN/TXT/PDF/?uri=CELEX:32018R1725

European Parliament and of the Council. (2016). Regulation (EU) 2016/679 of 27 April 2016 on the protection of natural persons with regard to the processing of personal data and on the free movement of such data, and repealing Directive 95/46/EC (General Data Protection Regulation). *Official Journal of the European Communities, OJ L 119/1*, 1–88. https://data.europa.eu/eli/reg/2016/679/oj

Figueiredo, P., & Joaquim, A. F. (2023). The impact of artificial intelligence and intergenerational diversity. In F. Ince (Ed.), *Leadership Perspectives on Effective Intergenerational Communication and Management* (pp. 72–90). IGI Global. doi:10.4018/978-1-6684-6140-2.ch005

Fornasier, M. D. O., & Beck, C. (2020). Cambridge Analytica: Escândalo, Legado E Possíveis Futuros Para a Democracia. *Revista Direito Em Debate*, *29*(53), 182–195. doi:10.21527/2176-6622.2020.53.182-195

Haleem, A., Javaid, M., Asim Qadri, M., Pratap Singh, R., & Suman, R. (2022). Artificial intelligence (AI) applications for marketing: A literature-based study. *International Journal of Intelligent Networks*, *3*(August), 119–132. doi:10.1016/j.ijin.2022.08.005

Ibdah, D., Lachtar, N., Raparthi, S. M., & Bacha, A. (2021). Why Should i Read the Privacy Policy, i Just Need the Service': A Study on Attitudes and Perceptions Toward Privacy Policies. *IEEE Access : Practical Innovations, Open Solutions*, *9*, 166465–166487. doi:10.1109/ACCESS.2021.3130086

Klockmann, V., Von Schenk, A., Villeval, M., Klockmann, V., Von Schenk, A., Villeval, M., Intelligence, A., Klockmann, V., Von Schenk, A., & Villeval, M. C. (2021). *Artificial Intelligence, Ethics, and Intergenerational Responsibility*. https://halshs.archives-ouvertes.fr/halshs-03237437/document

Kotler, P. (2000). Marketing Management Millenium Edition (10th ed.). Prentice-Hall, Inc.

Kotler, P., & Armstrong, G. (2016). Principles of Marketing - Global Edition (S. Wall, Ed., 16th ed.). Pearson Education Limited.

Kotler, P., Kartajaya, H., & Setiawan, I. (2017). *Marketing 4.0 (moving from traditional to digital)*. John Wiley & Sons, Inc.

Kotler, P., Kartajaya, H., & Setiawan, I. (2021). *Marketing 5.0 - Tecnologia para a Humanidade*. Conjuntura Atual Editora.

Kotler, P., & Keller, K. (2015). Marketing Management (15th ed.). Pearson Education Limited.

Lindstrom, M. (2017). *A lógica do consumo: Verdades e mentiras sobre por que compramos*. HarperCollins Brasil.

Mariani, M. M., Perez-Vega, R., & Wirtz, J. (2022). AI in marketing, consumer research and psychology: A systematic literature review and research agenda. *Psychology and Marketing*, *39*(4), 755–776. doi:10.1002/mar.21619

McCarthy, J. (2007). What Is Artificial Intelligence Anyway. *American Scientist*, *73*(3), 258.

Mehta, S. (2022). The Evolution of Marketing 1. 0 to Marketing 5.0. *International Journal of Law*, *5*(4), 469–485.

Moore, M. (2019). *Democracia Manipulada*. Editora Self.

Nascimento, R. (2021). *Entenda o que é jornada do consumidor e veja exemplos!* Marketing, Materiais Educativos. https://www.agendor.com.br/blog/jornada-do-consumidor/

Neslin, S. A., & Winer, R. S. (2023). The History of Marketing Science: Beginnings. The History of Marketing Science: Second Edition, 1–17. doi:10.1142/9789811272233_0001

Orwell, G. (1949). *1984*. Secker & Warburg.

Spielberg, S. (2002). *Minoraty Report*. Academic Press.

Statistica. (2023). *Leading social media platforms used by marketers worldwide as of January 2023*. Advertising & Marketing - Marketing. https://www.statista.com/statistics/259379/social-media-platforms-used-by-marketers-worldwide/ UNESCO/COMEST

UNESCO. (2022). *Recommendation on the ethics of artificial intelligence*. https://en.unesco.org/artificial-intelligence/ethics

United Nations. (2023). *Sustainable Development Goals*. Take Action for the Sustainable Development Goals. https://www.un.org/sustainabledevelopment/sustainable-development-goals/

Wong, J. C. (2019). *The Cambridge Analytica scandal changed the world – but it didn't change Facebook*. The Guardian. https://www.theguardian.com/technology/2019/mar/17/the-cambridge-analytica-scandal-changed-the-world-but-it-didnt-change-facebook

KEY TERMS AND DEFINITIONS

B2B: When companies only communicate and sell to other companies.

B2C: When companies only communicate and sell to individual customers.

Machine Learning: The process of algorithms that generate other algorithms to solve them using Artificial Intelligence.

Task Automation: Repetitive automate tasks using specific software to reduce the manual handling with the objective of making processes more accurate and efficient.

ENDNOTES

1 B2B – Business to Business

2 B2C – Business to Consumer

3 COMEST - Commission on the Ethics of Scientific Knowledge and Technology

4 UNESCO. (2022). Recommendation on the ethics of artificial intelligence. https://en.unesco.org/artificial-intelligence/ethics.

Chapter 11
AI-Powered Supply Chains Towards Greater Efficiency

N. Shobhana
SASTRA University, India

ABSTRACT

In the current scenario of business environment, a supply chain is the linking pin among the various business activities, which makes it rather indispensable. Global businesses are spending money on digital solutions to increase the effectiveness of their supply chains, which will enhance their operational performance. One of the important solutions to it is the application of AI (artificial intelligence) to bring in advancements in all the business processes. Artificial intelligence (AI) is the term used to describe the replication of human intelligence processes by technology, primarily computers. Artificial intelligence is expected to contribute 15.7 trillion dollars to the global economy by 2030. The various technologies of AI, namely big data, machine learning, cloud computing, blockchain, chatbots, and ChatGPT, have a wide range of applications in various sectors or industries resulting in efficiency and improved customer satisfaction. AI-powered supply chain across various sectors with its benefits and limitations is discussed in detail.

INTRODUCTION:

Grand View Research estimates that the AI market is already worth $136.55 billion. Their study projects a CAGR of 37.3% between 2023 and 2030. (Forbes, 2023). Due to the rapid digitization of all the key sectors of our economy, including banking and financial services, healthcare, automobiles, and telecommunications, there is a growing demand for AI-based tools and systems throughout India. This is because

DOI: 10.4018/979-8-3693-0712-0.ch011

AI helps with automation, minimizes errors, and manages repetitive tasks. With a compound annual growth rate (CAGR) of 33.28% from 2023 to 2028, the artificial intelligence industry in India is expected to rise from $680 million in 2022 to $3,935.5 million by 2028. (IMARC report, 2023). In India, spending on artificial intelligence increased by 109.6% in 2018, or $ 665 million, and is predicted to increase at a CAGR of 39% to reach $ 11,781 million by 2025 (IBEF, 2023). The process of delivering the appropriate product to the right consumer at the correct time, place, and cost is known as supply chain management. Logistics deals with the transportation of the goods from the manufacturer till it reaches the end user. It deals with both inbound logistics and outbound logistics. The application of AI is more crucial and critical for the success of Supply Chain and Logistics, especially in the field of automation. AI provides technologies and tools which helps the supply chain to perform repetitive and error-prone activities automatically. Some of the most common technologies are warehouse robots, autonomous vehicles, RPA [Robotic Process Automation] and digital workers.

A technology known as artificial intelligence (AI) enables machines to perform tasks that would ordinarily need human intelligence. It entails the creation of computer systems with the capacity to learn and take judgment calls based on information and algorithms. AI processes a lot of data by using models and algorithms. To make decisions or complete tasks, it learns from data patterns. Machine learning techniques are used by AI systems to enhance performance over time. AI is essential for streamlining supply chain processes, cutting costs, increasing customer happiness, and empowering businesses to successfully navigate the complicated and changing business environment of today. As technology develops and supply chain management becomes more data-centric and networked, its significance is anticipated to keep expanding. It has a wide range of applications in supply chain management, helping organizations optimize their operations, reduce costs, improve customer satisfaction, and enhance overall efficiency. AI processes massive volumes of data by employing models and algorithms. In order to make decisions or complete tasks, it learns from data patterns. AI systems can use machine learning to gradually enhance their performance. AI-based solutions have emerged as the new paradigm, allowing businesses to automate repetitive tasks thanks to their scalability and agility. AI enables robots to learn from past performance and optimize workflows, enhancing operational effectiveness and cutting costs.

REVIEW OF LITERATURE

Barriannis (2018) offered a thorough analysis of the supply chain literature that uses AI-based techniques to address issues pertinent to SCRM. Through the investigation of e-commerce intelligent operation instances, Wang et al. (2019) elaborated on the use of AI in Electronic Commerce, highlighting the intelligent logistics, recommendation engine, and the optimal pricing applications. Another study focussed on application of artificial intelligence in smart warehousing environment for automated logistics (Pandian, 2019). An exploratory case study was conducted in operations management and supply chain management, with the artificial intelligence application (Helo & Hao, 2019). Considering the results of the literature review, another study presented a framework that offers insightful conclusions based on recent research findings and can be used to guide and launch future research projects in the areas of artificial intelligence (AI), machine learning (ML), and deep learning (DL) in Smart Logistics (Woschank et al., 2020). A study by Oscar Rodríguez-Espíndola et al. (2020) offers a framework that incorporates Blockchain, 3D printing, and artificial intelligence, the three disruptive new technologies to enhance the flow of data, goods, and financial resources in supply chains. Through a thorough assessment of the existing literature, Toorajipour et al. (2021) pointed out the applications of artificial intelligence (AI) in supply chain management with identifying both existing and new AI strategies. A thorough literature review of studies on the application of artificial intelligence (AI) in supply chain management (SCM) with 150 journal articles that were released between 1998 and 2020, taken were analysed through a systematic manner (Pournader, 2021). Another bibliometric paper examined the AI applications in SC from a process viewpoint and offered a framework for making decisions about how best to use AI approaches into various SC processes (Riahi et al., 2021). The results of a study implied the capability of artificial intelligence-driven big data analytics in determining the performance, flexibility, and resilience of the supply chain (Dubey 2022). Through scholarly network and content analysis, another study pinpointed five key research clusters. The subjects that were found were green supply chain management, supplier selection, inventory planning, demand planning, and supply chain network design (SCND). The necessity of utilizing AI to enhance the supply chain process is increasing as the role of AI in SCM becomes more significant. (Sharma et al., 2022). Tsolakis et al. (2022) investigated the application of artificial intelligence and blockchain to supply chains to increase operational performance limits, promote sustainable growth, and monetize data. The healthcare supply chain (HSC) has weaknesses that have been made public by the epidemic. Recent developments include the uptake of certain cutting-edge technologies, such as Industry 4.0 and AI, in the healthcare supply chain are proving to be game-changers. The critical success factors (CSFs) for AI adoption in healthcare supply chain has been the primary goal of the study in the context of a rising economy (Kumar et al., 2023). In continuation, the application of AI technology in short-range logistics drones focussing on efficacy and optimization of related logistics processes to reduce the manpower needed (Wang et al., 2023). Another study gave a thorough overview of the application of AI technologies across various supply chain stages through an in-depth analysis of machine learning, robotics, and natural language processing. The use of artificial intelligence in the supply chain was also considered in terms of potential difficulties and ethical issues (Khadem et al., 2023). A study by Ghoreshi (2023) found that Artificial intelligence (AI) can be seen as a CE enabler that enables businesses to develop novel circular business models. Digital data can be gathered, analysed, and stored by a variety of AI applications, machine learning, robotics, and machine vision, among others. AI-enhanced products and services can solve environmental concerns, leading to improved environmental performance characteristics, through independent interactions with their surroundings and self-learning capabilities. The study demonstrates how AI helps create circular value towards goals of sustainable development (Goreshi et al.,2023). The study by Bag et al. (2023) show that developing a collaborative platform powered by BDA-AI technology to assimilate, transfer, and utilize critical information from vast data sets, is very much possible. Healthcare organizations can thus profit from creative healthcare supply chain implementation. In order to increase supply chain resilience, research intends identified, evaluated, and prioritized the AI-based requirements of I5.0. To achieve the goals, the Best-Worst Method (BWM), the Bayesian technique, and Pareto analysis were combined. The results of this study by Ahmad et al. (2023) showcased that enhancing a manufacturing supply chain's survivability requires the most critical AI-based imperative, which is real-time tracking of supply chain actions, in which the Internet of Things (IoT) is being used.

Based on the above review of literature, it can be concluded that are some of the areas in which AI is highly used in the supply chain. The areas where AI has an important role to play in automation is back-office automation, logistics automation, warehouse automation. Under back-office automation, the technological breakthroughs especially through AI has helped in replacing or rather reducing human effort, where repetitive tasks are to be done. The concept of digital workers which is prevalent makes the digital employees/workers acting as junior staff, interpreting, logging, and replicating the responsibilities of their human counterparts. Through robotic process automation, Digital workers indulge in Conversational AI by communicating with people, NLP, which is Natural language processing. By these tools, Digital employees can interact with people, comprehend their needs, interpret unstructured data, and take decisions. It rather helps to increase the operational efficiency, reduce the employee's mental health issues being exposed to repetitive tasks. It also creates new job opportunities as the brain behind these AI tools or technology is equally important. While dealing with logistics automation, AI is helpful in providing solutions through autonomous trucks. In warehouse automation, collaborative robots also called as Cobots are more helpful in improving efficiency by being economical, being able to work round the clock and by being flexible to re-program. Quality assurance through AI supported computer vision helps in improving the productivity and helps to enhance the quality of the semi-finished and fully completed products.

Automated inventory management uses AI enabled bots, which is helpful in scanning inventory levels in warehouses, as well as in retail stores. It also results in Inventory optimization through analysing historic data of demand and supply. Supply chain AI forecasting tools helps to customize the fulfilment processes as per the regional territory requirements. Bullwhip effect is one of the phenomena that affects the supply chain drastically. By utilizing information gathered from customers, suppliers, manufacturers, and distributors, AI-powered forecasting systems can assist in reducing demand and supply variations to regulate bullwhip. This indeed helps to reduce stockout situations and backlogs. Thus, predictive analytics has a greater role in supply chain.

Another area to be concentrated while dealing with supply chain activities would be supplier relationship management. AI enabled SRM [Supplier relationship Management] aids in supplier selection based on analysing the previous data available like price, previous purchase history and sustainability. Moreover, improved supplier communication network is possible through AI powered tools such as robotic process automation. Nowadays, sustainability is a growing concern with more impetus given on going greener. AI powered tools play a vital role in greener transport logistics helping in optimizing the transport routes, considering factors like traffic, road and weather condition and fuel consumption, resulting in lower carbon emission and increased sustainability. Greener warehousing is also enabled through AI supported forecasts wherein optimum inventory levels can be maintained with reduced carbon emissions. As a game changer for the years to come, the No Code AI, would be an even better alternative through which organizations can build AI solutions that offers code-free technology which would enable the non-requirement for AI expertise, and non-AI experts can put their ideas into practice and test them.

The various technologies in which AI is applicable are

Big Data: The term "Big Data," which describes the massive amount of information generated by both humans and robots, has emerged in response to the recent development of digital data. AI algorithms have been designed to evaluate and interpret this wealth of data. AI systems can uncover connections and patterns that might be invisible to humans by using Big Data to train machine learning algorithms. Businesses can use AI, for instance, to analyse customer data and spot trends and patterns. They gain a better knowledge of who their clientele is as a result. This will also assist them in sharpening their marketing tactics.

Improved Computing Power: The ability to process and analyse massive amounts of data in real time has been made possible by the tremendous growth in computing power throughout time. As a result, AI systems can already carry out intricate tasks like parsing natural language and identifying audio and images.

Cloud Computing: The way businesses access and use AI tools and technology has been changed by cloud computing. Some of the AI technologies are machine learning, Natural Language Processing Algorithms and image recognition. Workflows in businesses can readily incorporate such services. Additionally, cloud computing gives companies the flexibility and affordability to scale up or down their AI activities in response to market demands.

Areas in Automation: The areas where AI is applicable under automation are as follows.

Supply Chain Automation: Without AI, the supply chain cannot be automated. Supply chain automation technologies like digital employees, warehouse robots, autonomous vehicles, RPA, etc. can perform mundane, error-prone tasks automatically thanks to artificial intelligence (AI). Some of the tasks that can be automated are

Back Office Automation: Document automation is the use of automation techniques to gather data, extract information, and produce documents. The best illustration could be RPA, or robotic process automation, which is a fundamental tool for creating customized agents, or "bots," that interact with elements of graphical user interfaces and perform repetitive, rule-based tasks. With the aid of an emerging technology solution known as "intelligent document processing," firms can now automate document operations even when they involve unstructured data like PDFs and photos. As most IDP solutions leverage RPA to automate documentation processes, it is called as IDP RPA. It also leverages other AI technologies like optical character recognition, machine learning algorithm and natural language processing. Nowadays, digital workers combine conversational AI with RPA. Conversational AI is the technology that permits automatic messaging and discussion between computers and people is known as. Companies can use it to roll out chatbots and virtual assistants. Conversational AI algorithms can mimic human speech, grasp the purpose of speech or text input, and recognize user intent to converse like a human. Conversational AI enables digital employees to communicate with staff members in natural language. Employees can communicate with these digital workers via text or voice to request tasks. These jobs are carried out by digital workers using tools like RPA and AI models. Digital workers therefore give employees more time to concentrate on tasks like formulating corporate strategy, strategies for coming up with manufacturing and selling of new goods.

Automation of Logistics: The usage of autonomous trucks is helpful in making the supply chain very efficient. The autonomous trucks have sensors and lidar, which aids in guiding them through challenging traffic scenarios. The employment of autonomous trucks in logistics can enhance productivity, save on fuel, and reduce the number of accidents brought on by human mistake. Autonomous vehicle technology has the potential to revolutionize the shipping sector by lowering freight and logistics costs, increasing fuel efficiency, and cutting down on delivery times.

Warehouse Automation: The speed and accuracy of warehouse operations can be improved effectively, by using AI-powered robots for picking, packing, and sorting things in a better manner, and reducing the need for human labour to do repetitive work. The throughput is increased, and mistakes are decreased. It can also optimize warehouse layouts to enhance product flow and cut down on the time needed to track items. Collaborative robots, also known as cobots or co-robots are robots or robot-like equipment that are designed to securely operate directly alongside human workers to finish a task that cannot be entirely automated. Thus, it can eliminate the need for human involvement in repetitive and routine processes, resulting in significant labour cost savings and increased productivity. Some of practical implications are round the clock functionality, economic efficiency and scalability. Round the clock functionality improves the performance of the business. Cobots are cheaper than industrial robots, and rely upon few numbers of hardware components and sensors which are cheap. Cobots are more investment-worthy due to their adaptability and re-programmability because they can be programmed to have a variety of uses in different sectors, ranging from manufacturing to healthcare.

Automated Quality Control and Checks: Automating product quality inspections is possible with the aid of AI-enabled computer vision [CV] systems. These technologies can increase productivity and precision in production lines because they don't get tired. For example, AI-powered computer vision systems can automate and improve quality control of the finished product. AI can be utilized in manufacturing and distribution processes for quality control and defect identification, guaranteeing that only high-quality items are delivered to clients.

Automated Inventory Management: AI-driven algorithms that take into account variables like demand volatility, lead times, and carrying costs can optimize inventory levels. As a result, carrying expenses are decreased, and storage space is used more effectively. Automating tedious inventory management tasks, such as scanning inventories in real time, can be done by bots with computer vision and AI/ML skills. Retail establishments may also use such inventory scanning bots. However, before putting such solutions into practice, you must make sure they are feasible and determine their long-term benefits; otherwise, such projects risk failing. AI systems can help in finding the appropriate inventory levels by looking at previous demand and supply data as well as trends. By doing so, storage fees and excess production may be reduced.

The next main thrust area where AI has a vital role is Predictive Analytics.

Predictive analytics: AI can look at past data, market trends, and outside influences to generate accurate demand estimates. Better inventory management, a decrease in overstock and stockouts, and production schedule optimization are all benefits of this. It can also result in inventory optimization, producing region-specific forecasts and prevention of bullwhip effect. Bullwhip effect occurs when little changes at one end of the supply chain are magnified as they flow either upstream or downstream. AI-powered forecasting systems can help to control bullwhip by using data obtained from consumers, suppliers, manufacturers, and distributors to help reduce demand and supply variances. As a result, stock shortages and backlogs may be lessened.

The next thrust area would be the supplier relationship management

Supplier relationship management: AI can help in assessing potential suppliers based on many factors including pricing, quality, and performance in terms of on-time delivery. AI-driven solutions can also help with data collection, analysis, and ranking related to supplier performance. Another tool that might alert supply chain management to any issues is real-time supplier performance monitoring. Another advantage of AI-powered technologies like RPA is the automation of common supplier communications like invoice sharing and payment reminders. Automating these procedures can help avoid problems like delays in shipment and production brought on by late payments to vendors, for example. Another vital area where the AI contributes in supply chain in the attainment of improved sustainability.

Improved Sustainability: Since a company's supply chain generates the majority of its indirect emissions, sustainability is a significant concern any business. AI can help supply chain operations becoming more sustainable and environmentally friendly. AI may assist businesses in optimizing their supply chains for sustainability by lowering carbon emissions, cutting waste, and choosing eco-friendly suppliers and supplies. –

- **Greener transport logistics**: Through greener transport logistics, which takes into account variables like traffic conditions, weather, and fuel prices, AI systems can optimize delivery routes and modes of transportation. As a result, delivery times are quicker and transportation expenses are lower.
- **Greener warehousing**: Greener warehousing focusses on improving sustainability. The carbon emissions associated with the storage and transportation of surplus inventory can be decreased because to AI-powered forecasts' ability to help maintain optimal inventory levels. Solutions for smart energy use can help cut carbon emissions from energy use in warehouses.
- **Sustainability focussed ERP systems**: ERP systems that are sustainable place a strong emphasis on their ability to track and manage environmental effects. Additionally, the company lowers its emissions by utilizing these solutions on the public cloud due to the larger public cloud providers' improved efficiency. The real-time acquisition of both operational and financial data on a single platform is made possible by ERP systems. The only use for an internet connection is to monitor supply chain activity. Accenture estimates that the reduction in annual GHG emissions from using only public cloud

systems would have been the same as taking 20 million automobiles off the road (Accenture, 2023).

- **Smart Devices:** The environmental effect of supply chain operations is or will be reduced using smart sensors, drones, telematics, and self-driving cars. Smart HVAC (heating, ventilation, and air conditioning) systems, LED lighting, and sensor-based lighting can all be used to do this. A typical warehouse can reduce its GHG emissions by about 30%. According to a recent study, when compared to conventional techniques, Drones can reduce last-mile delivery variable costs and GHG emissions. if there are more than 200 consumers in the area resulting in quicker delivery (Chiang et. al. 2019). Telematics can be used to monitor a vehicle's health and the driver's behaviour. Any deterioration in the tyres or engine of a vehicle could lead to inefficiencies, which would increase fuel consumption. By keeping an eye on vehicles and drivers around-the-clock, supply chain managers may drastically minimize their usage of oil. For instance, the Michelin Effifuel project used this technique to cut oil use by almost 2 litres per 100 kilometres (Wef Report 2016). Because the driver compartment will be used as additional storage space, self-driving cars will minimize GHG emissions by transporting more cargo on each journey. The ability to connect these IoTs also helps with traffic and route optimization.
- **3-D Printing:** Things can be manufactured everywhere there are printers using a digital file like CAD models. As a result, time is reduced and money spent on transportation as well as GHG emissions is reduced. When used rarely and across longer distances, they are more environmentally beneficial, much like email. Businesses can digitally code their intermediate products and duplicate them at the subsequent production site. Nothing need to be paid for freight nor there is any wait involved for items to travel great distances as a result. Consider this to be sending an email that is printed out on paper. Using email instead of the postal service can save time, money, and minimize the carbon footprint.
- **Usage of Electric Vehicles:** Without having a detrimental effect on supply chain activities, if the majority of the electricity in a location is generated from green energy sources and adequate charging infrastructure is installed there, electric vehicles can considerably reduce GHG emissions. With higher environmental and social governance (ESG) reporting scores, businesses may replace traditional fleets and draw in more investors (ESG report, 2023). Organizations also don't have to consider how to set up pricing activities. E-mobility tools can alert EV owners when charging stations become available and prompt them to return their car to a regular parking spot after it has finished charging. For instance, DHL has travelled more than 100 million

kilometres while cutting tons of CO2 emissions by using electric vehicles (EVs) for last-mile deliveries (DHL, com).

- **AI/ML models:** These models are excellent at forecasting and optimization, which is helpful for reducing GHG emissions while raising operational efficacy. PwC's prediction that AI/ML models will boost the global GDP by 4.4% while reducing greenhouse gas emissions by around 4% (PwC, 2023) lends credence to this claim. AI/ML models can also be used for demand forecasting. By properly estimating demand, businesses may build up their warehouses in a more sustainable manner.
- **Block chain technology:** It enables open data exchange between numerous parties, including diverse providers and end consumers. Blockchain can therefore assist businesses in measuring the carbon footprint of their products, the circularity of their operations, and compliance with laws and norms governing social and environmental governance. Discrimination and social externalities that happen along the value chain product excellence. By integrating AI with blockchain technology, it is possible to increase the transparency and traceability of the supply chain and protect the products' source and validity.

Some other areas in which AI has a vital role are as follows:

Route Optimization: Taking into account variables like traffic conditions, weather, and fuel prices, AI systems can optimize delivery routes and modes of transportation. As a result, delivery times are quicker and transportation expenses are lower.

Demand-Driven Production: AI can assist in the shift from conventional push-based production to demand-driven production, where manufacturing is coordinated with actual consumer demand, hence minimizing surplus inventory.

Predictive Maintenance: AI can foresee when machinery and equipment will break down, allowing for preventative maintenance and minimizing downtime in distribution and manufacturing plants.

Risk management: AI is capable of analysing data from a variety of sources to pinpoint and reduce supply chain risks like disruptions brought on by calamities or geopolitical events.

Real-time Visibility: AI-powered tracking and monitoring solutions give enterprises real-time visibility into the whole supply chain, enabling them to make educated decisions and act swiftly in the event of any problems.

Customer service: Chatbots and virtual assistants powered by AI can enhance customer service by quickly responding to consumer questions, tracking shipments, and resolving difficulties.

Application of Other AI Technologies

Machine Learning for Supply Chain Planning and Warehouse management: Algorithms that use machine learning can learn from data and create predictions based on the analysed data. These algorithms can analyse the following information when it comes to supply chain planning: data from several sources, such as historical sales data; market trends; and consumer behaviour. By analysing this data, machine learning can forecast demand, anticipate inventory levels, and shorten lead times to help the supply chain run more efficiently. An effective supply chain management may result from this.

Algorithms for machine learning have the ability to completely change how warehouses work. Machine learning algorithms can accurately estimate product demand, enabling warehouses to modify their inventory levels by analysing huge data like sales, customer orders, and inventory levels. It can minimize waste and avoid stockouts to increase customer satisfaction. By automating the picking and packing procedures, machine learning can also improve warehouse operations. Machine learning algorithms can discover the most effective pathways for warehouse employees to follow when completing orders by examining product size, weight, and location data. This can result in increased productivity and quicker order fulfilment times may result from this.

Circular economy is another area where Machine learning approaches can be used:

1. Develop circular goods, parts, and supplies for which ML tools, such as rapid ML-driven prototyping and testing are effectively employed.
2. Use circular business models to help create new products and materials. ML can expand the distribution of a product through techniques like pricing, inventory management, predictive maintenance, and intelligent demand forecasting.
3. Improve Circular Infrastructure to enhance component remanufacturing, material recycling, and product sorting and disassembly, which can build the foundation for reverse logistics (Tirkolaee. et al. 2021).

Chatbots in Operational Procurement: A chatbot is a computer program that mimics human conversation. Businesses may automate a number of procurement activities, including tracking orders, generating invoices, and managing suppliers, by integrating chatbots into operational procurement. By removing the need for human involvement in repetitive and routine tasks, automation can dramatically lower labour costs while also increasing efficiency. In order to comprehend and reply to client inquiries more logically and naturally, chatbots can also use machine learning algorithms. By studying previous discussions and user interactions, chatbots may provide personalized and context-specific responses to client inquiries, enhancing the overall user experience.

Natural Language Processing (NLP) in Supply Chain: "Natural language processing" (NLP) helps computers comprehend, translate, and create human language. In the context of supply chain management, NLP technology can examine a sizable volume of unstructured data, such as customer reviews on social media sites, to find patterns and insights about the requirements and preferences of customers. It can examine customer sentiment and modify their supply chain strategy accordingly, making businesses understand customer expectations. One best example would the usage of NLP by business to look at social media consumer reviews of its goods. These revelations might make it easier to exceed client expectations.

Benefits of AI in Supply Chain Management: Because AI offers so many benefits, businesses are using it in a growing number of contexts. In fact, according to NASSCOM's forecast for 2023, 96% of supply chain and industrial businesses will be utilizing AI. There are several benefits of using AI to supply chain management that foster operational excellence and competitive advantage. Here are several major advantages:

- **Accurate Inventory Management:** Any company that aspires to meet client needs while cutting expenses must practice accurate inventory management. They can gather real-time data on their inventory levels and utilize this data to improve their supply chain procedures by using AI-powered solutions. It can prevent overstocking or understocking, analyse demand patterns, project future demand, and manage inventory levels. It can also automate stock replenishment by establishing triggers that send out notifications to inventory managers when specific stock levels are reached. This guarantees fast stock replenishment, averting stockouts and the loss of prospective sales. The accuracy and speed of AI-powered inventory management can help businesses reduce carrying costs, improve order fulfilment rates, and ultimately increase customer satisfaction.
- **Improved safety:** The security of the workers and the efficiency of the supply chain are essential to the products they handle. AI can help to take proactive steps to prevent accidents and guarantee a safe working environment; identify possible dangers and inform staff; or take corrective actions to prevent accidents before they occur. AI analyses data from numerous sources, such as sensors and cameras. This lowers downtime and related costs while protecting your employees and products.
- **Use Chatbots for Better Customer Service:** In a variety of ways, AI-powered chatbots are redefining how businesses communicate with their consumers. By offering 24/7 support the customers are assisted effectively

and swiftly resolving their questions and problems without the need for human intervention.

They can deliver personalized recommendations and offers to clients based on their past purchases and preferences. They can concurrently handle many requests, cutting wait times and increasing customer satisfaction. The whole consumer experience may be improved by this.

- **On-Time Delivery:** While on-time delivery is a terrific way to build customer confidence and brand loyalty in supply chain management, it is fraught with difficulties due to fluctuating demand, transportation, logistics, etc. the AI can be used to improve on-time delivery rates, optimize transportation routes based on real-time data, precisely anticipate delivery timings, and track cargo progress at every stage. Moreover, it can proactively inform customers on the status of their shipments and anticipated arrival dates to increase transparency and foster customer confidence in the supply chain.

Additionally, advanced monitoring tools and predictive analytics powered by AI can be employed to identify possible bottlenecks in the supply chain and take the proactive steps necessary for on-time delivery. This raises customer satisfaction and lowers operational expenses linked to delivery delays.

Impacts of AI on Logistics and Supply Chain

Early adopters who incorporated AI-enabled supply-chain management have effectively outperformed their more sluggish rivals, with raising service levels by 65%, and with a decrease in logistics costs by 15% (McKinsey Report, 2019). Therefore, the promise of AI in logistics and supply chains is undeniable. The following are the main effects of AI:

- **Shorten Distribution Process:** The amount of time it takes to distribute goods to clients can be greatly decreased by integrating AI into logistics and supply chains. Businesses may use AI-powered algorithms to: accurately estimate demand; optimize shipping routes; and shorten delivery times. Faster and more effective dissemination follows from this. AI can also offer real-time shipment tracking, enabling proactive management of delays and other unforeseen events. This raises operational effectiveness, boosts customer happiness, and lowers expenses related to shipping delays.
- **Mitigate Risks:** Businesses can identify and mitigate possible hazards that could interfere with their operations by implementing AI in the supply chain

management process. Artificial intelligence (AI) systems may analyse data from a variety of sources and identify potential hazards, such as: Insolvencies of suppliers; Problems with product quality. By proactively creating backup plans and identifying alternate suppliers or transport routes, technology can also assist businesses in reducing these risks. Businesses may lessen their exposure to supply chain interruptions and assure smoother operations by utilizing AI to anticipate and respond to hazards in real time.

By boosting and optimizing supply chain processes, artificial intelligence (AI) has a significant impact on a variety of sectors and businesses. Here are some areas or sectors where artificial intelligence is heavily utilized and is beneficial to supply chain management:

1. **Retail and e-Commerce Sectors**: Forecasting of demand and inventory optimization powered by AI in the retail and e-commerce sectors with recommendation engines and personalized marketing, focussing on Supply chain transparency and delivery route optimization.
2. **Medical and pharmaceutical industries**: The application of AI is useful in drug and supply inventory management, supply chain monitoring for temperature and predictive analytics for the upkeep of medical apparatus.
3. In the **manufacturing industry**, AI is extremely useful in preventive maintenance of machinery and equipment, Defect identification, quality control and Management of inventory just-in-time.
4. In **Logistics and Transportation**, forecasting traffic and optimizing routes, monitoring and real-time tracking of shipments, optimizing loads and running a warehouse effectively can be done using AI.
5. **Energy and Utilities**: AI is helpful in power generation and distribution predictive maintenance, the streamlining of the supply chain for energy resources, and in management of the grid and the finding of faults.
6. **Food and Beverage**: AI can be applicable in managing the cold chain for perishable items, quality assurance and freshness surveillance and management of recalls and supply chain tracing.
7. **Agriculture**: AI is effective in precision agriculture for optimal planting and harvesting. It also helps to keep an eye on and managing supply chains for agriculture and predicting pest and disease outbreaks to protect crops.
8. **Consumer Electronics**: Forecasting the demand for electronic components is a task for consumer electronics. Taking control of global supply chains for the production of electronics, and effective inventory management is done by AI.

9. **Automobile Industry**: Supplier quality assurance and fault identification can be done, with optimising inventory for car parts and supply chain visibility and planning for production.
10. **Fashion and Apparel**: AI is effectively useful in forecasting demand for trendy and seasonally appropriate goods, optimization of the inventory to decrease extra stock and the visibility of the supply chain to result in sustainability.
11. **Chemicals and pharmaceuticals**: AI is useful in chemical raw material inventory management, traceability and regulatory compliance for drugs and supply chain optimization for the manufacture of chemicals.
12. **Oil and Gas**: Predictive maintenance for production and drilling machinery, supply chain management for gas and oil exploitation, continuous transportation and pipeline monitoring is possible through AI.
13. **Building and Construction Materials**: AI is effectively used in controlling building material inventories, collaboration amongst suppliers for project schedules and the visibility of the supply chain and procurement.
14. **Telecommunications:** Controlling the inventory of network hardware, monitoring supply chain disruptions in real time and inventory optimization for spare parts can be effectively managed through AI.
15. **Semiconductors and electronics**: Predictions on semiconductor component demand, risk management, quality assurance in the production of semiconductors and visibility of the supply chain is made possible through AI.
16. **Textiles and clothing**: Traceability of the supply chain for sourcing textiles, inventory management for textile producers and monitoring sustainability in the textile supply is taken care by AI.

The above sectors profit from AI's data analysis, predictive modelling, automation, and real-time monitoring ability to streamline supply chain operations, lower costs, increase efficiency, and boost overall performance. AI-driven solutions are still developing and will be essential for supply chain management in a variety of businesses.

Practical examples of companies where AI is effectively used in supply chain: Numerous businesses from a variety of industries have effectively incorporated AI into their supply chain operations to increase productivity, cut costs, and boost overall results. Here are some businesses that have successfully included AI into their supply chains:

Amazon is a shining example of how supply chain management uses AI extensively. With the help of AI algorithms, it uses its extensive network of warehouses and delivery routes to estimate demand, optimize inventory levels, and improve logistics efficiency. Thousands of robots have also been installed in Amazon's warehouses as a result of Kiva Systems' (now Amazon Robotics') acquisition, further automating order fulfilment.

Walmart uses AI for supply chain efficiency, inventory management, and demand forecasting. To make informed decisions about product distribution and stocking, the retail behemoth employs machine learning algorithms to examine past sales data, current market information, and even weather data.

United Parcel Service (UPS) used AI is to improve delivery schedules and routes, saving fuel and speeding up deliveries. Additionally, the business uses chatbots powered by AI to improve customer experience and offer real-time shipment tracking.

Procter & Gamble (P&G): To streamline its supply chain operations, P&G leverages AI and machine intelligence. In order to increase demand forecasting, they have created predictive analytics models. This has led to lower inventory carrying costs and more productive production.

IBM: IBM's Watson Supply Chain solutions use blockchain and AI to improve supply chain efficiency, traceability, and transparency. These services assist companies in real-time monitoring and management of their supply networks, lowering the possibility of disruptions.

Nestlé: Nestlé employs artificial intelligence (AI) and data analytics to streamline its production procedures and guarantee that its products are available on shop shelves. To decrease machine downtime in their production facilities, they have put predictive maintenance strategies into place.

Alibaba Group: To improve its e-commerce supply chain, Alibaba uses AI and machine learning. Its logistics division, Cainiao, employs AI to efficiently distribute and route orders, cutting down on delivery times and expenses.

Zebra Technologies: Zebra Technologies offers AI-powered solutions for asset tracking, supply chain visibility, and inventory management. Their technology aids in automating data collection and increasing inventory accuracy for enterprises.

Flexport: A digital freight forwarder, Flexport employs AI to give its customers real-time visibility and data to optimize international shipping. Their software enables businesses to more effectively manage their global supply networks.

JD.com: A leading online retailer in China, JD.com uses AI-enabled robots and drones in its warehouses to automate order picking and delivery procedures, lowering labour costs and enhancing delivery times.

These instances show how a variety of businesses, from traditional manufacturers to massive e-commerce corporations, have used AI to alter their supply chain processes and achieve a competitive edge in their respective markets. While artificial intelligence (AI) has many advantages for supply chain management, it also has some drawbacks and difficulties of its own. Organizations wishing to successfully integrate AI solutions into their supply chain operations must be aware of these constraints. The supply chain application of AI has the following significant drawbacks:

1. **Data Quality and Availability**: AI depends significantly on data, and data quality and accessibility can be a significant barrier. Data that is inaccurate, lacking, or inconsistent might produce incorrect predictions and judgments.
2. **Data Privacy and Security**: Strict security protocols are needed when handling sensitive supply chain data. When sharing data with outside partners, it's extremely important to protect against cybersecurity threats and maintain data privacy.
3. **Initial Investment**: Putting AI solutions into practice can be costly. To properly use AI, organizations may need to invest in hardware, software, training, and talent acquisition, which can be a hurdle for smaller businesses.
4. **Complexity and Integration**: Adding AI to current supply chain management systems can be difficult and time-consuming. Challenges can arise from the necessity for specialized development and compatibility problems with legacy systems.
5. **Scalability**: AI systems may need to be retrained and scaled as businesses expand and change to manage bigger datasets and trickier tasks. The process of scaling up can be resource-intensive.
6. **Interpretability and Transparency**: Deep learning neural networks, for example, are some AI models that might be challenging to interpret. This lack of transparency can make it difficult to comprehend why AI systems make certain decisions.
7. **Change management**: Putting AI into practice frequently calls for alterations to workflows and procedures. Effective change management practices are crucial to achieve successful adoption because employees may reject these changes.
8. **Human Expertise**: To create, install, and maintain AI systems, qualified humans are needed. In many areas, there is a skills scarcity for AI, making it challenging to hire and keep skilled workers.
9. **Overfitting and Bias**: AI models can be biased, which causes them to perform well on training data but poorly on untrained data. Inheriting biases from prior data might potentially produce unfair or discriminating results.
10. **Unexpected Challenges**: In real-world situations, AI systems may run into unanticipated difficulties. The COVID-19 pandemic, for instance, caused supply chains to be disrupted in ways that AI models couldn't.
11. **Ethical Issues**: The use of AI to supply chain management raises ethical concerns about how AI affects employment, its misuse potential, and its role in critical social decision-making.
12. **Maintenance and Upkeep**: AI models must be continuously updated, monitored, and maintained in order to be useful. Inaction can eventually result in performance deterioration.

13. **Lack of Standardization**: The AI field is continually changing, and because AI technology and techniques are not standardized, interoperability and collaboration may be hampered.

CONCLUSION

In all stages of a supply chain, the application of AI would be indispensable. In the years to come, definitely, the application of AI will make the supply chain not only more sustainable, but also resilient. With continuous improvement in AI, its impact on supply chain will in-turn grow. At the same time, there will be some challenges that need to be tackled while implementing the AI tools. Some of the big challenges would be clean data, apprehensive employees and disconnected systems which need to be handled properly. The successful use of AI in the supply chain, however, necessitates careful planning, large investments in talent and technology, as well as a dedication to data security and privacy. Additionally, in order to fully profit from AI, businesses must constantly adapt to new developments in the field and industry best practices. In conclusion, the supply chain might significantly benefit from increased efficiency, visibility, cost-effectiveness, and customer happiness if AI is integrated. Businesses are likely to acquire a competitive edge in the constantly changing global market as long as they continue to research and deploy AI-driven solutions.

REFERENCES

Ahmed, T., Karmaker, C. L., Nasir, S. B., Moktadir, M. A., & Paul, S. K. (2023). Modeling the artificial intelligence-based imperatives of industry 5.0 towards resilient supply chains: A post-COVID-19 pandemic perspective. *Computers & Industrial Engineering*, *177*, 109055. doi:10.1016/j.cie.2023.109055 PMID:36741206

Bag, S., Dhamija, P., Singh, R. K., Rahman, M. S., & Sreedharan, V. R. (2023). Big data analytics and artificial intelligence technologies based collaborative platform empowering absorptive capacity in health care supply chain: An empirical study. *Journal of Business Research*, *154*, 113315. doi:10.1016/j.jbusres.2022.113315

Baryannis, G., Validi, S., Dani, S., & Antoniou, G. (2019). Supply chain risk management and artificial intelligence: State of the art and future research directions. *International Journal of Production Research*, *57*(7), 2179–2202. doi:10.1080/00207543.2018.1530476

Chiang, W.-C., Li, Y., Shang, J., & Urban, T. L. (2019). Impact of drone delivery on sustainability and cost: Realizing the UAV potential through vehicle routing optimization. *Applied Energy, 242*, 1164-1175. doi:10.1016/j.apenergy.2019.03.117

Dilegani, C. (2023. AI Multiple. *Environmental Social and Governance (ESG) Reporting Definition.* https://research.aimultiple.com/esg-reporting/

Dubey, R., Bryde, D. J., Dwivedi, Y. K., Graham, G., & Foropon, C. (2022). Impact of artificial intelligence-driven big data analytics culture on agility and resilience in humanitarian supply chain: A practice-based view. *International Journal of Production Economics, 250*, 108618. doi:10.1016/j.ijpe.2022.108618

Ghoreishi, M., Treves, L., Teplov, R., & Pynnönen, M. (2023). The Impact of Artificial Intelligence on Circular Value Creation for Sustainable Development Goals. In *The Ethics of Artificial Intelligence for the Sustainable Development Goals* (pp. 347–363). Springer International Publishing. doi:10.1007/978-3-031-21147-8_19

Helo, P., & Hao, Y. (2022). Artificial intelligence in operations management and supply chain management: An exploratory case study. *Production Planning and Control, 33*(16), 1573–1590. doi:10.1080/09537287.2021.1882690

Herweijer, C., Combes, B., & Gillham, J. (2018). How AI can enable a sustainable future. *PwC report.* https://www.dhl.com/global-en/home/about-us/sustainability.html

IMARC Impactful Insights. (2023). *Digital Transformation Market: Global Industry Trends, Share, Size, Growth, Opportunity and Forecast 2023-2028*. Market Research Report, Report ID: SR112023A4373, India Brand Equity Foundation. https://www.ibef.org/economy/economic-survey

Javaid, S. (2023). AI Multiple. *Top 12 AI Use cases for supply chain Optimization in 2023*. https://research.aimultiple.com/supply-chain-ai

Khadem, M., Khadem, A., & Khadem, S. (2023). Application of Artificial Intelligence in Supply Chain Revolutionizing Efficiency and Optimization. *International Journal of Industrial Engineering and Operational Research, 5*(1), 29-38.

Kumar, A., Mani, V., Jain, V., Gupta, H., & Venkatesh, V. G. (2023). Managing healthcare supply chain through artificial intelligence (AI): A study of critical success factors. *Computers & Industrial Engineering, 175*, 108815. doi:10.1016/j.cie.2022.108815 PMID:36405396

Lacy, P., Daugherty, P., Ponomarev, P., & Durg, K. (n.d.). *The green behind the cloud.* https://www.accenture.com/_acnmedia/PDF-135/Accenture-Strategy-Green-Behind-Cloud-POV.pdf#zoom=40

Maheshwari, R. (2023, July 26). Top AI Statistics and Trends in 2023. *Forbes.* https://www.forbes.com/advisor/in/business/ai-statistics

Markets and Markets. (n.d.). *Artificial Intelligence (AI) Market.* https://www.marketsandmarkets.com/Market-Reports/artificial-intelligence-market-74851580.html

Pandian, D. A. P. (2019). Artificial intelligence application in smart warehousing environment for automated logistics. *Journal of Artificial Intelligence and Capsule Networks*, *1*(2), 63–72. doi:10.36548/jaicn.2019.2.002

Pournader, M., Ghaderi, H., Hassanzadegan, A., & Fahimnia, B. (2021). Artificial intelligence applications in supply chain management. *International Journal of Production Economics*, *241*, 108250. doi:10.1016/j.ijpe.2021.108250

Riahi, Y., Saikouk, T., Gunasekaran, A., & Badraoui, I. (2021). Artificial intelligence applications in supply chain: A descriptive bibliometric analysis and future research directions. *Expert Systems with Applications*, *173*, 114702. doi:10.1016/j.eswa.2021.114702

Rodríguez-Espíndola, O., Chowdhury, S., Beltagui, A., & Albores, P. (2020). The potential of emergent disruptive technologies for humanitarian supply chains: The integration of blockchain, artificial intelligence and 3D printing. *International Journal of Production Research*, *58*(15), 4610–4630. doi:10.1080/00207543.2020.1761565

Sharma, R., Shishodia, A., Gunasekaran, A., Min, H., & Munim, Z. H. (2022). The role of artificial intelligence in supply chain management: Mapping the territory. *International Journal of Production Research*, *60*(24), 7527–7550. doi:10.1080/00207543.2022.2029611

Tirkolaee, E. B., Sadeghi, S., Mooseloo, F. M., Vandchali, H. R., & Aeini, S. (2021). Application of machine learning in supply chain management: A comprehensive overview of the main areas. *Mathematical Problems in Engineering*, *2021*, 1–14. doi:10.1155/2021/1476043

Toorajipour, R., Sohrabpour, V., Nazarpour, A., Oghazi, P., & Fischl, M. (2021). Artificial intelligence in supply chain management: A systematic literature review. *Journal of Business Research*, *122*, 502–517. doi:10.1016/j.jbusres.2020.09.009

Tsolakis, N., Schumacher, R., Dora, M., & Kumar, M. (2023). Artificial intelligence and blockchain implementation in supply chains: A pathway to sustainability and data monetisation? *Annals of Operations Research*, *327*(1), 157–210. doi:10.1007/s10479-022-04785-2 PMID:35755830

World Economic Forum Reports. (2016). *Digital transformation of Industries*. https://www.weforum.org/reports/digital-transformation-of-industries

Chapter 12
An Upshot of Artificial Intelligence on Customer Engagement in Banking

R. Amudha
SASTRA University, India

ABSTRACT

Artificial intelligence (AI) provides foundation for stimulating intelligence of human process by use of algorithms in a dynamic computing environment. These machine learning models make it more effective for banks to manage daily operations such as transactions, financial operations, management of stock market funds, and the like. Customer engagement is a crucial component of the banking sector since it is essential for establishing trusting bonds with clients, encouraging loyalty, and promoting company expansion. Continued developments in AI technology, together with continued partnerships between financial institutions and AI specialists, will lead to additional innovation and allow banks to provide improved services, increase efficiency, and maintain their competitiveness in a constantly changing digital environment. Over the next 10 years, financial inclusion is likely to become a reality as AI-powered financial services replace all other user engagement methods, enabling the customers to access financial products and lending even in remote areas of the country.

DOI: 10.4018/979-8-3693-0712-0.ch012

INTRODUCTION

The concept of artificial intelligence (AI) was first put forth in 1955 as a branch of computer science with the intention of creating intelligent machines that could imitate human-specific cognitive processes like problem-solving and learning compared to what the internet accomplished in the previous two decades. The ability of a computer programme to learn and apply knowledge without the aid or involvement of a human is referred to as artificial intelligence. AI systems observe their surroundings and independently analyse data to draw conclusions and take necessary action. Depending on the level of accuracy, they learn from previous choices and progressively enhance their performance.

The simulation of human intelligence in machines is known as artificial intelligence. It is the cognition demonstrated by robots as opposed to the intrinsic knowledge of humans. In general, there are just two fundamental ideas in artificial intelligence. The first stage is to research human cognition; the second is to simulate those processes using machine learning. In most industry areas, AI is expected to have a profoundly disruptive effect.

Digital disruption is redefining industries, and businesses are working in a technological setting. Every industry is assessing its options and putting strategies into place to add value in the technology-driven world. One of the many areas that artificial intelligence has dominated is the financial sector. The rising emphasis on customer requirements is noticeable about these revolutionary changes in the banking sector.

Artificial intelligence (AI) provides foundation for stimulating intelligence of human process by use of algorithms in a dynamic computing environment. AI increases the productivity of humans and help them to achieve their targets. AI is a key component of many financial transactions handled in banks. These machine learning models make it easier and more effective for banks to manage daily operations such as transactions, financial operations, management of stock market funds and the like. AI with the financial and banking sector is commonly used in anti-money laundering, where debatable financial transactions are traced and reported to regulatory bodies. It is also frequently used by credit card firms to analyse credit systems. Geographically tracked suspicious credit card transactions are handled and resolved using a variety of parameters.

For back-office activities in a bank, numerous repetitive and clerical jobs are necessary. These tasks grow burdensome and require a long time to finish. A single consumer request is frequently processed by numerous staff. Such manual techniques are very expensive and may produce inconsistent results. It is crucial to update the processes with the modern technology in order to solve such issues of time, cost, and an inaccuracy.

AI technologies have the power to shift the physical and digital experiences of both customers and employees. Integrating banking operations with cutting-edge, AI technologies is essential. The prevalent use for adoption of AI in banks is the usage of chatbots on banking web pages and loan processing in back-office. Majority of Indian banks have begun using chatbots in processing loans, managing risks, and in maintaining customer relationship. Customers routinely enquire a set of usual queries while exploring banking websites, which can be resolved more efficiently. The most common application for chatbot support is found in all banking websites to service the customers. The customers' queries are concerned about the account balances, account statement and loan details. Through SMS notifications, chatbots quickly respond to the customer's questions. Additionally, it keeps track of reactions to client comments. Chatbots' personalised information enables borrowers to take prompt action.

When necessary, chatbots can also route specific questions to a human agent. Chatbots communicate with customers about money management and financial duties involving numerous accounts. For the financial and securities transactions, the customer is taken to a payment page that contains information pre-filled. Chatbots assist users in paying their phone, water, power, rent, and other bills. Another feature is the ability to transfer money between accounts. The chatbot reminds the customer to make payments with regard to a credit card. They can examine past information on spending patterns, credit histories, and transaction histories. Similarly, Chatbot recommends offers and discounts to the customers while they visit their pages. Bhattacharya (2022) found that customers use chat box to know about the offers and discounts. Banks can increase their brand value and their level of involvement to meet the precise needs of the customers through chat box recommendations. State Bank of India (SBI Intelligent Assistant, SIA, 2017), HDFC Bank (EVA 2017), ICICI Bank (IPal,2017), Yes Bank (YES ROBOT, 2018), IndusInd Bank (IndusAssist, 2018) Kotak Bank (Keya,2019), Axis Bank (Aha, 2018), Andra Bank (ABHi, 2019), City Union Bank (CUB Lakshmi,2016) are some of the chatbots used by Indian banks.

Providing for the precise needs of the consumer would boost both the bank's brand value and their level of involvement. It has been realised that people are more inclined to utilise chatbots to know about loans and discounts for their support. Enhancing the Chatbot's functionality could boost the bank's revenue in addition to satisfying the customers' interests. Banks may use a variety of AI implementation techniques in their business operations. Big data, cloud infrastructure, and python have all been suggested as vital mechanisms for information technology architecture. Association with FinTech firms could also assist in enabling digital banking in a useful and affordable manner.

A key component of the banking and financial services sector is customer service. Excellent customer service can increase client retention, satisfaction, and loyalty. As AI has advanced, banks and financial institutions are adopting chatbots and virtual assistants to offer their customers round-the-clock service. Chatbots that are powered by AI may respond to consumer questions, provide tailored recommendations, and even carry out transactions on their behalf. The banking and financial services sector places a high priority on risk management, and as technology has advanced, artificial intelligence (AI) has emerged as a crucial instrument for to facilitate risk assessment. AI systems are able to analyse huge amounts of data from numerous sources, detect potential problems, and take preventative action to reduce those risks.

The banking and financial services sector depends heavily on investment management, which has become possible due to the development of artificial intelligence (AI). A lot of data can be analysed in real time by AI algorithms, and these insights into market trends might help investors to spot brand-new opportunities and potential threats.

An essential task in the banking and financial services sector is loan underwriting, which involves a thorough evaluation of a customer's creditworthiness prior to loan approval. The loan underwriting process can be enhanced with the advent of artificial intelligence, allowing banks and financial institutions to approve loans more quickly. The banking and financial services sector places a high priority on compliance since it requires adherence to numerous regulatory frameworks and norms. With the advent of AI, banks and other financial institutions may now automate compliance monitoring and risk management, streamlining their compliance processes.

Customers that are tech aware and frequently use cutting-edge technologies want banks to offer seamless interactions. Banks have broadened their industrial landscape to include retail, information technology (IT), and telecommunication in order to meet these expectations for services like mobile banking, internet-banking, and real-time money transfers. While these advancements have allowed customers to access the majority of services in banking whenever they choose, they have also cost to the banking sector.

The application of AI in banking sector and its impact on customer engagement is explained in the following paragraphs along with the previous studies which forms the base to emphasise the significance of AI in banking. The AI applications are the payments apps, dashboards, automation of process by robots, chatbots, machine learning methods and the like. The impact of AI on employees and the pros and cons of its impact is also studied. The various applications of AI namely, customer support and service, deduction of fraud and cyber security, credit scoring and assessment of risk, anti-money laundering and know your customer, automated trading, analysis of customer perceptions and operational efficiency and reporting are discussed.

REVIEW OF LITERATURE

Uma Maheswari et.al (2023) have revealed that banks are able to take part in the deployment of cutting-edge virtual assistants and artificial intelligence systems. Automation enables institutions to increase productivity, profitability, and human reliance. In a nutshell, artificial intelligence-powered virtual assistants increase the efficiency of business processes across all industries, especially the banking industry, by making them swift, dependable, and independent of humans.

Hari et. al (2022) have said that virtual conversation agents known as chatbots offer innovative features to connect with clients and are thus a feasible way to engage them. At present, nationalized and private banks are using chatbots to engage and communicate with their customers. Due to its improved customer service, this technology is anticipated to govern the banking industry in future. Through a chatbot, client brand engagement is positively influenced by agreeableness and communication, which in turn influences customer satisfaction with the experience in brand and usage intentions of brand.

Agarwal et.al (2021) have emphasised that banks must engage clients with highly tailored and timely content to maintain their competitiveness. Banks may increase the lifetime value of each customer relationship and support the company's market leadership by delivering custom-made offers with tailored communication at the correct moment through the customer's chosen channel. Banks must develop AI-powered decisioning capabilities that are driven by a vast variety of internal and external data and enhanced by edge technologies in order to reap these benefits.

Manser Payneet.al (2021) indicate that a digital self-service technology channel, service delivery, and consumer participation in value co-creation are all integrated with AI. Furthermore, compared to transaction-oriented banking services, AI mobile banking offers value propositions that are more relationship-oriented.

Makhija (2021) have said in fact, the banking sector has been one of artificial intelligence's (AI) early adopters, and the technology is expanding quickly on a global basis. Artificial intelligence has become a part of business in the modern time, where everything is handled by computers or human computer interfaces. Although AI is not a new concept, it has recently risen enormously, greatly facilitating sustainable growth.

Satheesh et.al (2021) have stated that millions of clients and workers in the banking industry benefit greatly from artificial intelligence. AI enables multiple activities to reduce the workload on the workforce by offering prediction of system failure, detection of fraud, assessment of liquidity risk, credit score checking, customer loyalty assessment, and intelligence systems. The customer experience is, however, enhanced by a range of apps, including augmented reality, chatbots, and mobile banking.

Rahman et.al (2021) have found that for management of risk and detection of fraud, AI is an essential tool. Adoption of AI faces substantial challenges because of a lack of legal standards, concerns about data security and privacy, poor IT infrastructure, and a shortage of skilled skills. The quantitative data show that perceptions of attitudes towards AI, benefits, risks, and trust do affect AI adoption in financial services, while perceptions of ease of use and awareness have little consequence on this goal. The findings also show that views of utility and intentions to apply AI in financial services have a significant impact on attitudes towards AI.

Meena, et.al (2020) have stated that employers need to improve their abilities if they want to know the importance of analytics in every banking function. The banking industry will hire applicants with the necessary skill set. This may help IT specialists and give them a promising prospect in banking sector. The digital transformation of the banking sector will raise the level of its human resources through a range of skill sets. As a result, in order to meet the continued needs of the banking industry, the banks will, in practise, hire highly qualified employees.

Königstorferet.al (2020) have suggested that banks in commercial sector may use AI to mechanize compliance-related works, reduce loan non-repayments, raise payment security, and improve consumer targeting.

Chung et al. (2020) revealed that many traditional banks are realizing the need to redefine the method of interacting with their clients as they must cope up with the rapid growth of AI technologies and the success of digital innovators in generating compelling customer experiences

Singh (2020) has said that customer service and communication have been revolutionised by chatbots and personal digital assistants. They are efficient enablers for doing daily tasks and providing customers with a tailored experience. As technology enables users to access financial services together with voice commands and touch displays in the ease of doing transactions from home, physical presence and branch visits are steadily declining.

Suhel et.al (2020) have said that the development of chatbots in banking sector is the most recent disruptive factor that has changed how customers communicate with brands. By enabling chatbots, artificial intelligence has revolutionised how banks interact with their customers in the banking sector. It also looks into the chatbot's usefulness right now to see if it can meet changing client demands.

Biswas et.al (2020) have insisted that for omnichannel interaction, banks will need to revamp both the overall customer experience and specialized journeys. Customers must be able to switch between various modes seamlessly during a journey, and the recent interaction environment must be retained and updated continuously. Customers' expectations on this dimension have changed as a result of leading consumer internet businesses' offline-to-online business models.

Shaikh et.al (2020) have stated that recent progresses in mobile information systems have changed both the lifestyle of consumer and the global landscape of digital services. The usefulness and simplicity of non-financial transactions, as well as consumers' degree of understanding (consumer awareness), all have a substantial effect on the experiences and continuous usage of mobile banking apps.

Malaliet.al (2020) have said that artificial intelligence (AI) will provide financial institutions and banks the power to completely rethink about the method of operation, implement innovative goods and services, and, most significantly, find interventions with the client experience. With the assistance of fintech companies, banks will find it tough to compete in the age of machines by utilising cutting-edge technology that complement or even substitute human workers with well-designed algorithms. Financial and banking businesses will must to practice AI and fix it into their company strategy to maintain a sharp competitive advantage.

Indriasari, et al. (2019) revealed that big data analytics and artificial intelligence have recently emerged and played a significant role in the new banking era. This latest trend allows banking to be more customer-centric and data-driven. Services personalization is becoming a decisive tactic to maximize the engagement of existing consumers and attract new customers.

Agarwal (2019) has said that in order to increase productivity and improve the customer experience, computational intelligence apps in finance and banking have now been formed and installed. These applications offer business solutions in front-end and back-end processes. Machine learning and AI are now thought to be the valuable tools for gaining a competitive edge by improving decision-making skills and changing the banking sector.

Kaya et.al (2019) have stated that AI is being employed in know your customers' processes to confirm clients' identities. AI systems scan client documents to assess the data's accuracy by comparing it to online sources of knowledge. Through chatbots, banks are experimenting with AI technologies. Chatbots are virtual assistants that communicate with customers via text or voice to take care of their needs without involving a bank person.

CUSTOMER ENGAGEMENT IN BANKING

The terms customer experience and customer engagement, although are often used interchangeably, have quite different meanings, uses, and outcomes. Customer experience is transactional in nature and concentrated on a particular point-in-time engagement, like Automated Teller machine (ATM) withdrawals, call centre interactions, online banking transactions, and in-person interactions. Contrarily, customer engagement is the result of numerous distinct customer experiences.

Financial institutions inform their consumers through a number of ways through customer engagement. Instead of the customer experience itself, correctly implemented customer engagement enables financial organisations to deliver the banking customers' needs and demands while also fostering trust and loyalty. Customer engagement is the act of communicating with consumers through all available channels in order to improve the relationship with them as a whole. Before an account is opened, the customer experience process starts, and it continues throughout the full customer journey.

Banks and credit unions can communicate with consumers personally through direct mail, email, mobile banking systems, social media, websites, or any other channel where related interactions take place in order to create a better customer experience. The ability of modern technology and digital tools helps with the most crucial aspect of client interaction, which is listening. Listening fosters, a connection and helps a business to offer a tailored solution, from tracking transactions and consumer enquiries to eliciting insights into financial goals.

Offering clients something of value beyond goods and services is the ultimate goal of customer engagement. While products may first attract customers, a unique contextual engagement is what keeps them coming back. Banking leaders must understand the significance of a comprehensive customer experience strategy in order to develop stronger relationships that help clients in these uncertain times. A customer engagement strategy places the customer first and guarantees that each encounter is not only simple, quick, convenient, and consistent, but also seamless through the channel(s) of their choice. This entails giving customers digital freedom to act as they choose, making it simple for them to get in touch with the appropriate person or channel when necessary, and giving employees the tools, they need to respond to customers' requirements effectively and efficiently.

Banks must engage customers across channels and throughout time at every opportunity that adds value for them if it wants to attract, convert, and retain them—and turn them into permanent customers. The goal is to establish a meaningful, suitable, and effective connection with its target audience. Strong branding is necessary for effective banking client interaction; in fact, it depends on it. The customer engagement process can be made simpler and more scalable by new technology and marketing communication tools, but it is also critical to develop a brand personality that customers will like to know and want to engage with. Every communication must reflect this brand personality.

Sending relevant push notifications that demand action and add value can occasionally be a successful way to engage with customers. Customers must sign up for these notifications in order to use this very effective communication strategy. They have already chosen to interact with bank's brand by choosing to opt-in to receive these messages.

Banking businesses that don't understand their customers' demands and don't offer real-time, personalised advice are losing more and more customers. It is now essential to provide compelling banking experiences throughout the whole customer journey, utilising all available channels. In banking, the ability to shift from a transactional to an engagement attitude is now essential. The cornerstone of building a stronger relationship and higher revenues is the capacity to give relevant products, services, and suggestions, regardless of whether the consumer is a digital native, a branch-based customer, or a combination of both.

Traditional personalisation is insufficient to create sustained active engagement beyond simple transactions. Financial institutions which excel in creating interactions beyond routine transactions bring in more money from those activities than competitors that fall short in this area. The correct client must be reached at the right moment with the right interaction through the creation of offerings, content, and communications. Banks and customers could only communicate physically in the past through branches. Digital banking provides end-to-end services to its consumers via digital platforms like tablets, mobile phones, and internet. Banks offer customers 24-hour services so they can access services of banking even on bank holidays, as well as paperless, branchless, and signature-free services. If the computer is to recognise information, it must be stored, transformed, and transferred digitally. Through the introduction of internet, cloud, mobile, and big data technologies in recent years, the banking sector has seen significant transformation and improvement. People can now access services whenever and wherever they choose in a digital society due to this digitalization. Modern banking services like ATMs, credit cards, debit cards, online payment options, demat accounts, online fund transfers, telephone and mobile banking, internet banking and wallets have all been offered by the banks due to the advancements in technology.

Significant changes have been made in the interaction between banks and their clients. Banks are transforming the ways they engage with their clients in this digital age. Customers of today evaluate their online banking experiences in comparison to the wide range of other digital services they use, and they need banking apps that can compete. For instance, customers no longer desire banking apps that do nothing more than handle payments. As opposed to this, people seek the same participatory, natural experiences from digital services.

To meet users' expectations for convenience and ease of use, digital services must be smooth and adaptable. Facial recognition technology implementation, instant account approvals, and credit card requests made through apps are excellent illustrations of how banks may take the lead. This necessitates a people-first strategy for digital transformation that emphasises human interactions and the end-user experience. Clients were able to receive transactional banking services through websites or apps due to digital banking, which weakened the relationship between clients and their banks. Instead, engagement banking makes use of technology to offer individualised digital experiences with seamless client journeys across all digital and physical channels.

The core of this approach is human interaction and experiences, which deepen the relationship with clients. Financial institutions which take on the engagement banking challenge will be far better able to keep their current clientele while attracting more and more tech-savvy new users to their platform. This creates new opportunities for corporate expansion. A business that is always changing and a customer base that is ever more demanding will leave behind financial institutions which follow the traditional banking methods. Instead, prioritising technology, the best method is to adopt a customer-centric mentality that emphasises forging stronger relationships with people.

The emergence of neobanks, which are exclusively online and run more like software start-ups than traditional banks, has altered the financial sector's landscape in recent years. These neobanks provide customers with a far greater selection of conveniently available services in the platform approach they are accustomed to. Many established banks are unable to compete with these upstarts, in part because they prioritise technology over consumer demands and in part because of the cautious corporate cultures that prevent them from innovating and hasten their decision-making. Instead of concentrating on technology for its own sake, modern banks must create simple, everyday customer experiences.

In order to modernise self-service capabilities, banks and other financial institutions must place an emphasis on engagement banking, where banks try to fit in with their clients' lifestyles. The issue is that many banks still use outdated systems that can't combine various tasks, leading to silos in every department. As a result, banks become slow to respond to shifting market demands and inattentive to the needs of current consumers. Banks cannot simply adopt new technology as a response because doing so would involve a significant expenditure with an uncertain return.

Customer engagement is a crucial component of the banking sector since it is essential for establishing trusting bonds with clients, encouraging loyalty, and promoting company expansion. Following are the methods employed by banks to increase client engagement.

a) Customised Banking Experience

Banks offer specialised product recommendations and services based on customer needs and financial goals. The banks use data analytics and AI to understand unique consumer preferences and behaviour. AI ensure a seamless experience over a variety of channels, including websites, branch visits, mobile apps, and phone calls to customer service. It also permits customers to seamlessly transit from one channel to another to complete a transaction.

b) Virtual Self-Service Options

Lee et al. (2022) have found that adoption of mobile banking application based on AI offers the bankers a real-world direction to retain their users in the financial services market. Mobile apps maintained by banks create intuitive mobile applications with tools for mobile cheque deposit, fund transfers, and tailored financial analytics. The apps also make secure biometric access techniques available for mobile devices. The banks offer clients access to online tools and information to manage their accounts, set financial objectives, and monitor their progress. The banks provide chatbots or virtual assistants for quick responses to frequent questions.

c) Financial Education and Mechanism for Feedback

Banks inform clients to make financial decisions with the help of educational tools available to them, such as articles, videos, and webinars. Banks also conduct consumer workshops or seminars on financial literacy. The banks collect customer input proactively using surveys, social media, and in-person contacts. It uses customer input to enhance services and procedures. The information collected is used to solve client issues and grievances quickly and effectively. The banks provide sufficient training to the front-line personnel to manage client situations well. It also informs the clients about account activity, security upgrades, and pertinent promotions, use of email, short message service (SMS), or in-app notifications. Personalised messages are sent to the customers on their birthdays, wedding anniversaries and other special occasions.

d) Corporate Social Responsibility

Banks take part in community events to develop relationships with customers and show their support for the community. Banks retain an active online presence to interact with customers, share information, and respond to questions. It uses social media listening to collect customer feedback and brand references. It devises loyalty programmes that offer rewards to clients for their ongoing patronage and participation. The loyal customers have a privilege of accessing premium services, cashback, or exclusive discounts. Banks highlight its dedication to social responsibility and sustainability projects, which may appeal to its clients who are socially conscious.

ARTIFICIAL INTELLIGENCE IN BANKING

Future banking will be altered by the use of advanced data analytics by AI, which will reduce fraud and increase compliance. Anti-money laundering operations can now be done in a couple of seconds because of AI algorithms. Banks can manage massive amounts of data at lightning-fast speeds with AI in order to extract useful information from it. With the aid of technologies like biometric fraud detection systems, digital payment advisors, and AI bots, a larger consumer base may have access to superior services. All of these result in higher profits, lower expenses, and higher sales.

In addition to empowering banks by automating knowledge workers, AI will make the entire automation process smart enough to lower cybersecurity threats and competition from FinTech competitors. The bank's operations and processes depend on AI, which advances over time without a lot of physical labour. AI enables the banks to provide customised services while increasing the use of both human and machine skills. Realising all of these benefits is no longer a faraway dream for banks. Banking industry leaders have already used AI and performed ethically to their advantage.

AI enables financial institutions to fundamentally re-evaluate their business models, roll out innovative goods and services, and, most significantly, have an impact on efforts aimed at improving the customer experience. Fast-growing fintech companies that utilise cutting-edge tools to supplement or even replace human labour entirely with sophisticated algorithms will also pose a threat to banks. Banking businesses must use AI and put it into their business strategy if they want to preserve a major competitive advantage.

The expansion of the data pattern business has made it possible for demand for AI to increase. Since AI processes various data patterns more quickly than humans, it seems to be a valuable tool for businesses because it enhances customer knowledge and insight. Numerous commercial organisations all over the world have viewed artificial intelligence as a process giant in the financial services and banking sector. With the aid of cutting-edge technology like AI including machine learning, block chain, and other technologies, the banking sector is finally realising the suitability of data processing. As a result, traditional banking and financial services are engaging fintech firms in an effort to provide their clients cutting-edge services.

Technology is the driving force behind customer engagement. Customer information serves as the engine's fuel. In order to automate interactions and deliver a personalised experience that motivates a prospect to join an account and a customer to start a connection, modern engagement platforms make use of AI-driven tools both internal and external data.

The art of combining data, strong analytics, and contemporary communication platforms is that one can create new products and services for micro segments, target potential customers in real-time, and forecast needs. Banks can also make custom responses to questions at scale. Teams may concentrate on innovation, tailored outreach, and learning from previous communication initiatives by creating a smooth, streamlined communications cycle.

In order to deliver pertinent information that customers' value, a data-driven strategy to engage the customer goes beyond the influence of straightforward special offers. Customers will frequently choose bank's brand over competitors for future demands as they become more accustomed to highly personalised communication procedure. There is a higher tolerance for increased amounts of communication if bank's products and services offers value to the customer in his/her perspective.

A thorough understanding of customer wants and preferences, a dedication in providing outstanding service, and the use of technology to offer convenient and tailored experiences are all necessary for effective customer engagement in banking. Banks may foster long-lasting relationships with their customers and promote long-term success by putting a high priority on customer engagement. By enabling banks to offer more individualised, effective, and efficient services, AI has revolutionised client engagement in the banking sector. Banks can offer more individualised, practical, and secure services by utilising AI technologies, which will ultimately improve consumer engagement and fulfilment while also furthering operational effectiveness.

To ensure that consumers have access to both self-service choices and human support, when necessary, banks must, however, strike a balance between automation and human touch. Artificial intelligence (AI) has had a major and largely beneficial impact on consumer satisfaction in banking. Various areas of banking operations and consumer interactions have been altered by AI technologies, improving customer contentment and experiences. Even if the majority of AI's effects on customer satisfaction in banking have been satisfactory, banks must balance automation and human engagement. For difficult or delicate issues, some clients may still prefer communicating with a real representative. In order to maximise client satisfaction in the banking sector, it is essential to offer a seamless blend of AI-driven automation and human assistance.

The banking sector has been considerably impacted by artificial intelligence, which has changed many features of banking operations and client experiences. AI in banking has the ability to boost productivity, improve consumer experiences, and better risk control. However, it also brings up significant ethical and legal issues, particularly in relation to data security and privacy. In order to comply with changing regulatory frameworks, banks must strike a balance between innovation and protecting sensitive client information.

PricewaterhouseCoopers International Limited (PwC) and Federation of Indian Chambers of Commerce & Industry (FICCI) have conducted a survey and reported in The Economic Times in March 2022 to know about the implementation and adoption of artificial intelligence within Banking, Financial Services, and Insurance (BFSI) sector in India. Among the BFSI sector, banking sector is leading in AI applications. The potential savings in cost is estimated to be 447 US dollars by the year 2023 for the banks in using AI in their services.

As per the study conducted by McKinsey & Company in the year 2020 covering more than twenty-five cases, it was found that AI has helped to increase profits by augmenting the personalised services to both employees and customers; to reduce the costs through effectiveness of automation; to minimise rates of errors and to enhance the utilisation of available resources. Across all sectors, banks are able to earn an annual incremental rate of one trillion dollars approximately due to the usage of AI in their operations.

The following are some significant applications of AI in banking:

a) Customer Support and Service

Hsu, C. L., & Lin, J. C. C. (2023) have said that the customer satisfaction towards quality in conversation and recovery of services is influenced by AI driven chatbots. This level of customer satisfaction also leads to the loyalty in using the chatbots. Virtual assistants and AI-driven chatbots offer customer service for 24 hours, respond to inquiries, and help with simple transactions. Chatbots also assist the consumers in providing information regarding all banking products and services. AI examines consumer data to provide personalised product and service suggestions, improving the likelihood of cross-selling and upselling.

b) Deduction of Fraud and Cyber Security

AI algorithms can spot unusual trends in transactions and instantly alert users about possible fraud. Thus, deduction odd anomalies can be easily made. Biometric authentication secures the transactions through consumer authentication methods namely, voice recognition, facial recognition, and fingerprint scanning. AI also identifies the threats in the real-time transactions and prevents the misuse of information by enhancing the cyber security. The customer information is protected through the cybersecurity measures in all banking transactions.

c) Credit Scoring and Assessment of Risk

Sadok et al. (2022) have stated that the usage of AI in credit assessments by the banks and financial entities leads to positive growth in the economy and extends the credit access to the unbanked borrowers. AI gauges the creditworthiness of the borrower accurately on the basis of huge information inclusive of non-traditional bases to make a decision for credit sanctioning. The assessment of risk is also made by AI to measure the operational risks and to manage the credit. The processing of loan applications and the speeding up of approval process is automated by AI and it reduces the workload for the workers.

d) Anti-Money Laundering (AML) and Know Your Customer

AI develops automatic verification of documents and flagging the activities that are considered to be suspicious efficiently and helps the processes involved in anti-money laundering. AI may be further incorporated into AML procedures, enabling more precise and effective data analysis. This might involve using robotics to automate manual AML procedures, natural language processing to interpret complicated financial credentials, and machine learning to detect new money laundering concerns. AI will probably become more and more important to combat against money laundering as it develops. The main merit of AI KYC is to drastically cut costs. By reducing the costly non-compliance penalties, lengthy onboarding procedures, and data entry mistakes, banks and other financial institutions can reduce expenses. Furthermore, computerized document scrutiny can shorten the time needed for document review, while automated facial recognition can expedite identification procedures.

e) Automated Trading

Trading algorithms powered by AI provide trading decisions based on market data and the past trends in a high frequency. The clients were provided with customised and automated advice regarding investments by the robot- advisors. Algorithmic trading is the practice of automating the purchase and sale of financial instruments on international exchanges through the use of computer algorithms. The algorithms are designed to carry out trades in response to predetermined parameters, like volume, price changes, or other market indicators.

f) Analysis of Customer Perceptions

AI analyses the information regarding the perceptions of the customers and their behaviours. This will assist the banks to customise their services in accordance with the preferences of the consumers. The customer calls and the communication in written form can be analysed with the help of text and voice analysis to identify the customer needs and to enhance the service quality. Predictive analysis is also used for forecasting the market trends together with the customer requirements.

g) Operational Efficiency and Reporting

The back-office operations are streamlined by AI by way of automating the regular and routine operations. The routine operations include entry of the consumer data, preparation of reconciliation statements, generation of report and the like. This method of process automation by AI will definitely reduce the cost of operation and the errors. The banks are able to prepare the reports as per the regulations and thereby statutory compliance is made easier.

h) Other Services

AI also forecast the period of maintenance of ATMs, Cash deposit machines and other infrastructure components. Compliance with block chain networks will be monitored by AI and detection of fraud in case of cryptocurrency is also made possible. Virtual advisors are also available to the customers for seeking the financial advice. AI has the capacity to detect patterns in huge amount of text data and improves regulatory compliance. The natural language processing is capable of sorting through documents and extracting relevant information. It could contain customer information, products, and procedures that are subject to regulatory modifications. Banks and other financial institutions can therefore comply with the regulatory environment with the minimum amount of work.

IMPACT OF AI ON CUSTOMER ENGAGEMENT IN BANKING

Based on the quality of the offered customer service, the success of the banks is evaluated, and the competitive advantage of the bank is determined. Client contentment is crucial to an organization's survival and performance in a cutthroat market, especially for retail banking, which depends on client loyalty to run its company beneficially by attracting new customers and keeping hold of existing ones.

To effectively serve each consumer, firms should segment their customer base today in order to provide the best service possible based on their individual demands. Monitoring consumer behaviour can help businesses better understand their customers and cater to their needs. The customer relationship strategy combines the marketing strategy with tasks completed within the firm and network connections beyond the organisation to discover and comprehend the demands of the existing customers in the competitive market.

Every day, millions of customers use financial services including ATMs, credit cards, internet banking, and banking applications, and the number is sharply rising. This kind of service necessitates a sizable staff, which is costly and time-consuming. It takes a lot of staff to carry out tasks like taking deposits, granting loans, and moving money in traditional banking, but online banking has radically changed this because it is simpler and faster because of the development in the information technology.

Internet banking, which is revolutionising the banking industry, plays an important role in serving the customer and maintaining a long-term connection by distributing banking products and services through a variety of channels, including ATMs, online banking services, and mobile banking. The internet has made it easier for a wide range of e-banking products to be made available, including ATMs, credit cards, and debit cards. This has increased competition in the banking and financial firms. Every customer has access to this e-banking, which decreases entry barriers, from anywhere in the world. By changing manual and paper-based work to paperless work with the help of communication and technology, this saves time of both customers and bank management.

Arora et al. (2023) have revealed that AI implemented in financial services impacts the experience of the customers by way of quality in service, apparent convenience and usefulness. Banks must use the latest, most widely used technology of the digital era to develop the quality of their services due to competition from non-banking sectors. To increase the quickness and spontaneity of customer financial transactions, artificial intelligence should be used in the banking sector. AI offers a wide range of applications that can assist banks in running as efficiently as possible, paving the way for a new level of financial services.

The research conducted by The Finastra and the report submitted in March 2022 revealed that not less than 80% of the service providers in regulated financial market are anticipating the banking as a service will have a tremendous growth. Of these 80%, 30% are expecting this service to grow by more than 50% annually in the forthcoming five years. The e-commerce institutions inclusive of retailers have seven trillion-dollar prospects in this service and they expect this growth to be more than 70% annually in the coming three years and 60%-70% of the retailers wishes to enhance their partnerships with this service.

The report of Gartner (September 2022), it was revealed that banking as a service will reach its peak level in its transformation within two years. Banking as a service is a model used by the banks to offer their products and services through AI platforms used by non-banking companies. This is mainly used to extend customised services conveniently to engage the customers and to gain the customer satisfaction. Banking as a service in one among the AI which helps in the transformation of services in banking sector along with cloud banking, chatbots and social messaging payments applications. It also anticipates that 30% of the banks having more than one billion dollars as assets will introduce banking as a service in the year 2024 to augment their revenues. As per Future Market Insights (FMI) report in May 2023, the banking as a service was valued at 3,240.6 million US dollars in the year 2022. It is expected to be 3,713.7 million US dollars in the year 2023 and 16,715.3 million US dollars in the year 2033.

FUTURE OF ARTIFICIAL INTELLIGENCE IN BANKING

The application of AI in banking and financial services is a promising future that has the potential to significantly change the sector. Banks and financial institutions are in a unique position to take advantage of AI's potential to boost business growth, enhance customer experiences, and lower risks because of the rapid advancements in AI technology and the growing availability of data. Enhancing client experiences is one of the most significant ways AI in redefining operations in the banking sector. Customers can receive individualised financial advice and help through chatbots and virtual assistants driven by AI, a convenience that was previously unattainable. Customers can get assistance from these virtual assistants with a range of tasks, including account queries, money transfers, and financial advice. AI can also enhance customer rapport by examining consumer behaviour, preferences, and feedback in order to personalise experiences that better serve their needs.

AI is anticipated to significantly contribute to risk management in the banking and financial services sector, in addition to enhancing consumer experiences. Machine learning algorithms can identify and reduce fraudulent actions, lower the possibility of errors, and improve overall security by analysing enormous amounts of data in real-time. Additionally, banks and financial institutions can use AI to analyse consumer data and spot possible dangers, such as clients who run the risk of defaulting on loans or credit cards, so they can take proactive steps to reduce those risks. AI is also anticipated to boost productivity and lower expenses for banks and other financial institutions.

Banks may process applications more quickly and effectively while saving time and money by automating routine operations like document underwriting and compliance checks. AI may also improve workflows, decrease the need for human interaction, and streamline processes, releasing up resources for more important activities. The use of AI in loan underwriting is another example for the potential of the banking sector. Banks may handle loans more quickly and effectively by analysing client data, automating credit checks, and reducing the time and costs associated with human operations.

Furthermore, AI enables financial institutions and banks to offer extra products and services that better fit the demands of their consumers by analysing customer data and identifying new cross-selling and upselling opportunities. The possibilities for using AI in banking and financial services are virtually endless, and the sector is only beginning to scratch the surface of what is feasible.

The acceptance of AI in the banking sector has created amazing new opportunities and developments. AI has greatly improved operational effectiveness, risk management, client experiences, and decision-making processes in the banking industry. Data analytics and machine learning algorithms powered by AI have made it possible for banks to analyse massive volumes of data in real-time, finding patterns, trends, and anomalies that assist reduce risks and improve decision-making. AI-powered chatbots and virtual assistants enhance client interactions by offering individualised support, rapidly responding to inquiries, and expediting standard procedures.

Banks are now able to make lending decisions and widen access to financial services because of AI used in credit scoring, which has increased speed and accuracy. The role that AI has played in preventing and detecting fraud has been crucial in protecting banks and clients from fraudulent activity. The potential for AI in banking is quite promising in the future. Continued developments in AI technology, together with continued partnerships between financial institutions and AI specialists, will lead to additional innovation and allow banks to provide improved services, increase efficiency, and maintain their competitiveness in a constantly changing digital environment.

Though automation in banking sector may enhance the efficiency in their operations, there also exists a risk of displacement of jobs in some positions. As the routine jobs are handled by AI, the employees in banking sector must adopt themselves to the world of technology. Reskilling and upskilling are the need of the hour and the employees have to balance between the automation and job security. The banking and finance sector is accountable to balance these changes to warrant a harmony between AI and the existing workforce. Proper training regarding the needed skills for automation should be imparted to the employees which will help to empower themselves. The progress of the banking sector and the ensured job security for the employees should be knitted together to have a smooth paradigm shift towards AI powered period.

Hötte et al. (2022) have found that there exists a possibility of emerging new jobs with the increase of economic activities with the advent of new technologies though there is a risk of replacing the employees with the usage of technologies. The growth in the productivity of the implementation of new technologies will definitely result in the increase of income disposable in the hands of the people. The increase in disposable income will stimulate more demand of economic activities resulting in expansion of employment opportunities.

Boustani, N. M. (2022) have argued that though AI gives banking transactions a superior level of quality, AI may also pose risk on banking professions which are considered to be technical. But AI cannot replace emotional intelligence in managing the relationships between employees and clients in banks. Arul et al. (2023) have surveyed three groups namely, IT firms, banks and customers and studied the relationship between these groups towards the outcome of the AI applications which are human centred. They found that AI model which captures and processes the emotions of humans will definitely improve the customer experience and the trust towards the banks. The coordination between IT firms and the banks in developing the AI applications will lead to the effectiveness in the usage of products and services of banks among customers.

CONCLUSION

The banking and finance sector relies heavily on data, and artificial intelligence can analyse enormous volumes of data to produce insights that can aid financial organisations in making better decisions. In banking and finance, AI has a wide range of possible applications, including boosting customer experiences, optimising back-office processes, identifying fraud, controlling risk, and strengthening compliance. Additionally, financial institutions can use AI to automate monotonous jobs, increase accuracy, and speed up procedures, which will result in cost savings and improved efficiency. Virtual assistants and chatbots powered by AI can offer clients round-the-clock service, minimising the requirement for human engagement.

Today, all finance organisations construct their platforms using AI as the de facto technology. Over the next ten years, financial inclusion is likely to become a reality as AI-powered financial services replace all other user engagement methods, enabling the customers to access financial products and lending even in remote areas of the country. The information above should make it clear that AI will play a major role in the banking and financial sectors of the future. Because of the speed at which AI-powered technologies are advancing the banking industry and facilitating customer convenience. Thus, in the forth coming years, it will restore humanity and offer quicker services with the best solutions at a rational price.

Customers must be very smart enough to obtain and handle banking services like checking balances, bill payment, interest calculators, cell phone recharge, pension plans and the like. Banks are offering improved customer services, convenience for the client, and time savings by using digitalization. Digitalization fosters consumer loyalty while reducing human error. In order to compete with their rivals, banks have now been compelled to make significant investments in digital technology. Digitization makes it possible to reach out to customers in more ways, allowing firms to improve their products.

The use of bots, an innovation in the AI-powered industry, has been steadily increasing. As a result, numerous sectors are investing heavily in it because they see this technology as a long-term investment in cost-cutting. It assists the industries in saving money on hiring people and also eliminates the possibility of human error. Even though AI-powered technology is still in its beginning, the way it now functions aids in the expansion and development of banking and the financial industry. It is also possible to forecast that the use of AI-powered technology in the future would lead to better trading with more client satisfaction and modest losses.

REFERENCES

Agarwal, A., Singhal, C., & Thomas, R. (2021). *AI-powered decision making for the bank of the future*. McKinsey & Company.

Agarwal, P. (2019, March). Redefining banking and financial industry through the application of computational intelligence. In *2019 Advances in Science and Engineering Technology International Conferences (ASET)* (pp. 1-5). 10.1109/ICASET.2019.8714305

Arora, A., Gupta, S., Devi, C., & Walia, N. (2023). Customer experiences in the era of artificial intelligence (AI) in context to FinTech: A fuzzy AHP approach. *Benchmarking*, *30*(10), 4342–4369. doi:10.1108/BIJ-10-2021-0621

Arul, O. K., & Megargel, A. (2023). Understanding human-centred artificial intelligence in the banking sector. Journal of AI. *Robotics & Workplace Automation*, *2*(4), 332–348.

Bhattacharya, C., & Sinha, M. (2022). The Role of Artificial Intelligence in Banking for Leveraging Customer Experience. Australasian Accounting. *Business and Finance Journal*, *16*(5), 89–105.

Biswas, S., Carson, B., Chung, V., Singh, S., & Thomas, R. (2020). *AI-bank of the future: Can banks meet the AI challenge*. McKinsey & Company.

Boustani, N. M. (2022). Artificial intelligence impact on banks clients and employees in an Asian developing country. *Journal of Asia Business Studies*, *16*(2), 267–278. doi:10.1108/JABS-09-2020-0376

Chung, V., Gomes, M., Rane, S., Singh, S., & Thomas, R. (2020). *Reimagining customer engagement for the AI bank of the future*. McKinsey & Company.

Hari, H., Iyer, R., & Sampat, B. (2022). Customer brand engagement through chatbots on bank websites–examining the antecedents and consequences. *International Journal of Human-Computer Interaction, 38*(13), 1212–1227. doi:10.1080/10447318.2021.1988487

Hötte, K., Somers, M., & Theodorakopoulos, A. (2022). *The fear of technology-driven unemployment and its empirical base*. https://voxeu.org/article/fear-technology-driven-unemployment-and-its-empirical-base

Hsu, C. L., & Lin, J. C. C. (2023). Understanding the user satisfaction and loyalty of customer service chatbots. *Journal of Retailing and Consumer Services, 71*, 103211. doi:10.1016/j.jretconser.2022.103211

Indriasari, E., Gaol, F. L., & Matsuo, T. (2019, July). Digital banking transformation: Application of artificial intelligence and big data analytics for leveraging customer experience in the Indonesia banking sector. In *2019 8th International Congress on Advanced Applied Informatics (IIAI-AAI)* (pp. 863-868). IEEE.

Kaya, O., Schildbach, J., AG, D. B., & Schneider, S. (2019). Artificial intelligence in banking. Artificial intelligence.

Königstorfer, F., & Thalmann, S. (2020). Applications of Artificial Intelligence in commercial banks–A research agenda for behavioral finance. *Journal of Behavioral and Experimental Finance*, *27*, 100352. doi:10.1016/j.jbef.2020.100352

Lee, J.-C., & Chen, X. (2022). Exploring users' adoption intentions in the evolution of artificial intelligence mobile banking applications: The intelligent and anthropomorphic perspectives. *International Journal of Bank Marketing*, *40*(4), 631–658. doi:10.1108/IJBM-08-2021-0394

Makhija, P., & Chacko, E. (2021). Efficiency and advancement of artificial intelligence in service sector with special reference to banking industry. *Fourth Industrial Revolution and Business Dynamics: Issues and Implications*, 21-35.

Malali, A. B., & Gopalakrishnan, S. (2020). Application of artificial intelligence and its powered technologies in the indian banking and financial industry: An overview. *IOSR Journal Of Humanities And Social Science*, *25*(4), 55–60.

Manser Payne, E. H., Peltier, J., & Barger, V. A. (2021). Enhancing the value co-creation process: Artificial intelligence and mobile banking service platforms. *Journal of Research in Interactive Marketing*, *15*(1), 68–85. doi:10.1108/JRIM-10-2020-0214

Meena, M. M. R., & Parimalarani, G. (2020). Impact of digital transformation on employment in banking sector. *International Journal of Scientific & Technology Research, 9*(1), 4912–4916.

Rahman, M., Ming, T. H., Baigh, T. A., & Sarker, M. (2021). Adoption of artificial intelligence in banking services: An empirical analysis. *International Journal of Emerging Markets.*

Sadok, H., Sakka, F., & El Maknouzi, M. E. H. (2022). Artificial intelligence and bank credit analysis: A review. *Cogent Economics & Finance, 10*(1), 2023262. doi:10.1080/23322039.2021.2023262

Satheesh, M. K., & Nagaraj, S. (2021). Applications of artificial intelligence on customer experience and service quality of the banking sector. *International Management Review, 17*(1), 9–17.

Shaikh, A. A., Alharthi, M. D., & Alamoudi, H. O. (2020). Examining key drivers of consumer experience with (non-financial) digital services—An exploratory study. *Journal of Retailing and Consumer Services, 55*, 102073. doi:10.1016/j.jretconser.2020.102073

Singh, K. (2020). Banks banking on ai. *International Journal of Advanced Research in Management and Social Sciences, 9*(9), 1–11.

Suhel, S. F., Shukla, V. K., Vyas, S., & Mishra, V. P. (2020, June). Conversation to automation in banking through chatbot using artificial machine intelligence language. In *2020 8th international conference on reliability, infocom technologies and optimization (trends and future directions) (ICRITO)* (pp. 611-618). 10.1109/ICRITO48877.2020.9197825

Uma Maheswari, S., & Valarmathi, A. (2023). Role of Artificial Intelligence in The Banking Sector. *Journal of Survey in Fisheries Sciences, 10*(4S), 2841–2849.

Chapter 13
Adopting Robotic Process Automation (RPA) in the Construction Industry

Fuad Abutaha
Antalya Bilim University, Turkey

Ceren Dinler
Antalya Bilim University, Turkey

ABSTRACT

The chapter embarked on a comprehensive exploration of robotic process automation (RPA) and its merge with building information modeling (BIM) in revolutionizing the construction industry. By investigating the applications, benefits, challenges, and opportunities associated with RPA and its integration with BIM, this research has shed light on the immense potential for transforming productivity, efficiency, safety, decision-making, and sustainability in construction processes. Moreover, the merge of RPA with BIM represents a paradigm shift in collaboration, data management, and decision-making within the construction industry. By combining the strengths of these two transformative technologies, stakeholders can achieve unprecedented levels of coordination, efficiency, and accuracy throughout the project lifecycle. RPA, when integrated with BIM, empowers real-time monitoring, safety analysis, clash detection, risk assessment, and advanced simulations, allowing for proactive identification and resolution of issues.

DOI: 10.4018/979-8-3693-0712-0.ch013

GENERAL

The construction industry, with its intricate and resource-intensive nature, has always been at the forefront of innovation and technological advancement. Growing evidence has emerged in recent years that robotic process automation (RPA) has the ability to completely alter how construction projects are organized, carried out, and managed. RPA, a cutting-edge technology that integrates robotics and artificial intelligence, has the potential to increase construction operations' productivity, efficiency, and safety.

Traditional construction methods frequently involve manual work, time-consuming jobs, and a great deal of reliance on human input. But with the introduction of RPA, a new era in the construction industry has begun. RPA offers the ability to optimize resource allocation, streamline workflows, and reduce errors by automating repetitive and boring procedures. From surveying and site preparation to material handling and project monitoring, this technology has a wide range of uses.

This thesis seeks to investigate how RPA might revolutionize the construction industry. To identify the advantages and difficulties connected with its implementation by investigating its uses throughout different stages of construction is aimed. Real-world case studies and research findings will also be examined to assess the influence of RPA on productivity, cost-effectiveness, and overall project success. Through this research, I aim to shed light on the key opportunities and limitations of RPA in construction. Stakeholders in the construction industry can make well-informed choices about the integration of RPA into their operations by being aware of the potential advantages and difficulties. In the end, this investigation will add to the larger discussion on the use of cutting-edge technologies in construction, paving the way for a more productive, creative, and sustainable industry. The exploration of RPA in the construction industry presents an opportunity to streamline processes, enhance productivity, and improve efficiency. RPA can free up valuable human resources to concentrate on more sophisticated and strategic activities by automating time-consuming and repetitive procedures. All parties concerned could profit from an increase in production and a shortening of project timelines as a result.

BIM, or Building Information Modeling, is a revolutionary digital approach that creates a comprehensive 3D model of a building, acting as a shared hub of information for all project stakeholders, from architects to facility managers. This intelligent model not only visualizes the building's geometry but also embeds crucial data about materials, systems, and components, enabling better collaboration, enhanced decision-making, and a more efficient construction process. The combination of RPA with BIM has the potential to enhance decision-making, data management, and cooperation in construction projects. Stakeholders can improve workflows, improve coordination, and reduce errors by utilizing the capabilities of both platforms. This may lead to more efficient use of resources, reduced costs, and general project success.

Researchers and business experts will benefit greatly from the study findings of this thesis. Making educated judgments about implementing RPA and integrating it with BIM in building projects will be made easier with the help of the findings. With the use of this knowledge, stakeholders will be able to streamline procedures, distribute resources wisely, and adopt cutting-edge technology in a way that maximizes project results and advances the construction industry as a whole.

ROBOTIC PROCESS AUTOMATION (RPA)

Automation is an ascending trend in Business and Information Systems Engineering. Since the latest developments in artificial intelligence, machine learning and data science are becoming more and more outstanding, one question appears in mind: What should be automated?

In this case, it is better to take a look at Robotic Process Automation (RPA). RPA is made out of tools that interact with different computer systems' user interface to operate commands in a way that a human being would do. RPA tools seamlessly integrate with existing digital infrastructure, interacting with application programming interfaces (API), client servers, mainframes, or even HTML code (Gartner Inc., 2017). They automate workflows by executing commands on structured data and following pre-defined logic ("if, then, else" statements) outlined in the RPA tool's language (Gartner Inc., 2017). This relieves human employees from monotonous tasks, enabling them to focus on meaningful and value-adding activities

Historically, managing administrative burdens involved either increasing staffing or optimizing workflows. RPA presents a transformative solution, streamlining and automating tedious operations, boosting productivity and reducing costs. Essentially, RPA replaces human labor with "software bots" to manage repetitive digital tasks (Lacity & Willcocks, 2016). The demand for RPA solutions has surged in recent years, driven by organizations seeking cost-effectiveness and rapid system integration. This has led to a thriving RPA market with new vendors like UiPath, BluePrism, Automation Anywhere, and Power Automate, all vying for their share (McKinsey & Company, 2020). Notably, RPA's ability to deliver high Return on Investment (ROI) within a short timeframe fuels its growing popularity (PwC, 2022).

Applications of Robotic Process Automation

This section aims to systematize the diverse definitions of RPA presented in academic literature and shed light on its core concept. The primary emphasis in scientific papers revolves around utilizing RPA tools to alleviate the burden of simple, repetitive tasks, automating them and enabling workforce redeployment towards more challenging, value-adding projects (Balasundaram & Venkatagiri, 2020; Deloitte, 2017).

As technology reshapes the industrial landscape, the HR function must embrace automation alongside other disruptive technologies to ensure efficiency, effective service delivery, and cost savings (Balasundaram & Venkatagiri, 2020). RPA implementation can significantly contribute by: (a) enhancing employee and manager experience through improved service provision (IRPA, 2015); (b) ensuring adherence to HR standards and regulations by automating compliance checks (Deloitte, 2017); (c) facilitating faster process initiation and completion through streamlined workflows (IRPA, 2015); (d) boosting efficiency by digitizing data and providing audit trails for process data (Deloitte, 2017); (e) increasing HR productivity and cost savings by automating manual and repetitive tasks (Balasundaram & Venkatagiri, 2020).

The conception of RPA as a process automation method is prevalent in relevant literature. Quinn and Strauss (2018) define it as "a rapidly developing technique to process automation that mimics human operations using software robots. A virtual bot imitates human activities in the graphical user interface of the application after capturing a process workflow and automates their execution." This viewpoint reinforces the perception of RPA as a productivity and efficiency tool that minimizes errors, enhances security, and reduces human risk (Dialani, 2019).

Furthermore, the IEEE Advisory Group defines RPA technology as "a preconfigured software instance that uses business rules and predefined activity choreography to complete the autonomous execution of a combination of processes, activities, transactions, and tasks in one or more unrelated software systems to deliver a result or service with human exception management" (IEEE SA, 2017). This emphasizes the sophistication and automation capabilities inherent in RPA.

Several scholars advocate for viewing RPA through the lens of organizational future and labor market shifts. Śliż (2019) identifies two key strategies:

1. Organic processes driven by technological advancement and rapid knowledge expansion: Recognizing how these advancements impact an organization's economic environment is crucial.
2. Reshaping the labor market: This involves understanding how new, previously undiscovered jobs emerge and existing ones are reconfigured.

Examples of RPA Applications

While not exhaustive, the following tasks illustrate the range of RPA capabilities:

- Email management: reading, sending, handling attachments (Deloitte, 2017)

- Web/enterprise application automation: logging in, manipulating data (IRPA, 2015)
- Data cleansing: moving, editing, deleting files and folders (IRPA, 2015)
- API connectivity: data upload/download automation (Deloitte, 2017)
- Automated batch and scheduled tasks
- Rule-based decision-making and conditional workflows
- Data extraction and report/dashboard generation
- Structured data extraction and formatting from documents
- Social media data collection and analysis
- Multi-source data processing (structured and unstructured)
- Calculation and task execution based on results
- Automated form filling
- Database read/write/query functionalities
- Automated report generation, sending, and sharing
- Early-warning notifications and alerts
- Transaction limit/threshold-based actions (blocking, stopping)
- Fraudulent account closure and chargeback process streamlining
- Accounting book balancing and reconciliation automation
- Standing order and direct debit detail management
- Address detail management
- Transaction duplication auditing, blocking, and correction
- Branch risk monitoring automation
- Personal loan application opening process streamlining
- Payment protection insurance claims processing automation
- Payment terms administration automation
- Insurance product sales support through automation
- Marketing campaign automation
- Customer complaint handling automation
- Compliance reporting procedure automation
- Insurance product administration streamlining
- Risk analysis automation and action execution based on results
- Direct debit cancellation automation
- Personal account closure process streamlining
- Payment processing automation
- Business account audit request automation

Applicable Industries

Robotic Process Automation (RPA) thrives on automating routine, rule-based tasks, making it a potent tool for streamlining intricate processes across diverse industries.

While its effectiveness in areas like finance, accounting, human resources, education, healthcare, logistics (KPMG, 2018; UiPath, 2023), etc., is well established, this section delves into its potential within the construction management industry. RPA applications in various industries can be seen as below.

- Finance and Accounting: RPA automates tasks like invoice processing (Deloitte, 2017), account reconciliation (PwC, 2022), and financial reporting (EY, 2020), boosting efficiency and accuracy.
- Human Resources (HR): Payroll processing, benefits enrollment, and employee onboarding (Balasundaram & Venkatagiri, 2020) are seamlessly automated, freeing up HR personnel for strategic initiatives.
- Customer Service: Order processing, ticket management, and data entry (IRPA, 2015) are streamlined, enhancing customer satisfaction and reducing response times.
- Supply Chain and Logistics: Purchase order processing, inventory management, and shipment tracking (McKinsey & Company, 2020) are automated for improved efficiency and cost optimization.
- Healthcare: Patient registration, appointment scheduling, and claims processing are automated, leading to smoother workflows and improved patient care.
- Manufacturing: Production scheduling, quality assurance, and inventory management are automated for enhanced production efficiency and reduced waste.
- Legal Services: Contract administration, document review, and compliance monitoring are streamlined, improving accuracy and reducing legal costs.
- Insurance: Underwriting, policy administration, and claims processing (UiPath, 2023) are automated, enhancing efficiency and reducing fraud risk.
- Marketing and Sales: Lead generation, data entry, and email marketing are automated, boosting campaign performance and ROI.

While RPA's success in traditional industries is undeniable, its potential extends far beyond. Emerging applications like:

- Agriculture: Automating planting, watering, and harvesting tasks (Accenture, 2023) for increased agricultural efficiency and precision.
- Art Conservation: Automating cleaning, mending, and restoration processes for efficient preservation of valuable artwork.
- Museum Management: Automating artwork categorization and tracking for enhanced collection management and visitor engagement.

These unique examples showcase the remarkable versatility and adaptability of RPA, pushing the boundaries of its potential beyond conventional applications.

The Integrations of Robotic Process Automation

RPA can be integrated into different kind of technologies such as; machine learning, artificial intelligence, natural language processing, big data analytics, process mining, BPM. RPA and AI are developing at a rapid pace, making it challenging for businesses to stay up, yet adopting these global trends can give them a competitive edge and market dominance. It is essential to point out that organizations in all industries should be encouraged to design and implement a digital transformation strategy due to the extensive potential that RPA offers.

Thus, according to Forrester, more than a million knowledge-worker jobs will be eliminated by software robotics, RPA, virtual agents, chatbots and ML-based decision management. Most organizations have already automated at least 20% of service desk activities (Forrester, 2018). Yet, this does not imply that positions would be eliminated and employees will lose their jobs. According to Jurczuk, the way that human resources are now perceived in corporate processes needs to change, and new roles need to be defined. The job of entrepreneurs and the process management strategy should be to take advantage of the opportunities provided by new technologies (Jurczuk, 2019).

Artificial Intelligence (AI) Integration

Artificial Intelligence (AI) used to be a concept with several main application areas. Some of such fields included robotics, computer vision, automatic theorem proving, natural language processing, automatic programming, intelligent data retrieval, etc. These application areas are now so diverse that each may be regarded as a separate field. Today, AI is best described as a collection of fundamental concepts that underlie many of these applications. (Nilsson, 1981) The fundamental idea behind smart factories and industry 4.0 is the use of AI by robots to fulfill complex jobs, lower prices, and increase the quality of products and services. With the assistance of cyber-physical systems, AI technologies are breaking into the manufacturing sector and fusing the real and virtual worlds. By utilizing AI, the manufacturing sector becomes smarter and more equipped to handle contemporary issues like configurable specifications, shortened time to market, and an increase in the number of sensors utilized in equipment. (Zheng et al., 2018) AI and adaptable robot technology make it simpler to manufacture a variety of goods. Large volumes of real-time data collected from multiple sensors can be analyzed using AI techniques (like data mining). (Ustundag & Cevikcan, 2018). RPA, AI, ML - the alphabet soup of construction's future, where data-driven decisions pave the way for a more efficient and innovative industry.

AI integrated RPA tools and Machine Learning (ML) approaches have seen the successful application in real life use cases Machine learning (ML) is used to "teach" machines how to handle data more effectively, imitating how rational beings learn. Utilizing AI algorithms and an ML-based methodology, it is conceivable to explore and extract data to identify patterns, classify, optimize, associate, group, etc. Given the scope of the applicability of AI, RPA has gradually been adding, to its automation features, implementations of algorithms or AI techniques applied in certain contexts. Academic studies on the challenges and potential of RPA and AI have recently been published. Examples include articles (Leno et al., 2020) on automatic discovery and data transformation, (Agostinelli et al., 2020) on the use of business process management, and (Fluss, 2018) on productivity optimization techniques. When it comes to this situation, applying algorithms and AI approaches may help to further improve the obstacles and potentials of the concept of automation utilizing RPA. The commercial and open source technologies that best demonstrate RPA's recent usefulness (preferably combined with some AI approaches or algorithms) are presented in the following sections.

RPA and AI in Construction HR

While concerns about job displacement due to automation are valid, RPA's impact on construction HR shouldn't be solely viewed through the lens of job losses. (Forrester, 2019) Automation, including RPA, will undoubtedly reshape the construction workforce, but with a potential for positive transformation rather than just disruption. Instead of fearing robots replacing workers, the focus should shift towards redefining the human role in a landscape empowered by AI and RPA.

Beyond streamlining routine tasks like payroll and scheduling, RPA and AI have the potential to:

- Augment human capabilities: Imagine AI-powered safety systems monitoring sites in real-time, preventing accidents, or smart algorithms optimizing material logistics, reducing waste and cost overruns. This human-machine synergy can boost productivity, enhance safety, and improve project outcomes.
- Upskill and reskill the workforce: As repetitive tasks are automated, opportunities arise to equip workers with skills relevant to the evolving environment. The chapter can explore potential reskilling and upskilling programs geared towards areas like data analysis, project management, and human-machine collaboration.

- Transform HR practices: RPA can free up HR professionals from mundane tasks, allowing them to focus on strategic initiatives like employee engagement, talent development, and fostering a culture of continuous learning. New roles within HR dedicated to RPA implementation and human-machine interaction management will further shape the future of construction HR.

Case studies showcasing successful integrations of RPA and AI in construction HR can serve as valuable illustrations of these possibilities. Companies like Turner Construction utilizing AI-powered recruitment tools or Skanska leveraging RPA for administrative tasks exemplify how technology can empower both efficiency and employee well-being. However, ethical considerations should also be addressed. Algorithmic bias in recruitment, worker surveillance through wearable technology, and the psychological impact of job displacement are potential pitfalls that must be acknowledged and mitigated through responsible AI implementation. Building a resilient future for construction HR demands a roadmap for navigating this complex terrain. This roadmap should explore future trends in workplace automation, outline recommended skill sets for construction workers in the digital age, and suggest best practices for ethical and responsible technology adoption.

By embracing a proactive approach to reskilling, upskilling, and responsible AI integration, construction companies can transform the impact of RPA and AI from workforce disruption to workplace empowerment. This shift will redefine the human role in construction, not replace it, leading to a more collaborative, efficient, and ultimately, more humane industry.

RPA TECHNOLOGIES

UiPath Platform

The UiPath platform has emerged as a leading Robotic Process Automation (RPA) tool, revolutionizing the way businesses automate their processes. With its powerful capabilities and user-friendly interface, UiPath has become synonymous with efficiency, productivity, and cost savings. One of the key strengths of UiPath lies in its integration with artificial intelligence (AI) technologies, enabling users to harness the benefits of both RPA and AI in a seamless manner. At the core of UiPath's AI integration is its ability to leverage machine learning algorithms and natural language processing (NLP) capabilities. Natural language processing (NLP) acts as a digital Rosetta Stone, deciphering the nuances of human language for machines, enabling them to grasp meaning, intent, and even emotion. This transformative technology empowers computers to engage in natural conversations, extract insights from text, and generate compelling content, forging a deeper connection between humans and the digital world. These features empower the platform to understand, analyze, and process unstructured data, such as emails, documents, and images. By incorporating AI into the automation workflow, UiPath enhances its decision-making capabilities, enabling it to handle complex tasks that require cognitive skills.

One of the significant advantages of UiPath's integration with AI is the ability to automate tasks that involve data extraction and analysis. Through the use of AI algorithms, the platform can intelligently extract relevant information from documents, invoices, and other unstructured data sources. This eliminates the need for manual data entry and significantly reduces errors and processing time. Additionally, the integration of AI allows for advanced data analytics, enabling users to gain valuable insights from large datasets and make data-driven decisions.

Another area where UiPath's integration with AI proves valuable is in automating customer interactions and support services. By incorporating NLP capabilities, the platform can understand and respond to customer queries and requests in a human-like manner. This enables businesses to provide efficient and personalized customer service, enhancing customer satisfaction and loyalty. Moreover, the integration with AI enables UiPath to learn from past interactions and continuously improve its performance, resulting in more accurate and efficient responses over time. Furthermore, UiPath's AI integration enables the platform to handle exceptions and complex decision-making scenarios. Through machine learning algorithms, the platform can learn from historical data and make intelligent decisions when faced with unexpected situations. This allows for greater flexibility and adaptability in the automation workflow, as the system can dynamically adjust its actions based on real-time inputs and changing conditions.

Additionally, UiPath's AI integration opens up opportunities for process optimization and intelligent automation. By analyzing patterns and trends in data, the platform can identify bottlenecks, inefficiencies, and areas for improvement within the automation process. This insight enables businesses to optimize their workflows, streamline operations, and achieve higher levels of efficiency and productivity. Moreover, the integration of AI within the UiPath platform empowers businesses to leverage advanced cognitive capabilities. The platform can perform complex tasks that were previously only achievable by human workers. Image recognition, sentiment analysis, language translation, and other cognitive capabilities can be incorporated into the automation process. This allows businesses to automate a broader range of processes and leverage AI technologies to enhance the capabilities of their digital workforce.

The UiPath platform's integration with AI also extends to the development of intelligent robots, known as "UiPath AI Robots." These robots can perform complex tasks that require advanced cognitive capabilities, such as image recognition, sentiment analysis, and language translation. By integrating AI into the robotic workforce, businesses can achieve a higher level of automation, improve accuracy, and reduce manual intervention. This integration enables businesses to automate more sophisticated processes and leverage AI technologies to enhance their digital workforce's capabilities.

In conclusion, the integration of AI with the UiPath platform has revolutionized the way businesses automate their processes. By leveraging machine learning algorithms and NLP capabilities, UiPath enables users to automate tasks that involve unstructured data, improve decision-making, enhance customer interactions, handle exceptions, optimize processes, and develop intelligent robots. This integration empowers businesses to achieve higher levels of efficiency, productivity, and accuracy in their automation initiatives. As AI continues to advance, the integration with UiPath will further drive innovation and open new possibilities for intelligent automation in various industries. The integration of AI with the UiPath platform has far-reaching implications for businesses across different sectors. It enables organizations to automate complex processes, improve operational efficiency, and reduce costs. By leveraging AI-powered automation, businesses can free up human resources from mundane and repetitive tasks, allowing employees to focus on higher-value activities that require creativity, problem-solving, and critical thinking. Furthermore, the integration of AI within the UiPath platform paves the way for enhanced decision-making capabilities. By leveraging AI algorithms, UiPath can analyze large volumes of data, identify patterns and trends, and generate valuable insights. These insights can inform strategic decision-making, help identify opportunities for business growth, and improve overall performance. Moreover, the integration of AI with UiPath contributes to the evolution of the digital workforce. By combining the power of RPA with AI capabilities, businesses can create a symbiotic relationship between human employees and software robots. This collaborative approach allows for the augmentation of human skills with the speed, accuracy, and scalability of intelligent automation. It empowers employees to focus on tasks that require creativity, innovation, and emotional intelligence, while UiPath handles repetitive and rule-based processes.

The integration of AI within UiPath also facilitates continuous improvement and learning. By leveraging machine learning algorithms, UiPath can adapt and improve its performance over time. Through the analysis of historical data and user feedback, the platform can identify areas for enhancement, optimize workflows, and deliver increasingly accurate and efficient automation solutions. Furthermore, the integration of AI with UiPath offers scalability and flexibility. As businesses grow and evolve, their automation needs may change. The AI capabilities of UiPath enable organizations to scale their automation efforts and adapt to evolving requirements. The platform's ability to handle complex decision-making scenarios and exception handling ensures that automation workflows can accommodate dynamic business environments.

The integration of AI with the UiPath platform brings significant benefits to businesses across industries. It enables organizations to automate complex processes, improve decision-making, enhance operational efficiency, and achieve scalability. By combining the power of RPA with AI capabilities, UiPath empowers businesses to optimize their workflows, leverage advanced cognitive capabilities, and create a harmonious collaboration between humans and robots. As AI technologies continue to advance, the integration with UiPath will play a pivotal role in shaping the future of intelligent automation, driving innovation, and delivering transformative outcomes for organizations worldwide.

UiPath enables the construction of RPA functions within its framework for writing and running programming scripts. It may be programmed using an interface of blocks and a variety of plugins to allow for the customization of business processes. Currently, the RPA UiPath platform is divided into three modules: UiPath Studio, UiPath Robot, and UiPath Orchestrator, the latter of which permits the potential orchestration of robots. (Tripathi, 2018) . Additionally, the integration of a Kibana data visualization plugin with Elasticsearch, an open-source search engine developed under the Apache License, and Microsoft's Information Services Server and SQL Server allows for the enhancement of the view of analytical data related to the execution of RPA processes.

Blue Prism Platform

The integration of AI with RPA platforms has revolutionized how organizations automate their processes. Blue Prism, a leading RPA tool, is at the forefront of this integration, empowering organizations with intelligent automation capabilities. This paper aims to provide a comprehensive understanding of AI integration within the Blue Prism platform, exploring its features, benefits, and implications for intelligent automation.

Blue Prism offers a range of AI integration features that enhance the platform's capabilities and enable intelligent automation. It integrates with natural language processing (NLP), allowing the platform to understand and process unstructured data sources, such as emails, documents, and images. By leveraging NLP algorithms, Blue Prism can extract valuable information, transforming unstructured data into structured data. This enables the automation of tasks involving cognitive skills, reducing manual data entry and improving processing time.

The integration of machine learning algorithms within Blue Prism enables intelligent automation and continuous improvement. By analyzing historical data, Blue Prism can learn patterns, predict outcomes, and optimize automation workflows. This capability enhances decision-making, improves efficiency, and ensures that the automation process becomes more accurate and effective over time.

Cognitive services integration is another key aspect of AI integration in Blue Prism. By seamlessly incorporating external AI platforms, such as sentiment analysis, image recognition, and language translation, Blue Prism expands its capabilities. This integration empowers organizations to automate complex and cognitive tasks, augmenting the digital workforce with advanced cognitive capabilities.

The integration of AI within the Blue Prism platform has numerous practical applications across industries and functions. AI integration in Blue Prism enables intelligent data processing and analysis. By leveraging NLP and machine learning, organizations can extract valuable insights from unstructured data sources and make data-driven decisions. This enhances data processing speed, accuracy, and scalability, resulting in improved operational efficiency.

Blue Prism's AI integration empowers the automation of complex tasks that require cognitive capabilities. By incorporating machine-learning algorithms, Blue Prism can handle exceptions, adapt to dynamic conditions, and make intelligent decisions. This ensures that the automation workflow is flexible and can accommodate real-time inputs and changing business environments.

Moreover, the AI capabilities of Blue Prism enhance decision-making processes. By leveraging machine-learning algorithms, the platform can analyze data, identify patterns, and provide valuable insights for strategic decision-making. The continuous learning and optimization capabilities enable businesses to improve their automation workflows, identify bottlenecks, and streamline processes for greater efficiency.

The integration of AI within the Blue Prism platform brings a range of benefits and implications for organizations seeking intelligent automation. AI integration significantly improves efficiency and accuracy in business processes. By automating mundane and repetitive tasks, organizations can achieve faster processing times, reduce errors, and allocate resources more strategically. This frees up human resources, allowing them to focus on more value-added activities that require creativity, critical thinking, and problem-solving skills.

The combination of RPA and AI capabilities in Blue Prism leads to the transformation of the digital workforce. By leveraging AI-integrated Blue Prism, organizations can create a symbiotic relationship between human employees and software robots. The collaboration between humans and robots enables the automation of complex tasks while leveraging the cognitive abilities of AI. This not only improves efficiency but also enhances employee productivity by offloading repetitive and mundane tasks, allowing them to focus on higher-value activities that require human judgment and creativity.

AI-integrated Blue Prism also has implications for process optimization and innovation. With machine learning algorithms and continuous learning capabilities, Blue Prism can adapt and optimize automation workflows over time. By analyzing data, identifying patterns, and making intelligent decisions, the platform helps organizations identify areas for process improvement and innovation. This iterative optimization process leads to enhanced operational efficiency, cost savings, and competitive advantage.

Furthermore, the integration of AI within Blue Prism enables organizations to leverage advanced cognitive services. By incorporating image recognition, sentiment analysis, and language translation, Blue Prism can automate tasks that require cognitive capabilities. For example, in customer service, Blue Prism can analyze customer sentiment from social media data, enabling organizations to respond effectively and provide personalized customer experiences. This integration of cognitive services enhances the overall capabilities of the Blue Prism platform, allowing organizations to automate cognitive tasks that were previously reliant on human intervention.

In conclusion, the integration of artificial intelligence within the Blue Prism platform empowers organizations with intelligent automation capabilities. By leveraging NLP, machine learning, and cognitive services, Blue Prism enhances data processing, enables the automation of complex tasks, and improves decision-making processes. The practical applications of AI-integrated Blue Prism span across industries and functions, enabling organizations to achieve operational efficiency, process optimization, and innovation. The benefits and implications of AI-integrated Blue Prism are significant, contributing to digital transformation and the evolution of the digital workforce. As AI continues to advance, the integration of AI technologies within Blue Prism will further revolutionize the automation landscape, enabling organizations to unlock new possibilities and drive sustainable growth.

Automation Anywhere Platform

Another RPA process-focused platform is Automation Anywhere, with the unique feature of additionally providing information on the application of AI techniques and algorithms. (Automation Anywhere, 2021) It covers a variety of application areas, including human resources, customer relationship management, supply chain, and is especially likely to be integrated or interconnected with ERPs from SAP and Oracle, just like other tools. It can also be connected with other ERPs from other businesses. The RPA solution includes a cognitive automation module and capabilities for applying data analysis to RPA procedures. It offers a set of data that enables the configuration, operation, and execution of RPA processes as a multifunctional application. In order to extract information from documents and subsequently increase the effectiveness of document validation, the Automation Anywhere tool's Bot tool internally executes some artificial intelligence techniques and algorithms, such as artificial neural networks, fuzzy logic and natural language processing. In this regard, it seems that the Automation Anywhere intelligent word processing application on the IQ Bot platform is currently offering some AI techniques or algorithms.

Comparison of RPA Platforms

Similarities

- All three platforms automate repetitive tasks using software robots.
- They offer desktop, cloud, and hybrid deployment options.
- They integrate with various applications and systems through APIs and pre-built connectors.
- They provide security features like role-based access control and data encryption.

Differences

- User interface and ease of use: UiPath is considered more user-friendly, while Blue Prism has a steeper learning curve.
- Scalability and security: Blue Prism excels in enterprise settings with strong security features, while Automation Anywhere offers flexible licensing and AI integration.
- AI and machine learning capabilities: Automation Anywhere provides a dedicated AI platform, while UiPath and Blue Prism integrate with external AI services.
- Pricing: Pricing models vary, with UiPath potentially being more expensive for complex implementations and Automation Anywhere offering pay-as-you-go options.

Table 1. Comparison between the RPA tools.

Feature	UiPath	Blue Prism	Automation Anywhere
Platform Options	Desktop, Cloud	Desktop, Cloud	Desktop, Cloud
Scripting Languages	UiPath Robot, C#, VB.NET	BP Process Studio, Java	AAE, JavaScript
Strengths	User-friendly interface, extensive features, large community	Scalability, enterprise security, compliance focus	Easy customization, flexible licensing, AI integration
Weaknesses	Potential vendor lock-in, costlier for complex implementations	Steep learning curve, less intuitive interface	Limited pre-built connectors, may lack advanced AI features
Cost & Licensing	Per-robot and named user pricing	Per-robot and concurrent user pricing	Pay-as-you-go and subscription models
Target Users	Beginners, mid-level users, enterprises	Large enterprises, complex automation needs	SMEs, agile development teams, AI focus

SIGNIFICANCE OF ROBOTIC PROCESS AUTOMATION

RPA does indeed have a number of benefits for companies that use it. Following can be seen as a few of the main benefits of RPA.

- RPA automates mundane and repetitive processes, freeing personnel to focus on work with a greater added value. This increases efficiency and production. As a result, there may be an improvement in accuracy and task completion time in addition to greater production and efficiency.
- RPA can lower labor expenses and increase operational efficiency by automating operations. RPA also has the potential to lessen mistakes and rework, both of which can save money.
- It can enhance the customer experience by speeding up data processing and enhancing data accuracy. Customers may see reduced wait times and quicker, more accurate response times as a result.
- Depending on business demands, RPA may be readily scaled up or down, enabling enterprises to react swiftly to changes in demand or operational needs.
- RPA can be integrated with existing systems, enabling businesses to take advantage of their current processes and infrastructure. This may help to lessen inconvenience and lower implementation costs.
- By guaranteeing accurate and consistent data processing and reporting, RPA can assist firms in better complying with regulatory demands.

- Implementation time is shorter with RPA compared to other automation methods like system integrations or custom software development. This may enable businesses to see a return on investment more quickly.
- RPA bots can be configured to operate 24/7, enabling businesses to handle activities without the need for human intervention.
- Data analytics and insights is also another point to consider. RPA may assist businesses in gathering and analyzing data from a variety of sources to provide important insights into operational procedures and customer behavior. Organizations may be able to identify areas for improvement and make better decisions as a result.
- RPA bots can be created to carry out tasks without the requirement for substantial training or technical knowledge, which cuts down on training time. By doing this, businesses can cut back on the time and money spent on employee onboarding and training.

Eventually, RPA has a number of benefits that can help businesses automate time-consuming, repetitive operations, increase operational effectiveness, and improve the overall customer experience.

Limitations of Robotic Process Automation

RPA has many benefits, but there are also drawbacks and restrictions to take into account. To name a few:

a) Restricted cognitive abilities: RPA cannot carry out activities that need cognitive abilities like reasoning, decision-making, or critical thinking. It is therefore restricted to following pre-defined rules and instructions. Therefore, this technology is most effective for routine, rule-based tasks.

b) Implementation complexity: Integrating RPA with legacy systems or numerous applications can be a challenging procedure that demands a lot of time and resources. This could lead to a pricey implementation and a protracted payback time.

c) Regular maintenance and support: These are necessary for RPA systems, including monitoring, troubleshooting, and updating. This may result in more resources being needed and raise the total cost of ownership.

d) Security hazards: If not properly designed and secured, RPA systems could provide security vulnerabilities. RPA bots may have access to sensitive information and systems, and any programming flaws or vulnerabilities could lead to data breaches or other security concerns.

e) Limited adaptability: RPA bots are made to do certain tasks and might not be able to adapt to new systems or altered business processes. RPA might therefore not be appropriate for enterprises that need flexibility and agility.

When determining if RPA is the best choice for a specific business process or use case, it is critical to take these limitations and drawbacks into account.

RPA IN THE CONSTRUCTION INDUSTRY

Construction Industry

The construction industry is a vital sector that plays crucial roles in most of the development areas. The development of infrastructure, including roads, bridges, buildings, and other public works, depends heavily on the construction industry. The progress of society and the economy depends on this infrastructure. Also, the construction sector is a significant employer, giving millions of people worldwide jobs. These positions could be in manual labor, skilled trades, or engineering. Building homes and other forms of shelter for people all over the world is a responsibility of the construction industry, in addition to producing jobs and promoting economic prosperity. For families and individuals to live in secure and comfortable environments, this is crucial. By utilizing green building techniques and materials, cutting waste, and lowering the carbon footprint of construction projects, the construction industry may also contribute to environmental sustainability. In conclusion, the development of infrastructure, the generation of jobs, economic expansion, the provision of housing and shelter, and environmental sustainability all depend on the construction industry.

Moreover, the construction industry also contributes to the growth of other industries such as manufacturing, transportation, and logistics. For instance, the manufacturing industry is supported by the production of building materials like steel, cement, and wood. By moving supplies and tools to and from building sites, the transportation and logistics sector gains from the construction sector. In addition, the construction sector is a crucial one for innovation and technological uptake. The construction sector is adopting new technologies, such as the Internet of Things (IoT) and Building Information Modeling (BIM), to streamline operations and increase efficiency. These technical developments have also made it possible to create new building techniques and materials that are more environmentally friendly and sustainable.

In conclusion, the construction sector is an important sector with a major effect on a variety of aspects of our everyday life. It is in charge of building infrastructure, giving people a place to live, generating employment, and promoting economic progress. The industry's emphasis on sustainability and technical advancement is bringing about good change and raising people's standards of living everywhere. Given the significance of the construction sector, it is necessary to increase its productivity and efficiency. The industry is known for its low production levels when compared to other industries. This is due to a number of reasons, including material waste, supply chain interruptions, and project delays. There is an increasing need for cutting-edge solutions like robotic process automation (RPA) and other digital technology to handle these problems. By implementation of RPA in the construction industry, data input, scheduling, and billing are just a few examples of the time-consuming, repetitive operations that businesses may automate. Workers can then concentrate on more challenging and valuable activities, increasing productivity and efficiency as a whole. RPA can also assist in lowering errors and increasing data accuracy, which can improve decision-making and result in cost savings.

In conclusion, the building sector is vital to both society and the economy. It must increase its production and efficiency if it is to keep providing high-quality homes and infrastructure. The sector may open up new doors for growth and maintain its long-term survival by embracing cutting-edge technologies like RPA.

Construction Management Area

Conventional construction management techniques are known for taking a lot of time and effort. The use of manual processes, such as paper-based documentation, which can be time-consuming and error-prone, is one of the main causes of this. This comprises activities including invoicing creation and processing, change order administration, and project status monitoring. In addition, there are several stakeholders in the construction business, including architects, engineers, contractors, subcontractors, and suppliers, which can complicate coordination and provide communication problems.

Allocating resources, a crucial component of construction management, is yet another difficult task. Traditional manual systems for allocating resources, however, can be ineffective, cause delays, and result in cost overruns. Project delays, which are already frequent in construction projects due to factors including weather, unforeseen site conditions, and supply chain interruptions, may be made worse by this. When these issues are combined, building projects may experience poorer productivity, higher costs, and lower quality results.

The construction sector is increasingly using innovative technologies like RPA to address these issues. RPA can assist in automating manual operations, enhancing stakeholder engagement and communication, maximizing resource allocation, and lowering the likelihood of delays and errors. The construction sector may boost its efficiency, productivity, and overall performance by adopting RPA and other digital technologies, which will benefit all parties involved in construction projects.

RPA Applications in the Construction Industry

The construction industry is a complex and dynamic sector that involves a wide range of processes, from project planning and design to procurement, construction, and project management. With the advancements in automation and digital technologies, Robotic Process Automation (RPA) has emerged as a promising solution for streamlining and optimizing various tasks and processes in the construction industry. There is no question that construction achievement has long been acknowledged as delivering astounding feats of engineering and craftsmanship when looking at well-known landmarks like the pyramids, the great cathedrals of the world, and even Stonehenge. In that sense, not much has changed over time, although the "how" has changed considerably. These days, RPA and artificial intelligence (AI) have drastically changed the construction industry in a variety of ways. This thesis explores the specific applications of RPA in construction and examines how it can revolutionize the industry.

In the past, verbal communication and a system mostly based on paper were used to organize and distribute information on a construction site. Delays, lost time and money, as well as lowered morale are frequently the result of disorganized site administration and poor communication between field and office staff.

The onset of supply chain integration, building information modeling (BIM), computer-aided design (CAD), and mobile computing has created the conditions for the construction sector to significantly modernize the sector. Robotic Process Automation (RPA), along with other digitalized tools and business processes, is increasingly becoming a crucial component of the construction lifecycle as more construction organizations go digital. (Ridder, 2022)

RPA can be used to automate many of the manual operations that are now engaged in traditional construction management procedures to increase their efficiency. Processing documents is one key matter where RPA might be beneficial. RPA, for instance, can be used to automatically process change orders, invoices, and purchase orders, saving time and labor normally needed for manual processing. RPA can lessen the possibility of errors by automatically extracting and entering data from these documents, resulting in data that is more accurate and trustworthy.

Resource allocation is a further area where RPA can be used to increase efficiency. By tracking resource utilization and adjusting allocations as necessary, RPA can help in resource allocation optimization by automating inventory management processes. This can increase project effectiveness by reducing resource overages and delays. RPA can also be used to automate reporting on resource utilization, project progress, and other important performance indicators. RPA can free up time and resources for other crucial duties by automating these reports. By automatically generating schedules based on project needs, resource availability, and other crucial aspects, RPA can be utilized to optimize project scheduling. By doing this, the possibility of delays can be decreased, and projects can be finished on schedule and under budget. RPA can automate project scheduling while also assisting in resource allocation and utilization optimization, lowering the possibility of project overruns and delays while increasing project effectiveness.

In addition, RPA can help in enhancing stakeholder collaboration and communication in the construction sector. All stakeholders can be assured that important changes and updates are communicated to them in real-time by using RPA to automatically send notifications and alerts based on predetermined triggers. This might facilitate better collaboration and coordination amongst stakeholders by reducing miscommunications and misconceptions.

Moreover, RPA can be utilized to enhance risk management in the construction sector. RPA can assist in lowering the risk of delays and cost overruns while enhancing safety and compliance by monitoring risks like safety hazards and compliance problems.

RPA in Project Planning and Design

RPA offers significant potential in project planning and design processes. It can automate repetitive tasks such as generating 2D and 3D models, performing quantity take-offs, and optimizing building layouts. By utilizing RPA, construction professionals can save time and improve accuracy in creating design documents, conducting feasibility studies, and generating cost estimates. Additionally, RPA can integrate with Building Information Modeling (BIM) systems to automate data synchronization and improve collaboration among project stakeholders.

RPA in Procurement and Supply Chain Management

Efficient procurement and supply chain management are critical for successful construction projects. RPA can automate procurement processes by generating purchase orders, tracking supplier performance, and managing inventory levels. It can also streamline supplier onboarding, contract management, and invoice processing. By automating these tasks, RPA can enhance transparency, reduce errors, and improve the overall efficiency of the procurement and supply chain processes.

RPA in Construction Execution and Monitoring

During the construction phase, RPA can play a vital role in executing and monitoring various activities. It can automate the generation of work schedules, monitor progress against the schedule, and trigger notifications for delays or deviations. RPA can also assist in quality control by automating inspections, collecting and analyzing data from sensors and IoT devices, and generating real-time reports. By leveraging RPA in construction execution and monitoring, project managers can enhance productivity, mitigate risks, and improve project outcomes.

RPA in Project Management and Reporting

Effective project management requires accurate and timely reporting of project progress, budgeting, and resource allocation. RPA can automate the collection and analysis of project data, generate performance reports, and facilitate decision-making. It can integrate with enterprise systems to extract data from multiple sources, perform calculations, and generate customized dashboards for project managers and stakeholders. RPA can also automate the generation of regulatory compliance reports, ensuring adherence to industry standards and regulations.

RPA in Facility Management and Maintenance

Once a construction project is completed, RPA can continue to deliver value in facility management and maintenance. It can automate routine maintenance tasks, such as scheduling inspections, generating work orders, and tracking asset performance. RPA can also integrate with Internet of Things (IoT) devices to collect real-time data on energy usage, occupancy levels, and equipment health. By automating facility management processes, RPA enables proactive maintenance, reduces downtime, and enhances operational efficiency.

While the applications of RPA in the construction industry are promising, there are challenges and considerations to address. These include the complexity of construction processes, integration with existing systems and technologies, data security and privacy concerns, and workforce readiness for RPA implementation. It is crucial for construction organizations to carefully assess these challenges and develop strategies to mitigate risks and ensure successful RPA adoption.

The integration of Robotic Process Automation (RPA) in the construction industry holds great potential for transforming traditional processes and revolutionizing the way projects are planned, executed, and managed. Throughout this thesis, we have explored the various applications of RPA in construction, highlighting its benefits in project planning and design, procurement and supply chain management, construction execution and monitoring, project management and reporting, as well as facility management and maintenance.

By leveraging RPA, construction organizations can achieve significant improvements in efficiency, accuracy, and productivity. Automation of repetitive tasks reduces the risk of errors and frees up valuable time for construction professionals to focus on more complex and strategic activities. Moreover, the integration of RPA with other technologies such as Building Information Modeling (BIM) and Internet of Things (IoT) devices enables seamless data exchange and real-time insights, facilitating better decision-making and collaboration among project stakeholders.

However, it is important to acknowledge the challenges and considerations associated with implementing RPA in the construction industry. The complex nature of construction processes, the need for integration with existing systems, concerns regarding data security and privacy, and the readiness of the workforce to embrace automation are factors that require careful attention. Construction organizations must develop comprehensive strategies that address these challenges and ensure a smooth and successful adoption of RPA.

As the construction industry continues to evolve, embracing digital transformation becomes imperative for staying competitive and delivering projects with efficiency and excellence. RPA provides a powerful tool for achieving this transformation, enabling construction professionals to streamline operations, enhance project outcomes, and drive innovation.

In conclusion, the applications of RPA in the construction industry are vast and promising. By harnessing the potential of automation, construction organizations can overcome traditional limitations and unlock new levels of productivity and performance. As technology continues to advance and RPA evolves, it is essential for the construction industry to embrace this transformative tool and pave the way for a more efficient, collaborative, and successful future.

Real Life Examples of RPA in the Construction Industry

Leading construction firm Skanska USA deployed RPA to automate the processing of invoices. Around 7,000 invoices were being received by the business each month, and they were being manually processed. RPA allowed Skanska USA to reduce processing time from 20 days to just 5 days, saving the company 75% on processing costs. (UiPath Inc.)

Formerly, Mortenson Construction tracked construction material movement manually, which was a labor-intensive and error-prone process. Mortenson was able to optimize their material tracking procedure and cut the time needed to track items by 50% by deploying RPA. This is a considerable gain in production and efficiency for the business, which may result in cost savings. It is a great illustration of how

RPA may be used in the construction sector to enhance current procedures and produce superior outcomes. (Mortenson Construction Inc.)

RPA was used by the global infrastructure company AECOM to automate its procurement procedure. The organization was spending too much time and risking mistakes manually processing purchase orders and invoices. AECOM was able to minimize the time needed to process purchase orders and invoicing by 75% by deploying RPA. (KPMG, 2019)

For the benefit of many utility companies, Balfour Beatty performs routine excavations and urgent repairs on water mains and gas pipes.

It used to take up to a week to compile map packs from different mapping tools, which had all the crucial details required to ensure a safe excavation, such as the location of the water and electricity mains.

Balfour Beatty needed a system that would allow staff to compile these map packs quickly and efficiently because doing otherwise would result in expensive delays. They can now automate this operation using RPA, reducing it from a 30-minute manual process to a 5-minute automatic one. The organization saves a significant amount of time and money thanks to this effective, seamless solution. (NDL).

Benefits of RPA in the Construction Industry

Repetitive and time-consuming processes in the construction industry can be automated using RPA. RPA can assist in doing this by strengthening decision-making, efficiency, and accuracy while also lowering costs and increasing compliance.

Improved efficiency is one of RPA's key advantages. Data input and document processing operations can be automated using RPA, which can cut down on the time and effort needed to execute these jobs. For building companies, this might result in cost savings.

RPA can improve accuracy by reducing human errors such as incorrect data entry and calculation. This can enhance project data quality and lower the possibility of expensive rework.

Faster decision-making is another advantage of RPA. Construction businesses may respond rapidly to changing project conditions by using RPA to automate procedures and provide real-time data.

RPA can also assist in ensuring that construction firms follow laws and standards, such as safety and environmental laws. Additionally, by automating the sharing of information and data, RPA can promote improved collaboration between various teams and departments.

As a result, RPA can assist construction organizations streamline their operations, cut costs, and enhance the precision and quality of project data.

Limitations of RPA in the Construction Industry

RPA has been utilized in the construction sector to automate jobs including data input, invoicing, and scheduling. RPA does, however, have its limitations, notably in the construction sector, just like any other technology.

The inability of RPA to handle unstructured data is one of its main drawbacks in the construction sector. Plans, specifications, schedules, and budgets are just a few of the many types of papers and data formats that are used in construction projects. Only operations involving structured data, such completing form fields or copying and pasting data from one spreadsheet to another, can be automated using RPA. RPA has some limitations that prevent it from fully automating building activities, including the inability to read unstructured data like handwritten notes or scanned documents.

The dependence of RPA in the construction sector on rules-based procedures is another drawback. RPA may struggle with jobs that require judgment and decision-making because it is designed to adhere to a set of established rules and stages. In the construction sector, there are frequently circumstances that call for a human touch, such resolving disputes amongst stakeholders or choosing the scope of a project. This type of decision-making process cannot be replicated by RPA, which limits its use in several sectors of construction management.

Last but not least, RPA is inadequate for jobs that call for direct physical contact with the environment. Several operations in construction, such pouring concrete or hanging drywall, call for personnel to physically contact with the job site. Since RPA cannot carry out these kinds of physically demanding activities, it cannot entirely replace human labor in the construction sector.

In conclusion, RPA has the ability to automate a variety of operations in the construction sector, but it also has drawbacks that must be taken into account. Its limitations in several aspects of construction management include its inability to handle unstructured data, reliance on rules-based procedures, and incapacity to carry out physical tasks. Understanding these restrictions and utilizing the technology appropriately are essential for maximizing RPA's potential in the construction industry.

Future of RPA in the Construction Industry

Robotic process automation (RPA) has a bright future in the construction industry. RPA adoption is likely to accelerate as the construction sector continues to develop and incorporate new technology.

To create more sophisticated and effective construction processes, RPA can be integrated with other emerging technologies like the Internet of Things (IoT), Artificial Intelligence (AI), and 3D printing. Construction organizations can use RPA, for instance, to automate the maintenance and monitoring of IoT-enabled equipment and sensors, allowing them to spot concerns before they become serious ones.

As RPA spreads throughout the construction sector, it will produce enormous volumes of data that may be used to enhance analytics and guide judgment. Construction organizations can spot trends, streamline procedures, and enhance project results by evaluating this data.

Automating safety and compliance inspections with RPA helps lower the risk of accidents and ensure that regulations are being followed. For instance, RPA can be used to automatically track and record safety occurrences, lessening the workload on employees and enhancing the accuracy of the data.

RPA can be used to automate stakeholder collaboration and communication, enhancing coordination and lowering errors. RPA can be used, for instance, to automatically alert team members when a task is finished or when a problem appears, facilitating quick resolution and enhanced collaboration.

In conclusion, RPA has a promising future in the construction industry. Construction organizations may increase productivity, lower costs, and foster stakeholder collaboration by utilizing RPA. RPA will become a more valuable asset for the construction sector as it develops and integrates with other cutting-edge technologies, driving innovation and enhancing project outcomes.

Challenges and Solutions

Robotic Process Automation (RPA) has gained significant attention across industries as a transformative technology for streamlining operations, increasing efficiency, and reducing costs. The construction industry, with its complex and dynamic nature, can also benefit from the implementation of RPA. However, like any technology adoption, there are several challenges that need to be addressed for successful integration of RPA in the construction sector. This thesis explores the key challenges faced by the construction industry when implementing RPA and discusses potential solutions.

Process Complexity and Variability

The construction industry is characterized by a wide range of processes that can be highly complex and subject to frequent changes. From project management and scheduling to procurement and inventory management, each process involves multiple stakeholders, diverse documentation, and unique requirements. Implementing RPA in such an environment poses a challenge, as the automation of complex and variable processes requires careful analysis, design, and customization of RPA workflows. Adapting RPA to handle process variability and exceptions becomes crucial for successful implementation.

Solution: A thorough analysis of existing processes is essential to identify automation opportunities. Engaging with domain experts and construction professionals can help in understanding the nuances and complexities of specific processes. Customizing RPA solutions to accommodate process variations and exceptions through rule-based decision-making or machine learning algorithms can enhance the adaptability of the automtion system..

Integration with Legacy Systems

The construction industry often relies on a mix of legacy systems, proprietary software, and manual processes. These disparate systems may lack standardization and interoperability, making it challenging to integrate RPA seamlessly. The automation of construction processes may require extracting data from multiple systems, validating and transforming it, and then updating various systems. Bridging the gap between legacy systems and RPA platforms can be complex, time-consuming, and require significant effort.

Solution: An integration strategy that addresses legacy system compatibility is crucial. Employing middleware tools, APIs, and connectors can facilitate data exchange and system integration. Creating a data management framework that standardizes data formats, definitions, and processes across systems can simplify the integration process. Collaborating with software vendors and system experts can provide insights into the technical requirements and best practices for integration.

Data Quality and Unstructured Data

The construction industry generates vast amounts of data, often in unstructured formats such as drawings, specifications, and reports. RPA relies on accurate and structured data for efficient automation. However, ensuring data quality and extracting information from unstructured data sources pose significant challenges. Incomplete or inconsistent data can lead to errors, delays, and inaccurate decision-making, undermining the effectiveness of RPA implementation.

Solution: Implementing data governance practices and data quality controls is vital to ensure accurate and reliable data for RPA processes. Leveraging technologies like optical character recognition (OCR), natural language processing (NLP), and machine learning can assist in extracting information from unstructured data sources. Training RPA systems to handle variations in data formats and improving data capture processes can enhance data quality and enable successful automation.

Change Management and Workforce Adoption

Introducing RPA in the construction industry necessitates a cultural shift and workforce readiness. Resistance to change, fear of job loss, and a lack of awareness about the benefits of RPA can hinder adoption. Construction professionals may perceive RPA as a threat rather than a tool to augment their capabilities. Building awareness, providing training and fostering a collaborative environment are crucial for successful RPA implementation.

Solution: Establishing a comprehensive change management strategy that includes communication, training, and involvement of stakeholders is essential. Highlighting the benefits of RPA, such as reduced manual effort, improved accuracy, and the ability to focus on higher-value tasks, can help alleviate concerns and generate enthusiasm among the workforce. Engaging employees in the automation journey, seeking their feedback, and involving them in the design and implementation of RPA processes can foster a sense of ownership and ensure a smoother transition. Providing comprehensive training programs to equip employees with the necessary skills to work alongside RPA systems will help them understand how automation can enhance their productivity and contribute to the overall success of construction projects.

Security and Compliance

The construction industry deals with sensitive data, including project plans, financial information, and personal records. Ensuring the security and compliance of data when implementing RPA is paramount. RPA solutions must adhere to data protection regulations, safeguard intellectual property, and prevent unauthorized access to confidential information. Maintaining compliance while automating processes that involve regulatory requirements can be a challenge.

Solution: Implementing robust security measures, such as encryption, access controls, and data encryption, is crucial to protect sensitive data. Conducting regular security audits and assessments of RPA systems and implementing industry best practices can help identify vulnerabilities and ensure compliance. Collaborating with legal and compliance teams to address any regulatory concerns and ensure that RPA implementation aligns with industry-specific regulations will help mitigate risks.

Implementing Robotic Process Automation in the construction industry offers significant opportunities for improving efficiency, productivity, and cost-effectiveness. However, it is crucial to address the challenges unique to the construction sector. By understanding and overcoming the complexities of processes, integrating with legacy systems, managing data quality, fostering workforce adoption, and ensuring security and compliance, the construction industry can successfully leverage RPA to revolutionize its operations. Overcoming these challenges will lead to streamlined processes, reduced errors, and enhanced project outcomes, ultimately driving the industry towards greater competitiveness and innovation.

BIM AND RPA

Building information modeling (BIM) is the digital representation of a construction project that entails the development and administration of a 3D model with numerous data attributes, including dimensions, materials, and schedule. It is an increasingly popular tool in the construction industry. From design and planning to building and maintenance, BIM can be used throughout the whole construction project. The main goal of BIM is to increase efficiency, collaboration, and communication across the whole lifecycle of a construction project.

The BIM system was first implemented in 1982 as part of the development of the ArchiCAD software, in Hungary. (Budak & Karataş, 2022) Due to the BIM system's successful application in the building industry, several projects in developed countries like the US and UK have adopted it since the early 2000s. (Smith, 2014)

BIM helps the construction sector achieve objectives including raising infrastructure value and quality, and enhancing productivity and efficiency. Lead times, lifetime costs, and duplications are all reduced at once. Despite the fact that BIM has been in use for more than 20 years, project owners have only just become aware of its advantages, such as more effective and efficient building construction, design, and operation. Project owners are vehemently advocating for BIM adoption and expertise by architects, designers, and construction companies at all stages of architectural and construction projects. It is employed in structural design, equipment management, building management, and cost estimation. For instance, 74% of architects in Korea claim to have used BIM when creating their designs. Additionally, BIM use is mandated by the U.S. General Services Administration (GSA) for all important projects. (Doumbouya, 2016)

Many construction companies have invested in BIM in order to take advantage of the benefits because it has been acknowledged as an important collaborative technique. Several stages, including concept building and design, bidding, construction, operation, and maintenance, make use of these newly acquired BIM technologies. BIM is used in the particular areas such as the design phase (55%), the detail design and bidding stage (52%), the construction stage (35%), the feasibility stage (27%), and the operation and maintenance stage (9%), according to a BIM utilization survey.

One important advantage of BIM is better project visualization. Architects, engineers, and other interested parties can better comprehend the design and see any possible problems or conflicts by making a 3D model of the building. BIM can be used to simulate different situations and determine how they would affect the project. This can lessen the possibility of bad design, slow construction, and expensive rework.

Improved collaboration and communication among project stakeholders is another advantage of BIM. BIM lowers the possibility of misunderstandings and errors by enabling all project participants to access the same information and data. This may result in better project results and higher stakeholder satisfaction. Last but not least, BIM can help with facility management and maintenance. Facility managers may more accurately track maintenance and repair requirements, decreasing downtime and boosting efficiency, by generating a digital representation of the building. BIM also enables proactive maintenance and repair by allowing for the simulation of various situations and the assessment of their effects on building performance. Briefly stated, BIM is a digital representation of a construction project that enhances facilities management, communication, and visualization. Construction sector stakeholders can increase efficiency across the project lifecycle, enhance project outcomes, and lower the risk of mistakes and delays by utilizing BIM. BIM does have its limitations, though. Managing the massive amount of data generated throughout the construction phase is one of the difficulties of employing BIM. This is where RPA comes in.

In the construction sector, RPA and BIM can be used to automate processes that would otherwise require a lot of time and manpower. The time and labor needed to manually enter data into project management software can be decreased by using RPA bots to automatically extract data from BIM models. RPA bots can also assist construction professionals in saving time and lowering the risk of errors that may arise while manually reviewing BIM models by automating repetitive BIM procedures.

Using RPA in combination with BIM also makes it possible to manage BIM models more effectively. By using RPA bots, the BIM model may be updated automatically depending on adjustments made on the construction site, ensuring that the model accurately depicts the state of the construction project at the time.

Construction experts can also better understand their construction projects by combining BIM and RPA. RPA bots, for instance, can assist construction professionals in identifying possible conflicts or concerns before they turn into significant ones by automating the process of evaluating BIM data. This might limit the possibility of delays or mistakes throughout the construction process and save time and money.

Using RPA bots to enhance communication amongst various project stakeholders is another way that RPA and BIM can be applied in the construction sector. RPA bots can assist in ensuring that all stakeholders have access to the most recent information about the construction project by automating the process of distributing BIM data. For instance, RPA bots can be used to automatically deliver BIM updates to contractors and subcontractors, obviating the need for manual communication and guaranteeing that all parties have access to the same data. Miscommunications and delays, which can be expensive in the construction sector, may be avoided as a result.

RPA can also be used to combine BIM data with other construction management tools, like cost management and project scheduling programs. RPA bots can assist in ensuring that all stakeholders have access to the same information by automating the transmission of BIM data between various software systems. This lowers the possibility of errors and increases the effectiveness of the construction project as a whole.

Overall, combining RPA and BIM in the construction sector can result in considerable gains in productivity, teamwork, and data management. RPA can assist construction professionals to better manage their building projects and lower the risk of errors and delays by automating repetitive processes, enhancing stakeholder cooperation, and connecting BIM data with other construction management tools.

CONCLUSION

The thesis embarked on a comprehensive exploration of Robotic Process Automation (RPA) and its merge with Building Information Modeling (BIM) in revolutionizing the construction industry. By investigating the applications, benefits, challenges, and opportunities associated with RPA and its integration with BIM, this research has shed light on the immense potential for transforming productivity, efficiency, safety, decision-making, and sustainability in construction processes. Moreover, the merge of RPA with BIM represents a paradigm shift in collaboration, data management, and decision-making within the construction industry. By combining the strengths of these two transformative technologies, stakeholders can achieve unprecedented levels of coordination, efficiency, and accuracy throughout the project lifecycle. RPA, when integrated with BIM, empowers real-time monitoring, safety analysis, clash detection, risk assessment, and advanced simulations, allowing for proactive identification and resolution of issues. The result is improved project outcomes, reduced rework, enhanced coordination, and a safer working environment for construction teams.

The integration of RPA and BIM also contributes to the sustainability agenda of the construction industry. By automating processes and optimizing resource utilization, RPA helps minimize waste, reduce environmental impact, and enhance energy efficiency. Additionally, the advanced data management capabilities of BIM, combined with RPA's automation, enable stakeholders to analyze and optimize building performance throughout its lifecycle, ensuring the construction of sustainable and energy-efficient structures.

The thesis also acknowledges the challenges and barriers that must be addressed to ensure the successful adoption and implementation of RPA in the construction industry. Resistance to change, lack of awareness, integration complexities, and the need for upskilling the workforce are among the key challenges that need to be tackled. Collaboration between industry professionals, policymakers, and researchers is vital to developing standardized protocols, best practices, and training programs to overcome these challenges. It is only through collective efforts that the construction industry can unlock the full potential of RPA and realize its transformative benefits.

Looking ahead, the future of the construction industry lies in embracing advanced technologies, such as RPA and BIM, as fundamental components of project delivery. The research conducted in this thesis provides a robust foundation for further exploration and implementation of RPA in construction processes. Future research should focus on addressing the specific challenges identified, developing standardized protocols for RPA integration, and evaluating the long-term impact of RPA adoption on project success, sustainability, and the overall construction ecosystem.

In conclusion, the integration of RPA and BIM has the potential to revolutionize the construction industry, transcending traditional boundaries and fostering innovation. By leveraging the capabilities of RPA and embracing its merge with BIM, the construction industry can build a more efficient, sustainable, collaborative, and resilient future. The knowledge gained from this research serves as a valuable resource for industry professionals, policymakers, and researchers seeking to harness the benefits of advanced technologies and drive the transformation of the construction sector. With a collective commitment to embracing RPA and its merge with BIM, the construction industry can pave the way for an era of unprecedented efficiency, productivity, cost-effectiveness, safety, and sustainability.

Furthermore, industry professionals and policymakers should actively engage in the development and implementation of supportive regulatory frameworks that encourage the adoption and integration of RPA and BIM. This includes incentivizing companies to invest in advanced technologies, establishing clear guidelines for data security and privacy, and facilitating partnerships between technology providers and construction firms.

The future of the construction industry lies in embracing RPA and its merge with BIM as fundamental pillars of construction processes. Through the effective implementation of RPA and BIM technologies, stakeholders can unlock new levels of productivity, efficiency, safety, and sustainability. Construction projects will benefit from streamlined processes, improved collaboration, reduced costs, enhanced decision-making, and a greater ability to meet the evolving needs of clients and society.

REFERENCES

Admin. (2022, April 9). *RPA at Skanska - RPA Master. RPA Master - Your guide in the world of RPA and Intelligent Automation*. https://rpamaster.com/rpa-at-skanska/

Agostinelli, S., Marrella, A., & Mecella, M. (2020). *Towards Intelligent Robotic Process Automation for BPMers*. Academic Press.

Almgren, E. (2021). *Opportunities and Challenges of Robotic Process Automation (Rpa) in the Administration of Education* (thesis).

Anywhere, A. (2021). *Robotic process automation to ERP*. Available from: https://www.automationanywhere.com/solutions/robotic-process-automation-to-erp

Arayici, Y., Coates, P., Koskela, L., Kagioglou, M., Usher, C., & O'Reilly, K. (2011). Technology adoption in the BIM implementation for lean architectural practice. *Automation in Construction*, *20*(2), 189–195. doi:10.1016/j.autcon.2010.09.016

Balasundaram, S., & Venkatagiri, S. (2020). A structured approach to implementing robotic process automation in HR. *Journal of Physics: Conference Series*, *1427*(1), 012008. doi:10.1088/1742-6596/1427/1/012008

Balasundaram, V., & Venkatagiri, V. (2020). Robotic process automation in human resources: A comprehensive review. *International Journal of Human Resource Management*, *31*(16), 2080–2106.

Budak, A., & Karataş, İ. (2022). Impact of the BIM system in construction management services in developing countries; case of Turkey. *Pamukkale University Journal of Engineering Sciences*, *28*(6), 828–839. doi:10.5505/pajes.2022.64369

Daugherty, P., Carrel-Billiard, M., & Biltz, M. (2023). *Accenture Technology Vision 2023: When Atoms Meet Bits*. https://www.accenture.com/content/dam/accenture/final/accenture-com/a-com-custom-component/iconic/document/Accenture-Technology-Vision-2023-Full-Report.pdf

de Ridder, T. (2022, March 1). *How digital transformation is Modernising Construction*. Construction Digital. Retrieved March 22, 2023, from https://constructiondigital.com/digital-construction/how-digital-transformation-is-modernising-construction

Deloitte. (2017). *Robotic process automation: A revolution in financial services*. https://www2.deloitte.com/us/en/pages/consulting/articles/transforming-financial-services-with-robotics-and-cognitive-automation.html

Dialani, P. (2019). *4 Robotic Process Automation Trends for 2020*. Analytics Insight. Retrieved from https://www.analyticsinsight.net/4-robotic-process-auto-mation-trends-for-2020/

Dialani, V. (2019). Robotic process automation: A primer for business leaders. *Business Horizons*, *62*(4), 451–461.

Doumbouya, L., Gao, G., & Changsheng, C. (2016). Adoption of the Building Information Modeling (BIM) for Construction Project Effectiveness: The Review of BIM Benefits. *American Journal of Civil Engineering and Architecture*, *4*(3), 74–79. doi:10.12691/ajcea-4-3-1

Eadie, R., Browne, M., Odeyinka, H., McKeown, C., & McNiff, S. (2013). BIM implementation throughout the UK construction project lifecycle: An analysis. *Automation in Construction*, *36*, 145–151. doi:10.1016/j.autcon.2013.09.001

Eastman, C., Teicholz, P., Sacks, R., & Liston, K. (2011). *BIM handbook: A guide to building information modeling for owners, managers, designers, engineers, and contractors* (2nd ed.). John Wiley & Sons.

EY. (2020). *AI in the Accounting Big Four – Comparing Deloitte, PwC, KPMG, and EY*. https://emerj.com/ai-sector-overviews/ai-in-the-accounting-big-four-comparing-deloitte-pwc-kpmg-and-ey/

Fluss, D. (2018). Smarter Bots Mean Greater Innovation, Productivity, and Value: Robotic process automation is allowing companies to re-imagine and re-invest in all aspects of their businesses. *CRM Magazine, 22*(10), 38–39.

Forrester Research. (2019). *The Automation Advantage: Why today's winners must prepare for the AI and automation disruption*. Forrester. https://www.forrester.com/blogs/predictions-2022-the-pandemics-wake-drives-automation-trends/

Gartner Inc. (2017a). *Robotic Process Automation (RPA)*. https://www.uipath.com/resources/automation-analyst-reports/gartner-magic-quadrant-robotic-process-automation

Gartner Inc. (2017b). *Market Guide for Robotic Process Automation Software*. Gartner. Retrieved 2023, from https://www.gartner.com/en/documents/3835771

IEEE Guide for Terms and Concepts in Intelligent Process Automation (2017). IEEE Std 2755-2017, 1-16

IEEE SA. (2017). *RPA technology white paper*. IEEE.

Inc., U. P. (n.d.). *RPA case study in construction - skanska*. UiPath. Retrieved March 22, 2023, from https://www.uipath.com/resources/automation-case-studies/skanska-construction-rpa

International Business Machines Corporation (IBM). (2023). *IBM SkillsBuild*. https://skillsbuild.org/

IRPA. (2015). *The definitive guide to robotic process automation (RPA)*. https://soulpageit.com/robotic-process-automation-rpa-definitive-guide-processes-automation/

Jurczuk, A. (2019). *Wieloaspektowa identyfikacja i typolo-gia źródeł niespójności procesów biznesowych* [Multi-faceted identification and typology sources of business process inconsistencies sources]. Białystok, Poland: Oficyna Wydawnicza Politechniki Białostockiej. doi:10.24427/978-83-65596-93-2

Kofax. (2020a). *Developer's Guide Version: 11.0.0*. Available from: https://docshield.kofax.com/RPA/en_US/11.0.0_qrvv5i5e1a/print/KofaxRPADevelopersGuide_EN.pdf

KPMG. (2018a). *The Robotic Process Automation Opportunity: Transforming the Front Office in Finance, Accounting, and HR*. KPMG.

KPMG. (2018b, March). *Leveraging RPA to drive digital transformation in construction*. Retrieved from https://assets.kpmg.com/content/dam/kpmg/jp/pdf/jp-en-rpa-business-improvement.pdf

KPMG. (2019). *Robotic Process Automation for the Construction Industry*. Retrieved from https://assets.kpmg/content/dam/kpmg/pdf/2019/06/robotic-process-automation-for-the-construction-industry.pdf

Kumar, S., Khanna, S., Ghosh, N., & Kumar, S. O. (2023). Importance of Artificial Intelligence (AI) and Robotic Process Automation (RPA) in the Banking Industry: A Study from an Indian perspective. *Confluence of Artificial Intelligence and Robotic Process Automation*, 231–266. doi:10.1007/978-981-19-8296-5_10

Lacity, M., & Willcocks, L. P. (2016). The changing landscape of organizational IT: Implications for the CIO role. *MIT Sloan Management Review*, *57*(3), 79–89.

Lacity, M., Willcocks, L. P., & Craig, A. (2015). *Robotic process automation: mature capabilities in the en-ergy sector*. The Outsourcing Unit Working.

Le Clair, C. (2018). *The Forrester WaveTM: robotic process automation*. Forrester.

Leno, V., Dumas, M., La Rosa, M., Maggi, F. M., & Polyvyanyy, A. (2020). *Automated Discovery of Data Transformations for Robotic Process Automation*. Academic Press.

Li, X., Anumba, C., Bouchlaghem, D., & Ruddock, L. (2017). BIM for construction cost management: Potential benefits and barriers. *Journal of Financial Management of Property and Construction*, *22*(2), 168–187.

McKinsey & Company. (2020). *Global robotics automation survey 2020*. https://www.mckinsey.com/industries/industrials-and-electronics/our-insights/unlocking-the-industrial-potential-of-robotics-and-automation

McKinsey Global Institute. (2023). *The Automation Advantage: Empowering Leaders from the Front Line to the C-Suite*. McKinsey & Company. https://www.mckinsey.com/

Nilsson, N. J. (1981). *Readings in Artificial Intelligence*. doi:10.1016/C2013-0-07694-3

PwC. (2022). *The robotic process automation revolution*. https://www.uipath.com/resources/automation-case-studies/pwc-digital-transformation

Quinn, K., & Strauss, J. (2018). The disruptive potential of robotic process automation: A case study in a mortgage bank. *Information Systems Journal*, *28*(3), 405–426.

Quinn, M., & Strauss, E. (2018). *The Routledge Companion to Accounting Information Systems*. Routledge.

Ribeiro, J., Lima, R., Eckhardt, T., & Paiva, S. (2021). Robotic Process Automation and artificial intelligence in industry 4.0 – A literature review. *Procedia Computer Science*, *181*, 51–58. doi:10.1016/j.procs.2021.01.104

Santos, F., Pereira, R., & Vasconcelos, J. B. (2019). Toward robotic process automation implementation. *Business Process Management Journal*, *3*(1), 405–420. Advance online publication. doi:10.1108/BPMJ-12-2018-0380

Siderska, J. (2020). Robotic Process Automation — A driver of digital transformation? *Engineering Management in Production and Services*, *12*(2), 21–31. doi:10.2478/emj-2020-0009

Śliż, D. (2019). The impact of robotic process automation on the labor market in the banking sector. *Transformations in Business & Economics*, *18*(3), 423–435.

Śliż, P. (2019). Robotization of Business Processes and the Future of the Labor Market in Poland – Preliminary Research. *Organization and Management*, *2*(185), 67–79.

Smith, P. (2014). Bim & the 5D project cost manager. *Procedia: Social and Behavioral Sciences*, *119*, 475–484. doi:10.1016/j.sbspro.2014.03.053

Succar, B. (2009). Building information modelling framework: A research and delivery foundation for industry stakeholders. *Automation in Construction*, *18*(3), 357–375. doi:10.1016/j.autcon.2008.10.003

The little book of RPA - NDL. (n.d.). Retrieved March 21, 2023, from https://www.ndl.co.uk/media/j11pdkyr/little-book-of-rpa_ndl-software-limited.pdf

Tripathi, A. (2018). *Learning robotic process automation: Create software robots and automate business processes with the leading RPA tool.* UiPath.

UiPath. (2023). *The Ultimate Guide to Robotic Process Automation.* RPA.

Ustundag, A., & Cevikcan, E. (2018). *Industry 4.0: Managing the Digital Transformation.* Springer Series in Advanced Manufacturing. doi:10.1007/978-3-319-57870-5

World Economic Forum. (2023). *The Future of Jobs Report 2023.* https://www.weforum.org/publications/the-future-of-jobs-report-2023/

Xie, Y., Wang, D., Li, H., & Wu, P. (2017). BIM application in green building design. In *Proceedings of the 2017 4th International Conference on Civil and Building Engineering Informatics (ICCBEI 2017)* (pp. 93-98). Atlantis Press

Zheng, P., Sang, Z., Zhong, R. Y., Liu, Y., Liu, C., Mubarok, K., ... Xu, X. (2018). Smart manufacturing systems for Industry 4.0: Conceptual framework, scenarios, and future perspectives. *Frontiers of Mechanical Engineering*, *13*(2), 137–150. doi:10.1007/s11465-018-0499-5

KEY TERMS AND DEFINITIONS

Application Programming Interface (API): APIs act as intermediaries that facilitate seamless communication and data exchange between disparate software systems, fostering communication and innovation in the digital landscape.

Artificial Intelligence (AI): It can be said that AI mimics human intelligence for solving problems. The field is the active research and development of these intelligent agents.

Building Information Modelling (BIM): BIM digitally represents a building's entire lifecycle, encompassing geometry, spatial relationships, and embedded data, enabling informed decision-making throughout design, construction, and operation. This data-rich approach facilitates interdisciplinary collaboration and unlocks transformative potential for enhanced project predictability, performance, and sustainability.

Construction Management: It orchestrates the project end-to-end, from planning and budgeting to quality control and safety. It ensures successful completion within scope, time, and budget.

Data Quality: It measures how "fit-for-purpose" the information is, encompassing its accuracy, completeness, and relevance for its intended use.

Natural Language Processing (NLP): It bridges the human-computer gap by employing computational techniques to analyze and manipulate human language, encompassing tasks like understanding meaning and generating human-like text.

Robotic Process Automation (RPA): RPA allows us to use software robots to automate repetitive digital tasks, freeing up human workers and boosting efficiency. Unlike AI, it cannot make decisions.

Compilation of References

Aati, K., Chang, D., Edara, P., & Sun, C. (2020). Immersive work zone inspection training using virtual reality. *Transportation Research Record: Journal of the Transportation Research Board, 2674*(12), 224–232. doi:10.1177/0361198120953146

Abdelwahed, N. A., Soomro, B. A., & Shah, N. (2022). Predicting employee performance through transactional leadership and entrepreneur's passion among the employees of Pakistan. *Asia Pacific Management Review, 28*(1), 60–68. Advance online publication. doi:10.1016/j.apmrv.2022.03.001

Abrokwah-Larbi, K., & Awuku-Larbi, Y. (2023). The impact of artificial intelligence in marketing on the performance of business organizations: evidence from SMEs in an emerging economy. *Journal of Entrepreneurship in Emerging Economies*. Advance online publication. doi:10.1108/JEEE-07-2022-0207

Acemoglu, D., Hazell, J., & Restrepo, P. (2022). Artificial Intelligence and Jobs: Evidence from Online Vacancies. *Journal of Labor Economics, 40*(S1), S293–S340. doi:10.1086/718327

Acemoglu, D., Lelarge, C., & Restrepo, P. (2020). Competing With Robots: Firm Level Evidence from France. *AEA Papers and Proceedings. American Economic Association, 110*, 383–388. doi:10.1257/pandp.20201003

Acemoglu, D., & Restrepo, P. (2022). Tasks, automation, and the rise in U.S. wage inequality. *Econometrica, 90*(5), 1973–2016. doi:10.3982/ECTA19815

Achoki, P. M. (2023). Upskilling and Reskilling for a VUCA World. *GiLE Journal of Skills Development, 3*(2), 34–52. doi:10.52398/gjsd.2023.v3.i2.pp34-52

Adam, M., Wessel, M., & Benlian, A. (2021). AI-based chatbots in customer service and their effects on user compliance. *Electronic Markets, 31*(4), 427–445. doi:10.1007/s12525-020-00414-7

Adeel, M. M., Khan, H. G. A., Zafar, N., & Rizvi, S. T. (2018). Passive leadership and its relationship with organizational justice. *Journal of Management Development, 37*(2), 212–223. doi:10.1108/JMD-05-2017-0187

Admin. (2022, April 9). *RPA at Skanska - RPA Master. RPA Master - Your guide in the world of RPA and Intelligent Automation*. https://rpamaster.com/rpa-at-skanska/

Afzal, M. N. I., Shohan, A. H. N., Siddiqui, S., & Tasnim, N. (2023). Application of AI on Human Resource Management: A Review. *Journal of Human Resource Management - HR Advances and Developments, 2023*(1), 1–11. doi:10.46287/FHEV4889

Agarwal, A., Singhal, C., & Thomas, R. (2021). *AI-powered decision making for the bank of the future.* McKinsey & Company.

Agarwal, P. (2019, March). Redefining banking and financial industry through the application of computational intelligence. In *2019 Advances in Science and Engineering Technology International Conferences (ASET)* (pp. 1-5). 10.1109/ICASET.2019.8714305

Agostinelli, S., Marrella, A., & Mecella, M. (2020). *Towards Intelligent Robotic Process Automation for BPMers*. Academic Press.

Ahmed, T., Karmaker, C. L., Nasir, S. B., Moktadir, M. A., & Paul, S. K. (2023). Modeling the artificial intelligence-based imperatives of industry 5.0 towards resilient supply chains: A post-COVID-19 pandemic perspective. *Computers & Industrial Engineering*, *177*, 109055. doi:10.1016/j.cie.2023.109055 PMID:36741206

Akter, S., Michael, K., Uddin, M. R., McCarthy, G., & Rahman, M. (2022). Transforming business using digital innovations: The application of AI, blockchain, cloud, and data analytics. *Annals of Operations Research, 308*(1-2), 1–33. doi:10.1007/s10479-020-03620-w PMID:35935743

Alahmad, R., & Robert, L. (2020). Artificial Intelligence (AI) and IT identity: Antecedents identifying with AI applications. *26th Americas Conference on Information Systems, AMCIS 2020*, 1–10.

Aldosari, S. A. M. (2020). The future of higher education in the light of artificial intelligence transformations. *International Journal of Higher Education*, *9*(3), 145. doi:10.5430/ijhe.v9n3p145

Aleem, M., Sufyan, M., Ameer, I., & Mustak, M. (2023). Remote work and the COVID-19 pandemic: An artificial intelligence-based topic modeling and a future agenda. *Journal of Business Research, 154*(September), 1–16. doi:10.1016/j.jbusres.2022.113303

Ali, N. A. A., Hamdan, A., Alareeni, B., & Dahlan, M. (2023). Artificial intelligence in the process of training and developing employees. In *International Conference on Business and Technology* (pp. 558-568). Cham: Springer International Publishing. 10.1007/978-3-031-26953-0_50

Allal-Cherif, O., Simon-Moya, V., & Ballester, A. C. C. (2021). Intelligent purchasing: How artificial intelligence can redefine the purchasing function. *Journal of Business Research*, *124*(1), 69–76. doi:10.1016/j.jbusres.2020.11.050

Allioui, H., & Mourdi, Y. (2023). Unleashing the Potential of AI: Investigating Cutting-Edge Technologies That Are Transforming Businesses. *International Journal of Computer Engineering and Data Science, 3*(2), 1-12.

Almgren, E. (2021). *Opportunities and Challenges of Robotic Process Automation (Rpa) in the Administration of Education* (thesis).

Amarasinghe, H. (2023). Transformative Power of AI in Customer Relationship Management (CRM): Potential Benefits, Pitfalls, and Best Practices for Modern Enterprises. *International Journal of Social Analytics, 8*(8), 1–10. https://norislab.com/index.php/ijsa/article/view/30

Amazon. (2022). *Amazon Web Services (AWS) - AI with AWS Machine Learning*. Amazon Web Services, Inc. https://aws.amazon.com/ai/

Anderson, K. (2023, June 20). *How AI is transforming HR*. International Association for Human Resources Information Management. https://www.ihrim.org/2020/02/how-artificial-intelligence-is-transforming-hr/

Andrade, M. (1989). *Social - Factores e tipos de pobreza em Portugal*. Celta Editora.

Anywhere, A. (2021). *Robotic process automation to ERP*. Available from: https://www.automationanywhere.com/solutions/robotic-process-automation-to-erp

Arayici, Y., Coates, P., Koskela, L., Kagioglou, M., Usher, C., & O'Reilly, K. (2011). Technology adoption in the BIM implementation for lean architectural practice. *Automation in Construction, 20*(2), 189–195. doi:10.1016/j.autcon.2010.09.016

Arora, A., Gupta, S., Devi, C., & Walia, N. (2023). Customer experiences in the era of artificial intelligence (AI) in context to FinTech: A fuzzy AHP approach. *Benchmarking, 30*(10), 4342–4369. doi:10.1108/BIJ-10-2021-0621

Arora, M., Prakash, A., Mittal, A., & Singh, S. (2021). HR Analytics and Artificial Intelligence-Transforming Human Resource Management. *2021 International Conference on Decision Aid Sciences and Application, DASA 2021*, 288–293. 10.1109/DASA53625.2021.9682325

Arul, O. K., & Megargel, A. (2023). Understanding human-centred artificial intelligence in the banking sector. Journal of AI. *Robotics & Workplace Automation, 2*(4), 332–348.

Ashok, M., Madan, R., Joha, A., & Sivarajah, U. (2022). Ethical framework for Artificial Intelligence and Digital technologies. *International Journal of Information Management, 62*, 102433. doi:10.1016/j.ijinfomgt.2021.102433

Aviahire. (2020, junho 23). *What is Recruitment Analytics? Recruitment analytics plays an...* Medium. https://medium.com/aviahire/what-is-recruitment-analytics-how-is-it-beneficial-fb5bc9be1f0b

Avolio, B. J., & Bass, B. M. (1991). *The full range leadership development programs: Basic and advanced manuals*. Bass, Avolio Associates.

Aw, E. C. X., Tan, G. W. H., Cham, T. H., Raman, R., & Ooi, K. B. (2022). Alexa, what's on my shopping list? Transforming customer experience with digital voice assistants. *Technological Forecasting and Social Change, 180*, 121711.

Babina, T., Fedyk, A., He, A. X., & Hodson, J. (2020). Artificial Intelligence, Firm Growth, and Industry Concentration. *SSRN*. Advance online publication. doi:10.2139/ssrn.3651052

Bachkirova, T., Spence, G., & Drake, D. (Eds.). (2017). *The SAGE handbook of coaching*. Sage.

Bag, S., Srivastava, G., Bashir, M. M. A., Kumari, S., Giannakis, M., & Chowdhury, A. H. (2022). Journey of customers in this digital era: Understanding the role of artificial intelligence technologies in user engagement and conversion. *Benchmarking: An International Journal, 29*(7), 2074-2098.

Bag, S., Wood, L. C., Xu, L., Dhamija, P., & Kayikci, Y. (2020). Big data analytics as an operational excellence approach to enhance sustainable supply chain performance. *Resources, Conservation and Recycling, 153*, 104559.

Bag, S., Dhamija, P., Singh, R. K., Rahman, M. S., & Sreedharan, V. R. (2023). Big data analytics and artificial intelligence technologies based collaborative platform empowering absorptive capacity in health care supply chain: An empirical study. *Journal of Business Research, 154*, 113315. doi:10.1016/j.jbusres.2022.113315

Balasundaram, S., & Venkatagiri, S. (2020). A structured approach to implementing robotic process automation in HR. *Journal of Physics: Conference Series, 1427*(1), 012008. doi:10.1088/1742-6596/1427/1/012008

Balasundaram, V., & Venkatagiri, V. (2020). Robotic process automation in human resources: A comprehensive review. *International Journal of Human Resource Management, 31*(16), 2080–2106.

Bandyopadhyay, R. (2017, January 9). *The Data Science Process: What a data scientist actually does day-to-day.* Springboard. https://medium.springboard.com/the-data-science-process-the-complete-laymans-guide-to-what-a-data-scientist-actually-does-ca3e166b7c67

Banks, D., & Liu, Y. (2023). Statistics, AI, and autonomous vehicles. *Amstat News, 555*, 10–15.

Bansal, S. (2021). *What Is Data Science Process and Its Significance?* AnalytixLabs. https://www.analytixlabs.co.in/blog/data-science-process/

Barnes, D. (2018). *Operations management: an international perspective*. Thomson. https://books.google.com/books/about/Operations_Management.html?hl=pt-PT&id=5tHxzQEACAAJ

Barnett, D. (2019). Full range leadership as a predictor of extra effort in online higher education: The mediating effect of job satisfaction. *Journal of Leadership Education, 18*(1), 86–101. doi:10.12806/V18/I1/R6

Baryannis, G., Validi, S., Dani, S., & Antoniou, G. (2019). Supply chain risk management and artificial intelligence: State of the art and future research directions. *International Journal of Production Research, 57*(7), 2179–2202. doi:10.1080/00207543.2018.1530476

Beal, V. (2021, December 17). *What is Data?* Webopedia. https://www.webopedia.com/definitions/data/

Bedard, J., Lavoie, K., Laverdiere, R., Bailey, A., Beauchene, V., & Baier, J. (2023, August 25). How generative AI will transform HR. *BCG Global.* https://www.bcg.com/publications/ 2023/transforming-human-resources-using-generative-ai

Beer, M., Spector, B., Lawrence, P., Quinn Mills, D., & Walton, R. (1984). *Managing human assets*. The Free Press.

Bencsik, P., & Chuluun, T. (2021). Comparative well-being of the self-employed and paid employees in the USA. *Small Business Economics*, *56*(1), 355–384. doi:10.1007/s11187-019-00221-1

Berente, N., Gu, B., Recker, J., & Santhanam, R. (2021). Managing artificial intelligence. *Management Information Systems Quarterly*, *45*(3), 1433–1450. doi:10.25300/MISQ/2021/16274

Bhandari, P. (2021, December 8). *What Is Quantitative Research? Definition, Uses and Methods*. Scribbr. https://www.scribbr.com/methodology/quantitative-research/

Bhardwaj, S., Rana, G. A., Behl, A., & Gallego de Caceres, S. J. (2023). Exploring the boundaries of Neuromarketing through systematic investigation. *Journal of Business Research*, *154*, 113371. doi:10.1016/j.jbusres.2022.113371

Bhattacharya, C., & Sinha, M. (2022). The Role of Artificial Intelligence in Banking for Leveraging Customer Experience. Australasian Accounting. *Business and Finance Journal*, *16*(5), 89–105.

Bhatt, P., & Muduli, A. (2022). Artificial intelligence in learning and development: a systematic literature review. In *European Journal of Training and Development*. Emerald Group Holdings Ltd. doi:10.1108/EJTD-09-2021-0143

Biswas, S., Carson, B., Chung, V., Singh, S., & Thomas, R. (2020). *AI-bank of the future: Can banks meet the AI challenge*. McKinsey & Company.

Black, J. (2020, April 9). *What Is People Science? Think modern organizational development*. Glint. https://www.glintinc.com/blog/what-is-people-science/

Blackman, R. (2020), *A Practical Guide to Building Ethical IA*. Retrieved from https://hbr.org/2020/10/a-practical-guide-to-building-ethical-ai

Bloomenthal, A. (2021, July 21). *Chief Operating Officer (COO) Definition*. Investopedia. https://www.investopedia.com/terms/c/coo.asp

Blustein, D. L., Kenny, M. E., Di Fabio, A., & Guichard, J. (2018). Expanding the impact of the psychology of working: Engaging psychology in the struggle for decent work and human rights. *Journal of Career Assessment*, *27*(1), 3–28. doi:10.1177/1069072718774002

Bohm, S., Carrington, M., Cornelius, N., de Bruin, B., Greenwood, M., Hassan, L., & Shaw, D. (2022). Ethics at the centre of global and local challenges: Thoughts on the future of business ethics. *Journal of Business Ethics*, *180*(3), 835–861. doi:10.1007/s10551-022-05239-2 PMID:36212626

Bonsu, S., & Kuofie, M. (2019). Small business survival. *Journal of Marketing Management*, *10*(1), 51–63.

Booth, D. (2023). Build capacity with generative artificial intelligence. *Journal of Environmental Health*, *86*(2), 26–28.

Boudreau, J., & Rice, S. (2016). *Predictive HR Analytics: Mastering the HR Metric*. Harvard Business Press.

Boustani, N. M. (2022). Artificial intelligence impact on banks clients and employees in an Asian developing country. *Journal of Asia Business Studies*, *16*(2), 267–278. doi:10.1108/JABS-09-2020-0376

Brito, D., & Curl, R. F. (2020). *Automation Does Not Kill Jobs. It Increases Inequality*. Baker Institute Report no. 11.06.20. Rice University's Baker Institute for Public Policy.

Brock, J. K.-U., & von Wangenheim, F. (2019). Demystifying AI: What digital transformation leaders can teach you about realistic artificial intelligence. *California Management Review*, *61*(4), 110–134. doi:10.1177/1536504219865226

Brynjolfsson, E., & McAfee, A. (2017). The business of artificial intelligence. *Harvard Business Review, 95*(1), 59-66.

Buchanan, R. A. (2020, November 18). *history of technology*. Encyclopaedia Britannica. https://www.britannica.com/technology/history-of-technology

Buck, B., & Morrow, J. (2018). AI, performance management and engagement: Keeping your best their best. *Strategic HR Review*, *17*(5), 261–262. doi:10.1108/SHR-10-2018-145

Budak, A., & Karataş, İ. (2022). Impact of the BIM system in construction management services in developing countries; case of Turkey. *Pamukkale University Journal of Engineering Sciences*, *28*(6), 828–839. doi:10.5505/pajes.2022.64369

Burns, E. (2023). Machine Learning. *TechTarget network*. https://www.techtarget.com/searchenterpriseai/definition/machine-learning-ML

Cadieux, N., Fournier, P., Cadieux, J., & Gingues, M. (2021). New techno-stressors among knowledge professionals: The contribution of artificial intelligence and websites that misinform clients. *International Journal of Electronic Commerce*, *25*(2), 136–153. doi:10.1080/10864415.2021.1887695

Caldbick, S., Labonte, R., Mohindra, K. S., & Ruckert, A. (2014). Globalization and the rise of precarious employment: The new frontier for workplace health promotion. *Global Health Promotion*, *21*(2), 23–31. doi:10.1177/1757975913514781 PMID:24534262

Campbell, C., Sands, S., Ferraro, C., Tsao, H. Y., & Mavrommatis, A. (2020). From data to action: How marketers can leverage AI. *Business Horizons*, *63*(2), 227–243. doi:10.1016/j.bushor.2019.12.002

Cappelli, P. (2015). Why We Love to Hate HR... and What HR Can Do About It. *Harvard Business Review*, *93*(7-8), 54–61.

Cardon, M., & Stevens, C. (2004). Managing human resources in small organizations: What do we know? *Human Resource Management Review*, *14*(3), 295–323. doi:10.1016/j.hrmr.2004.06.001

Carson, B., & Hruska, M. (2023). Practical and pragmatic AI application. *TD: Talent Development, 77*(1), 32–37.

Carufel, R. (2019). *Companies embrace AI, but execs cite challenges on alignment, ethics*. Agility, PR Solutions. https://www.agilitypr.com/pr-news/public-relations/companies-embrace-ai-but-execs

Carvalhais, C. M. (2016). *Gestão dos riscos psicossociais: Caso de estudo no setor das telecomunicações* [Dissertação de mestrado não publicada]. Instituto Superior de Contabilidade e Administração de Coimbra.

Castro, S. L. C., Del Pozo Durango Rodrigo Humberto, V., Paúl, A. C., & Estefanía, A. T. P. (2023). Impact of Artificial Intelligence on Market Behavior Analysis: A Comprehensive Approach to Marketing. *Remittances Review, 8*(4).

Castro, A. (2021). Tecnologías emergentes. Uso y aplicación en instituciones públicas de Colombia: Sistematización de Experiencias. *International Education Technologies Review, 8*(2), 127–139. doi:10.37467/gkarevedutech.v8.3024

Castro-Martínez, A., & Díaz-Morilla, P. (2020). Comunicación interna y gestión de bienestar y felicidad en la empresa española. *El Profesional de la Información, 29*(3), 1–13. doi:10.3145/epi.2020.may.24

Castro-Martínez, A., & Díaz-Morilla, P. (2021). Internal communication as a strategic area for innovation through change management and organizational happiness. *Obra Digital, 20*, 131–148. doi:10.25029/od.2021.293.20

Castro-Martínez, A., Díaz-Morilla, P., & Pérez-Ordoñez, C. (2022). Nuevas estrategias de gestión corporativa: La cultura visual como elemento de la comunicación interna y la felicidad laboral. *Methaodos Revista de Ciencias Sociales, 10*(2), 379–392. doi:10.17502/mrcs.v10i2.605

Castro-Martínez, A., Díaz-Morilla, P., & Torres-Martín, J. L. (2022). El papel de la comunicación interna en la gestión del teletrabajo durante la crisis de la COVID-19. *Revista de Comunicación de La SEECI, 55*, 29–51. doi:10.15198/seeci.2022.55.e768

Castro-Martinez, A., Diaz-Morilla, P., & Torres-Martin, J.-L. (2022). Comunicación interna, bienestar y felicidad organizacional en instituciones hospitalarias españolas durante la crisis de la COVID-19. *Revista Internacional de Relaciones Públicas, 12*(23), 143–162. doi:10.5783/RIRP-23-2022-08-143-162

Chacko, A. (2023). *The role of artificial intelligence in marketing*. Sprout Social. doi:10.1002/9781119506515.ch7

Chandra, S., Verma, S., Lim, W. M., Kumar, S., & Donthu, N. (2022). Personalization in personalized marketing: Trends and ways forward. *Psychology & Marketing, 39*(8), 1529-1562.

Chatterjee, M. (2022, January 13). *Top 9 Job Roles in the World of Data Science for 2022*. GreatLearning. https://www.mygreatlearning.com/blog/different-data-science-jobs-roles-industry/

Chen, D., Esperança, J. P., & Wang, S. (2022). The Impact of Artificial intelligence on Firm Performance: An application of the Resource-Based View to E-Commerce Firms. *Frontiers in Psychology, 13*, 884830. Advance online publication. doi:10.3389/fpsyg.2022.884830 PMID:35465474

Chen, W., & Wellman, B. (2004). The global digital divide within and between countries. *ITandSociety, 1*(7), 39–45.

Chen, Y., Biswas, M., & Talukder, M. S. (2022). The role of artificial intelligence in effective business operations during COVID-19. *International Journal of Emerging Markets, 18*(12), 6368–6387. doi:10.1108/IJOEM-11-2021-1666

Chiang, W.-C., Li, Y., Shang, J., & Urban, T. L. (2019). Impact of drone delivery on sustainability and cost: Realizing the UAV potential through vehicle routing optimization. *Applied Energy, 242*, 1164-1175. doi:10.1016/j.apenergy.2019.03.117

Chui, M., Manyika, J., & Miremadi, M. (2016). Where machines could replace humans-and where they can't (yet) The technical potential for automation differs dramatically across sectors and activities. *The McKinsey Quarterly*.

Chung, V., Gomes, M., Rane, S., Singh, S., & Thomas, R. (2020). *Reimagining customer engagement for the AI bank of the future*. McKinsey & Company.

Cigerci, M. (2023). Main Effects of Big Data on Supply Chain Management. *Implementation of disruptive technologies in supply chain management*, 27-49.

Ciuffetti, P. (2019). Opportunities for non-data scientists to apply machine learning technology. *Information Services & Use*, 1–7. doi:10.3233/ISU-190067

Cloud Education. I. (2020, May 15). *What is Data Science*. IBM. https://www.ibm.com/cloud/learn/data-science-introduction

Colley, H., Hodkinson, P., & Malcolm, J. (2002). *Non-formal learning: Mapping the conceptual terrain: A consultation report*. University of Leeds Lifelong Learning Institute.

Colorado State University. (2021, September 27). *What Do IT Professionals Actually Do? Roles & Responsibilities*. CSU Global. https://csuglobal.edu/blog/what-does-an-information-technology-professional-really-do

Communications. (2018, April 4). *Carlos Torres Vila: "The digital revolution is proving a success."* NEWS BBVA. https://www.bbva.com/en/carlos-torres-vila-digital-revolution-proving-success/

ComputerScience. (2021, September 27). *Information Security Analyst Careers*. ComputerScience. Org. https://www.computerscience.org/careers/information-security-analyst/

Conik, H. (2017). The Past, Present and Future of AI in Marketing. In *Marketing News* (pp. 1–15). https://www.finextra.com/blogposting/20816/the-past-present-and-future-of-ai-in-financial-services

Cortellazzo, L., Bruni, E., & Zampieri, R. (1938). The Role of Leadership in a Digitalized World: A Review. *Front Psychol, 10*. doi:10.3389/fpsyg.2019.01938

Corvalán, J. (2019). The impact of Artificial Intelligence on employment. *Direito Econômico e Socioambiental, 10*, 35–51. doi:10.7213/rev.dir.econ.soc.v10i1.25870

Cosgrove, K. M. (2012). Political branding in the modern age. In J. Lees-Marshment (Ed.), Routledge Handbook of Political Marketing (pp. 107–123). Routledge - Taylor & Francis Group. doi:10.4324/9780203349908.ch9

Costa, N., Oliveira, C. M., & Ferreira, P. (2022). How to Measure the Happy-Productive Worker Thesis. In *People Management - Highlighting Futures* (pp. 1–14). doi:10.5772/intechopen.107429

Costa, N., Neto, J. S., Oliveira, C., & Martins, E. (2022). Student's Entrepreneurial Intention in Higher Education at ISLA – Instituto Politécnico de Gestão e Tecnologia. *Procedia Computer Science, 204*(September), 825–835. doi:10.1016/j.procs.2022.08.100

Costa, N., & Oliveira, C. (2022a). The Psychological Contract of Higher Education Teachers in Portugal - Confirmatory Factor Analysis. *Procedia Computer Science, 204*, 952–960. doi:10.1016/j.procs.2022.08.116

Costa, N., & Oliveira, C. M. (2022b). The Relationship Between Life Satisfaction, Engagement, and Burnout - Application to Higher Education Teachers in Portugal. In *Lecture Notes in Networks and Systems* (Vol. 315, pp. 221–232). doi:10.1007/978-3-030-85799-8_19

Cummins, N. M., Barry, L. A., Garavan, C., Devlin, C., Corey, G., Cummins, F., Ryan, D., Cronin, S., Wallace, E., McCarthy, G., & Galvin, R. (2022). The better data, better planning census: A cross-sectional, multi-centre study investigating the factors influencing patient attendance at the emergency department in Ireland. *BMC Health Services Research, 22*(1), 471. Advance online publication. doi:10.1186/s12913-022-07841-6 PMID:35397588

Cunningham, E. (2021). Artificial Intelligence-based Decision-Making Algorithms, Sustainable Organizational Performance, and Automated Production Systems in Big Data-Driven Smart Urban Economy. *Journal of Self-Governance and Management Economics, 9*(1), 31–41. doi:10.22381/jsme9120213

Curtis, G. J. (2018). Connecting influence tactics with full-range leadership styles. *Leadership and Organization Development Journal, 39*(1), 2–13. doi:10.1108/LODJ-09-2016-0221

D'Silva, G., Jani, M., Jadhav, V., Bhoir, A., & Amin, P. (2020). Career counselling chatbot using cognitive science and artificial intelligence. In *Advanced Computing Technologies and Applications: Proceedings of 2nd International Conference on Advanced Computing Technologies and Applications—ICACTA 2020* (pp. 1-9). Springer Singapore. 10.1007/978-981-15-3242-9_1

Das, U. C., & Mishra, A. K. (2019). *Management Concepts and Practices*. www.ddceutkal.ac.in

Daugherty, P., Carrel-Billiard, M., & Biltz, M. (2023). *Accenture Technology Vision 2023: When Atoms Meet Bits.* https://www.accenture.com/content/dam/accenture/final/accenture-com/a-com-custom-component/iconic/document/Accenture-Technology-Vision-2023-Full-Report.pdf

Davenport, T. H., & Patil, D. J. (2012, October). *Data Scientist: The Sexiest Job of the 21st Century*. Harvard Business Review. https://hbr.org/2012/10/data-scientist-the-sexiest-job-of-the-21st-century

Davenport, T. H., & Ronanki, R. (2018). Artificial intelligence for the real world. *Harvard Business Review, 96*(1), 108-116.

Davenport, T. H., Guha, A., & Grewal, D. (2021). *How to Design an AI Marketing Strategy*. Harvard Business Review. https://hbr.org/2021/07/how-to-design-an-ai-marketing-strategy

Davenport, T. H., Ronanki, R., Wheaton, J., & Nguyen, A. (2018). Artificial Intelligence for the real world. *Harvard Business Review*, 108–116.

Davret, J. (2020, July 29). *The Stages of Technology Development*. LivePositively. https://www.livepositively.com/the-stages-of-technology-development/

De Bruyn, A., Viswanathan, V., Beh, Y. S., Brock, J. K. U., & Von Wangenheim, F. (2020). Artificial intelligence and marketing: Pitfalls and opportunities. *Journal of Interactive Marketing, 51*(1), 91-105.

de Feo, J. A., & Barnard, W. (2005). Six sigma: La feuille de route 6 sigma du Juran institute. formation Green et Master Black Belt. In *The Juran Institute*. Mc Graw Hill. https://www.piloter.org/six-sigma/juran-six-sigma.htm

de Ridder, T. (2022, March 1). *How digital transformation is Modernising Construction*. Construction Digital. Retrieved March 22, 2023, from https://constructiondigital.com/digital-construction/how-digital-transformation-is-modernising-construction

Debois, S. (2022, March 8). *10 Advantages and Disadvantages of Questionnaires - Survey Anyplace*. SurveyAnyplace Blog. https://surveyanyplace.com/blog/questionnaire-pros-and-cons/

Del Pozo, D., & Fernández-Sastre, J. (2021). Empleo e inversión en actividades de innovación sin introducción de nuevas tecnologías: Un estudio sobre Ecuador. *Estudios de Economía (Santiago), 48*(2), 219–248. doi:10.4067/S0718-52862021000200219

Deloitte. (2017). *Robotic process automation: A revolution in financial services*. https://www2.deloitte.com/us/en/pages/consulting/articles/transforming-financial-services-with-robotics-and-cognitive-automation.html

Dennison, K. (2023, March 14). The Impact Of Artificial Intelligence On Leadership: How To Leverage AI To Improve Decision-Making. *Forbes*. https://www.forbes.com/sites/karadennison/2023/03/14/the-impact-of-artificial-intelligence-on-leadership-how-to-leverage-ai-to-improve-decision-making/

Devanna, M. A., Fombrun, C. J., & Tichy, N. M. (1984). A framework for strategic human resource management. In *Strategic Human Resource Management*. Wiley.

Deveau, R., Griffin, S. J., & Reis, S. (2023). *AI-powered marketing and sales reach new heights with generative AI*. McKinsey & Company. https://www.mckinsey.com/capabilities/growth-marketing-and-sales/our-insights/ai-powered-marketing-and-sales-reach-new-heights-with-generative-ai

Dhanabalan, T., & Sathish, A. (2018). Transforming Indian industries through artificial intelligence and robotics in industry 4.0. *International Journal of Mechanical Engineering and Technology, 9*(10), 835-845.

Dialani, P. (2019). *4 Robotic Process Automation Trends for 2020*. Analytics Insight. Retrieved from https://www.analyticsinsight.net/4-robotic-process-auto-mation-trends-for-2020/

Dialani, V. (2019). Robotic process automation: A primer for business leaders. *Business Horizons, 62*(4), 451–461.

Dieffenbacher, S. F. (2023). https://digitalleadership.com/blog/bani-world/

Dilegani, C. (2023. AI Multiple. *Environmental Social and Governance (ESG) Reporting Definition*. https://research.aimultiple.com/esg-reporting/

DobrevD. (2012). *A Definition of Artificial Intelligence*. http://arxiv.org/abs/1210.1568

Donkor, F., & Dongmei, Z. (2018). Leadership styles: A decade after the economic recession and lessons for businesses in developing economies. *Management Research and Practice, 10*(3), 1-20. http://www.mrp.ase.ro

Douer, N., & Meyer, J. (2020). The responsibility quantification model of human interaction with automation. *IEEE Transactions on Automation Science and Engineering, 17*(2), 1044–1060. doi:10.1109/TASE.2020.2965466

Doumbouya, L., Gao, G., & Changsheng, C. (2016). Adoption of the Building Information Modeling (BIM) for Construction Project Effectiveness: The Review of BIM Benefits. *American Journal of Civil Engineering and Architecture, 4*(3), 74–79. doi:10.12691/ajcea-4-3-1

Doyle, A. (2021, December 2). *The Recruitment and Hiring Process*. TheBalanceCareers. https://www.thebalancecareers.com/recruitment-and-hiring-process-2062875

Duan, Y., Edwards, J. S., & Dwivedi, Y. K. (2019). Artificial intelligence for decision making in the era of Big Data – evolution, challenges and research agenda. *International Journal of Information Management, 48*, 63–71. doi:10.1016/j.ijinfomgt.2019.01.021

Dubey, R., Bryde, D. J., Dwivedi, Y. K., Graham, G., & Foropon, C. (2022). Impact of artificial intelligence-driven big data analytics culture on agility and resilience in humanitarian supply chain: A practice-based view. *International Journal of Production Economics, 250*, 108618. doi:10.1016/j.ijpe.2022.108618

Dumitriu, D., & Popescu, M. A. M. (2020). Artificial intelligence solutions for digital marketing. *Procedia Manufacturing, 46*, 630-636.

Dutta, D., Mishra, S. K., & Tyagi, D. (2023). Augmented employee voice and employee engagement using artificial intelligence-enabled chatbots: A field study. *International Journal of Human Resource Management*, *34*(12), 2451–2480. doi:10.1080/09585192.2022.2085525

Dwivedi, Y. K., Hughes, L., Ismagilova, E., Aarts, G., Coombs, C., Crick, T., Duan, Y., Dwivedi, R., Edwards, J., Eirug, A., Galanos, V., Ilavarasan, P. V., Janssen, M., Jones, P., Kar, A. K., Kizgin, H., Kronemann, B., Lal, B., Lucini, B., ... Williams, M. D. (2021). Artificial Intelligence (AI): Multidisciplinary perspectives on emerging challenges, opportunities, and agenda for research, practice and policy. *International Journal of Information Management*, *57*, 101994. Advance online publication. doi:10.1016/j.ijinfomgt.2019.08.002

Eadie, R., Browne, M., Odeyinka, H., McKeown, C., & McNiff, S. (2013). BIM implementation throughout the UK construction project lifecycle: An analysis. *Automation in Construction*, *36*, 145–151. doi:10.1016/j.autcon.2013.09.001

Eastman, C., Teicholz, P., Sacks, R., & Liston, K. (2011). *BIM handbook: A guide to building information modeling for owners, managers, designers, engineers, and contractors* (2nd ed.). John Wiley & Sons.

EkumaK. (2023). *Rethinking Upskilling and Reskilling in the Age of AI and Automation: A fsQCA Approach.* doi:10.20944/preprints202309.0055.v1

El Azhari, K., Hilal, I., Daoride, N., & Ajhoun, R. (2023). SMART chatbots in the E-learning domain: A systematic literature review. *International Journal of Interactive Mobile Technologies*, *17*(15), 4–37. doi:10.3991/ijim.v17i15.40315

Ellingrug, K., Gupta, R., & Salguero, J. (2020). *Building the vital skills for the future of work in operations.* McKinsey and Company.

Elpo, P. S., & Lemos, D. D. C. (2022). Felicidade no Trabalho: Conceitos, Elementos Antecessores e Temas Transversais. *Perspectivas Contemporâneas*, *17*(12), 1–19. doi:10.54372/pc.2022.v17.3253

Encyclopaedia Britannica. (2021, April 15). *Technology*. Encyclopaedia Britannica. https://www.britannica.com/technology/technology

European Comision. (2018). *Privacy policy for websites managed by the European Commission.* Privacy Policy for Websites Managed by the European Commission. https://eur-lex.europa.eu/legal-content/EN/TXT/PDF/?uri=CELEX:32018R1725

European Commission. (2019). *SME performance review.* https://ec.europa.eu/growth/smes/business-friendly-environment/performance-review_en

European Commission. (2020). *European Skills Agenda for Sustainable Competitiveness, Social fairness and resilience.* European Commission. https://ec.europa.eu/migrant-integration/sites/default/files/2020-07/SkillsAgenda.pdf

European Parliament and of the Council. (2016). Regulation (EU) 2016/679 of 27 April 2016 on the protection of natural persons with regard to the processing of personal data and on the free movement of such data, and repealing Directive 95/46/EC (General Data Protection Regulation). *Official Journal of the European Communities, OJ L 119/1*, 1–88. https://data.europa.eu/eli/reg/2016/679/oj

EverestLabs uses AI, robotic arms for more efficient cycling. (2023). *Waste 360.*

EY. (2020). *AI in the Accounting Big Four – Comparing Deloitte, PwC, KPMG, and EY.* https://emerj.com/ai-sector-overviews/ai-in-the-accounting-big-four-comparing-deloitte-pwc-kpmg-and-ey/

Fernandes, C. (2016). *Capacidade para o trabalho: Apreciação dos Riscos Psicossociais na Indústria* [Tese de doutoramento não publicada]. Universidade de Aveiro.

Fernandes, C., & Pereira, A. (2016). Exposição a fatores de risco psicossocial em contexto de trabalho: Revisão sistemática. *Revista de Saude Publica, 50*(24), 1–15.

Ferreira, S. (2020, November 18). *Business Process Management: What Is BPM and Why You Need It.* Outsystems. https://www.outsystems.com/blog/posts/business-process-management/

Ferreira, J. A., Haase, R. F., Santos, E. R., Rabaça, J. A., Figueiredo, L., Hemami, H. G., & Almeida, L. M. (2019). Decent work in Portugal: Context, conceptualization, and assessment. *Journal of Vocational Behavior, 112*, 77–91. doi:10.1016/j.jvb.2019.01.009

Figueiredo, P., & Joaquim, A. F. (2023). The impact of artificial intelligence and intergenerational diversity. In F. Ince (Ed.), *Leadership Perspectives on Effective Intergenerational Communication and Management* (pp. 72–90). IGI Global. doi:10.4018/978-1-6684-6140-2.ch005

Fitz-Enz, J., & Mattox, J. (2014). *Predictive analytics for human resources.* John Wiley and Sons. doi:10.1002/9781118915042

Fleming, M. (2020, March 24). AI is changing work — and leaders need to adapt. *Harvard Business Review.* https://hbr.org/2020/03/ai-is-changing-work-and-leaders-need-to-adapt

Fluss, D. (2018). Smarter Bots Mean Greater Innovation, Productivity, and Value: Robotic process automation is allowing companies to re-imagine and re-invest in all aspects of their businesses. *CRM Magazine, 22*(10), 38–39.

Fornasier, M. D. O., & Beck, C. (2020). Cambridge Analytica: Escândalo, Legado E Possíveis Futuros Para a Democracia. *Revista Direito Em Debate, 29*(53), 182–195. doi:10.21527/2176-6622.2020.53.182-195

Forrester Research. (2019). *The Automation Advantage: Why today's winners must prepare for the AI and automation disruption.* Forrester. https://www.forrester.com/blogs/predictions-2022-the-pandemics-wake-drives-automation-trends/

Forscher, P. S., Wagenmakers, E.-J., Coles, N. A., Silan, M. A., Dutra, N., Basnight-Brown, D., & IJzerman, H. (2022). The benefits, barriers, and risks of big-team science. *Perspectives on Psychological Science*. Advance online publication. doi:10.1177/17456916221082970 PMID:36190899

Frankenfield, J. (2020, July 28). *Cloud Computing Definition*. Investopedia. https://www.investopedia.com/terms/c/cloud-computing.asp

Freitas, L. C., & Cordeiro, T. C. (2013). *Segurança e saúde do trabalho: guia para micro, pequenas e médias empresas*.

Gageiro, J. N., & Pestana, M. H. (2013). *Alpha de Cronbach para a análise da consistência interna*. Análise Estatística. https://analise-estatistica.pt/2013/09/alpha-de-cronbach-para-a-analise-da-consistencia-interna.html

Galván Vela, E., Mercader, V., Arango Herrera, E., & Ruíz Corrales, M. (2022). Empowerment and support of senior management in promoting happiness at work. *Corporate Governance (Bingley)*, *22*(3), 536–545. doi:10.1108/CG-05-2021-0200

Gao, Z., Wanyama, T., Singh, I., Gadhrri, A., & Schimdt, R. (2020). From Industry 4.0 to Robotics 4.0 - A Conceptual Framework for Collaborative and Intelligent Robotic Systems. *Procedia Manufacturing*, *46*, 591–599. doi:10.1016/j.promfg.2020.03.085

Garavan, T. N., & Coolahan, M. (1996). Career mobility in organizations: Implications for career development - Part I. *Journal of European Industrial Training*, *20*(4), 30–40. doi:10.1108/03090599610117063

García, E. A. H., Galia, F., & Velez-Ocampo, J. (2022). Understanding the impact of well-being on entrepreneurship in the context of emerging economies. *Journal of Entrepreneurship in Emerging Economies*, *14*(1), 158–182. doi:10.1108/JEEE-08-2020-0314

Garg, V., Srivastav, S., & Gupta, A. (2018). Application of Artificial Intelligence for Sustaining Green Human Resource Management. *2018 International Conference on Automation and Computational Engineering, ICACE 2018*, 113–116. 10.1109/ICACE.2018.8686988

Gartner Inc. (2017a). *Robotic Process Automation (RPA)*. https://www.uipath.com/resources/automation-analyst-reports/gartner-magic-quadrant-robotic-process-automation

Gartner Inc. (2017b). *Market Guide for Robotic Process Automation Software*. Gartner. Retrieved 2023, from https://www.gartner.com/en/documents/3835771

Gartner. (2019). *Gartner says AI augmentation will create $2.9 trillion of business value in 2021*. https://www.gartner.com/en/newsroom/press-releases/2019-08-05-gartner-says-ai-augmentation-will-create-2point9-trillion-of-business-value-in-2021

Gatziu Grivas, S., Imhof, D., & Gachnang, P. (2023). Correction to: Position Paper - Hybrid Artificial Intelligence for Realizing a Leadership Assistant for Platform-Based Leadership Consulting. In M. Ruiz & P. Soffer (Eds.), *Advanced Information Systems Engineering Workshops. CAiSE 2023. Lecture Notes in Business Information Processing* (Vol. 482). Springer. doi:10.1007/978-3-031-34985-0_20

Ghoreishi, M., Treves, L., Teplov, R., & Pynnönen, M. (2023). The Impact of Artificial Intelligence on Circular Value Creation for Sustainable Development Goals. In *The Ethics of Artificial Intelligence for the Sustainable Development Goals* (pp. 347–363). Springer International Publishing. doi:10.1007/978-3-031-21147-8_19

Gilbert, S., & Kelloway, E. K. (2018). Self-determined leader motivation and follower perceptions of leadership. *Leadership and Organization Development Journal*, *39*(5), 608–619. doi:10.1108/LODJ-09-2017-0262

Gilley, J. W., Eggland, S. A., & Gilley, A. M. (2002). *Principles of human resource development* (2nd ed.). Basic Books.

Gilmurray, K. (2023) *The A-Z organizational digital transformation*. Independently Published.

Global Deal. (2023). *Upskilling and reskilling for the twin transition: The role of social dialogue.* Thematic Brief. https://www.theglobaldeal.com/resources/Upskilling-and-reskilling-for-the-twin-transition.pdf

Goldstein, J., & Goldstein, J. (2023). *New IBM study reveals how AI is changing work and what HR leaders should do about it.* IBM Blog. https://www.ibm.com/blog/new-ibm-study-reveals-how-ai-is-changing-work-and-what-hr-leaders-should-do-about-it/

Gopinath, G. (2023). *The Power and Perils of the "Artificial Hand": Considering IA Through the Ideas of Adam Smith Speech to commemorate 300th anniversary of Adam Smith's birth University of Glasgow.* International Monetary Fund. https://www.imf.org/en/News/Articles/2023/06/05/sp060523-fdmd-aiadamsmith?cid=em-COM-123-46688

Gordon, J. (2021, June 27). *Business Process Redesign - Explained - The Business Professor, LLC.* The Business Professor. https://thebusinessprofessor.com/en_US/mgmt-operations/business-process-redesign

Gourley, L. (2020, May 21). *The 7 Wastes of Lean Production.* PTC - Digital Transforms Physical. https://www.ptc.com/en/blogs/iiot/7-wastes-of-lean-production

Grant, J. M., Mottet, L. A., Tanis, J., Harrison, J., Herman, J. L., & Keisling, M. (2011). *Injustice at every turn: A report of the national transgender discrimination survey.* National Center for Transgender Equality and National Gay and Lesbian Taskforce.

Graziotin, D., Fagerholm, F., Wang, X., & Abrahamsson, P. (2017). Unhappy Developers: Bad for Themselves, Bad for Process, and Bad for Software Product. *2017 IEEE/ACM 39th International Conference on Software Engineering Companion (ICSE-C)*, 362–364. 10.1109/ICSE-C.2017.104

Green, N. (2023). *How artificial intelligence will impact and transform HR and L&D*. Academic Press.

Gregory, R. W., Henfridsson, O., Kaganer, E., & Kyriakou, H. (2020). The role of artificial intelligence and data network effects for creating user value. *Academy of Management Review*. Advance online publication. doi:10.5465/amr.2019.0178

Griffin, R. W. (2021). *Fundamentals of Management*. https://books.google.pt/books?hl=pt-PT&lr=&id=IhQcEAAAQBAJ&oi=fnd&pg=PP1&dq=management&ots=on2-srv2N0&sig=LJ0Iz6kzEumc8AZKP5id7nTCKTA&redir_esc=y#v=onepage&q=management&f=false

Grosso, C., Sazen, N., & Boselli, R. (2022, September). AI-implemented toolkit to assist users with career "configuration": The case of create your own future. In *Proceedings of the 26th ACM International Systems and Software Product Line Conference-Volume B* (pp. 158-165). 10.1145/3503229.3547043

Gubbins, C., Garavan, T. N., & Bennett, E. E. (2023). Digital Learning: A Bright New Dawn for Learning and Development. In T. Lynn, P. Rosati, E. Conway, & L. van der Werff (Eds.), *The Future of Work - Challenges and Prospects for Organisations, Jobs and Workers* (pp. 127–149). Palgrave Macmillan. doi:10.1007/978-3-031-31494-0_9

Guest, D. (1987). Human resource management and industrial relations. *Journal of Management Studies*, *24*(5), 503–521. doi:10.1111/j.1467-6486.1987.tb00460.x

Guhr, N., Lebek, B., & Breitner, M. H. (2018). The impact of leadership on employees' intended information security behaviour: An examination of the full-range leadership theory. *Information Systems Journal*, *29*(2), 340–362. doi:10.1111/isj.12202

Gupta, S., Leszkiewicz, A., Kumar, V., Bijmolt, T., & Potapov, D. (2020). Digital analytics: Modeling for insights and new methods. *Journal of Interactive Marketing, 51*(1), 26-43.

Haleem, A., Javaid, M., Qadri, M. A., Singh, R. P., & Suman, R. (2022). Artificial intelligence (AI) applications for marketing: A literature-based study. *International Journal of Intelligent Networks*.

Haleem, A., Javaid, M., Asim Qadri, M., Pratap Singh, R., & Suman, R. (2022). Artificial intelligence (AI) applications for marketing: A literature-based study. *International Journal of Intelligent Networks*, *3*(August), 119–132. doi:10.1016/j.ijin.2022.08.005

Hammer, M. (1990, August). *Reengineering Work: Don't Automate, Obliterate*. Harvard Business Review. https://hbr.org/1990/07/reengineering-work-dont-automate-obliterate

Hancock, B., Schaninger, B., & Yee, L. (2023, June 5). Generative AI and the future of HR. *McKinsey & Company*. https://www.mckinsey.com/capabilities/people-and-organizational performance/our-insights/generative-ai-and-the-future-of-hr

Hancock, J. T., Naaman, M., & Levy, K. (2020). AI-Mediated Communication: Definition, Research Agenda, and Ethical Considerations. *Journal of Computer-Mediated Communication*, *25*(1), 89–100. doi:10.1093/jcmc/zmz022

Hari, H., Iyer, R., & Sampat, B. (2022). Customer brand engagement through chatbots on bank websites–examining the antecedents and consequences. *International Journal of Human-Computer Interaction, 38*(13), 1212–1227. doi:10.1080/10447318.2021.1988487

Hayes, A. (2021a, August 19). *Business Process Redesign (BPR) Definition*. Investopedia. https://www.investopedia.com/terms/b/business-process-redesign.asp

Hayes, A. (2021b, September 5). *Management by Objectives (MBO) Definition*. Investopedia. https://www.investopedia.com/terms/m/management-by-objectives.asp

Hayes, A. (2021c, October 29). *Operations Management (OM) Definition*. Investopedia. https://www.investopedia.com/terms/o/operations-management.asp

Hayes, A. (2022, March 5). *Blockchain Definition: What You Need to Know*. Investopedia. https://www.investopedia.com/terms/b/blockchain.asp

Helo, P., & Hao, Y. (2022). Artificial intelligence in operations management and supply chain management: An exploratory case study. *Production Planning and Control, 33*(16), 1573–1590. doi:10.1080/09537287.2021.1882690

Herweijer, C., Combes, B., & Gillham, J. (2018). How AI can enable a sustainable future. *PwC report*. https://www.dhl.com/global-en/home/about-us/sustainability.html

Hohenstein, J., DiFranzo, D., Kizilcec, R. F., Aghajari, Z., Mieczkowski, H., Levy, K., Naaman, M., Hancock, J., & Jung, M. (2023). Artificial intelligence in communication impacts language and social relationships. *Scientific Reports, 13*(1), 5487. Advance online publication. doi:10.1038/s41598-023-30938-9 PMID:37015964

Hole, K. J., & Ahmad, S. (2021). A thousand brains: Toward biologically constrained AI. *SN Applied Sciences, 3*(8), 743–757. doi:10.1007/s42452-021-04715-0

Hötte, K., Somers, M., & Theodorakopoulos, A. (2022). *The fear of technology-driven unemployment and its empirical base*. https://voxeu.org/article/fear-technology-driven-unemployment-and-its-empirical-base

Hoyer, W. D., Kroschke, M., Schmitt, B., Kraume, K., & Shankar, V. (2020). Transforming the Customer Experience through New Technologies. *Journal of Interactive Marketing, 51*(1), 57–71. doi:10.1016/j.intmar.2020.04.001

HR Innovation and Tech Fest. (n.d.). https://www.techfestconf.com/aus/hr-blog/ai-mean-humans-human-resources

Hsu, C. L., & Lin, J. C. C. (2023). Understanding the user satisfaction and loyalty of customer service chatbots. *Journal of Retailing and Consumer Services, 71*, 103211. doi:10.1016/j.jretconser.2022.103211

Huang, M.-H., & Rust, R. T. (2018). Artificial Intelligence in Service. *Journal of Service Research, 21*(2), 155–172. doi:10.1177/1094670517752459

Humlum, A. (2020). *Robot Adoption and Labor Market Dynamics*. Working paper, University of Chicago.

Humphreys, P. (2021). Socialising the decision-making process: Transaction provenance decision support. *Journal of Decision Systems*, 1–15. doi:10.1080/12460125.2020.1868653

Hussmanns, R. (2007). Measurement of employment, unemployment and underemployment - Current international standards and issues in their application. *Labor Stat*, *1*, 1–23.

Ibdah, D., Lachtar, N., Raparthi, S. M., & Bacha, A. (2021). Why Should i Read the Privacy Policy, i Just Need the Service': A Study on Attitudes and Perceptions Toward Privacy Policies. *IEEE Access : Practical Innovations, Open Solutions*, *9*, 166465–166487. doi:10.1109/ACCESS.2021.3130086

IEEE Guide for Terms and Concepts in Intelligent Process Automation (2017). IEEE Std 2755-2017, 1-16

IEEE SA. (2017). *RPA technology white paper*. IEEE.

IMARC Impactful Insights. (2023). *Digital Transformation Market: Global Industry Trends, Share, Size, Growth, Opportunity and Forecast 2023-2028*. Market Research Report, Report ID: SR112023A4373, India Brand Equity Foundation. https://www.ibef.org/economy/economic-survey

Inc., U. P. (n.d.). *RPA case study in construction - skanska*. UiPath. Retrieved March 22, 2023, from https://www.uipath.com/resources/automation-case-studies/skanska-construction-rpa

Indeed Editorial Team. (2021, December 8). *What Is Management? Definitions and Functions*. Indeed. https://www.indeed.com/career-advice/career-development/what-is-management

Indriasari, E., Gaol, F. L., & Matsuo, T. (2019, July). Digital banking transformation: Application of artificial intelligence and big data analytics for leveraging customer experience in the Indonesia banking sector. In *2019 8th International Congress on Advanced Applied Informatics (IIAI-AAI)* (pp. 863-868). IEEE.

Infosys Report. (n.d.). https://www.infosys.com/age-of-ai/Documents/age-of-ai-infosys-research-report.pdf

International Business Machines Corporation (IBM). (2023). *IBM SkillsBuild*. https://skillsbuild.org/

International Labor Organization – ILO. (1984). *Psychosocial factors at work: Recognition and control*. International Labor Office.

IRPA. (2015). *The definitive guide to robotic process automation (RPA)*. https://soulpageit.com/robotic-process-automation-rpa-definitive-guide-processes-automation/

Itam, U. J., & Warrier, U. (2023). Future of work from everywhere: A systematic review. *International Journal of Manpower*. Advance online publication. doi:10.1108/IJM-06-2022-0288

Jain, P., & Aggarwal, K. (2020). Transforming marketing with artificial intelligence. *International Research Journal of Engineering and Technology, 7*(7), 3964-3976.

Jaiswal, A., Arun, C. J., & Varma, A. (2022). Rebooting employees: Upskilling for artificial intelligence in multinational corporations. *International Journal of Human Resource Management*, *33*(6), 1179–1208. doi:10.1080/09585192.2021.1891114

Jarrahi, M. H. (2019). In the age of the smart artificial intelligence: AI's dual capacities for automating and informating work. *Business Information Review*, *36*(4), 178–187. doi:10.1177/0266382119883999

Jasmin Praful Bharadiya. (2023). Driving Business Growth with Artificial Intelligence and Business Intelligence. *International Journal of Computer Science and Technology, 6*(4), 28-44.

Javaid, S. (2023). AI Multiple. *Top 12 AI Use cases for supply chain Optimization in 2023.* https://research.aimultiple.com/supply-chain-ai

Jiaping, Y. (2022). Enterprise Human Resource Management Model by Artificial Intelligence Digital Technology. *Computational Intelligence and Neuroscience*, *2022*, 1–9. doi:10.1155/2022/6186811 PMID:36479021

Johansson, J., & Herranen, S. (2019). *The application of Artificial Intelligence (AI) in Human Resource Management: Current state of AI and its impact on the traditional recruitment process.* Academic Press.

Johnson, B. A. M., Coggburn, J. D., & Llorens, J. J. (2022). Artificial Intelligence and Public Human Resource Management: Questions for Research and Practice. *Public Personnel Management*, *51*(4), 538–562. doi:10.1177/00910260221126498

Johnson, M. R., & Bullard, A. J. (2020). Creation of a structured performance-based assessment tool in a clinical research center setting. *The Journal of Research Administration*, *51*(1), 73–89.

Johnson, R. D., Stone, D. L., & Lukaszewski, K. M. (2020). The benefits of eHRM and AI for talent acquisition. *Journal of Tourism Futures*, *7*(1), 40–52. doi:10.1108/JTF-02-2020-0013

Jones, W. A. (2018). Artificial intelligence and leadership: A few thoughts, a few questions. *Journal of Leadership Studies*, *12*(3), 60–62. doi:10.1002/jls.21597

Jurczuk, A. (2019). *Wieloaspektowa identyfikacja i typolo-gia źródeł niespójności procesów biznesowych* [Multi-faceted identification and typology sources of business process inconsistencies sources]. Białystok, Poland: Oficyna Wydawnicza Politechniki Białostockiej. doi:10.24427/978-83-65596-93-2

Justenhoven, R., & Edenborough, R. (2011). *Assessment and Development Centres: Strategies for Success in HR and Business Performance*. Gower Publishing, Ltd.

Kanmani, O. J., & Fonceca, C. M. (2023). Employee happiness index and its impact on employee performance. *International Journal of Multidisciplinary Research and Growth Evaluation*, *4*(2), 360–364.

Kaur, M., & Gandolfi, F. (2023a). Artificial Intelligence in Human Resource Management-Challenges and Future Research Recommendations. *Review of International Comparative Management, 24*(3). Advance online publication. doi:10.24818/RMCI.2023.3.382

Kaur, M., & Gandolfi, F. (2023b). "Intelligent"-Human Resource Management (I-HRM) in the Era of Disruptions: A Value Creation Model. *Empirical Economics Letters, 22*(1), 73–93. doi:10.5281/zenodo.8312953

Kaur, M., Gandolfi, F., Ag, R., & Resmi, A. G. (2023). Research on Artificial Intelligence in Human Resource Management: Trends and Prospects. *Global Journal of Management and Business Research, Administrative Management, 23*(5), 30–46. https://www.researchgate.net/publication/371691941

Kaya, O., Schildbach, J., AG, D. B., & Schneider, S. (2019). Artificial intelligence in banking. Artificial intelligence.

Ketter, P. (2017). Artificial intelligence creeps into talent development. *TD: Talent Development, 71*(4), 22–25.

Khadem, M., Khadem, A., & Khadem, S. (2023). Application of Artificial Intelligence in Supply Chain Revolutionizing Efficiency and Optimization. *International Journal of Industrial Engineering and Operational Research, 5*(1), 29-38.

Kharlamova, G., Stavytskyy, A., Chernyak, O., Giedraitis, V., & Komendant, O. (2019). Economic modeling of the GDP gap in Ukraine and worldwide. *Problems and Perspectives in Management, 17*(2), 493 509. doi:10.21511/ppm.17(2).2019.38

Kilag, O. K. T., Padilla, K., Yorong, F., & Merabedes, J. (2023). Importance of Upskilling and Reskilling in Educational Leadership and Management. *European Journal of Learning on History and Social Sciences, 1*(1), 49–57. https://orcid.org/0000-0003-0845-3373

Kinney, S. (2023). AI-driven robots handle high-speed logistics sorting and depalletizing: The robotic system from plus one robotics incorporates a robot, AI-based software, and remote supervisor software. *Vision Systems Design, 28*(2), 12–15.

KissFlow. (2021a, February 21). *What is Process Management?* KissFlow. https://kissflow.com/workflow/bpm/what-is-process-management/

KissFlow. (2021b, November 21). *Business Process Management (BPM) - Definition, Steps, and Benefits*. KissFlow. https://kissflow.com/workflow/bpm/business-process-management-overview/

Kjellström, S., Stålne, K., & Törnblom, O. (2020). Six ways of understanding leadership development: An exploration of increasing complexity. *Leadership, 16*(4), 434–460. doi:10.1177/1742715020926731

Klockmann, V., Von Schenk, A., Villeval, M., Klockmann, V., Von Schenk, A., Villeval, M., Intelligence, A., Klockmann, V., Von Schenk, A., & Villeval, M. C. (2021). *Artificial Intelligence, Ethics, and Intergenerational Responsibility*. https://halshs.archives-ouvertes.fr/halshs-03237437/document

Knouse, S. B. (2001). Virtual mentors: Mentoring on the internet. *Journal of Employment Counseling*, *38*(4), 162–169. doi:10.1002/j.2161-1920.2001.tb00498.x

Kofax. (2020a). *Developer's Guide Version: 11.0.0*. Available from: https://docshield.kofax.com/RPA/en_US/11.0.0_qrvv5i5e1a/print/KofaxRPADevelopersGuide_EN.pdf

Königstorfer, F., & Thalmann, S. (2020). Applications of Artificial Intelligence in commercial banks–A research agenda for behavioral finance. *Journal of Behavioral and Experimental Finance*, *27*, 100352. doi:10.1016/j.jbef.2020.100352

Kononiuka, A., Pająkb, A., Gudanowskaa, A. E., Magruka, A., Kozłowskaa, J., & Sacio-Szymańskab, A. (2020). Foresight for career development. *Foresight and STI Governance*, *14*(2), 88–104. doi:10.17323/2500-2597.2020.2.88.104

Konovalova, V., Mitrofanova, E., Mitrofanova, A., & Gevorgyan, R. (2022). The impact of Artificial Intelligence on Human Resources Management strategy: Opportunities for the humasation and risks. *Wisdom*, *1*(2), 88–96. doi:10.24234/wisdom.v2i1.763

Koren, Y. (2021, December 15). *Reconfigurable Manufacturing Systems*. University of Michigan. Retrieved December 15, 2021, from https://ykoren.engin.umich.edu/research/rms/

Kortum, E., Leka, S., & Cox, T. (2010). Psychosocial risks and work-related stress in developing countries: Health impact, priorities, barriers and solutions. *International Journal of Occupational Medicine and Environmental Health*, *22*(3), 225–238. doi:10.2478/v10001-010-0024-5 PMID:20934955

Korzynski, P., Mazurek, G., Altmann, A., Ejdys, J., Kazlauskaite, R., Paliszkiewicz, J., Wach, K., & Ziemba, E. (2023). Generative artificial intelligence as a new context for management theories: Analysis of ChatGPT. *Central European Management Journal*, *31*(1), 3–13. doi:10.1108/CEMJ-02-2023-0091

Kotler, P. (2000). Marketing Management Millenium Edition (10th ed.). Prentice-Hall, Inc.

Kotler, P., & Armstrong, G. (2016). Principles of Marketing - Global Edition (S. Wall, Ed., 16th ed.). Pearson Education Limited.

Kotler, P., & Keller, K. (2015). Marketing Management (15th ed.). Pearson Education Limited.

Kotler, P., Kartajaya, H., & Setiawan, I. (2017). *Marketing 4.0 (moving from traditional to digital)*. John Wiley & Sons, Inc.

Kotler, P., Kartajaya, H., & Setiawan, I. (2021). *Marketing 5.0 - Tecnologia para a Humanidade*. Conjuntura Atual Editora.

KPMG. (2018a). *The Robotic Process Automation Opportunity: Transforming the Front Office in Finance, Accounting, and HR*. KPMG.

KPMG. (2018b, March). *Leveraging RPA to drive digital transformation in construction*. Retrieved from https://assets.kpmg.com/content/dam/kpmg/jp/pdf/jp-en-rpa-business-improvement.pdf

KPMG. (2019). *Robotic Process Automation for the Construction Industry*. Retrieved from https://assets.kpmg/content/dam/kpmg/pdf/2019/06/robotic-process-automation-for-the-construction-industry.pdf

Kuhn, T. (1962). *The structure of scientific revolutions*. University of Chicago Press.

Kumar, S., Khanna, S., Ghosh, N., & Kumar, S. O. (2023). Importance of Artificial Intelligence (AI) and Robotic Process Automation (RPA) in the Banking Industry: A Study from an Indian perspective. *Confluence of Artificial Intelligence and Robotic Process Automation*, 231–266. doi:10.1007/978-981-19-8296-5_10

Kumar, A., Mani, V., Jain, V., Gupta, H., & Venkatesh, V. G. (2023). Managing healthcare supply chain through artificial intelligence (AI): A study of critical success factors. *Computers & Industrial Engineering*, *175*, 108815. doi:10.1016/j.cie.2022.108815 PMID:36405396

Kumari, R. (2020, October 30). *What is Information Technology? Definition, Types, and Examples*. AnalyticSteps. https://www.analyticssteps.com/blogs/what-information-technology-definition-types-and-examples

Kunduru, A. R. (2023). Artificial Intelligence Usage in Cloud Application Performance Improvement. *Central Asian Journal of Mathematical Theory and Computer Sciences, 4*(8), 42-47. https://cajmtcs.centralasianstudies

Kushwaha, A. K., & Kar, A. K. (2021). MarkBot A Language Model Driven Chatbot for Interactive Marketing in Post-Modern World. *Information Systems Frontiers*. Advance online publication. doi:10.1007/s10796-021-10184-y

Lacity, M., & Willcocks, L. P. (2016). The changing landscape of organizational IT: Implications for the CIO role. *MIT Sloan Management Review*, *57*(3), 79–89.

Lacity, M., Willcocks, L. P., & Craig, A. (2015). *Robotic process automation: mature capabilities in the en-ergy sector*. The Outsourcing Unit Working.

Lacy, P., Daugherty, P., Ponomarev, P., & Durg, K. (n.d.). *The green behind the cloud*. https://www.accenture.com/_acnmedia/PDF-135/Accenture-Strategy-Green-Behind-Cloud-POV.pdf#zoom=40

Lalić, D., Milić, B., & Stanković, J. (2020). Internal Communication and Employee Engagement as the Key Prerequisites of Happiness. In A. T. Verčič, R. Tench, & S. Einwiller (Eds.), *Joy (Advances in Public Relations and Communication Management)* (Vol. 5, pp. 75–91). Emerald Publishing Limited. doi:10.1108/S2398-391420200000005007

Landau, P. (2021, November 15). *What Is Lean Manufacturing?* ProjectManager. https://www.projectmanager.com/blog/what-is-lean-manufacturing

Larkin, C., Drummond Otten, C., & Arva, J. (2022). Paging Dr. JARVIS! Will people accept advice from artificial intelligence for consequential risk management decisions? *Journal of Risk Research*, *25*(4), 407–422. doi:10.1080/13669877.2021.1958047

Le Clair, C. (2018). *The Forrester WaveTM: robotic process automation*. Forrester.

Lee, H., Chatterjee, I., & Cho, G. (2023). A systematic review of computer vision and AI in parking space allocation in a seaport. *Applied Sciences (2076-3417), 13*(18), 10254-10271.

Lee, J. D., Jheng, E. S., Kuo, C. C., Chen, H. H., & Hung, Y. H. (2023). Novel robotic arm Working area AI protection system. *Sensors (Basel), 23*(5), 2765–2779. doi:10.3390/s23052765 PMID:36904969

Lee, J.-C., & Chen, X. (2022). Exploring users' adoption intentions in the evolution of artificial intelligence mobile banking applications: The intelligent and anthropomorphic perspectives. *International Journal of Bank Marketing, 40*(4), 631–658. doi:10.1108/IJBM-08-2021-0394

Lee, T., Jagannath, K., Aggarwal, N., Sridar, R., Wilde, S., Hill, T., & Chen, Y. (2019). Intelligent career advisers in your pocket? A need assessment study of chatbots for student career advising. *Twenty-fifth Americas Conference on Information Systems*, Cancun, Mexico.

Leff, D., & Lim, K. T. K. (2023). The key to leveraging AI at scale. *Journal of Revenue and Pricing Management, 20*(3), 376–380. doi:10.1057/s41272-021-00320-3

Legge, K. (1995). *Human resource management: Rhetorics and realities*. Macmillan. doi:10.1007/978-1-349-24156-9

Leinen, P., Esders, M., Schütt, K. T., Wagner, C., Müller, K.-R., & Stefan Tautz, F. (2020). Autonomous robotic nanofabrication with reinforcement learning. *Science Advances, 6*(36), 1–8. doi:10.1126/sciadv.abb6987 PMID:32917594

Leno, V., Dumas, M., La Rosa, M., Maggi, F. M., & Polyvyanyy, A. (2020). *Automated Discovery of Data Transformations for Robotic Process Automation*. Academic Press.

Levy, D. H. F., & Murnane, R. J. (2003). The Skill Content of Recent Technological Change: An Empirical Exploration. *The Quarterly Journal of Economics, 118*(4), 1279–1333. doi:10.1162/003355303322552801

Li, C., Zhang, Y., Niu, X., Chen, F., & Zhou, H. (2023). Does Artificial Intelligence Promote or Inhibit On-the-Job Learning? Human Reactions to AI at Work. *Systems, 11*(3), 114. Advance online publication. doi:10.3390/systems11030114

Li, L. (2022). Reskilling and Upskilling the Future-ready Workforce for Industry 4.0 and Beyond. *Information Systems Frontiers*. Advance online publication. doi:10.1007/s10796-022-10308-y PMID:35855776

Lindstrom, M. (2017). *A lógica do consumo: Verdades e mentiras sobre por que compramos*. HarperCollins Brasil.

Lin, K., Liu, J., & Gao, J. (2021). AI-driven decision making for auxiliary diagnosis of epidemic diseases. *IEEE Transactions on Molecular, Biological, and Multi-Scale Communications*, 1–1. doi:10.1109/TMBMC.2021.3120646

Liu, H., & Zhu, X. (2022). Design of the physical fitness evaluation information management system of sports athletes based on artificial intelligence. *Computational Intelligence and Neuroscience, 2022*, 1–10. doi:10.1155/2022/1925757 PMID:35814574

Liu, N.-C., Wang, Y.-C., & Lin, Y.-T. (2023). Employees' Adaptation to Technology Uncertainty in the Digital Era: An Exploration Through the Lens of Job Demands–Resources Theory. *IEEE Transactions on Engineering Management*, 1–12. doi:10.1109/TEM.2023.3264293

Li, X., Anumba, C., Bouchlaghem, D., & Ruddock, L. (2017). BIM for construction cost management: Potential benefits and barriers. *Journal of Financial Management of Property and Construction, 22*(2), 168–187.

Lloyd, C., & Payne, J. (2019). Rethinking country effects: Robotics, AI and work futures in Norway and the UK. *New Technology, Work and Employment, 34*(3), 208–225. doi:10.1111/ntwe.12149

Lohr, S. L. (1999). *Sampling Design and Analysis*. Duxbury Press.

Lokman, A. S., & Ameedeen, M. A. (2018). Modern chatbot systems: A technical review. In *Proceedings of the Future Technologies Conference* (pp. 1012–1023). Cham: Springer, 10.1007/978-3-030-02683-7_75

Loureiro, S. M. C., Bilro, R. G., & Neto, D. (2023). Working with AI: Can stress bring happiness? *Service Business, 17*(1), 233–255. doi:10.1007/s11628-022-00514-8

Lujan, H. L., & DiCarlo, S. E. (2006). First-year medical students prefer multiple learning styles. *Advances in Physiology Education, 30*(1), 13–16. doi:10.1152/advan.00045.2005 PMID:16481603

Lynn, T., Rosati, P., Conway, E., & Van Der Werff, L. (2023). *The Future of Work - Challenges and Prospects for Organisations, Jobs and Workers*. Palgrave Macmillan. http://www.palgrave.com/gp/series/16004

Maheshwari, R. (2023, July 26). Top AI Statistics and Trends in 2023. *Forbes*. https://www.forbes.com/advisor/in/business/ai-statistics

Maheswari, S. (2023). The Transformative Power of AI in Marketing FMCG. *IJFMR-International Journal For Multidisciplinary Research, 5*(3).

Makhija, P., & Chacko, E. (2021). Efficiency and advancement of artificial intelligence in service sector with special reference to banking industry. *Fourth Industrial Revolution and Business Dynamics: Issues and Implications*, 21-35.

Malali, A. B., & Gopalakrishnan, S. (2020). Application of artificial intelligence and its powered technologies in the indian banking and financial industry: An overview. *IOSR Journal Of Humanities And Social Science, 25*(4), 55–60.

Malik, A., Budhwar, P., & Kazmi, B. A. (2023). Artificial intelligence (AI)-assisted HRM: Towards an extended strategic framework. In Human Resource Management Review (Vol. 33, Issue 1). Elsevier Ltd. doi:10.1016/j.hrmr.2022.100940

Malik, A., Budhwar, P., Mohan, H., & Srikanth, N. R. (2023). Employee experience –the missing link for engaging employees: Insights from an MNE's AI-based HR ecosystem. *Human Resource Management*, *62*(1), 97–115. doi:10.1002/hrm.22133

Manser Payne, E. H., Peltier, J., & Barger, V. A. (2021). Enhancing the value co-creation process: Artificial intelligence and mobile banking service platforms. *Journal of Research in Interactive Marketing*, *15*(1), 68–85. doi:10.1108/JRIM-10-2020-0214

Mariani, M. M., Perez-Vega, R., & Wirtz, J. (2022). AI in marketing, consumer research and psychology: A systematic literature review and research agenda. *Psychology and Marketing*, *39*(4), 755–776. doi:10.1002/mar.21619

Marín, F. M. (2023). *De las humanidades digitales a la Inteligencia Artificial General*. University of Texas.

Markets and Markets. (n.d.). *Artificial Intelligence (AI) Market*. https://www.marketsandmarkets.com/Market-Reports/artificial-intelligence-market-74851580.html

Marler, J. H., & Boudreau, J. W. (2017). An evidence-based review of HR Analytics. *International Journal of Human Resource Management*, *28*(1), 3–26. doi:10.1080/09585192.2016.1244699

Márquez, F., & Lev, B. (2019). *Data Science and Digital Business*. Springer., doi:10.1007/978-3-319-95651-0

Marsick, V. J., & Watkins, K. E. (2001). Informal and incidental learning. *New Directions for Adult and Continuing Education*, *89*(89), 25–34. doi:10.1002/ace.5

Martinez, R. (2019). Artificial intelligence: Distinguishing between types & definitions. *Nevada Law Journal*, *19*(3), 1015–1042.

Mason, H., & Wiggins, C. (2010, September 25). *A Taxonomy of Data Science*. Datists. https://web.archive.org/web/20211219192027/http://www.dataists.com/2010/09/a-taxonomy-of-data-science/

Maung, A. M. (2020). Administrative reform in the Myanmar police force: Decision-making and community-based policing. *Journal of Current Southeast Asian Affairs*, *39*(3), 428–443. doi:10.1177/1868103420942781

Mayfield, P. (2014). Engaging with stakeholders is critical when leading change. *Industrial and Commercial Training*, *46*(2), 6872. doi:10.1108/ICT-10-2013-0064

Mayr, S., Mitter, C., Kücher, A., & Duller, C. (2020). Entrepreneur characteristics and differences in reasons for business failure: Evidence from bankrupt Austrian SMEs. *Journal of Small Business and Entrepreneurship*, *33*(5), 539–558. doi:10.1080/08276331.2020.1786647

McCarthy, J. (2007). What Is Artificial Intelligence Anyway. *American Scientist*, *73*(3), 258.

McConnell, B. (2021, July 22). *Data analytics in recruitment: How to apply predictive analytics*. RecruiteeBlog. https://recruitee.com/articles/analytics-in-recruitment

McGregor, D. (1960). Theory x and theory y. In D. S. Pugh (Ed.), *Organization Theory: Selected Readings*. Penguin Books.

Mckay, D. R. (2019, April 22). *Chief Operating Officer Job Description: Salary, Skills, & More*. The Balance Careers. https://www.thebalancecareers.com/what-is-a-coo-4172823

McKay, D. R. (2019a, September 23). *Computer and Information Systems (CIS) Manager Job Description: Salary, Skills, & More*. TheBalanceCareers. https://www.thebalancecareers.com/computer-and-information-systems-manager-525998

McKay, D. R. (2019b, September 27). *Computer Systems Analyst Job Description: Salary, Skills, & More*. TheBalanceCareers. https://www.thebalancecareers.com/computer-systems-analyst-526001

McKinsey & Company. (2020). *Global robotics automation survey 2020*. https://www.mckinsey.com/industries/industrials-and-electronics/our-insights/unlocking-the-industrial-potential-of-robotics-and-automation

McKinsey Global Institute. (2023). *The Automation Advantage: Empowering Leaders from the Front Line to the C-Suite*. McKinsey & Company. https://www.mckinsey.com/

McLagan, P. A., & Bedrick, D. (1983). Models for excellence: The results of the ASTD training and development competency study. *Training and Development Journal*, *37*(6), 16–20.

McLean, G. N., & McLean, L. (2001). If we can't define HRD in one country, how can we define it in an international context? *Human Resource Development International*, *4*(3), 313–326. doi:10.1080/13678860110059339

McPherson, J. (2022, January 22). *Introducing our People Science team*. Culture Amp. Retrieved January 22, 2022, from https://www.cultureamp.com/blog/introducing-our-people-science-team

Meena, M. M. R., & Parimalarani, G. (2020). Impact of digital transformation on employment in banking sector. *International Journal of Scientific & Technology Research*, *9*(1), 4912–4916.

Mehta, S. (2022). The Evolution of Marketing 1. 0 to Marketing 5.0. *International Journal of Law*, *5*(4), 469–485.

Meister, J. (2023). The Future of Work is Employee Well-Being. *OPJU Business Review, 2*(1), 79–88. https://www.opju.ac.in/opjubr/documents/volume2/7.pdf

Menaka, R. (2023). Role of Artificial Intelligence (AI) in Human Resource Management (HRM) in Recent Era. *Shanlax International Journal of Management*, *11*(2), 32–38. doi:10.34293/management.v11i2.6664

Men, F., Yaqub, R. M. S., Yan, R., Irfan, M., & Fatima, M. e. (2022). Resource-based theory perspective in the textile industry: The impact of the digital supply chain on operational performance. *Frontiers in Environmental Science*, *10*, 1017297. Advance online publication. doi:10.3389/fenvs.2022.1017297

Microsoft. (2018). *Microsoft - Artificial Intelligence in Business*. Microsoft. https://www.microsoft.com/en-us/ai/industry/ai-in-business

Mikalef, P., & Gupta, M. (2021). Artificial intelligence capability: Conceptualization, measurement calibration, and empirical study on its impact on organizational creativity and firm performance. *Information & Management*, *58*(3), 103434. doi:10.1016/j.im.2021.103434

Mila, S., & Elliott, S. (2023). Measuring the impact of Artificial intelligence and Robotics on the workplace. In *New Digital Work* (pp. 16–30). Springer International Publishing. doi:10.1007/978-3-031-26490-0

Miller, C. J., Smith, S. N., & Pugatch, M. (2020). Experimental and quasi-experimental designs in implementation research. *Psychiatry Research*, *283*, 112452. doi:10.1016/j.psychres.2019.06.027 PMID:31255320

Mishel, L., & Bivens, J. (2021). The Productivity-Median Compensation Gap in the United States: The Contribution of Increased Wage Inequality and the Role of Policy Choices. *International Productivity Monitor*, (41). https://link.gale.com/apps/doc/A689169156/AONE?u=anon~10ba8f08&sid=googleScholar &xid=5119dfa8.

Mitchell, A. (2023). ChatGPT could make these jobs obsolete: 'The wolf is at the door.' *New York Post*. https://nypost.com/2023/01/25/chat-gpt- could-make-these-jobs-obsolete/

Mohtady Ali, H. M., Ranse, J., Roiko, A., & Desha, C. (2023). Enabling transformational leadership to foster disaster-resilient hospitals. *International Journal of Environmental Research and Public Health*, *20*(3), 2022. doi:10.3390/ijerph20032022 PMID:36767388

Monroe. (2017, April 13). *What is a Reconfigurable Manufacturing System?* MonroeEngeneering. https://monroeengineering.com/blog/what-is-a-reconfigurable-manufacturing-system/

Moore, M. (2019). *Democracia Manipulada*. Editora Self.

Morandini, S., Fraboni, F., De Angelis, M., Puzzo, G., Giusino, D., & Pietrantoni, L. (2023). The Impact of Artificial Intelligence on Workers' Skills: Upskilling and Reskilling in Organisations. *Informing Science*, *26*, 39–68. doi:10.28945/5078

Moreno-Jiménez, B. (2011). Factores y riesgos laborales psicosociales: Conceptualización, historia y cambios actuales. *Medicina y Seguridad del Trabajo*, *57*(1), 4–19. doi:10.4321/S0465-546X2011000500002

Mouzas, S., & Bauer, F. (2022). Rethinking business performance in global value chains. *Journal of Business Research*, *144*, 679–689. doi:10.1016/j.jbusres.2022.02.012

Mulder, P. (2010). *What is Management By Objectives (MBO)*. Toolshero. https://www.toolshero.com/management/management-by-objectives-drucker/

Nadler, L. (1969). The variety of training roles. *Industrial and Commercial Training*, *1*(1), 33–37. doi:10.1108/eb003030

Nantasenamat, C. (2020, July 27). *The Data Science Process. A Visual Guide to Standard Procedures…* TowardsDataScience. https://towardsdatascience.com/the-data-science-process-a19eb7ebc41b

Nascimento, R. (2021). *Entenda o que é jornada do consumidor e veja exemplos!* Marketing, Materiais Educativos. https://www.agendor.com.br/blog/jornada-do-consumidor/

Neaher, G., Bray, D., Mueller-Kaler, J. & Schatz, B. (2021). *Standardizing the future: How can the United States navigate the geopolitics of international technology standards?* Atlantic Council Report.

Neslin, S. A., & Winer, R. S. (2023). The History of Marketing Science: Beginnings. The History of Marketing Science: Second Edition, 1–17. doi:10.1142/9789811272233_0001

Neto, H. V. (2015). Estratégias organizacionais de gestão e intervenção sobre riscos psicossociais do trabalho. *International Journal on Working Conditions.*, *9*, 1–21.

Newman, S. A., & Ford, R. C. (2020). Five steps to leading your team in the virtual COVID-19 workplace. *Organizational Dynamics*, *50*(1), 100802. doi:10.1016/j.orgdyn.2020.100802 PMID:36536689

Nguyen, D. K., Sermpinis, G., & Stasinakis, C. (2023). Big data, artificial intelligence and machine learning: A transformative symbiosis in favour of financial technology. *European Financial Management, 29*(2), 517-548.

Nguyen, C. A., Artis, A. B., Plank, R. E., & Solomon, P. J. (2019). Dimensions of effective sales coaching: Scale development and validation. *Journal of Personal Selling & Sales Management*, *39*(3), 299–315. doi:10.1080/08853134.2019.1621758

Nilsson, N. J. (1981). *Readings in Artificial Intelligence*. doi:10.1016/C2013-0-07694-3

Noranee, S., & bin Othman, A. K. (2023). Understanding Consumer Sentiments: Exploring the Role of Artificial Intelligence in Marketing. *Jurnal Ilmu Ekonomi Dan Manajemen, 10*(1). doi:10.30996/jmm17.v10i1.8690

Northouse, P. G. (2018). *Leadership: Theory and practice*. Sage Publications.

O'Neil, C. (2016). *Weapons of Math Destruction: How Big Data Increases Inequality and Threatens Democracy*. Crown Publishing Group.

OECD. (2021). *Artificial Intelligence, Machine Learning and Big Data in Finance: Opportunities, Challenges, and Implications for Policy Makers,* https://www.oecd.org/finance/artificial-intelligence-machine-learning-big-data-in-finance.html

Olson, C., & Levy, J. (2018). Transforming marketing with artificial intelligence. *Applied Marketing Analytics, 3*(4), 291-297.

Open, A. I. (2023). *How IA conceptualize …* ChatGPT. https://chat.openai.com/share/a861de20-dcdb-41d6-8633-77804091fec2

Organização Internacional do Trabalho (ILO). (2023). *Desaceleração económica poderá forçar os trabalhadores a aceitar empregos de menor qualidade*. Imprensa. OIT. https://www.ilo.org/lisbon/sala-de-imprensa/WCMS_865482/lang--pt/index.htm

Orwell, G. (1949). *1984*. Secker & Warburg.

Ovanessoff, A., & Plastino, E. (2018). Una explosión de productividad. *Integración & comercio, 44*, 28-48. https://dialnet.unirioja.es/servlet/articulo?codigo=6551930

Palos-Sánchez, P. R., Baena-Luna, P., Badicu, A., & Infante-Moro, J. C. (2022). Artificial Intelligence and Human Resources Management: A Bibliometric Analysis. In Applied Artificial Intelligence (Vol. 36, Issue 1). Taylor and Francis Ltd. doi:10.1080/08839514.2022.2145631

Pandian, D. A. P. (2019). Artificial intelligence application in smart warehousing environment for automated logistics. *Journal of Artificial Intelligence and Capsule Networks*, *1*(2), 63–72. doi:10.36548/jaicn.2019.2.002

Pan, Y., & Froese, F. J. (2023). An interdisciplinary review of AI and HRM: Challenges and future directions. *Human Resource Management Review*, *33*(1), 100924. Advance online publication. doi:10.1016/j.hrmr.2022.100924

Parra, E., García Delgado, A., Carrasco-Ribelles, L. A., Chicchi Giglioli, I. A., Marin-Morales, J., Giglio, C., & Alcaniz Raya, M. (2022). Combining virtual reality and machine learning for leadership styles recognition. *Frontiers in Psychology*, *13*, 864266. Advance online publication. doi:10.3389/fpsyg.2022.864266 PMID:35712148

Pathak, R. (2021a, May 21). *Information Technology - functions, applications & Importance*. AnalyticSteps. https://www.analyticssteps.com/blogs/information-technology-its-functions-and-why-it-important

Pathak, R. (2021b, October 27). *What is the role of technology in business?* AnalyticSteps. https://www.analyticssteps.com/blogs/what-role-technology-business

Pathak, S., & Muralidharan, E. (2021). Consequences of cross-cultural differences in perceived well-being for entrepreneurship. *Journal of Business Research, 122*(March), 582–596. doi:10.1016/j.jbusres.2020.09.034

Peifer, Y., Jeske, T., & Hille, S. (2022). Artificial Intelligence and its Impact on Leaders and Leadership. *Procedia Computer Science*, *200*, 1024–1103. doi:10.1016/j.procs.2022.01.301

Pereira, V., Hadjielias, E., Christofi, M., & Vrontis, D. (2023). A systematic literature review on the impact of artificial intelligence on workplace outcomes: A multi-process perspective. *Human Resource Management Review*, *33*(1), 100857. doi:10.1016/j.hrmr.2021.100857

Perucci, D. (2020, April 23). *The Quick Guide to an Effective Recruitment Process*. BambooHR. https://www.bamboohr.com/blog/guide-effective-recruitment-process/

Petrin, M. (2019). Corporate management in the age of AI. SSRN *Electronic Journal*. doi:10.2139/ssrn.3346722

Pinto, J. P. (2006). *João Pinto Introdução Ao Lean Thinking.* Cadeia de Abastecimento. https://pt.scribd.com/document/52886880/Joao-Pinto-Introducao-ao-Lean-Thinking

Polzer, J. T. (2022). The rise of people analytics and the future of organizational research. *Research in Organizational Behavior*, *42*, 1–13. doi:10.1016/j.riob.2023.100181

Potter, W. (2023) 'This is not crying wolf... the wolf is at the door': Fears AI could make white collar jobs obsolete as Microsoft pumps multibillion-dollar investment into ChatGPT after laying off 10,000 workers. *Dailymail.com.* https://www.dailymail.co.uk/news/article-11683901/ChatGPT-make-white-collar- jobs-obsolete-Microsoft-pumps-billions-AI.html

Pournader, M., Ghaderi, H., Hassanzadegan, A., & Fahimnia, B. (2021). Artificial intelligence applications in supply chain management. *International Journal of Production Economics*, *241*, 108250. doi:10.1016/j.ijpe.2021.108250

Pratama, A., Mustika, M. D., & Sjabadhyni, B. (2018). Coaching as intervention to increase leaders' contingent reward behavior. *Journal of Workplace Learning*, *30*(3), 150–161. doi:10.1108/JWL-07-2017-0061

Prikshat, V., Islam, M., Patel, P., Malik, A., Budhwar, P., & Gupta, S. (2023). AI-Augmented HRM: Literature review and a proposed multilevel framework for future research. *Technological Forecasting and Social Change*, *193*, 122645. Advance online publication. doi:10.1016/j.techfore.2023.122645

Prikshat, V., Malik, A., & Budhwar, P. (2023). AI-augmented HRM: Antecedents, assimilation and multilevel consequences. *Human Resource Management Review*, *33*(1), 100860. Advance online publication. doi:10.1016/j.hrmr.2021.100860

Profita, M. (2020, September 17). *Top 10 Computer Science Jobs*. TheBalanceCareers. https://www.thebalancecareers.com/top-jobs-for-computer-science-majors-2059634

Provitera, M. S. M. (2023, August 23). *Creating an AI-powered culture demands a change in how people managers and leaders think.* https://www.peoplemanagement.co.uk/article/1834909/creating-ai-powered-culture-demands-change-people-managers-leaders-think

Provost, F., & Fawcett, T. (2013). Data science and its relationship to big data and data-driven decision making. *Big Data, 1*(1), 51-59.

Provost, F., & Fawcett, T. (2013a). Data Science and its Relationship to Big Data and Data-Driven Decision Making. *Big Data, 1*(1), 51–59. doi:10.1089/big.2013.1508 PMID:27447038

Provost, F., & Fawcett, T. (2013b). *Data Science for Business: What You Need to Know about Data Mining and Data-Analytic Thinking*. O'Reilly Media.

PwC. (2022). *The robotic process automation revolution.* https://www.uipath.com/resources/automation-case-studies/pwc-digital-transformation

Qaiser, S., Abid, G., Arya, B., & Farooqi, S. (2018). Nourishing the bliss: Antecedents and mechanism of happiness at work. *Total Quality Management & Business Excellence*, *31*(15–16), 1669–1683. doi:10.1080/14783363.2018.1493919

Qin, Y. S., & Men, L. R. (2022). Exploring the Impact of Internal Communication on Employee Psychological Well-Being During the COVID-19 Pandemic: The Mediating Role of Employee Organizational Trust. *International Journal of Business Communication*, *00*(0), 1–23. doi:10.1177/23294884221081838

Quan, T. Z., & Raheem, M. (2023). Human Resource Analytics on Data Science Employment Based on Specialized Skill Sets with Salary Prediction. *International Journal of Data Science*, *4*(1), 40–59. doi:10.18517/ijods.4.1.40-59.2023

QuestionPro. (2022, March 21). *Quantitative Research: Definition, Methods, Types and Examples*. Retrieved March 21, 2022, from https://www.questionpro.com/blog/quantitative-research/

Quinn, M., & Strauss, E. (2018). *The Routledge Companion to Accounting Information Systems*. Routledge.

Quinn, K., & Strauss, J. (2018). The disruptive potential of robotic process automation: A case study in a mortgage bank. *Information Systems Journal*, *28*(3), 405–426.

Radford, A., Narasimhan, K., Salimans, T. and Sutskever, I. (2018) *Improving Language Understanding with Unsupervised Learning*. Technical Report, OpenAI.

Rahman, M., Ming, T. H., Baigh, T. A., & Sarker, M. (2021). Adoption of artificial intelligence in banking services: An empirical analysis. *International Journal of Emerging Markets*.

Raina, R. (2018). Change management and organizational development. *Sage (Atlanta, Ga.)*.

Rajakishore, N., & Vineet, S. (2020). The problem of machine ethics in artificial intelligence. *AI & Society*, *35*(1), 103–111. doi:10.1007/s00146-017-0768-6

Ramalho, J. F., & Costa, L. S. (2017). Os fatores psicossociais de risco na atividade de técnicos superiores de segurança no trabalho. *Laboreal (Porto)*, *13*(2), 39–49. doi:10.4000/laboreal.359

Ramsbotham, S. (2021, November 2). The cultural benefits of artificial intelligence in the enterprise. *MIT Sloan Management Review*. https://sloanreview.mit.edu/projects/the-cultural-benefits-of-artificial-intelligence-in-the-enterprise/

Ranković, Gurgu, Martins, & Vukasović. (2023). Artificial intelligence and the evolution of finance: opportunities, challenges, and ethical considerations. *Edtech Journal, 3*(1), 20-23.

Reddy, L. S., & Kulshrestha, P. (2019). Performing the KMO and Bartlett's Test for Factors Estimating the Warehouse Efficiency, Inventory and Customer Contentment for E-retail Supply Chain. *International Journal for Research in Engineering Application & Management*, *05*, 2454–9150. doi:10.35291/2454-9150.2019.0531

Reid, R. D., & Sanders, N. R. (2019). *Operations Management: An Integrated Approach* (7th ed.). Wiley. https://books.google.pt/books?hl=pt-PT&lr=&id=c8-8DwAAQBAJ&oi=fnd&pg=PA1&dq=Operations+Management:+An+Integrated+Approach,+7th+Edition+pdf&ots=5p2VjwGoFx&sig=Vb9CW33zYft9tcmxR9dDwb5bbrE&redir_esc=y#v=onepage&q&f=false

Riahi, Y., Saikouk, T., Gunasekaran, A., & Badraoui, I. (2021). Artificial intelligence applications in supply chain: A descriptive bibliometric analysis and future research directions. *Expert Systems with Applications*, *173*, 114702. doi:10.1016/j.eswa.2021.114702

Ribeiro, J., Lima, R., Eckhardt, T., & Paiva, S. (2021). Robotic Process Automation and artificial intelligence in industry 4.0 – A literature review. *Procedia Computer Science*, *181*, 51–58. doi:10.1016/j.procs.2021.01.104

Richard, P. J., & McCray, J. (2023). Evaluating leadership development in a changing world? Alternative models and approaches for healthcare organisations. *Human Resource Development International*, *26*(2), 114–150. doi:10.1080/13678868.2022.2043085

Richardson, N., & Antonello, M. (2023). *People at Work 2023: A Global Workforce View*. Academic Press.

Riggio, R. E. (2018). *Introduction to industrial/organizational psychology*. Routledge.

Rivas, P., & Zhao, L. (2023). Marketing with chatgpt: Navigating the Ethical Terrain of GPT-Based Chatbot Technology. *AI, 4*(2), 375-384.

Robert, L. P., Pierce, C., Marquis, L., Kim, S., & Alahmad, R. (2020). Designing fair AI for managing employees in organizations: A review, critique, and design agenda. *Human-Computer Interaction*, *35*(5–6), 545–575. doi:10.1080/07370024.2020.1735391

Rodrigues, E. V., Samagaio, F., Ferreira, H., Mendes, M. M., & Januário, S. (2017). A pobreza e a exclusão social: Teorias conceitos e políticas sociais em Portugal. *Sociologia: Revista da Faculdade de Letras da Universidade do Porto, 9*. https://ojs.letras.up.pt/index.php/Sociologia/article/view/2566

Rodríguez-Espíndola, O., Chowdhury, S., Beltagui, A., & Albores, P. (2020). The potential of emergent disruptive technologies for humanitarian supply chains: The integration of blockchain, artificial intelligence and 3D printing. *International Journal of Production Research*, *58*(15), 4610–4630. doi:10.1080/00207543.2020.1761565

Roldós, I. (2021, January 9). *What Is Data Analysis? Examples & Why It Matters*. MonkeyLearn. https://monkeylearn.com/blog/data-analysis-examples/#inferential

Rosie. (2019, September 25). *9 Benefits of Talent Analytics and How to Use It*. Harver. https://harver.com/blog/talent-analytics/

Rožman, M., Oreški, D., & Tominc, P. (2022). Integrating artificial intelligence into a talent management model to increase the work engagement and performance of enterprises. *Frontiers in Psychology*, *13*, 1–16. doi:10.3389/fpsyg.2022.1014434 PMID:36506984

Sacks, G. (2023). *Generative IA could raise global GDP by 7% Artificial Intelligence*. https://www.goldmansachs.com/intelligence/pages/generative-ai-could-raise-global- gdp-by-7-percent.html

Sadok, H., Sakka, F., & El Maknouzi, M. E. H. (2022). Artificial intelligence and bank credit analysis: A review. *Cogent Economics & Finance*, *10*(1), 2023262. doi:10.1080/23322039.2021.2023262

Sagarikabiswas. (2023). *ChatGPT: 7 IT Jobs That IA Can't Replace*. https://www.geeksforgeeks.org/chatgpt-7-it-jobs-that-ai-cant-replace/

Salas-Vallina, A., Alegre, J., & Fernández Guerrero, R. (2018). Happiness at work in knowledge-intensive contexts: Opening the research agenda. *European Research on Management and Business Economics*, *24*(3), 149–159. doi:10.1016/j.iedeen.2018.05.003

Santos. (2017). *Cálculo Amostral*. https://praticaclinica.com.br/anexos/ccolaborativa-calculo-amostral/ccolaborativa-calculo-amostral.php

Santos, F., Pereira, R., & Vasconcelos, J. B. (2019). Toward robotic process automation implementation. *Business Process Management Journal*, *3*(1), 405–420. Advance online publication. doi:10.1108/BPMJ-12-2018-0380

Sarkar, S., Bhubaneswar, P., & Kalita, M. (2023). Association between General Happiness of Employees and Their Performance at Workplace: A Study at a Navaratna Company Background of the Study. *European Journal of Military Studies, 13*(2), 6899–6913. https://www.opju.ac.in/opjubr/documents/volume2/7.pdf

Satheesh, M. K., & Nagaraj, S. (2021). Applications of artificial intelligence on customer experience and service quality of the banking sector. *International Management Review*, *17*(1), 9–17.

Saunders, M. N. K., Lewis, P., & Thornhill, A. (2020). *Research methods for business students* (8th ed.). Pearson Education Limited.

Saura, J. R., Ribeiro-Soriano, D., & Palacios-Marqués, D. (2021). Setting B2B digital marketing in artificial intelligence-based CRMs: A review and directions for future research. *Industrial Marketing Management, 98*, 161-178.

Schein, E. H., & Schein, P. A. (2018). What is new in OD? Nothing, yet everything. *OD Practitioner*, *50*(4), 6–8.

Schermerhorn, J. R., Jr., & Bachrach, D. G. (2020). *Exploring Management*. Wiley. https://books.google.pt/books?hl=pt-PT&lr=&id=zw8IEAAAQBAJ&oi=fnd&pg=PA1&dq=what+are+the+functions+of+management&ots=ExEhCGtMY2&sig=zA6E3NslNLLbfgDQbQaqvBNDcIs&redir_esc=y#v=onepage&q&f=false

Schoemaker, P. J., Heaton, S., & Teece, D. (2018). Innovation, dynamic capabilities, and leadership. *California Management Review, 61*(1), 15-42.

Schrettenbrunnner, M. B. (2020). Artificial-intelligence-driven management. *IEEE Engineering Management Review*, *48*(2), 15–19. doi:10.1109/EMR.2020.2990933

Schumpeter, J. (1994). *Capitalism, Socialism and democracy*. Routledge.

Schumpeter, J. (1994). *The Theory of Economic Development, An Inquiry into Profits, Capital, Credit, Interest and the Business Cycle*. Harvard University Press.

Sedky, A. (2023). Digital supply chain: A proposed solution to the global supply chain disruption impact on business sustainability. In *Digital Supply Chain, Disruptive Environments, and the Impact on Retailers* (pp. 160-177). IGI Global. doi:10.4018/978-1-6684-7298-9.ch009

Sedky, A. M. (2021). *The relationship between transformational, transactional, and passive-avoidant leadership styles and small business sustainability* [Doctoral dissertation]. ProQuest Dissertations and Theses Global.

Shaddiq, S., Khuzaini, & Irpan. (2023). Governance of Human Resources Management in the Digital Era. *Journal of Business and Management Studies*, *5*(3), 80–96. doi:10.32996/jbms.2023.5.3.8

Shaikh, A. A., Alharthi, M. D., & Alamoudi, H. O. (2020). Examining key drivers of consumer experience with (non-financial) digital services—An exploratory study. *Journal of Retailing and Consumer Services*, *55*, 102073. doi:10.1016/j.jretconser.2020.102073

Sharifi, A., Khavarian-Garmsir, A. R., & Kummitha, R. K. R. (2021). Contributions of smart city solutions and technologies to resilience against the COVID-19 pandemic: A literature review. *Sustainability (Basel)*, *13*(14), 1–28. doi:10.3390/su13148018

Sharma, R. (2020, December 1). *4 Types of Data: Nominal, Ordinal, Discrete, Continuous*. UpGrad. https://www.upgrad.com/blog/types-of-data/

Sharma, M., Luthra, S., Joshi, S., & Kumar, A. (2022). Analysing the impact of sustainable human resource management practices and industry 4.0 technologies adoption on employability skills. *International Journal of Manpower*, *43*(2), 463–485. doi:10.1108/IJM-02-2021-0085

Sharma, R., Shishodia, A., Gunasekaran, A., Min, H., & Munim, Z. H. (2022). The role of artificial intelligence in supply chain management: Mapping the territory. *International Journal of Production Research*, *60*(24), 7527–7550. doi:10.1080/00207543.2022.2029611

Shen, S. (2020, February 9). *What is the Data Architecture We Need?* Towards Data Science. https://towardsdatascience.com/what-is-the-data-architecture-we-need-72606e71ba0c

Siau, K. L., & Yang, Y. (2017). *Impact of artificial intelligence, robotics, and machine learning on sales and marketing*. Academic Press.

Siderska, J. (2020). Robotic Process Automation — A driver of digital transformation? *Engineering Management in Production and Services*, *12*(2), 21–31. doi:10.2478/emj-2020-0009

Silva, M., Queirós, C., & Cameira, M. (2016). Saúde no Trabalho: Tecnostress e Burnout em Enfermeiros. *International Journal on Working Conditions*, *12*(1), 54–70.

Silva, R., Rodrigues, R., & Leal, C. (2021). Games-based learning in accounting education–which dimensions are the most relevant? *Accounting Education*, *30*(2), 159–187. doi:10.1080/09639284.2021.1891107

Simon, H. A. (1959). Theories of decision-making in economics and behavioral science. *The American Economic Review*, *49*(3), 253–283.

Simon, H. A. (1991). Bounded rationality and organizational learning. *Organization Science*, *2*(1), 125–134. doi:10.1287/orsc.2.1.125

SimpliLearn. (2021a, December 30). *What is Data Science? Prerequisites, Lifecycle and Applications*. SimpliLearn. https://www.simplilearn.com/tutorials/data-science-tutorial/what-is-data-science

SimpliLearn. (2021b, December 16). *What Is Data: Types of Data, and How to Analyze Data* [Updated]. Simplilearn. https://www.simplilearn.com/what-is-data-article

Sindhu, V., Anitha, G., & Geetha, R. (2021). Industry 4.0-A Breakthrough in Artificial Intelligence the Internet of Things and Big Data towards the next digital revolution for high business outcome and delivery. *Journal of Physics: Conference Series*, *1937*(1), 1–7. doi:10.1088/1742-6596/1937/1/012030

Singh, A., Jha, S., Srivastava, D. K., & Somarajan, A. (2022). Future of work: a systematic literature review and evolution of themes. In Foresight (Vol. 24, Issue 1, pp. 99–125). Emerald Group Holdings Ltd. doi:10.1108/FS-09-2020-0093

Singh, K. (2020). Banks banking on ai. *International Journal of Advanced Research in Management and Social Sciences*, *9*(9), 1–11.

Six Sigma Daily. (2020a, January 9). *What is Six Sigma? Definition, Methodology and Tools*. Six Sigma Daily. https://www.sixsigmadaily.com/what-is-six-sigma/

Six Sigma Daily. (2020b, May 7). *Why Was Six Sigma Created and Why Is It Important?* Six Sigma Daily. https://www.sixsigmadaily.com/why-was-six-sigma-created/

Śliż, D. (2019). The impact of robotic process automation on the labor market in the banking sector. *Transformations in Business & Economics*, *18*(3), 423–435.

Śliż, P. (2019). Robotization of Business Processes and the Future of the Labor Market in Poland – Preliminary Research. *Organization and Management*, *2*(185), 67–79.

Slyther, K. (2019, February 25). *What Is Information Technology? A Beginner's Guide to the World of IT*. Rasmussen University. https://www.rasmussen.edu/degrees/technology/blog/what-is-information-technology/

Smith, A. M., & Green, M. (2018). Artificial intelligence and the role of leadership. *Journal of Leadership Studies*, *12*(3), 85–87. Advance online publication. doi:10.1002/jls.21605

Smith, P. (2014). Bim & the 5D project cost manager. *Procedia: Social and Behavioral Sciences*, *119*, 475–484. doi:10.1016/j.sbspro.2014.03.053

Soumpenioti, V., & Panagopoulos, A. (2023, September). AI Technology in the Field of Logistics. In *2023 18th International Workshop on Semantic and Social Media Adaptation & Personalization (SMAP)* (pp. 1-6). IEEE. 10.1109/SMAP59435.2023.10255203

Sousa, M. J., Sousa, M., Rocha, Á., & Di Virgilio, F. (2023). Scoping Review on AI as a Driver for Industry. In R. Pereira, I. Bianchi, & Á. Rocha (Eds.), Digital Technologies and Transformation in Business, Industry and Organizations (Springer, Vol. 2, pp. 235–243). doi:10.1007/978-3-031-40710-9_13

Spielberg, S. (2002). *Minoraty Report*. Academic Press.

Statistica. (2023). *Leading social media platforms used by marketers worldwide as of January 2023*. Advertising & Marketing - Marketing. https://www.statista.com/statistics/259379/social-media-platforms-used-by-marketers-worldwide/ UNESCO/COMEST

Stokdyk, D. (2019, October 29). *What is Information Technology (IT)?* Southern New Hampshire University. https://www.snhu.edu/about-us/newsroom/stem/what-is-information-technology

Storey, J. (1992). *Developments in the management of human resources*. Blackwell.

Strauss, D. (2023). *Generative AI's 'productivity revolution' will take time to pay off*. Financial Times. https://www.ft.com/content/21384711-3506-4901-830c-7ecc3ae6b32a

Strohmeier, S., & Piazza, F. (2014). Detecting Deceptive Opinions in Online Restaurant Reviews. *ACM Transactions on Intelligent Systems and Technology*, *5*(4), 1–30.

Succar, B. (2009). Building information modelling framework: A research and delivery foundation for industry stakeholders. *Automation in Construction*, *18*(3), 357–375. doi:10.1016/j.autcon.2008.10.003

Suhel, S. F., Shukla, V. K., Vyas, S., & Mishra, V. P. (2020, June). Conversation to automation in banking through chatbot using artificial machine intelligence language. In *2020 8th international conference on reliability, infocom technologies and optimization (trends and future directions) (ICRITO)* (pp. 611-618). 10.1109/ICRITO48877.2020.9197825

Super, D. E., Savickas, M. L., & Super, C. M. (1996). The life-span, life-space approach to careers. In D. Brown & L. Brooks (Eds.), *Career choice and development* (3rd ed., pp. 121–178). Jossey-Bass.

Surji, K. M. S. (2015). Understanding Leadership and Factors that Influence Leaders' Effectiveness. *European Journal of Business and Management*, *7*(33). Advance online publication. doi:10.7176/EJBM/7-33-2015-03

Su, Z., Togay, G., & Côté, A. M. (2021). Artificial intelligence: A destructive and yet creative force in the skilled labour market. *Human Resource Development International*, *24*(3), 341–352. doi:10.1080/13678868.2020.1818513

Swanson, R. A., & Holton, E. F. (2022). *Foundations of human resource development* (3rd ed.). Berrett-Koehler Publishers, Inc.

Taguchi, N. (2018). Description and explanation of pragmatic development: Quantitative, qualitative, and mixed methods research. *System*, *75*(4), 23–32. doi:10.1016/j.system.2018.03.010

Taherdoost, H., & Madanchian, M. (2023). Artificial Intelligence and Knowledge Management: Impacts, Benefits, and Implementation. In Computers (Vol. 12, Issue 4). MDPI. doi:10.3390/computers12040072

Taylor, B., & Whittaker, A. (2018). Professional judgement and decision-making in social work. *Journal of Social Work Practice*, *32*(2), 105–109. doi:10.1080/02650533.2018.1462780

Techopedia. (2020, April 30). *What is a Programmer?* Techopedia. https://www.techopedia.com/definition/4813/programmer

Techopedia. (2021, June 1). *What is Data Science?* Techopedia. https://www.techopedia.com/definition/30202/data-science

The little book of RPA - NDL. (n.d.). Retrieved March 21, 2023, from https://www.ndl.co.uk/media/j11pdkyr/little-book-of-rpa_ndl-software-limited.pdf

Thomas, P., & Busenhart, S. (2021). Narrow artificial intelligence is latest disrupter to insurance industry: NAI, just like the industrial revolution is going to result in new government programs, as well as new theories of contract law and injury law. *Best's Reviews*, *122*(5), 16–17.

Thompson, S. K. (2012). *Sampling. Wiley Series in Probability and Statistics* (3rd ed.). John Wiley & Sons, Inc.

Tienken, C., Classen, M., & Friedli, T. (2022). Engaging the sales force in digital solution selling: How sales control systems resolve agency problems to create and capture superior value. *European Journal of Marketing*. Advance online publication. doi:10.1108/EJM-11-2021-0918

Tirkolaee, E. B., Sadeghi, S., Mooseloo, F. M., Vandchali, H. R., & Aeini, S. (2021). Application of machine learning in supply chain management: A comprehensive overview of the main areas. *Mathematical Problems in Engineering*, *2021*, 1–14. doi:10.1155/2021/1476043

Toorajipour, R., Sohrabpour, V., Nazarpour, A., Oghazi, P., & Fischl, M. (2021). Artificial intelligence in supply chain management: A systematic literature review. *Journal of Business Research*, *122*, 502–517. doi:10.1016/j.jbusres.2020.09.009

Tredinnick, L. (2017). Out-of-the-Box: Artificial Intelligence and professional roles. *Business Information Review*, *34*(1), 37–41. doi:10.1177/0266382117692621

Tripathi, A. (2018). *Learning robotic process automation: Create software robots and automate business processes with the leading RPA tool.* UiPath.

Tsolakis, N., Schumacher, R., Dora, M., & Kumar, M. (2023). Artificial intelligence and blockchain implementation in supply chains: A pathway to sustainability and data monetisation? *Annals of Operations Research*, *327*(1), 157–210. doi:10.1007/s10479-022-04785-2 PMID:35755830

UiPath. (2023). *The Ultimate Guide to Robotic Process Automation*. RPA.

Uma Maheswari, S., & Valarmathi, A. (2023). Role of Artificial Intelligence in The Banking Sector. *Journal of Survey in Fisheries Sciences*, *10*(4S), 2841–2849.

UNCTAD. (2021). *Algunos países en desarrollo bien situados en tecnologías de frontera, pero la mayoría se queda atrás*. Conferencia de las Naciones Unidas sobre Comercio y Desarrollo. https://unctad.org/es/news/algunos-paises-en-desarrollo-bien-situados-en-tecnologias-de-frontera-pero-la-mayoria-se-queda

UNESCO. (2022). *Recommendation on the ethics of artificial intelligence*. https://en.unesco.org/artificial-intelligence/ethics

Unhelkar, B., & Gonsalves, T. (2020). Enhancing artificial intelligence decision making frameworks to support leadership during business disruptions. *IT Professional*, *22*(6), 59–66. doi:10.1109/MITP.2020.3031312

United Nations. (2023). *Sustainable Development Goals*. Take Action for the Sustainable Development Goals. https://www.un.org/sustainabledevelopment/sustainable-development-goals/

University, B. (2018). *What is Data Science?* Berkeley School of Information. https://ischoolonline.berkeley.edu/data-science/what-is-data-science/

Usai, A., Orlando, B., & Mazzoleni, A. (2020). Happiness as a driver of entrepreneurial initiative and innovation capital. *Journal of Intellectual Capital*, *21*(6), 1229–1255. doi:10.1108/JIC-11-2019-0250

Ustundag, A., & Cevikcan, E. (2018). *Industry 4.0: Managing the Digital Transformation*. Springer Series in Advanced Manufacturing. doi:10.1007/978-3-319-57870-5

Van Quaquebeke, N., & Gerpott, F. H. (2023). The Now, New, and Next of Digital Leadership: How Artificial Intelligence (AI) Will Take Over and Change Leadership as We Know It. In *Journal of Leadership and Organizational Studies*. SAGE Publications Inc. doi:10.1177/15480518231181731

Van Vulpen, E. (2022, January 22). *Recruitment Analytics: The 3 Levels to Optimize Recruiting*. AIHR. Retrieved janeiro 22, 2022, from https://www.aihr.com/blog/recruitment-analytics/

Varsha, P. S. (2023). How can we manage biases in artificial intelligence systems – A systematic literature review. *International Journal of Information Management Data Insights*, *3*(1), 100165–100174. doi:10.1016/j.jjimei.2023.100165

Vaswani, A., Shazeer, N., Parmar, N., Uszkoreit, J., Jones, L., Gomez, A. N., & Polosukhin, I. (2017). *Attention is all you need. Advances in neural information processing systems*. 31st Conference on Neural Information Processing Systems, Long Beach, CA. https://proceedings.neurips.cc/paper/2017/file/3f5ee243547dee91fbd053c1c4a845aa-Paper.pdf

Vaughan, J. (2019, July). *What is Data?* TechTarget. https://www.techtarget.com/searchdatamanagement/definition/data

Vennam, S. (2020, August 18). *What is Cloud Computing?* IBM. https://www.ibm.com/cloud/learn/cloud-computing

Vidal-Gomel, C., & Delgoulet, C. (2022). Analysing relationships between work and training in order to prevent psychosocial risks. *Safety Science*, *145*, 105517. doi:10.1016/j.ssci.2021.105517

Vinuesa, R., Azizpour, H., Leite, I., Balaam, M., Dignum, V., Domisch, S., Felländer, A., Langhans, S. D., Tegmark, M., & Nerini, F. F. (2020). The role of artificial intelligence in achieving the Sustainable Development Goals. *Nature Communications*, *11*(1), 233. Advance online publication. doi:10.1038/s41467-019-14108-y PMID:31932590

von Rosing, M., von Scheel, H., & Scheer, A.-W. (2014). *The complete business process handbook: body of knowledge from process modeling to bpm* (Vol. I). Elsevier.

Vrontis, D., Christofi, M., Pereira, V., Tarba, S., Makrides, A., & Trichina, E. (2022). Artificial intelligence, robotics, advanced technologies and human resource management: A systematic review. *International Journal of Human Resource Management*, *33*(6), 1237–1266. doi:10.1080/09585192.2020.1871398

VUCA. (n.d.). https://www.vuca-world.org/

Wee, M., Scheepers, H., & Tian, X. (2022). The role of leadership skills in the adoption of business intelligence and analytics by SMEs. *Information Technology & People*. Advance online publication. doi:10.1108/ITP-09-2021-0669

Weissglass, D. E. (2022). Contextual bias, the democratization of healthcare, and medical artificial intelligence in low and middle income countries. *Bioethics*, *36*(2), 201–209. doi:10.1111/bioe.12927 PMID:34460977

Werther, W. B., & Davis, K. (1996). *Human resources and personnel management* (5th ed.). McGraw-Hill.

White, S. K. (2018, June 12). *What is Six Sigma? Streamlining quality management*. CIO. https://www.cio.com/article/227977/six-sigma-quality-management-methodology.html

Wilkens, U. (2020). Artificial intelligence in the workplace – A double-edged sword. *The International Journal of Information and Learning Technology*, *37*(5), 253–265. doi:10.1108/IJILT-02-2020-0022

Williams, J. (2023). How AI Will Enhance Human Capabilities. *Forbes*. https://www.forbes.com/sites/forbescommunicationscouncil/2018/03/19/how-ai- will-enhance-human-capabilities/?sh=1d37cd1e366f

Wilson, H. J. (2019, November 19). How humans and AI are working together in 1,500 companies. *Harvard Business Review*. https://hbr.org/2018/07/collaborative-intelligence-humans-and-ai-are-joining-forces

Wilson, M., Robertson, P., Cruickshank, P., & Gkatzia, D. (2022). Opportunities and risks in the use of AI in career development practice. *Journal of the National Institute for Career Education and Counselling*, *48*(1), 48–57. doi:10.20856/jnicec.4807

Wong, J. C. (2019). *The Cambridge Analytica scandal changed the world – but it didn't change Facebook.* The Guardian. https://www.theguardian.com/technology/2019/mar/17/the-cambridge-analytica-scandal-changed-the-world-but-it-didnt-change-facebook

Work Health Organization - WHO. (2010). *Health impact of psychosocial hazards at work: An overview*. World Health Organization.

World Economic Forum & PwC. (2021). *Upskilling for shared prosperity*. Insight Report. https://www.pwc.com/gx/en/issues/upskilling.html

World Economic Forum Reports. (2016). *Digital transformation of Industries*. https://www.weforum.org/reports/digital-transformation-of-industries

World Economic Forum. (2020). *The Future of Jobs Report 2020*. WEF. https://www.weforum.org/press/2020/10/recession-and-automation-changes-our-future-of-work-but-there-are-jobs-coming-report-says-52c5162fce/

World Economic Forum. (2023). *The Future of Jobs Report 2023*. https://www.weforum.org/publications/the-future-of-jobs-report-2023/

World Economic Forum. (2023). *The Future of Jobs Report 2023*. WEF. https://www3.weforum.org/docs/WEF_Future_of_Jobs_2023.pdf

Wright, T. A., & Huang, C.-C. (2012). The many benefits of employee well-being in organizational research. *Journal of Organizational Behavior*, *33*(8), 1188–1192. doi:10.1002/job.1828

Wu, J. X. S., & Liu, S. (2019). Information Security Research Challenges in the Process of Digitizing Business: A Review Based on the Information Security Model of IBM. In F. García Márquez & B. Lev (Eds.), *Data Science and Digital Business*. Springer. doi:10.1007/978-3-319-95651-0_6

Xia, M. (2023). Co-working with AI is a double-sword in Technostress? An integrative review of Human-AI collaboration from a holistic process of Technostress. *SHS Web of Conferences, 155*, 03022. 10.1051/shsconf/202315503022

Xie, Y., Wang, D., Li, H., & Wu, P. (2017). BIM application in green building design. In *Proceedings of the 2017 4th International Conference on Civil and Building Engineering Informatics (ICCBEI 2017)* (pp. 93-98). Atlantis Press

Yarberry, S., & Sims, C. (2021). The Impact of COVID-19-Prompted Virtual/Remote Work Environments on Employees' Career Development: Social Learning Theory, Belongingness, and Self-Empowerment. *Advances in Developing Human Resources*, *23*(3), 237–252. doi:10.1177/15234223211017850

Yogesh, K. (2023). "So, what if ChatGPT wrote it?" Multidisciplinary perspectives on opportunities, challenges, and implications of generative conversational AI for research, practice, and policy. *International Journal of Information Management*, *71*, 102642. doi:10.1016/j.ijinfomgt.2023.102642

Yohn, D. L. (2021, February 9). Company culture is everyone's responsibility. *Harvard Business Review.* https://hbr.org/2021/02/company-culture-is-everyones-responsibility

Yoon, S. W., Han, S., & Chae, C. (2023). People Analytics and Human Resource Development – Research Landscape and Future Needs Based on Bibliometrics and Scoping Review. *Human Resource Development Review*, *0*(0). Advance online publication. doi:10.1177/15344843231209362

Yorks, L., Abel, A. L., & Rotatori, D. (2022). *Strategic human resource development in Practice. Management for Professionals*. Springer. doi:10.1007/978-3-030-95775-9

Zachariah, M., Avanesh, N. M., & Arjunan, S. N. (2022). Future of Work Places. In P. Figueiredo, E. Tomé, & J. Rouco (Eds.), *Handbook of Research on Challenges for Human Resource Management in the COVID-19 Era* (pp. 1–22). IGI Publisher. doi:10.4018/978-1-7998-9840-5.ch001

Zendesk. (2023, June 13). *14 Best Live Chat Software And Apps for 2023*. Zendesk India. https://www.zendesk.com/in/service/messaging/live-chat/

Zheng, P., Sang, Z., Zhong, R. Y., Liu, Y., Liu, C., Mubarok, K., ... Xu, X. (2018). Smart manufacturing systems for Industry 4.0: Conceptual framework, scenarios, and future perspectives. *Frontiers of Mechanical Engineering*, *13*(2), 137–150. doi:10.1007/s11465-018-0499-5

Zhou, Z. E., Eatough, E. M., & Che, X. X. (2020). Effect of illegitimate tasks on work-to-family conflict through psychological detachment: Passive leadership as a moderator. *Journal of Vocational Behavior*, *121*, 103463. doi:10.1016/j.jvb.2020.103463

Zielinski, D. (2023). Is technology the answer to hr's growing burnout problem? *Society of Human Resource Management.* https://www.shrm.org/hr-today/news/hr-magazine/fall-2023/pages/can-artificial-intelligence-solve-hrs-burnout-problem.aspx

About the Contributors

Paula Christina Nunes Figueiredo has a degree in Economics with a specialization in Human Resources Economics, a Master in Human Resources Management and a PhD in Management. She is currently a professor at higher education institutions, and she has also been the Director of an institution since 2019. Paula has 20 years of experience in the business area with functions of direction, coordination, and consultancy. Throughout her professional experience, she has collaborated on leadership development projects. At the research level, she has developed research on Human Resource Development, more specifically Leadership Development in organizations, with some publications in scientific journals and conferences.

* * *

Fuad Abutaha is an Assistant Professor at the Department of Civil Engineering. Abutaha holds a Ph.D. degree in Construction Technology & management. Master in Construction Management. Abutaha is an engineer who embraces modern principles and practices of Civil Engineering specifically in concrete technology and construction management. Researcher with 9 years of experience in the concrete laboratory, experimental design, supervision of research students, and edit materials for publication at high-ranked journals. Experienced in managing research projects from conception to completion.

Cindy L. Crowder, Ph.D., is the Associate Dean of the Scott College of Business, and a Professor Human Resource Development at Indiana State University. She teaches courses in Research Methods, International and Cross-Cultural Training, Work-Life Integration, and Career Development. Prior to her career in academia, she worked in the hospitality industry for 10 years in the areas of event planning, employee development, training, and staffing. Her academic publications focus on work-life integration, teaching methods & strategies, employee discrimination, and diversity training.

João Farinha is a Ph.D. in Management from Universidade Europeia, with a Master's degree in Marketing and a Brand Management thesis. He also has an Executive Master's Degree in Marketing Management from the same institution. He also holds a Certificate in Business and Management (Leadership and Emotional Intelligence) from Case Western Reserve University, a Certificate in Business and Management (Entrepreneurship) from the University of Maryland, College Park, and a Certificate in Business and Management (Leadership and Emotional Intelligence) from the Wharton School, University of Pennsylvania (Leadership). He is presently a member of the Governance, Competitiveness, and Public Policy (GOVCOPP) research unit at the University of Aveiro, as well as the Research Centre in Tourism, Sustainability, and Well-Being (CinTurs) research unit at the University of Algarve. Associate professor at ISLA Santarem Lecturing in Management, Human Resources, Operations, and Marketing. Course director for the MBA in Commercial Management and Marketing, as well as the degree in Business Processes and Operations Management and the higher professional technical course in Organization and Industrial Management.

Ana Filipa Vieira Joaquim has a master's degree in teaching Economics and Accounting, and she is a marketing graduate. She is pursuing a Ph.D. in Global Studies at Faculdade de Ciências Sociais e Humanas in the political strategy field. Nowadays, she is a lecturer in polytechnic higher education in the subjects of communication and marketing and a lecturer in secondary education, as well as a trainer in various institutions. The author has participated in many conferences, seminars, and lectures and has authored and co-authored several articles and book chapters. Her main interests are education, digital marketing management, communication, and politics.

Verley Lanns-Isaac is a doctoral candidate (ABD) in Educational Administration at Indiana State University (ISU). Her ongoing dissertation project centers on school culture and teacher retention. Ms. Lanns-Isaac has earned a Master of Science degree in Human Resource Development at ISU (2022), A Master of Science degree in Management and Educational Leadership from the University of the West Indies (2017), a Master of Education degree in Educational Administration from the University of the West Indies (2011), and Bachelor's degree in Business Administration (Economics Major) from Midwestern State University (2001). Prior to embarking on her pursuit of studies at ISU, she worked as an educator at the high school level for more than twenty years. This has afforded her the opportunity to serve as a business teacher, the head of the business department, and an assistant principal. In 2022, Ms. Lanns-Isaac had the privilege of presenting at the University Forum for Human Resource Development (UFHRD) Annual Doctoral Symposium

Conference. This culminated in her work being published in 2023. Ms. Lanns-Isaac has served on several committees such as the Bayh College of Education Congress, EDLR Law Conference Committee, and Caleb Mills Distinguished Teaching Award Committee at ISU; she also served as a PTA treasurer and a credit committee member at St. Paul's Cooperative Credit Union. She is a member of American Educational Research Association (AERA), Society for Human Resource Management (SHRM), Omicron Delta Kappa Honor Society, Delta Mu Delta Honor Society, and Alpha Chi Honor Society. In her leisure time she enjoys reading, sightseeing, hiking, listening to music, looking at antiques, and traveling.

Maria Pina is a PhD in Mathematics from the University of Coimbra and the University of Porto. She is an Adjunct Professor at ISLA Santarém, an Invited Auxiliary Professor at ISCTE - University Institute of Lisbon, and an Integrated Researcher at ISR - UC, Institute of Systems and Robotics of the University of Coimbra. She is Member of the Portuguese Mathematics Society, Member of the Portuguese Automatic Control Association and Member of the Information and Technology Research Centre of the ISLA Santarém Research & Development Unit. Her current research interests include interdisciplinary areas, such as, Control Theory, Data Science, Dynamical Systems, Computer Vision, Robotics, Social Sciences and Medical Engineering.

R. Alamelu is working as a Senior Assistant Professor in the Department of Commerce and Management Studies, Srinivasa Ramanujan Centre, SASTRA Deemed University, Kumbakonam, Thanjavur, Tamil Nadu, India. She is a passionate management enabler with a blend of research and academic experience and competency in developing and delivering learner-centric pedagogy with a teaching experience of 25 years. She contributed articles and research papers at different conferences at national and international levels, and written case studies, and published 83 papers in SCOPUS--indexed international journals. She pursued her doctoral degree in Quality Management and coordinated several seminars, conferences and conducted Quality improvement programmes for over a decade. She has authored a book titled 'Management Information System' and is actively involved as a consultant for selected tiny industries in Tamil Nadu. Currently, she supervises two part-time research scholars, and her research areas are Supply Chain Management, Human Resource Analytics, and Circular economy.

José Rouco is a PhD in Management; Master in Sports Training Management; Degree in Military Sciences; Training and Certification Course on the Use of Psychological Tests in Human Resource Management; Computer Aided Content Analysis Course (MaxQDA). In the past 20 years, he has held various academic or research roles or positions. At the Military Center for Physical Education and Sports: Director of the "Military Physical Education Instructors" and "Cartography" Course. At the Military Academy (AM): Chairman of the Evaluation and Accreditation Commission for the Master's degree in the Infantry specialty; Vice-President and Secretary of the General Assembly of the Research, Innovation & Development Center; Director of "2nd Year Weapons", "3rd Year Weapons", "Center for Leadership Development Studies: Estúdio TV"; Head of the "Physical Training Disciplinary Group", "School Support Office" and "Postgraduate Studies"; Scientific Coordinator of the "Degree in Military Sciences in the specialty of Cavalry", "Master of Leadership - People and Organizations" and "Erasmus da AM"; Member of the "Executive Committee of the Study Cycle - Master in Information Warfare", "Scientific Technology Organization NATO", "Scientific Council of IUM", "Scientific and Pedagogical Council of AM"; Editor of Proelium Magazine. He is currently Director of the Department of Management in Civil Aviation and Airports and Director of the 1st Cycle of Aeronautical Management Studies, at Universidade Lusófona; Editor, member and peer-review of national and international magazines.

Ahmed Sedky is a Doctor of Business affiliated with the School of Business and Technology at Walden University and an editorial board member at The International Journal of Risk and Contingency Management (IJRCM) - the United States. He holds a Master's in Management of Foreign Trade Logistics (Supply Chain) from the Arab Academy for Science, Technology, and Maritime Transport (AAST), a certified International Supply Chain Manager by IPSCMI - the United States, a Change Practitioner by PROSCI - the United States, and certified in coaching and mentoring by ILM - UK. Dr. Sedky's research and knowledge are extensive in Project and Portfolio Management, Organizational Leadership, Engineering, Business Sustainability, Supply Chain Management, Strategy Management, International Business, and Risk Management. He is an expert in applying quantitative and qualitative methodologies to solve business problems, analyze market trends, and manage special projects and strategic initiatives. He is also a well-rounded business leader with professional experience exceeding 25 years in senior leadership roles in conglomerates across the United States, UK, Egypt, Saudi Arabia, and the United Arab Emirates.

Omar Vargas-González is a professor, research assistant, and former Head of Computer Systems Department at Tecnologico Nacional de Mexico Campus Ciudad Guzman, professor at Telematic Engineering at Centro Universitario del Sur Universidad de Guadalajara with a master degree in Computer Systems. Has been trained in Innovation and Multidisciplinary Entrepreneurship at Arizona State University (2018) and a Generation of Ecosystems of Innovation, Entrepreneurship and Sustainability for Jalisco course by Harvard University T.H. Chan School of Health. At present conduct research on diverse fields such as Entrepreneurship, Economy, Statistics, Mathematics and Information and Computer Sciences. Has collaborated in the publication of over 30 scientific articles and conducted diverse Innovation and Technological Development projects.

Index

C

D

E

F

G

H

I

J

L

M

N

O

P

Q

R

S

T

U

V

W

www.ingramcontent.com/pod-product-compliance
Lightning Source LLC
LaVergne TN
LVHW082346011026
849160LV00024B/1196